Analysis of Socio-Economic Conditions

I0888331

Showcasing fuzzy-set theory, this book highlights the enormous potential of fuzzy logic in helping to analyse the complexity of a wide range of socio-economic patterns and behaviour.

The contributions to this volume explore the most up-to-date fuzzy-set methods for the measurement of socio-economic phenomena in a multi-dimensional and/or dynamic perspective. Thus far, fuzzy-set theory has primarily been utilised in the social sciences in the field of poverty measurement. These chapters examine the latest work in this area, while also exploring further applications including social exclusion, the labour market, educational mismatch, sustainability, quality of life and violence against women. The authors demonstrate that real-world situations are often characterised by imprecision, uncertainty and vagueness, which cannot be properly described by the classical set theory that uses a simple true–false binary logic. By contrast, fuzzy-set theory has been shown to be a powerful tool for describing the multi-dimensionality and complexity of social phenomena.

This book will be of significant interest to economists, statisticians and sociologists utilising quantitative methods to explore socio-economic phenomena.

Gianni Betti is Full Professor in Statistics and Economics at the Department of Economics and Statistics, University of Siena, Italy. He has worked on several projects for the World Bank and European Commission and has been closely involved with the development of the EU Statistics on Income and Living Conditions.

Achille Lemmi has been Full Professor in Statistics and Economics at the University of Siena, Italy. Presently he is Honorary Fellow of the Tuscan Universities Research Centre on Advanced Statistics for Sustainable and Equitable Development (TURC-ASESD) 'Camilo Dagum' at the University of Pisa, Italy.

Routledge Advances in Social Economics

Series Editor: John B. Davis, Marquette University

This series presents new advances and developments in social economics thinking on a variety of subjects that concern the link between social values and economics. Need, justice and equity, gender, cooperation, work poverty, the environment, class, institutions, public policy and methodology are some of the most important themes. Among the orientations of the authors are social economist, institutionalist, humanist, solidarist, cooperatist, radical and Marxist, feminist, post-Keynesian, behaviouralist, and environmentalist. The series offers new contributions from today's most foremost thinkers on the social character of the economy.

Publishes in conjunction with the Association of Social Economics.

History, Methodology and Identity for a 21st Century Social Economics
Edited by Wilfred Dolfsma, D. Wade Hands and Robert McMaster

Economics as Social Science
Economics Imperialism and the Challenge of Interdisciplinarity
Roberto Marchionatti and Mario Cedrini

How Social Forces Impact the Economy
Edited by Steven Pressman

The Gift in the Economy and Society
Perspectives from Institutional Economics and Other Social Sciences
Edited by Stefan Kesting, Ioana Negru and Paolo Silvestri

Analysis of Socio-Economic Conditions
Insights from a Fuzzy Multi-dimensional Approach
Edited by Gianni Betti and Achille Lemmi

For more information about this series, please visit: www.routledge.com/Routledge-Advances-in-Social-Economics/book-series/SE0071

Analysis of Socio-Economic Conditions

Insights from a Fuzzy Multi-dimensional Approach

Edited by
Gianni Betti and Achille Lemmi

Routledge
Taylor & Francis Group
LONDON AND NEW YORK

First published 2021
by Routledge
2 Park Square, Milton Park, Abingdon, Oxon OX14 4RN

and by Routledge
605 Third Avenue, New York, NY 10158

Routledge is an imprint of the Taylor & Francis Group, an informa business

British Library Cataloguing-in-Publication Data
A catalogue record for this book is available from the British Library

Library of Congress Cataloging-in-Publication Data
Names: Betti, Gianni, editor. | Lemmi, Achille, editor.
Title: Analysis of socio-economic conditions: insights from a fuzzy multidimensional aproach/edited by Gianni Betti and Achille Lemmi.
Description: Abingdon, Oxon; New York, NY: Routledge, 2021. | Series: Routledge advances in social economics | Includes bibliographical references and index.
Identifiers: LCCN 2020044788 (print) | LCCN 2020044789 (ebook) | ISBN 9780367514068 (hbk) | ISBN 9781003053712 (ebk)
Subjects: LCSH: Economics–Sociological aspects. | Fuzzy sets–Data processing. | Poverty–Measurement.
Classification: LCC HM548 .A535 2021 (print) | LCC HM548 (ebook) | DDC 306.3–dc23
LC record available at https://lccn.loc.gov/2020044788
LC ebook record available at https://lccn.loc.gov/2020044789

ISBN: 978-0-367-51406-8 (hbk)
ISBN: 978-0-367-51407-5 (pbk)
ISBN: 978-1-003-05371-2 (ebk)

Typeset in Sabon
by Deanta Global Publishing Services, Chennai, India

Book in Honour of Professor Vijay Verma

Contents

Illustrations

Figures

Tables

Contributors

Ali Asadi is Full professor in Agricultural Extension and Development at Faculty of Agricultural Economics and Development, University of Tehran, Iran. He has been the President of Iranian Agricultural Extension and Education Association for several years.

Besma Belhadj is Full Professor in Quantitative Methods at the Department of Quantitative Methods, FSEGT, University of Tunis El Manar, Tunisia. Her research interests are applied statistics, economic systems; microeconomics; mathematical and quantitative methods. She is the author of many research studies published, focusing on the problem of poverty, and many books in descriptive statistics, mathematical statistics, inference statistics, probability and mathematics.

Ilaria Benedetti is a research fellow of Economic Statistics at the Department of Economy, Engineering, Society and Business Organization, University of Tuscia, Italy. She has participated in various international research projects (MAKSWELL and COMUNIKOS in collaboration with Eurostat). She is a member of the SIS since 2018 and she serves several international journals as a reviewer.

Gaia Bertarelli is Research Fellow in Statistics at the Department of Economics and Management of the University of Pisa and a member of the Tuscany Interuniversity Centre ASESD 'Camilo Dagum'. She is involved in several European research projects and protocols with the Italian National Statistics Institute. Her research focuses mainly on sampling statistics and small area estimation models for poverty, inequality and living conditions measures.

Gianni Betti is Full Professor in Statistics and Economics at the Department of Economics and Statistics, University of Siena, Italy. He has worked on several projects for the World Bank and European Commission, and has been closely involved with the development of the EU Statistics on Income and Living Conditions.

Francesca Bettio is Full Professor of Economic Policy at the University of Siena. Her research focuses primarily on labour market and gender equality issues in Italy and Europe. She has a long track record of collaborating with the European Commission in the capacity of national expert and of lead coordinator of European expert networks on these issues. She is a founding member of the portal 'inGenere.it'.

Bruno Cheli is Associate Professor in Statistics and Economics at the University of Pisa, Italy. He is the author of several scientific publications on such topics as the analysis of income distribution, economic inequality and poverty, well-being and sustainability.

Alessandra Coli is Tenured Researcher in Economic Statistics at the Department of Economics and Management, University of Pisa, Italy. She has been Researcher at the Italian National Institute of Statistics for several years. Presently and on a temporary basis, she works as National Accounts Data Manager and Methodologist at Eurostat, Luxembourg.

Federico Crescenzi is a research fellow in statistics at the Department of Statistics, Computer Science and Applications, University of Florence, Italy. He has worked as Consultant for quality of life surveys supported by the World Bank and participated in the data analysis of the EU Statistics on Income and Living Condition survey.

Elisabetta Croci Angelini is Full Professor in Economic Policy at the Department of Political Science, Communication and International Relations, University of Macerata, Italy, where she teaches Development Economics. She has got a PhD in Economics at the European University Institute and has served as President of AISSEC, the Italian Association for the Study of Comparative Economic Systems.

Antonella D'Agostino is Associate Professor in Statistics and Economics at the Department of Management and Quantitative Studies, University of Napoli 'Parthenope', Italy. She was a member of several scientific projects and consulting for the International Labour Organization and Eurostat in the field of income, poverty and social exclusion.

Hanna Dudek is Associate Professor in Econometrics and Statistics at the Department of Econometrics and Statistics, Warsaw University of Life Sciences, Poland. She is a Member of the Polish Statistical Association. Her recent research focuses on multi-dimensional analysis of material deprivation and food insecurity.

José Espinoza-Delgado holds a PhD in Economics from the University of Goettingen in Germany. He is currently a postdoctoral researcher at the research centre 'Poverty, Equity and Growth in Developing Countries: Statistical Methods and Empirical Analyses' at the University of Goettingen and a Consultant to UNICEF New York on child poverty and gender equality. He is a member of the International Association for Research in Income and Wealth and the Development Studies Association.

Francesca Gagliardi is Researcher at the Department of Economics and Statistics, University of Siena. By the end of the PhD in Applied Statistics, she has been working on poverty measurement, variance estimation and sustainability. She has been involved in several European research project. She has been Consultant for OECD and Fondazione Brodolini.

Duccio Stefano Gazzei divides his professional activity between the University of Siena, where he is an Adjunct Professor in Statistics and Economics at the Department of Economics and Statistics, and the BNL BNP Paribas bank, where he is Manager, and Head of the Advocacy Analytics Lab.

Giulio Ghellini is Full Professor in Social Statistics at the Department of Economics and Statistics, University of Siena, Italy. He has directed several projects for Eurostat related to survey design and data quality of EU Statistics on Income and Living Conditions.

Caterina Giusti is Associate Professor of statistics at the Department of Economics and Management of the University of Pisa and member of the Tuscany Interuniversity Centre ASESD 'Camilo Dagum'. She is involved in the research and coordination activities of several projects funded by the European Commission. She is currently responsible for the coordination activities of the European Master in Official Statistics – Tender 2019–2021.

Albert Hizgilov has a MA in Economics from the Department of Economics, Bar-Ilan University, Israel. He is about to start a PhD in Economics that will focus on financial literacy and inclusion, with a special emphasis on measurement issues.

Aurora Hoxha is Full Professor in Accounting at the Department of Finance and Accounting, Agricultural University of Tirana, Albania. She has managed several projects funded by FAO, World Bank and European Commission, etc. and has closely worked with the development of the national accounting standards and their implementation to the Albanian companies.

Firas Kaabi is a pure mathematics student at the Department of Mathematics, University of Bordeaux, France. He is a medallist in PAMO 2016. His research interests are applied mathematics. He is the author of many research studies published and a mathematics book.

Hossein Khoshbakht received his PhD degree in Agricultural Development from the University of Tehran, Iran. Currently, he is a Visiting-Researcher at the University of Siena, Italy, where he is conducting research activities in the areas of poverty and inequality.

Tiziana Laureti is Full Professor of Economic Statistics at the Department of Economics, Engineering, Society and Business Organization, University of Tuscia, Italy. She carries out research activities with Istat for computing sub-national spatial price indexes using big data. She participates in various international research projects, including MAKSWELL project and INNOVAFRICA.

Achille Lemmi has been Full Professor in Statistics and Economics at the University of Siena, Italy. Presently he is Honorary Fellow of the Tuscan Universities Research Centre on Advanced Statistics for Sustainable and Equitable Development (TURC-ASESD) 'Camilo Dagum' at the University of Pisa, Italy.

Yang Liu has a PhD in Quantitative Methods for Economic Policy obtained at the Doctoral School of University of Macerata, Italy. He graduated at Northeast Forestry University (Harbin, China) and got a Master in International Politics and Economic Relations at Macerata University. He has contributed to the research of income distribution and trade, the belt and road Initiatives, healthcare and Traditional Chinese Medicine, education and growth.

Lorenzo Mori is a PhD student in statistics at the University of Bologna, Italy. He collaborates with Professor Gianni Betti of the University of Siena, Italy, in his studies on poverty and living conditions. He is interested in economic and social statistics.

Stéphane Mussard is Full Professor of Economics at the University of Nîmes, France, specialising in econometrics, machine learning and mathematical economics. He is the head of CHROME, an interdisciplinary laboratory dedicated to the research on risks science.

María Navarro is Professor in Economics at the Department of Applied Economics, at the University of Granada, Spain. She performed a PhD in Happiness Economics at the Department of Economic Theory and History at the University of Granada. Her research fields of interest are mainly well-being, inequality, deprivation and poverty.

Laura Neri is Associate Professor in Statistics and Economics at the Department of Economics and Statistics, University of Siena, Italy. Her research interests lie in the fields of social statistics like poverty and inequality, well-being, statistics on income and living conditions. On these topics, she has collaborated on projects of the World Bank's and of the European Commission.

Anh Dung Ngo is a Full Professor in Occupational Safety, Composites and Design at the Mechanical Engineering Department, École de Technologie Supérieure in Montréal, Québec, Canada. He is the founder of two research groups, one in Occupational Safety and one in Composite Materials.

Luigi Palumbo is a PhD Student in Economics, Management and Quantitative Methods at the University of Tuscia, Italy. He previously worked across Europe and Asia in global roles for a multinational company, and he founded companies in Italy and Hong Kong. His research interests are in fuzzy logic, big data, and machine learning applied to business topics.

Tomasz Panek is Full Professor at the Institute of Statistics and Demography of the Warsaw School of Economics, where he is Vice-Director. His research interests focus primarily on the issues of household living conditions, including the poverty, social inequalities, income inequalities and quality of life. He has participated in several dozen national and international research projects.

Nicoletta Pannuzi is head of the integrated system for Labour, Education and Training division at the Italian National Institute of Statistics. She has carried out teaching activities, cooperation, conferences and seminars, in Italy and abroad, and she is the author of scientific publications on socio-economic conditions of the population, with particular reference to well-being, labour, inequality and poverty.

María Noel Pi Alperin is a Research Scientist at the Luxembourg Institute of Socio-Economic Research (LISER). She is the Country Team Leader of the Survey of Health, Aging and Retirement in Europe and the principal investigator in several national projects. She has also been involved in projects for the European Commission.

Monica Pratesi is Full Professor of Statistics at the Department of Economics and Management of the University of Pisa, Holder of the Jean Monnet Chair 2019–2021 'Small Area Methods for Monitoring of Poverty and Living Conditions in EU', Director of the Tuscany Interuniversity Centre ASESD 'Camilo Dagum', President elected of the International Association of Survey Statisticians (IASS) and member of the Board of the European Master in Official Statistics.

Andrea Regoli is Associate Professor in Statistics and Economics at the University of Naples Parthenope, Italy. He worked at the Italian National Institute of Statistics and as a Consultant for the International Labour Organization (ILO). He is the author of several scientific publications on such topics as income distribution, economic inequality and poverty, quality of life and sustainability.

Angeles Sánchez is an Associate Professor in Economics at the University of Granada, Spain. She belongs to the Research Group of Public Economics (SEJ-393) at the University of Granada, where she has worked on several projects in cooperation with public and private institutions. Her research interests are the economics of inequality and social welfare.

Edmira Shahu (Ozuni) is Full Professor in Statistics at the Department of Mathematics and Informatics, Agricultural University of Tirana, Albania.

She has experience and skills in processing and analysing quantitative data, and she has participated in various studies and projects.

Jacques Silber received his PhD from the University of Chicago and is now a Professor Emeritus of Economics at Bar-Ilan University, Israel. He was the founding Editor of the *Journal of Economic Inequality* and in 2011–2013 was President of ECINEQ, the (International) Society for the Study of Economic Inequality. He edited the *Handbook on Income Inequality Measurement* and several other books and edited special issues of various academic reviews.

Wiesław Szczesny is Associate Professor Emeritus in Informatics at the Department of Computer Science, Warsaw University of Life Sciences, Poland. He has worked for the Institute of Computer Science of Polish Academy of Sciences, developing the methods of multi-dimensional data analysis, especially grade data analysis.

Elisa Ticci is Senior Researcher and teaches Public Economics and Development Economics at the Department of Political and International Sciences, University of Siena, Italy. She has worked as Research Assistant and Consultant on themes related to the development and gender economics for the UNICEF Office of Research Innocenti, World Bank and European University Institute. Recently, she has collaborated on a project on violence against women for the European Commission.

Nguyen Duy Phuong Tran is Lecturer at the Faculty of Mechanical Engineering, Ho Chi Minh City University of Technology, Vietnam. He is also a researcher at the Department of Mechanical Engineering, the École de Technologie Supérieure in Montréal, Canada. He specialises in modelling and simulation, manufacturing engineering, biomedical mechanical engineering and mechatronics.

Tony Venditti is Lecturer at the Department of Mechanical Engineering, École de Technologie Supérieure in Montréal, Canada. He specialises in risk assessment methods applied to industrial safety. He is also a Professional Engineer and Consultant with ASFETM, an accident prevention association in the province of Québec, Canada.

Vijay Verma† has been *Professore a Contratto*, University of Siena, Italy, and Director, International Social Research (ISR) Ltd. in London. He has worked for the development of statistics internationally, including with the United Nations, International Labour Office and Eurostat, and has been closely involved with two major survey research programmes in EU: the European Community Household Panel (ECHP) and EU-SILC.

Jan Zwierzchowski is Assistant Professor at the Institute of Statistics and Demography, Warsaw School of Economics. His research is situated in the fields of quality of life, policy evaluation and causation in statistics.

Foreword

When Gianni Betti asked me to write a foreword for this publication, I was happy to know that his fellow researchers were planning to honour Vijay's work.

Vijay loved maths as giving a theoretical diagram of the world, which can be applied to any aspect of the whole. He saw his role as developing and using the power of accurate statistics to present a clear picture of any social or economic situation to institutions, which have the power to improve the future through their policies.

Growing up in India informed and inspired Vijay's outlook on life, work and his understanding of the other person's situation. It gave him a clear insight into how cultural and economic factors shaped the lives of those around him, his family, schoolmates and neighbours. How religion and custom constrained the lives of his sister, aunts and female cousins. How education in a class of 80 children would permit only the most determined to gain a place at the front of the class to follow the teaching. How economic constraints curtailed the education of his friends and sent them out early to work. This led him to concentrate on his own education and to use it in an effort to influence social policy.

Vijay was generous in encouraging his colleagues and sharing his ideas and practical solutions for solving problems. He had the gift of being interested in and feeling at home with anyone and everyone. Vijay loved numbers and the people behind the numbers. He delighted in working with and supporting bright young minds, always interested in their lives and stories, thoughts and opinions. Vijay enjoyed long discussions with researchers, sparking their ideas, giving advice and suggesting new ways to turn concepts into applicable methods. This book presents research on topics Vijay was passionate about, using methods that he helped to develop. I want to thank Achille Lemmi and Gianni Betti for dedicating it to Vijay.

Gillian Verma

Foreword

1 A Book in Honour of Professor Vijay Verma

Gianni Betti and Achille Lemmi

This is the fourth book edited by Gianni Betti and Achille Lemmi; it contains a balance between theoretical/methodological and empirical chapters prepared by a group of contributors who are a mix of luminaries in socio-economic fields (Jacques Silber, Vijay Verma, Francesca Bettio, Stephan Mussard, Monica Pratesi, María Noel Pi-Alperin, Tomasz Panek, among others) and a group of young and very promising researchers.

In the first of the three previous books they co-edited, Betti and Lemmi assembled advanced thinking about the multi-dimensional measurement of poverty, including the theoretical background, applications to cross-sections and longitudinal aspects of multi-dimensional fuzzy poverty analysis, with particular attention to the transitory, or temporary, conditions that often occur during transitions to a market economy (Lemmi and Betti, 2006a).

Next, Betti and Lemmi (2008a) collected an impressive set of contributions that emerged from the conference in Certosa di Pontignano in May 2005 in honour of two social scientists at the turn of the twentieth century: C. Gini and M. O. Lorenz. In particular, the main themes that Betti and Lemmi (2008b) presented in this second book were related to: innovation in the theory and methods on income inequality and concentration analysis, decomposition of inequality and empirical applications in applied economic analysis worldwide. These research themes are a consistent and relevant part of the recent economic, econometric and statistical methods and applications in the international academic literature.

Finally, in the third book, Betti and Lemmi (2013a) proposed an up-to-date and innovative survey of new methods for estimating poverty at the local level, as well as the most recent multi-dimensional methods used to examine the dynamics of poverty (Betti and Lemmi, 2013b). They argued that the most useful measures of poverty and inequality for policymakers and researchers are finely disaggregated into small geographic units. This volume was the first attempt to compile the most recent research results about local estimates of multi-dimensional deprivation (Betti and Lemmi, 2013c).

This collection is dedicated to the memory of Professor Vijay Verma, who passed away in September 2018, and also contains his new research in Chapter 7 on the jack-knife repeated replication technique for variance estimates of fuzzy poverty measures, with a foreword from his wife, Gillian Verma.

Verma greatly contributed to the development of the fuzzy, multi-dimensional and longitudinal approach to poverty measurement; his original ideas and suggestions have inspired many researchers over the past two decades. Directly or indirectly, his ideas are found in most of the chapters in this book.

The relationship between Vijay Verma and this volume's editors evolved from purely academic links to a strong and long-lasting friendship, with common respect and trust. These common interests, in terms of research and a lust for life, drove Vijay to move from London to Siena in 2002; a few years later, Gillian joined Vijay, and they became fully 'Sienese'.

In the early 1990s, Lemmi presented the then-brand-new fuzzy approach to poverty measurement at a Eurostat meeting on official poverty in Stockholm, which had previously been discussed at the Italian National Institute of Statistics (Istat), accompanied by the Istat researchers Giuliana Coccia and Mauro Masselli. After the presentation, Achille desperately looked for a place to smoke a cigarette, finding an open space where a nice-looking bearded gentleman was puffing on his cigarette. Achille joined him, and they started to discuss the presentation and the new and interesting idea of fuzzy versus Boolean states. 'The bearded gentleman' offered Achille congratulations on both the presentation and the new ideas in it. Afterwards, Achille returned to Mauro, who exclaimed enthusiastically in Roman dialect: 'Anvedi! Avemo fatto un figurone! [Wow, we made a good impression!]. Do you know who he is? He is Vijay Verma, the father of ECHP [European Community Household Panel survey]'.

On that day, a fruitful collaboration began, under the direction of David Rose based at the Institute for Social and Economic Research (ISER) at the University of Essex, where several researchers from the University of Siena – Giulio Ghellini, Bruno Cheli, Nicoletta Pannuzi and Gianni Betti – later spent some months working with Vijay, under the supervision of Achille. This first collaboration ended with the first two seminal papers on the fuzzy-set approach to poverty measurement: Cheli et al. (1994) and Cheli and Lemmi (1995).

Gianni Betti first met Vijay Verma during the lectures that he delivered as part of the PhD course in applied statistics at the University of Florence during the academic year 1996–1997. Later, in November 1997, Gianni joined the ISER at the University of Essex, where Vijay was reproducing the British Household Panel Survey as the British ECHP. Vijay supervised Gianni in the calculation of special weights to be used in a pseudo-panel for estimating longitudinal equivalence scales (Betti, 1998), which became the basis for a collaboration to estimate the aggregated weights in the multi-dimensional and fuzzy approach. In the spring of 1998, Vijay and Gianni spent many mornings in Wivenhoe Park, one of the 'squares' at Essex University, defining the prevalence-correlation weights, first published in Betti and Verma (1998) and later presented at the sixth Islamic Countries Conference on Statistical Sciences in Lahore, Pakistan (Betti and Verma, 1999). Nearly a decade later, the paper was finally published, with some improvements, as Betti and Verma (2008).

The present collection gathers chapters of very high academic quality on multi-dimensional indices in the social sciences. Over the past three decades, several methodological studies in these fields have been developed, especially on poverty measurement, and multi-dimensional indices have recently become a key research topic in other fields, such as marital disruption, sustainability, violence against women, educational mismatch and quality of life. Most noteworthy is the use of fuzzy logic in these works. Fuzzy-set theory has been shown to be a powerful tool for describing the multi-dimensionality and complexity of social phenomena, replacing the classical crisp approach, which generally tends to overestimate or underestimate social dynamics.

Fuzzy-set theory, introduced by Zadeh in 1965, emerged in response to evidence that real situations are often characterised by imprecision, uncertainty and vagueness and cannot be described properly with the classical set theory, which represents reality with a simple true–false binary logic. Indeed, in the classical crisp approach, sets are characterised by sharp and clearly defined boundaries; thus, an item might fully belong or not belong at all to a set according to a bivalent condition. By contrast, in fuzzy-set theory, an item can belong to a set with partial degrees of membership between 0 and 1, not only with the extreme values.

For all these reasons, the objective of this collection is to explore the most up-to-date fuzzy-set methods for the measurement of socio-economic phenomena from a multi-dimensional and/or dynamic perspective. The chapters were selected based on three criteria: scientific quality, their ability to represent the leading paths in current scientific research, and the existence of a sort of scientific '*file rouge*' among the contributions in order to present a homogeneous, useful and updated group of discussions.

We invited the most authoritative researchers worldwide to submit high-quality original research and surveys as chapters on the fuzzy measurement of socio-economic phenomena. The main themes are related in particular to descriptions of the evolution and recent research findings on multi-dimensional fuzzy poverty and social exclusion (Part 1, consisting of Chapters 2–7), the extension of the fuzzy multi-dimensional method to measuring the quality of life (QoL; Part 2, comprising Chapters 8–13), and the extension of the methods to specific social science fields, such as the labour market, educational mismatch, sustainability, industrial processes and violence against women (Part 3, made up of Chapters 14–20).

After this introduction, in Chapter 2, Bruno Cheli, Achille Lemmi, Nicoletta Pannuzi and Andrea Regoli describe the 'Evolution of the Fuzzy-Set Approach to Multi-Dimensional Poverty Measurement'. The relevant key points in the chapter, which are preliminary to any discussion of the methods used for a multi-dimensional analysis of poverty, are the selection of the relevant dimensions and the indicators used to measure people's achievements in these dimensions. They also mention the related issue of the choice of deprivation thresholds and the weights assigned to each dimension, but they do not discuss them in a full way as done in Betti et al. (2008). Rather, they simply state that the binary distinction between a 'bad state' and a 'good state' is too sharp because deprivation is likely to occur in degrees. Beginning with this consideration, they retrace and update the fuzzy-set approach (Zadeh, 1965) for measuring multi-dimensional poverty, which leads to the integrated fuzzy and relative method. This chapter is not only the basic reference point for the remaining chapters in the first section but also a starting point in the development of a fuzzy approach to the measurement of any phenomenon in the social sciences.

Chapter 3, by José Espinoza-Delgado and Jacques Silber on 'Using Rippin's Approach to Estimate Multi-Dimensional Poverty in Central America', describes the mainstream approach to the measurement of multi-dimensional poverty in developing countries, which is insensitive to inequality among the poor and also overlooks intra-household inequality. Consequently, the authors of this chapter propose a departure from the mainstream approach and take an individual-based and inequality-sensitive view of multi-dimensional poverty when only dichotomised variables are available. They estimate multi-dimensional poverty among individuals between the ages of 18 and 59 living in Guatemala, El Salvador, Honduras, Nicaragua and Costa Rica. Overall, the most interesting finding is that people in Guatemala have the highest potential for multi-dimensional poverty, followed by those in Nicaragua; people in Costa Rica, by contrast, have by far the lowest probability of being poor. Honduras and El Salvador are in the middle, with Hondurans having a larger probability of multi-dimensional poverty than Salvadorans.

Chapter 4 analyses the measurement of poverty using the framework of the 2030 UN Agenda for Sustainable Development, in which one of the most important goals is to 'eradicate poverty, in all its forms and dimensions'. This has been particularly necessary since 2008, when the global financial crisis started, and 2015, with the failure to achieve the millennium development goal of halving extreme poverty in the world. The chapter authors, Gianni Betti, Federico Crescenzi and Francesca Gagliardi, respond to the question 'Can a neighbouring region influence poverty?' using a fuzzy and longitudinal approach. They also discuss the adoption of a longitudinal measure proposed by Verma et al. (2017), which is based on the fuzzy-set approach to multi-dimensional poverty: the 'fuzzy at-persistent-risk-of-poverty rate'. Then they estimate this measure at the regional level with small area estimation techniques by introducing a spatial correlation model. In this way, the approach takes into account whether a neighbouring region can influence poverty in all its forms and dimensions: the multi-dimensional dimension, the regional dimension and the longitudinal dimension.

In Chapter 5, Hossein Khoshbakht, Francesca Gagliardi and Ali Asadi use a multi-dimensional and fuzzy-set approach to measure poverty at the province level in Iran, offering the first attempt to use this approach for estimating poverty at the local level in that country. They go beyond conventional studies of poverty based simply on a dichotomy between those who are and are not poor defined in relation to a poverty line drawn only on the basis of income or total expenditure. They use the methodology in the Household Budget Survey in Iran, with a large set of indicators to examine the latent dimensions of non-monetary poverty for the period 2016–2017.

Another interesting application on an emerging country is reported in Chapter 6, 'China's Multi-dimensional Poverty and Trade', by Elisabetta Croci Angelini and Yang Liu. They explain that, over the past 40 years of reform and opening-up, China's economy has maintained rapid growth. Its achievements in poverty reduction have been remarkable: more than 700 million Chinese have been lifted out of poverty. Meanwhile, the volume of China's import and export trade has risen several fold, and, in 2017, China became the world's largest importer and exporter. By conducting an analysis at the provincial level, this chapter explores the links between poverty and trade and how poverty restricts participation in international trade. Assessments of poverty usually rely on a monetary variable, but in this chapter the authors adopt a multi-dimensional measurement of poverty calculated with a fuzzy-set methodology at the provincial level and compare it to the volume of trade, revealing an interesting relationship between multi-dimensional poverty and global trade.

Chapter 7, the final chapter in Part 1, presents the new and final research of Vijay Verma, in collaboration with Gianni Betti and Francesca Gagliardi. In this chapter, they further extend variance estimation to longitudinal multi-dimensional fuzzy poverty measures. The measures considered are based on fuzzy representations of individuals' propensity for deprivation in monetary and different non-monetary dimensions and are derived from sample surveys with complex designs and fairly large samples. In particular, the chapter adopts a new longitudinal measure based on the fuzzy-set approach to multi-dimensional poverty proposed by Verma et al. (2017): the 'fuzzy at-persistent-risk-of-poverty' rate. The authors present a practical methodology for variance estimation – in particular, the jack-knife repeated replication method – for multi-dimensional measures of poverty and deprivation of households and individuals in a longitudinal context. They quantitatively illustrate the calculation procedures and difficulties in producing reliable and robust estimates of sampling errors for such measures. Some of the problems encountered are identified, and solutions are provided in the context of actual conditions.

Part 2 is devoted to phenomena related to the quality of life. Over the past few decades, QoL has become a key issue in modern society and one of the most important goals for individuals. QoL implies, first, that the minimum conditions required for humans to thrive are met and, second, that opportunities and skills adequately match (Veenhoven, 2000; Betti, 2017).

On this basis, in Chapter 8, Antonella D'Agostino, Giulio Ghellini, María Navarro and Angeles Sánchez present an 'Overview of the Quality of Life in Europe'. They focus on the measurement of QoL in Europe, considering it a latent concept that can be studied as a foundational measurement model. That is, QoL is assumed to be defined by a set of indicators: objective or social indicators that reflect people's objective conditions within a given cultural or geographic area and indicators of subjective well-being that reflect individual judgements of well-being. In this light, the main goal is to show the utility of applying a fuzzy-set approach in this framework, using microdata collected through sample surveys.

The second aspect of QoL, financial literacy measurement, is addressed by Albert Hizgilov and Jacques Silber in Chapter 9. This chapter takes a multi-dimensional approach with a special emphasis on the fuzzy approach. Various weighting schemes (the weights given to the different aspects or questions related to financial literacy) are used to check whether selecting a specific weighting scheme has an impact on the overall degree of financial literacy. This study also places special emphasis on the fuzzy approach advocated by Rippin (2013) in the context of multi-dimensional poverty measurement.

An empirical illustration, based on data collected in a survey conducted by Israel's Central Bureau of Statistics in 2012, shows that, regardless of the weighting scheme adopted, financial literacy is higher among males, the relationship between age and financial literacy takes a U shape, and married people have a higher financial literacy score. Other things held constant, financial literacy is generally lower among Arab Muslims and among the unemployed, and it rises with education. Finally, it appears that the conclusions to be drawn from focusing on the Rippin approach do not depend on whether the attributes of financial literacy are substitutes or complements.

In Chapter 10, Hanna Dudek and Wiesław Szczesny focus their attention on multi-dimensional material deprivation (MD) in the four Visegrád Group (V4) countries, using zero-inflated beta regression modelling. This approach has many benefits. First, it enables the direct measurement of living standards by looking at the 'enforced lack' of 'necessities'. The 'enforced lack' approach means that an item is counted as lacking if people cannot afford it – distinguishing between those who choose not to obtain a specific item and those forced to forgo it because they lack the necessary economic resources. Thus, the lack of items is not due to lifestyle preferences and choice but, rather is the result of the enforced lack of items, that is, things that people would like to possess (have access to) but cannot afford. Analysing MD not only provides a broad picture of living standards but also captures elements of persistent poverty because the lack of goods is usually associated with a prolonged shortage of resources. Moreover, an analysis of common items in the European Union (EU) that captures the same aspect of deprivation enables comparability across countries. The chapter provides the first econometric evidence of the factors that affect household MD in the V4 countries using a fuzzy multi-dimensional approach. Moreover, it investigates the differences between the risk and the intensity of the extent to which both indicators are subject to the same determinants.

In Chapter 11, Gaia Bertarelli, Antonella D'Agostino, Caterina Giusti and Monica Pratesi present a multi-dimensional and fuzzy approach for measuring educational poverty (EP) in Italy. They extend previous work by providing a fuzzy multi-dimensional measure of EP based on digital as well as literacy and quantitative skills in the dimension 'friends and skills'. The first step consists of exploring the fuzzy nature of the phenomenon, as it results from four dimensions. Indeed, as the EP Index is multi-dimensional, the integrated fuzzy and relative methodology can be used under the assumption that EP is a vague predicate manifested in different shades and degrees (fuzzy concept), rather than an attribute that is simply present or absent for individuals. The chapter measures the degree of EP in the Italian regions and in local areas at the intersection of the regions by defining an overall EP fuzzy measure and four EP dimension-specific measures.

In Chapter 12, Tomasz Panek and Jan Zwierzchowski present fuzzy and multi-dimensional measures of the degree of social exclusion risk, providing evidence of social exclusion in the population over age 50 in Poland. Because of the progressive ageing of European society, the fight against the social exclusion of older people has become an increasing challenge in the EU member countries. Monitoring the threat of social exclusion among the elderly and exploring the factors which determine it is needed in order to develop an environment in which people can live well into old age. The chapter constructs a tool to help in achieving these goals. The authors propose a new methodology to measure the degree of social exclusion risk using a fuzzy multi-dimensional approach.

Chapter 13, the last chapter in Part 2, by Stéphane Mussard and María Noel Pi-Alperin, is on 'Socio-economic Health Inequality Indices: A Fuzzy Approach Applied to European Countries'. In this chapter, the authors propose a family of socio-economic health inequality indexes based on fuzzy sets. These indexes depend on two parameters: the first embodies the behaviour of the decision-maker with respect to income redistribution, and the second represents the sensibility of the decision-maker with respect to one exogenous risk factor. The indexes enable robust ranking between health deprivation matrices with respect to the risk factors studied. They are empirically applied to 13 European countries. It is shown that in many countries the level of education of parents is the main driver of risk that increases socio-economic health inequality.

Chapter 14, by Francesca Bettio, Gianni Betti and Elisa Ticci, begins Part 3 and is on 'The Fuzzy Perspective on Violence against Women:

Challenges and Advancements'. In this chapter, the authors discuss how the fuzzy-set approach advances the measurement of gender-based violence by accounting for the frequency and severity of these different acts in addition to their prevalence. As argued elsewhere (Bettio, Ticci and Betti, 2020), severity scales that enable going beyond prevalence measurement have long been proposed in the literature but suffer from limitations that can be overcome using fuzzy measurement, e.g. the costly gathering of information and various selectivity biases. One novel dimension of violence measurement that this chapter explores is aggregation measures. Separate fuzzy indexes for, respectively, physical, sexual and psychological violence can be aggregated into a single index by means of a simple average for the same individual and then for selected population sub-groups. Possible alternatives to this basic aggregation are standardising the index (with respect to the reference population group) or considering indexes of fuzzy intersections and fuzzy unions.

Chapter 15, by Tony Venditti, Nguyen Duy Phuong Tran and Anh Dung Ngo, offers an innovative approach for studying a system safety analysis of industrial processes. Industrial processes and machines (industrial systems) pose risks from equipment failure and worker accidents. Occupational laws and regulations, as well as safety codes and standards, call for risk assessment to effectively identify measures that prevent these risks from materialising. Risk assessment involves identifying the risk factors and estimating their importance in terms of their associated probability of occurrence and the severity of the consequences they can present. Probabilities are commonly expressed in terms of linguistic expressions (e.g. 'very low', 'low', 'moderate' and 'high'). Therefore these assessments are subjective and vague. Other methods, such as fault trees, are also often used to identify the combinations of events which can lead to accident-prone events. If data are available, such as failure and human error probabilities, the probability of occurrence of accidents could be calculated. But in real life, these values are not usually known. Furthermore, these analyses are often performed without full knowledge of the processes being examined. So, a degree of uncertainty is associated with the data and the knowledge used in the analyses. In these situations, fuzzy numbers are an attractive method for dealing and taking into account this uncertainty. A numerical fuzzy probability assessment or linguistic expression, instead of a single data point, can instead belong to several sets in various degrees of memberships. Using the rules of fuzzy logic, a fuzzy number can then be calculated as a single number encapsulating the underlying associated uncertainty. In this chapter, fuzzy concepts are explained and applied to industrial risk estimation methods and fault tree analysis.

Chapter 16, by Bruno Cheli, Alessandra Coli and Andrea Regoli, discusses 'A Fuzzy Approach to the Measurement of Employment and Unemployment'. This takes a new perspective using fuzzy sets, unlike other analyses of the workforce, which are traditionally based on a clear-cut distinction between those who are employed and those who are unemployed, which form complementary sets. However, this distinction appears too rigid because it obscures all the nuances between people who are fully employed and those who work only occasionally but need to, or wish to, work more. Furthermore, this way of proceeding involves a significant loss of statistical information, which could be used for portraying and measuring the phenomenon more accurately. In the chapter, employment is considered not as a simple condition that is either present or absent but, rather, as a matter of degree. In logical terms, this implies moving from a Boolean conception to a 'fuzzy' one. The final goal is to define fuzzy measures of employment and unemployment using the available information on the weekly number of hours worked and on the need or desire of workers to work more hours.

In Chapter 17, Besma Belhadj and Firas Kaabi explore 'The Relationship between Employment and Poverty Using Fuzzy Regression', with models linking poverty to employment. Sometimes, ordinary linear regression models, such as the model linking poverty to employment, do not satisfy the conditions under which a least-squares estimator would be consistent. In these cases, a consistent estimator needs to be found. For these reasons, Belhadj and Kaabi construct estimators for a linear fuzzy regression model and establish consistency in these estimators.

In Chapter 18, Lorenzo Mori and Duccio Stefano Gazzei propose a new approach using fuzzy clustering for geo-marketing. Marketing techniques encompass many subjects: neuroscience yielded neuro-marketing, which focuses on channels for emotional communication; out of digitisation grew digital marketing, which played a decisive role in the development of e-commerce; finally, others include relationship marketing, buzz marketing and guerrilla marketing. In this chapter, the authors are mainly interested in geo-marketing, which uses geo-location to plan and implement marketing activities. Interest has grown in techniques to determine the particular geographic zone where potential consumers live, work, or do something else. This chapter uses consumer data from a big Italian bank with a simple but efficient technique to divide customers into different clusters. Eurisko segmentation logic is a method that enables clustering of the population using socio-demographic information.

In Chapter 19, Francesca Gagliardi, Laura Neri, Edmira Shahu and Aurora Hoxha investigate 'Satisfaction in Higher Education: A Multi-Dimensional and Fuzzy Approach'. In this chapter, they measure satisfaction in higher education using a multi-dimensional and fuzzy methodology. As a complex phenomenon, satisfaction is difficult to measure in general because many factors are involved in its definition, and a univariate indicator offers a limited view of the concept. In their analysis, the authors identify three dimensions to describe student satisfaction. To overcome the over-simplification of a binary variable, they calculate a degree of membership in the set of those who are satisfied, based on these three dimensions. The findings in this chapter suggest that some dimensions are more informative than others, confirming that this approach yields useful results that can also help in designing policies.

Finally, in Chapter 20, Luigi Palumbo, Tiziana Laureti and Ilaria Benedetti discuss 'A Multi-dimensional Clustering on Fuzzy Metrics to Classify CPG Pricing and Price Promotion Strategies: The Case of Pasta in Italy'. Although retailers compete along many dimensions, pricing strategy is clearly one of the most important drivers for increasing sales, especially in consumer packaged goods (CPG). Previous studies reveal that the classification of pricing and price promotion strategies involves complexity that cannot be reduced to a binary choice between high reliance on price promotion (HiLo) and an everyday-low-price (EDLP) approach. This chapter offers a fuzzy and multi-dimensional framework for analysing price promotion strategies in the CPG market over time and geographic regions using a dataset of weekly prices and price promotions for pasta brands across different retailers and regions in Italy. Retailers' promotional strategies are divided into five dimensions: price level, price variability, price promotion frequency, price promotion intensity and price promotion variability. Membership functions are designed to transform those metrics into fuzzy measures. The authors obtain nine groups which identify different pricing and price promotion strategies and describe their distribution across brands, retailers and geographic regions.

References

Betti G. (1998), *Intertemporal equivalence scales and cost of children using BHPS*. ERSC Research Centre on Micro-Social Change Working Papers. Paper 11/98. University of Essex, Colchester.

Betti G. (2017), What impact has the economic crisis had on quality of life in Europe? A multi-dimensional and fuzzy approach. *Quality & Quantity*, 51(1), pp. 351–364.

Betti G., Cheli B., Lemmi A., Verma V. (2008), The fuzzy set approach to multi-dimensional poverty: the case of Italy in the 1990s, in Nanak Kakwani and Jacques Silber (eds.), *Quantitative approaches to multi-dimensional poverty measurement*. New York: Palgrave MacMillan, pp. 30–48.

Betti G., Lemmi A. (2008a), *Advances on income inequality and concentration measures*. London: Routledge.

Betti G., Lemmi A. (2008b), Editors' introduction, in G. Betti, A. Lemmi (eds.), *Advances on income inequality and concentration measures*. London: Routledge, pp. 3–11.

Betti G., Lemmi A. (2013a), *Poverty and social exclusion: new methods of analysis*. London: Routledge/Taylor & Francis Group.

Betti G., Lemmi A. (2013b), Introduction, in G. Betti, A. Lemmi (eds.), *Poverty and social exclusion: new methods of analysis*. London: Routledge/Taylor & Francis Group, pp. 1–6.

Betti G., Lemmi A. (2013c), Poverty and social exclusion in 3D. Multidimensional, longitudinal and small area estimation, in G. Betti and A. Lemmi (eds.), *Poverty and social exclusion: new methods of analysis*. New York: Routledge/Taylor & Francis Group, pp. 301–315.

Betti G., Verma V. (1998), *Measuring the degree of poverty in a dynamic and comparative context: a multi-dimensional approach using fuzzy set theory*. Working Paper no. 22. Dipartimento di Metodi Quantitativi, Università di Siena.

Betti G., Verma V. (1999), Measuring the degree of poverty in a dynamic and comparative context: a multi-dimensional approach using fuzzy set theory. *Proceedings of the ICCS-VI*, 11, pp. 289–301, Lahore, Pakistan, August 27–31.

Betti G., Verma V. (2008), Fuzzy measures of the incidence of relative poverty and deprivation: a multi-dimensional perspective. *Statistical Methods and Applications*, 12(2), pp. 225–250.

Bettio F., Ticci E., Betti G. (2020), A fuzzy index and severity scale to measure violence against women. *Social Indicators Research*, 148(1), pp. 225–249.

Cheli B., Ghellini G., Lemmi A., Pannuzi N. (1994), Measuring poverty in the countries in transition via TFR method: the case of Poland in 1990–1991. *Statistics in Transition*, 1, pp. 585–636.

Cheli B., Lemmi A. (1995), A 'Totally' fuzzy and relative approach to the multi-dimensional analysis of poverty. *Economic Notes*, 24, pp. 115–134.

Lemmi A., Betti G. (2006a), *Fuzzy set approach to multi-dimensional poverty measurement*. New York: Springer.

Lemmi A., Betti G. (2006b), Introduction, in A. Lemmi, G. Betti (eds.), *Fuzzy set approach to multi-dimensional poverty measurement*. New York: Springer, pp. 1–7.

Rippin N. (2013), *Considerations of efficiency and distributive justice in multi-dimensional poverty measurement*. PhD dissertation, George-August-Universität Göttingen, Germany. https://www.die-gdi.de/uploads/media/Rippin_Efficiency_and_Distributive_Justice_Online_Publication.pdf.

Veenhoven R. (2000), The four qualities of life. *Journal of Happiness Studies*, 1, pp. 1–39.

Verma V., Betti G., Gagliardi F. (2017), Fuzzy measures of longitudinal poverty in a comparative perspective, *Social Indicators Research*, 130(2), pp. 435–454.

Zadeh L.A. (1965), Fuzzy sets. *Information and Control*, 8, pp. 338–353.

2 Evolution of the Fuzzy-Set Approach to Multi-Dimensional Poverty Measurement

Bruno Cheli, Achille Lemmi, Nicoletta Pannuzi and Andrea Regoli

Multi-Dimensional Poverty Measurement: The-State-of-Art

The spectrum of poverty measurements is wide and varies from purely monetary indicators to more or less sophisticated models based on non-monetary measures (Alkire and Foster, 2011; UNECE, 2017; Aaberge et al., 2017; Atkinson, 2017; Atkinson et al., 2017). Measurement choices often remain implicit even though they can have a profound impact on results and related policies (Haughton and Khandker, 2009; Brucker et al., 2015; Ravallion, 2016; Jenkins, 2018; Berger et al., 2018; Atkinson, 2019).

The most traditional approach focuses on measuring monetary poverty, which includes conventional poverty analyses using information on household income or consumption expenditure, and more recently also on wealth (Brandolini et al., 2010; Meyer and Sullivan, 2011; Azpitarte, 2012; OECD, 2013; Jolliffe and Espen, 2016; Serafino and Tonkin, 2017; Brewer et al., 2017; Kuypers and Marx, 2018). In this framework, poverty is defined as a lack of strictly economic resources, indeed monetary, under the hypothesis that income or, more generally, monetary resources are able to interpret and capture all the aspects that contribute to determining the conditions of material hardship. Economic resources allow people to satisfy their needs and pursue many other goals that they deem important.

The advantages and disadvantages of this approach are well known (Nelson, 2012; Neckermann et al., 2016), but – across all – its simplicity and direct policy links (especially with monetary transfer policies) still make it the most common and widespread approach for measuring poverty and monitoring its dynamics.

Measures of poverty based on income or consumption expenditure are still the only ones available, for example, in the United States, Japan or Canada, while in Europe the income-based poverty indicator (the so-called *at-risk-of-poverty* indicator) has been available since 1995, and in 2004 it was juxtaposed and integrated with the material deprivation and low-work-intensity indicators (Eurostat, 2012). For several decades (starting from Townsend, 1979; Sen, 1980; Atkinson and Bourguignon, 1982), in fact, it has been widely acknowledged that reality is much more complex and that poverty, specifically, is a phenomenon concerning a plurality of dimensions (Ravallion, 2011; Stiglitz et al., 2018; World Bank, 2018). The problem of multi-dimensionality is mainly represented by the identification of the relevant dimensions, the availability of adequate and reliable information on them and the method of putting the information together (Duclos et al., 2006; Ferreira and Lugo, 2013; Alkire and Foster, 2011; Lustig, 2011; Labonté et al., 2011; Maasoumi and Lugo, 2008; Alkire and Foster, 2007). Therefore, for many years, this limit has also led to the predominance of uni-dimensional poverty measures, especially within the official statistics.

Measures of poverty that exceed the exclusive use of monetary indicators have been developed in different conceptual contexts, referring to different terms such as exclusion, inclusion or social cohesion, deprivation or 'capability' poverty (Back, 2018; Garner and Short, 2015). The latter approach, which arises from the fundamental contribution of Amartya Sen (1993), is what defines the most complete and robust conceptual reference for the development of multi-dimensional poverty measures (Chiappero-Martinetti, 2000). Nevertheless, the theoretical literature on multi-dimensional measurement is still far from being consolidated.

Finally, it is now commonly accepted that income-poor people do not necessarily have to be deprived in other dimensions. For example, in countries where some public services (such as education or health care services) are provided for free or at subsidised prices by the national social security system, even households with very low levels of income may have good health conditions and attain high levels of education for their children, or, in other words, an acceptable standard of living. There is an emerging consensus that multi-dimensional measures of poverty should complement monetary ones. Despite the fascination represented by the possibility of calculating a composite indicator that facilitates spatial and temporal comparisons and between population subgroups, the excessive aggregation of dimensions and indicators results in an extremely significant informative and analytical loss, even threatening to frustrate the use of multi-dimensional measures. Keeping the dimensions distinct or considering them as appropriate aggregations can help to identify the most critical or serious aspects of poverty and put in place more targeted and effective intervention policies (see Box at the end of the section).

The consensus on the fact that poverty must be seen and measured as a multi-dimensional phenomenon is also enshrined in the 2030 UN Agenda for Sustainable Development which identifies the reduction of poverty in 'all its forms and dimensions' among the objectives to be achieved. In particular, Target 1.2 of the SDGs (Sustainable Development Goals) states that by at least 2030 the number of men, women and children of all ages living in poverty should be halved, considered in all its dimensions and calculated according to national definitions (Loewe and Rippin, 2016; United Nations, 2015).

Several multi-dimensional poverty indicators have been developed over time, and they can be broadly classified into two groups: i) *aggregate indicators* and ii) *composite indicators*. In the former case, the information for each item is considered at the individual level, and an individual multi-dimensional measure of poverty is calculated and subsequently aggregated to provide a collective measure. In the latter case, the information for each item is considered at the aggregate level and then it is combined.

Two main examples are represented by the 'people at-risk-of-poverty or social exclusion' indicator, developed at the European level and published by Eurostat as a EU2020 indicator,[1] and the Multi-dimensional Poverty Index (MPI), developed by the Oxford Poverty and Human Development Initiative (OPHI). Even if they are conceptually different, both approaches need to define threshold levels (for one or more indicators) in order to classify each unit as poor or non-poor.

To summarise, whatever the approach, the choice of the indicators is intertwined with the definition of the respective deprivation thresholds. In multivariate analyses these problems may be amplified by the consideration of intangible dimensions for which it may be even more contentious to identify minimum thresholds (Thorbecke, 2013).

More complex and sophisticated models are also found in the literature, in order to obtain a comprehensive description of the various facets of a complex phenomenon, through a suitable synthesis of the associated elementary indicators. In this framework, Structural Equation Modelling (SEM) offers a powerful yet little explored platform for measuring poverty (Ningaye et al., 2013; Voth-Gaeddert and Oerther, 2014). Among others, particularly promising is the recent development in partial least square-path modelling (PLS-PM) that could help with building Model Based Composite Indicators, providing a better measure of complex social phenomena (Lauro et al., 2018).

The relevant key points, which are preliminary to any discussion of the methods for the multi-dimensional analysis of poverty, are: the selection of the relevant dimensions; the indicators used to measure people's achievements in these dimensions, and the related issue of the choice of deprivation thresholds; and the weights assigned to each dimension. However, we do not aim to discuss these in this chapter. We simply want to remark how the binary distinction between a 'bad state' and a 'good state' is too sharp, since deprivation is likely to occur in degrees. Starting from this consideration, we retrace and update the fuzzy-set approach (Zadeh, 1965) for measuring multi-dimensional poverty, which leads to the IFR (Integrated Fuzzy and Relative) method.

Box - Severe Deprivation and At-Risk-Of-Poverty Indicators Across Europe at the Regional Level

The map on the left displays the severe material deprivation (SMD) rate by geographical region, whereas the map on the right refers to the at-risk-of-poverty (AROP) rate (see Figure 2.1). The maps show how the two indicators – related to different dimensions – draw different geographical profiles of hardship at the territorial level. Looking at the map on the left, the worst situations (highlighted by the darkest areas) are observed in regions of Greece, Bulgaria and Hungary and in North Macedonia, whereas the map on the right shows that the highest AROP rates are found in regions of Italy, Spain and Romania. The incidence of deprivation/poverty highlighted by the two indicators sometimes agree and sometimes do not. In particular, the regions of Southern Italy and the regions of Romania outside Bucharest occupy the worst positions on both rankings. It is evident that using different indicators of poverty (in addition to the income dimension) at a disaggregated territorial level to the maximum extent possible helps to draw a more comprehensive and faithful picture of this phenomenon. Nevertheless, the level of geographical disaggregation is not the same for every country, even though it is extremely useful for dealing with specific local intervention policies. If direct estimations are not reliable, it would be recommended to reconstruct them with small area estimation methods (Guadarrama et al., 2014; Pratesi, 2016).

Poverty as a Fuzzy Concept

The fuzzy-set approach is a valid instrument to measure multi-dimensional poverty, and it offers the additional advantage of overcoming the use of unavoidably arbitrary poverty thresholds. In such a way, it avoids extreme simplifications and loss of statistical information, deriving from the rigid poor/non-poor dichotomy.

Moreover, a number of contributions to poverty research agree in stating that the fuzzy-set approach can be used to analyse poverty in a consistent way with the Sen's capability approach (Sen, 1993).

The fuzzy-set approach takes into account the vagueness of the concept of poverty, which does not mean to view it as semantically ambiguous (Chiappero Martinetti, 2008). The notion that poverty is an either/or condition was brought into question some 50 years ago by Watts (1968), who claimed that there is a continuous gradation as one crosses any particular poverty line. As Qizilbash (2006) argued, poverty meets all the following requirements of a vague or fuzzy predicate: i) there are 'borderline' situations where individuals cannot be unequivocally classified as poor or non-poor; ii) there is not a sharp boundary to separate the poor from the non-poor; iii) the Sorites paradox holds: an increase of 0.01 euros in the monetary resources of a poor may lift him out of the poverty while his real condition remains the same. Two additional sources of vagueness are represented: first, by the lack a consensus regarding the threshold below which an individual can be treated as definitely poor; and second by the fact that the

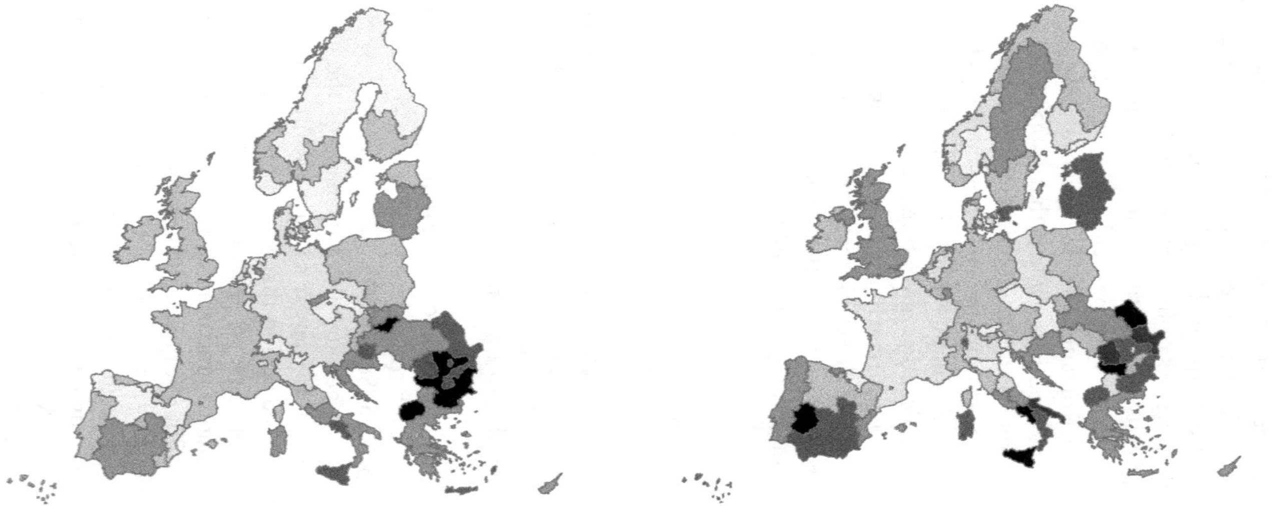

Figure 2.1 Severe material deprivation rate by NUTS region (left) and at-risk-of poverty rate by NUTS region (right). Year 2018. *Source:* https://ec.europa.eu/eurostat/data/database Data refer to the EU27 countries plus the United Kingdom, Norway, Switzerland and North Macedonia. The Nomenclature of Territorial Units for Statistics (NUTS) is used at its most disaggregated level, which is usually the NUTS2 level. Nevertheless, for some countries (namely Austria, Belgium, France, Germany, Portugal and the United Kingdom) the information is available at the country level (NUTS0) only.

variables used in poverty analyses (income, consumption and other deprivation indicators) are likely to be subject to measurement errors (Chakravarty, 2006; Zheng, 2015). These considerations lead to the identification of a grey area, where households and individuals are neither completely poor nor completely non-poor.

A phenomenon with such characteristics cannot be properly addressed through a crisp classification into poor and non-poor, based on the setting of a poverty threshold acting as a clear cut-off line, which constitutes the current practice of the poverty measurement. For example, based on the World Bank's $1.90-a-day (2011 PPP prices) International Poverty Line (World Bank, 2018), a person who commands over $1.91 is regarded as being undoubtedly non-poor just like another person whose resources are by far larger than the poverty line.

The fuzzy-set approach rejects the traditional dichotomy between poor and non-poor. The fuzziness is accounted for via a poverty membership function, measured on a scale from 0 to 1 – whereby 1 means full membership to the set of the poor and 0 full non-membership – which allows for a blurry (as opposed to sharp) vision of the concept of poverty. The conventional classification into a rigid dichotomy according to the traditional approach to poverty can then be viewed as a special case of the fuzzy conceptualisation of poverty, where the membership function equals 1 for those below the poverty line and 0 for those above the poverty line.

Moreover, the degree of membership can be considered as the relative risk of becoming poor in the future. Therefore, when the focus is on the people who are more vulnerable, the measures derived from a fuzzy logic lend themselves to being used fruitfully by policies aiming at preventing poverty. In the traditional approach, letting the poverty line change only identifies 'border areas' where people near the poverty line are located. For example, switching from a poverty line defined as 60% of the median equivalised income (which corresponds to the official Eurostat definition) to a threshold defined as 50% of the same income summary value can identify people who were classified as poor according to the former threshold and non-poor according to the latter threshold and, in general, to detect whether and to what extent the poverty measurement is sensitive to the choice of threshold (Lemmi et al., 2019).

An early attempt to incorporate the fuzzy-set theory (Zadeh, 1965) into poverty measurements and analyses at the methodological level (and in a multi-dimensional framework) was made by Cerioli and Zani (1990). Their original proposal was later developed by Cheli and Lemmi (1995), creating the so-called *totally fuzzy and relative* (TFR) approach. This approach avoids the need for poverty thresholds, defining a membership function as logically and economically founded, based on the relative position of every individual in the distribution of a specific indicator in a given context, which is summarised by the distribution function. Drawing on this approach, Betti et al. (2006a, 2006b) included the concentration (inequality) measure in the membership function, as defined by the Gini-Lorenz approach. The Betti et al. contribution, known as the *integrated fuzzy and relative* (IFR) approach, will be described in the next section.

Besides the specifications used in the TFR and IFR approaches, different membership function definitions have been proposed in several applications (Cerioli and Zani, 1990; Dombi, 1990; Chakravarty, 2006; Belhadj, 2011; Abdullah, 2011; Betti and Lemmi, 2013a; Zheng, 2015; Betti, 2017). These include: i) a simple monotone linear function; ii) a trapezoidal-shaped function, which incorporates the choice of two threshold values, so that any individual with a value below the lower threshold is counted as poor while any individual with a value above the upper threshold is counted as non-poor; iii) a nonlinear function, such as an inverted S-shaped function (sigmoid or logistic curve), which also requires identifying the crossover point of whose membership value equals 0.5; iv) other nonlinear curves, such as a Gaussian or an exponential function; v) and functions based on the experts' judgement.

Interest in the study of multi-dimensional poverty and deprivation using a fuzzy method was further supported by a recent analysis that aimed to search for a fuzzy counterpart to Alkire and Foster's Multi-dimensional Poverty Index (Kobus, 2018). The greatest contribution of this study was the removal of the dual cut-off of the MPI methodology, which relies strongly on the definition of a fixed threshold for every single indicator as well as for the final deprivation score.

The Integrated Fuzzy and Relative Method

Fuzzy Approach to the Measurement of Monetary Poverty ('Fuzzy Monetary')

The conventional approach based on a poverty line can be viewed as a special case of the fuzzy approach, where the membership function (MF) equals 1 for those below the poverty line and 0 for those above the poverty line. In fact, if we consider a poverty measure based on income, the membership function (μ) may be seen as:

$$\mu_i = 1 \text{ if } y_i < z,$$
$$\mu_i = 0 \text{ if } y_i \geq z,$$

where y_i is the equivalised income of individual i, and z is the poverty line.

In what has been called the TFR approach, Cheli and Lemmi (1995) define the MF in the fuzzy set of the poor as:

$$\mu_i = 1 - F(y_i) \tag{2.1}$$

where $F(y_i)$ is the cumulated distribution function of income calculated for individual i. In this way, the degree of poverty measured by μ_i equals 1 for the poorest and 0 for the richest person in the population and simply depends on each individual's position in the income distribution (which justifies the term 'totally relative'), therefore implying an ordinal approach to poverty measurement. Moreover, this approach can also be seen as 'totally fuzzy' as it defines the degree of poverty in fuzzy terms for every level of income.

The degree of poverty of generic individual i as specified in Equation (2.1) has a precise economic meaning. In particular, it represents the proportion of individuals whose level of income is higher than y_i.

Equation (2.1) provides the individual measure of deprivation of each statistical unit. By aggregating all these values, we obtain a collective index referring to the overall population, which is given by:

$$FM = (1/n)\sum \mu_i \tag{2.2}$$

Equation (2.2) represents the fuzzy proportion of poor people according to the monetary variable Y, where the symbol FM stands for *fuzzy monetary*.[2]

It must be noticed that the FM index specified in Equation (2.2) is always equal to approximately 0.5.[3] In fact it represents the sample estimate of $E[1 - F(y_i)] = 1 - E[F(y_i)]$, where $F(\ )$ is uniformly distributed in the interval [0,1] so that its mean is 0.5. At first glance, this fact might appear to be a drawback, as when we compute the FM index over different samples or populations we always get the same value. However, since we work in a purely relative context, we cannot (and we don't aim to) obtain a cardinal poverty measure for the surveyed population. We just evaluate which subgroups are better off and which ones are worse off by comparing the values of the FM index computed for each one.

In the case of international comparisons, we should consider the union of the various national samples and compute the individual memberships as specified in Equation (2.1) on this pooled sample. Hence we would compare the values of the FM index computed for each country based on the corresponding national sample.

In order to facilitate the comparison with the conventional poverty rate, Cheli (1995) proposed to raise the MF as specified in Equation (2.1) to some power $\alpha \geq 1$:

$$\mu_i = \left[1 - F(y_i)\right]^{\alpha} \tag{2.3}$$

Increasing the value of exponent α implies giving more weight to the poorer end of income distribution. In fact, being in general $0 < 1 - F(y_i) < 1$, as α increases μ decreases more for those who are less poor compared to those who are poorer. The value of α in Equation (2.3) is arbitrary and implies a political choice. Its introduction essentially aims at facilitating comparisons between the fuzzy measures and the conventional ones; for this reason the value of parameter α can be determined so that the FM index computed for the overall sample is equal to the proportion of the population below the official poverty line.

Betti and Verma (1999) define the fuzzy monetary indicator (*FM*), using a somewhat refined version of Equation (2.1), namely:

$$\mu_i = \left[1 - L(y_i)\right]^{\alpha} \tag{2.4}$$

where $L(y_i)$ represents the ordinate of the Lorenz curve of income for the *i*th individual. Hence, $1 - L(y_i)$ represents the *share of the total equivalised income* received by all individuals less poor than individual *i* and it varies from 1 for the poorest to 0 for the richest individual. $1 - L(y_i)$ can be expected to be a more sensitive indicator of the actual disparities in income, compared to $1 - F(y_i)$. This is illustrated in Figure 2.2, where the two MF definitions, represented in Equations (2.3) and (2.4), are compared (for $\alpha = 1$) by means of the Lorenz diagram.

Moreover, it may be noted that while the mean of $1 - F(y_i)$ values is always 0.5, as we already pointed out, the mean of $1 - L(y_i)$ equals $(1 + G)/2$, where G is the Gini index of the distribution. The more concentrated the income the greater $1 - L(y_i)$ is when compared to $1 - F(y_i)$.

However, recognising that both definitions of the MF are meaningful, effective and theoretically founded, Betti et al. (2006a) proposed to combine them as follows:[4]

$$FM_i = \mu_i = \left[1 - F(y_i)\right]^{\alpha - 1}\left[1 - L(y_i)\right]; \alpha \geq 1 \tag{2.5}$$

Henceforth we denote the income-based membership function by FM_i in order to distinguish it from the one calculated from non-monetary indicators (FS_i), which we describe in the next section.

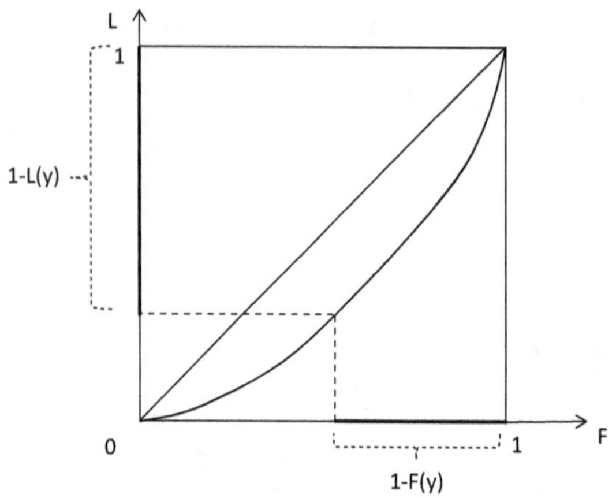

Figure 2.2 Membership functions as specified in Equations (2.1) and (2.4) in comparison.

Equation (2.5) integrates the original TFR approach, as specified in Equation (2.1), with the information on income shares $[1 - L(y_i)]$ which is directly connected to the Gini inequality index. This is what we refer to as the IFR approach.

The *FM* index obtained by averaging the μ values in Equation (2.5) is expressible as a function of the generalised Gini index G_α:

$$FM = (1/n)\sum \mu_i = \frac{\alpha + G_\alpha}{\alpha \cdot (\alpha + 1)} \tag{2.6}$$

where G_α is defined (in the continuous case) as:

$$G_\alpha = \alpha \cdot (\alpha + 1) \cdot \int_0^1 [1 - F(y)]^{\alpha - 1} [F(y) - L(y)] dF \tag{2.7}$$

G_α corresponds to the standard Gini index when $\alpha = 1$, and it weights the distance $[F(y) - L(y)]$ between the line of perfect equality and the Lorenz curve through the individual's position in the income distribution, giving more weight to its poorer end.

Fuzzy Approach to the Measurement of Non-Monetary Poverty ('Fuzzy Supplementary')

The living standard of the population can also be measured by means of a variety of non-monetary indicators referring to different domains (or dimensions), such as housing conditions, possession of durable goods, general financial situation, perception of hardship, expectations, etc. Quantification and combination of a large set of indicators of this kind involves a number of steps, models and assumptions.

First, from all the available indicators, a selection has to be made of those which are substantively meaningful and useful for the analysis of deprivation. This is a substantive as well as a statistical question.

Second, it is useful to identify the underlying dimensions and to group the indicators accordingly. Taking into account the manner in which different indicators may be grouped together adds to the richness of the analysis; ignoring such dimensionality can result in misleading conclusions (Whelan et al., 2001).

Betti et al. (2006a, 2006b) proposed to measure non-monetary deprivation in a way entirely analogous to the fuzzy monetary method, as described in the previous section.[5] On the basis of this approach, the membership function corresponding to Equation (2.5) would be:

$$FS_i = \mu_i = [1 - F(s_i)]^{\alpha - 1} [1 - L(s_i)]; \alpha \geq 1 \tag{2.8}$$

where *FS* stands for *fuzzy supplementary*; s_i represents the endowment of the overall supplementary items evaluated for individual *i*, $F(s_i)$ and $L(s_i)$ are the corresponding values of the distribution function and the Lorenz curve (of *s*), respectively, whereas α is a parameter to be determined so as to make the overall non-monetary deprivation rate numerically identical to the official head-count ratio of the poor.

In order to construct the fuzzy supplementary index defined in Equation (2.8) one has to begin by grouping the items into *dimensions* as mentioned at the beginning of this section. Individual items indicating non-monetary deprivation often take the form of simple 'yes/no' dichotomies (such as the presence or absence of an enforced lack of certain goods or facilities). However, some items may involve three or more ordered categories, reflecting different degrees of deprivation. Consider the case of C ordered categories (c=1,2,...,C) of some deprivation indicator, with $c = 1$ representing the most deprived and $c = C$ the least deprived situation. Let c_i be the category to which individual *i* belongs and let d_{ki} represent the deprivation score of individual *i* for what concerns item *k*, belonging to dimension δ. The d_{ki} deprivation score can be calculated in two different ways, represented by Equations (2.9) and (2.10):[6]

$$d_{ki} = (C - c_i)/(C - 1); 1 \le c_i \le C \tag{2.9}$$

$$d_{ki} = [1 - F(c_i)]/[1 - F(1)]; 1 \le c_i \le C \tag{2.10}$$

Equation (2.9) is based on the assumption that the rank of the categories represents an equally-spaced metric variable, whereas in Equation (2.10) the ranks are replaced by the distribution function of the *k*th item calculated for the *i*th individual.

Note that in the case of a dichotomous indicator (C = 2), which is by far the most common situation, d_{ki} is dichotomous too and takes a value of 1 (in cases of deprivation) or 0 (otherwise) for both Equations.

Now notice that if d_{ki} measures the specific deprivation for item *k*, $(1 - d_{ki})$ reflects the endowment for the same item.

The score for any individual *i* – that reflects her global endowment (or non-deprivation) – for what concerns dimension δ ($s_{\delta i}$) is computed as a weighted mean of the specific endowments for any item *k* belonging to δ (δ = 1,...,Δ):

$$s_{\delta i} = \sum_{k \in \delta} w_k (1 - d_{ki}) \Big/ \sum_{k \in \delta} w_k \tag{2.11}$$

the w_k weights are defined as a product of two factors:

$$w_k = w_k^{(a)} \cdot w_k^{(b)} \tag{2.12}$$

where $w_k^{(a)}$ depends only on the distribution of item *k* in the population and is defined as a decreasing function of the proportion of deprived in this item; on the other side, $w_k^{(b)}$ considers the correlation between k and the other items (in the dimension concerned) in order to reduce the redundancy produced by highly correlated indicators.[7]

By averaging $s_{\delta i}$ over dimensions we can obtain the overall deprivation score for the ith individual:

$$s_i = \sum_{\delta=1}^{\Delta} s_{\delta i} / \Delta \tag{2.13}$$

The s_i scores are used in Equation (2.8) to derive the fuzzy supplementary measure FS_i for each individual.

Finally, by averaging all the FS_i, we obtain a collective index of non-monetary deprivation that is called *Fuzzy Supplementary* (FS).

Monetary and Non-Monetary Poverty in Combination: Manifest and Latent Deprivation

In the IFR approach the two measures – FM_i concerning income (or monetary) poverty (Equation (2.5)), and FS_i concerning the overall non-monetary deprivation (Equation (2.8)) – may be combined to construct composite measures indicating the extent to which income poverty and non-monetary deprivation overlap. This is done by using the fuzzy-set union and intersection that we briefly describe below, together with the complement that is used for measuring longitudinal poverty (see the next section).

Given a fuzzy set A with membership function μ_A, its standard complement $\bar{A}$ is defined by the membership function $\bar{\mu}_A = 1 - \mu_A$ which can be interpreted as the degree to which a given element does not belong to A.

There is more than one way in which the fuzzy-set union and intersection can be formulated, each representing an equally valid generalisation of the corresponding crisp set operations. The IFR approach uses composite measures of monetary and non-monetary poverty that are based on the *min* and *max* operators,[8] as we describe below.

Given two fuzzy sets, A and B, with membership functions μ_A and μ_B, respectively, their union defines a new fuzzy set whose membership function can be specified as the maximum of the two membership functions, namely:

$$\mu(A \cup B) = \max(\mu_A, \mu_B) \tag{2.14}$$

On the other hand, the membership function in the intersection of A and B can be defined as the minimum of μ_A and μ_B, that is:

$$\mu(A \cap B) = \min(\mu_A, \mu_B) \tag{2.15}$$

Considering the two fuzzy sets of the income-poor and the non-monetary deprived whose membership functions are FM_i and FS_i, respectively, they can be combined to define two different measures, called manifest and latent deprivation.

For any individual i, the measure of *manifest deprivation* (M_i) is specified as follows:

$$M_i = \min(FM_i, FS_i) \tag{2.16}$$

On the other side, the measure of *latent deprivation* (L_i) is defined as the *maximum* of the two memberships FM_i and FS_i as follows:

$$L_i = \max(FM_i, FS_i) \tag{2.17}$$

The corresponding collective measures (M and L) for the whole population and for specific sub-populations can be obtained by averaging Equations (2.16) and (2.17).

In this context, it is useful to measure the overlapping degree of the two indices, by means of M to L ratio, which ranges from 0 to 1. When there is no overlap (i.e. when the subpopulation subject to income poverty is entirely different from the subpopulation subject to non-monetary deprivation), the above-mentioned ratio equals 0. On the contrary, when there is complete overlap, i.e. when each individual is subject to exactly the same degree of income poverty and of non-monetary deprivation ($FM_i = FS_i$), the M to L ratio equals 1.

Fuzzy Longitudinal Measures of Deprivation

P_t represents the fuzzy set of the poor at time t with membership function μ_t, and $\bar{P}_t$ represents its complement, which is the non-poor set, with membership function $\bar{\mu}_t = 1 - \mu_t$ (t = 1,2,...,T). Fuzzy longitudinal measures of deprivation across time require the specification of joint membership functions of the type:

$$I_T = \mu(P_1 \cap P_2 \cap \ldots \cap P_T) \tag{2.18}$$

and

$$U_T = \mu(P_1 \cup P_2 \cup \ldots \cup P_T) \tag{2.19}$$

where the first expression is the membership in the intersection of T cross-sectional fuzzy sets, whereas the second expression refers to their union. Using the *min* and *max* operators for intersection and union, respectively, the above longitudinal measures can be calculated as follows:

$$I_T = \min(\mu_1, \mu_2, \ldots \mu_t, \ldots, \mu_T) \tag{2.20}$$

$$U_T = \max(\mu_1, \mu_2, \ldots \mu_t, \ldots, \mu_T) \tag{2.21}$$

In other words, I_T represents the individual's propensity to be poor at all T periods, whereas U_T is the propensity to be poor in *at least one* of the T periods. Furthermore, the propensity to be *never poor* over all T periods is the complement of U_T, that is $\bar{U}_T = 1 - U_T$. The same result is obtained by considering the intersection of non-poor sets:

$$\begin{aligned}\bar{I}_T &= \min\left(\bar{\mu}_1, \bar{\mu}_2, \ldots \bar{\mu}_t, \ldots \bar{\mu}_T\right) \\ &= 1 - \max\left(\mu_1, \mu_2, \ldots \mu_t, \ldots, \mu_T\right) = 1 - U_T \end{aligned} \tag{2.22}$$

Furthermore, a measure that quantifies the 'exiting from poverty' event at time t after being poor until then requires the definition of the following membership function:

$$\mu\left(P_1 \cap \ldots \cap P_{t-1} \cap \bar{P}_t\right) = \max\left[0, \min\left(\mu_1, \ldots, \mu_{t-1}\right) - \mu_t\right], \quad t = 2, 3, \ldots, T \tag{2.23}$$

whereas the 're-entering into poverty' at time t following poverty experiences up to $t - 2$ and a non-poverty experience at $t - 1$ is based on the following membership function:

$$\begin{aligned}\mu\left(P_1 \cap \ldots \cap P_{t-2} \cap \bar{P}_{t-1} \cap P_t\right) &= \mu\left[(P_1 \cap \ldots \cap P_{t-2} \cap P_t) \cap \bar{P}_{t-1}\right] \\ &= \max\left[0, \min\left(\mu_1, \ldots, \mu_{t-2}, \mu_t\right) - \mu_{t-1}\right]; \text{ for } t = 3, 4, \ldots, T \end{aligned} \tag{2.24}$$

The corresponding rates for the population are computed by simply averaging the above individual contributions.

Recent Developments in Investigating the Accuracy of Fuzzy Poverty Estimates

The most recent studies on fuzzy measures focus on their sampling errors and also when referring to complex sample designs. In particular, the contributions mentioned below converge in finding that fuzzy measures present a smaller sampling error than conventional measures of poverty.

The method proposed by Verma et al. (2013) and Betti and Lemmi (2013b) aims to improve the sampling accuracy of fuzzy poverty indicators for sub-national areas by accumulating the information in a rotational panel design. Longitudinal poverty and multi-dimensionality are combined with estimation at the local level through small area estimation techniques to produce a cumulative 3D measure of fuzzy poverty.

The estimation of standard errors for fuzzy poverty measures from sample surveys with complex designs drove the study by Betti et al. (2018), the first paper that addressed the computation of accurate standard errors for fuzzy measures. They presented a robust computational methodology through the jack-knife repeated replication (JRR) procedure for variance estimation for multi-dimensional measures of poverty and deprivation through the IFR approach. The substantive finding of their paper was that fuzzy measures tend to be subjected to a smaller sampling error than conventional measures of poverty for a given sample size and design.

Through Monte Carlo simulation, Kim (2015) examined the sampling distribution of three fuzzy measures of poverty: TFR and IFR, as well as the measure derived from Cerioli and Zani's (1990) approach. He found that the three measures have very small confidence intervals and are quite robust to measurement errors. The IFR measure has some advantages over the other measures because, for relatively small sample sizes, it produces more accurate estimates than the other measures. Furthermore, as for the identification of the poor, the IFR measure has strong consistency, whereas the other measures considerably underestimate the number of people with very high membership function values.

Final Remarks

One challenge of poverty measurement consists in identifying who is poor. Such operation is traditionally accomplished by using poverty lines, both in the unidimensional and multi-dimensional framework, thus losing the ambiguity underlying the complex nature of poverty.

In contrast, fuzzy-set theory is able to capture the dimension of uncertainty that classical logic and crisp sets are unable to grasp, without competing with probability. They are, in fact, alternative tools for measuring two different types of uncertainty, that can complement each other.

A significant literature now applies the fuzzy-set approach to poverty measurement, and it also includes policy applications. Among others, Chiappero Martinetti (2006) emphasised several advantages of the fuzzy approach, namely: the possibility of using both quantitative and qualitative variables within the same approach; the opportunity of using multi-dimensional information for different wellbeing domains; and the chance to make poverty and wellbeing comparisons in a plurality of evaluative spaces. The fuzzy-set method also allows to aggregate across domains by making use of the union, intersection and average operators which satisfy a specific set of properties. Moreover, there are also recent fuzzy reformulations of a variety of multi-dimensional poverty indexes, including the Foster-Greer-Thorbecke (FGT) class of poverty measures (Chakravarty, 2019).

However, some complications remain due to the fact that, in every phase of the research conducted according to these methodologies, it is necessary to be aware of the impact that certain methodological choices may have on the results. These choices may refer, for example, to the shape of the membership functions or the aggregation operations. Therefore, a high interpretative capacity is necessarily required at each step, in order to better fill the gap between the richness and intrinsic vagueness of the theoretical multi-dimensional poverty concept on the one side, and their formal and empirical representation on the other side. In particular, the choice of a given membership function should be supported by sensitivity analyses or robustness tests also in terms of policy-relevant results (Alkire et al., 2015).

To summarise, a fuzzy approach to poverty may complement and encompass the traditional approach, handling vagueness and complexity, and, mostly, strengthening the connection between theory and data analysis, considering that '*in social investigation and measurement, it is undoubtedly more important to be vaguely right than to be precisely wrong*' (Sen, 1985).

Notes

1 An alternative indicator has been proposed by Guio, Gordon and Marlier, who suggested a list of 13 items (six of them already included in the previous indicator) and also a separate indicator for children aged less than 16 years old based on 18 items (Guio et al., 2016). For a critical evaluation of the EU 2020 Poverty and Social Exclusion indicators see Maître et al. (2013).
2 The name 'Fuzzy Monetary' was introduced later by Betti and Verma (1999) and Cheli and Betti (1999).
3 This happens when we average the μ values over the whole sample. By contrast, when we do it for specific subgroups (such as different geographical regions) the *FM* index will take values greater or less than 0.5.
4 Again, parameter α is chosen by the authors so that the mean of the MF (Equation 2.5) is equal to the official head count ratio of the poor.
5 This idea had been originally proposed by Betti and Verma (1999) who applied it to Equation (2.4).
6 Equation (2.9) was used in the first papers on the IFR approach (Betti et al., 2006a; 2006b; 2008) whereas Equation (2.10) was introduced later (see for instance Betti et al., 2015).
7 For a complete description of this weighting system see Betti and Verma (1999) or Betti et al. (2008).
8 The reasons that justify this choice are discussed in Betti et al. (2006a, 2006b).

References

Aaberge R., Bourguignon F., Brandolini A., Ferreira F.G., Gornick J.C., Hills J., Jäntti M., Jenkins S.P., Marlier E., Micklewright J., Nolan B., Piketty T., Radermacher W.J., Smeeding T.M., Stern N.H., Stiglitz J.E., Sutherland H. (2017). Tony Atkinson and his legacy, *Review of Income and Wealth*, 63(3), 412–444.

Abdullah L. (2011). Poverty lines based on fuzzy sets theory and its application to Malaysian data, *Social Indicators Research*, 104(1), 117–127.

Alkire S., Foster J.E. (2007). *Counting and Multi-dimensional Poverty Measurement*, Oxford Poverty and Human Development Initiative, Oxford Department of International Development, University of Oxford, 'Working Paper' No. 7.

Alkire S., Foster J.E. (2011). Understandings and misunderstandings of multidimensional poverty measurement, *Journal of Economic Inequality*, 9, 289–314.

Alkire S., Foster J.E., Seth S., Santos M.E., Roche J.M., Ballon P. (2015). *Multidimensional Poverty Measurement and Analysis*, Oxford: Oxford University Press.

Atkinson A.B. (2017). *Monitoring Global Poverty. Report of the Commission on Global Poverty*. Washington, DC: The World Bank.

Atkinson A.B. (2019). *Measuring Poverty around the World*. Princeton, NJ: Princeton University Press.

Atkinson A.B., Bourguignon, F. (1982). The comparison of multi-dimensionated distributions of economic status, *Review of Economic Studies*, 49, 183–201.

Atkinson A.B., Guio A.-C., Marlier E. (eds.) (2017). *Monitoring Social Inclusion in Europe. 2017 Statistical Books Edition*. Luxembourg: Eurostat.

Azpitarte F. (2012). Measuring poverty using both income and wealth: A cross-country comparison between the U.S. and Spain, *Review of Income and Wealth*, *58*(1), 24–50.

Bak C.K. (2018). Definitions and measurement of social exclusion – a conceptual and methodological review, *Advances in Applied Sociology*, 8(5), 2018.

Belhadj B. (2011). New fuzzy indices of poverty by distinguishing three levels of poverty, *Research in Economics*, 65(3), 221–231.

Berger L.M., Cancian M., Magnuson K. (2018). Anti-poverty policy innovations: New proposals for addressing poverty in the United States, *The Russell Sage Foundation Journal of the Social Sciences*, 4(3), 1–19.

Betti G. (2017). What impact has the economic crisis had on quality of life in Europe? A multi-dimensional and fuzzy approach, *Quality & Quantity*, 51(1), 351–364.

Betti G., Cheli B., Lemmi A., Verma V. (2006a). On the construction of fuzzy measures for the analysis of poverty and social exclusion, *Statistica & Applicazioni*, IV, numero speciale 1, 77–97.

Betti G., Cheli B., Lemmi A., Verma V. (2006b). Multidimensional and longitudinal poverty: An integrated fuzzy approach, in Lemmi A., Betti G. (eds.), *Fuzzy Set Approach to Multidimensional Poverty Measurement*. New York: Springer Science+Business Media, LLC, pp. 111–137.

Betti G., Cheli B., Lemmi A., Verma V. (2008). The fuzzy set approach to multi-dimensional poverty: The case of Italy in the 1990s, in Kakwani N., Silber J. (eds.), *Quantitative Approaches to Multi-dimensional Poverty Measurement*. London: Palgrave MacMillan, pp. 30–48.

Betti G., Gagliardi F., Lemmi A., Verma V. (2015). Comparative measures of multi-dimensional deprivation in the European Union, *Empirical Economics*, 49(3), 1071–1100.

Betti G., Gagliardi F., Verma V. (2018). Simplified Jackknife variance estimates for fuzzy measures of multi-dimensional poverty, *International Statistical Review*, 86(1), 68–86.

Betti G., Lemmi A. (2013a). *Poverty and Social Exclusion: New Methods of Analysis*. London: Routledge/Taylor & Francis Group.

Betti G., Lemmi A. (2013b). Poverty and social exclusion in 3D. Multi-dimensional, longitudinal and small area estimation, in Betti G., Lemmi A. (eds.), *Poverty and Social Exclusion. New Methods of Analysis*. London: Routledge/Taylor & Francis Group.

Betti G., Verma V. (1999). Measuring the degree of poverty in a dynamic and comparative context: A multi-dimensional approach using fuzzy set theory, *Proceedings ICCS-VI*, 11, 289–301, Lahore, Pakistan.

Brandolini A., Magri S., Smeeding T. (2010). Asset-based measurement of poverty, *Journal of Policy Analysis and Management*, 29(2), 267–284.

Brewer M., Etheridge B., O'Dea C. (2017). Why are households that report the lowest incomes so well-off? *The Economic Journal*, 127(605), F24–F49. https://doi.org/10.1111/ecoj.12334

Brucker D.L., Mitra S., Chaitoo N., Mauro J. (2015). More likely to be poor whatever the measure: Working-age persons with disabilities in the United States, *Social Science Quarterly*, 96(1), 273–296.

Cerioli A., Zani S. (1990). A fuzzy approach to the measurement of poverty, in Dagum C., Zenga M. (eds.), *Income and Wealth Distribution, Inequality and Poverty, Studies in Contemporary Economics*. Berlin: Springer Verlag, pp. 272–284.

Chakravarty S.R. (2006). An axiomatic approach to multidimensional poverty measurement via fuzzy sets, in Lemmi A., Betti G. (eds.), *Fuzzy Set Approach to Multidimensional Poverty Measurement*. New York: Springer, pp. 49–72.

Chakravarty S.R. (2019). An axiomatic approach to multi-dimensional poverty measurement via fuzzy sets, in Chakravarty S. (eds.), *Poverty, Social Exclusion and Stochastic Dominance. Themes in Economics (Theory, Empirics, and Policy)*. Singapore: Springer, pp. 123–141.

Cheli B. (1995). Totally Fuzzy and Relative Measures of Poverty in Dynamic Context, *Metron*, 53, 183–205.

Cheli B., Betti G. (1999). Fuzzy Analysis of Poverty Dynamics on an Italian Pseudo Panel, 1985-1994, *Metron*, 57, 83–103.

Cheli B., Lemmi A. (1995). A 'Totally' fuzzy and relative approach to the multi-dimensional analysis of poverty, *Economic Notes*, 24, 115–134.

Chiappero-Martinetti E. (2000). A multi-dimensional assessment of wellbeing based on Sen's functioning approach, *Rivista Internazionale di Scienze Sociali*, 108, 207–239.

Chiappero-Martinetti E. (2006). Capability approach and fuzzy set theory: Description, aggregation and inference issues, in Lemmi A., Betti G. (eds.), *Fuzzy Set Approach to Multidimensional Poverty Measurement*. New York: Springer, pp. 93–113.

Chiappero-Martinetti E. (2008). Complexity and vagueness in the capability approach: Strengths or weaknesses? In Comim F., Qizilbash M., Alkire S. (eds.), *The Capability Approach: Concepts, Applications and Measures*. Cambridge: Cambridge University Press.

Dombi J. (1990). Membership function as an evaluation, *Fuzzy Sets and Systems*, 35(1), 1–21.

Duclos J.-Y., Sahn D., Younger S. (2006). Robust multi-dimensional poverty comparisons, *Economic Journal*, 116(514), 943–968.

Eurostat (2012). Measuring material deprivation in the EU indicators for the whole population and child-specific indicators, *2012 Methodologies and Working Papers Edition*. Luxembourg: Eurostat.

Ferreira F.H.G., Lugo M.A. (2013). Multi-dimensional poverty analysis: Looking for a middle ground (English), *The World Bank Research Observer*, 28(2), 220–235.

Garner T.I., Short K.S. (eds.) (2015). Measurement of poverty, deprivation, and economic mobility, *Research on Economic Inequality, Emerald Publishing Ltd*, 23, number rein.2015.23, July.

Guadarrama M., Molina I., Rao J.N.K. (2014). A comparison of small area estimation methods for poverty mapping, *Statistics In Transition New Series And Survey Methodology Joint Issue: Small Area Estimation 2014*, 17(1), 41–66.

Guio A.-C., Gordon D., Marlier E., with Fahmy E., Nandy S., Pomati M. (2016). Improving the measurement of material deprivation at the European Union level, *Journal of European Social Policy*, 26(3), 219–333.

Haughton J., Khandker S.R. (2009). *Handbook on Poverty and Inequality*. Washington, DC: The International Bank for Reconstruction and Development/ The World Bank.

Jenkins S.P. (2018). *Perspectives on Poverty in Europe*. Social Policy Working Paper 03-18, London: LSE Department of Social Policy.

Jolliffe D., Espen B.P. (2016). Estimating international poverty lines from comparable national thresholds, *Journal of Economic Inequality*, 14(2), 185–198.

Kim S.G. (2015). Fuzzy multi-dimensional poverty measurement: An analysis of statistical behaviors, *Social Indicators Research*, 120, 635–667.

Kobus M. (2018). Fuzzy multi-dimensional poverty index, Studia Ekonomiczne, *Economic Studies*, 3(XCIV), 314–331.

Kuypers S., Marx I. (2018). Estimation of joint income-wealth poverty: A sensitivity analysis, *Social Indicators Research*, 136(1), 117–137.

Labonté R., Hadi A., E Kauffmann, X. (2011). *Indicators of Social Exclusion and Inclusion: A Critical and Comparative Analysis of the Literature*. PHIRN Working Papers. 2.

Lauro N.C., Grassia M.G., Cataldo R. (2018). Model based composite indicators: New developments in partial least squares-path modeling for the building of different types of composite indicators, *Social Indicators Research*, 135(2), 421–455.

Lemmi A., Grassi D., Masi A., Pannuzi N., Regoli A. (2019). Methodological choices and data quality issues for official poverty measures: Evidences from Italy, *Social Indicators Research*, 141(1), 299–330.

Loewe M., Rippin N. (eds.) (2016). *The Sustainable Development Goals of the Post 2015 Agenda: Comments on OWG and SDSN Proposals*. Bonn: German Development Institute.

Lustig N. (2011). Multidimensional indices of achievements and poverty: What do we gain and what do we lose? An introduction to the JOEI forum on multi-dimensional poverty, *Journal of Economic Inequality*, 9(2), 227–234.

Maasoumi E., Lugo M.A. (2008). The information basis of multivariate poverty assessments, in Kakwani N., Silber J. (eds.), *Quantitative Approaches to Multi-dimensional Poverty Measurement*. New York: Palgrave Macmillan, pp. 1–29.

Maître B., Nolan B., Whelan C.T. (2013). *A Critical Evaluation of the EU 2020 Poverty and Social Exclusion Target: An Analysis of EU-SILC 2009*. Working Papers 2013 09, Geary Institute, University College Dublin.

Meyer B.D., Sullivan J.X. (2011). Further results on measuring the wellbeing of the poor using income and consumption, *Canadian Journal of Economics*, 44(1), 52–87.

Neckerman K.M., Garfinkel I., Teitler J.O., Waldfogel J., Wimer C. (2016). Beyond income poverty: Measuring disadvantage in terms of material hardship and health, *Academic Pediatrics*, 16(3 Suppl), S52–S59.

Nelson G. (2012). Measuring poverty: The official U.S. measure and material hardship, *Poverty & Public Policy*, 3, 5–5. doi:10.2202/1944-2858.1077.

Ningaye P., Alexi T.Y., Virginie T.F. (2013). Multi-poverty in Cameroon: A structural equation modeling approach, *Social Indicators Research*, 113, 159–181.

OECD (2013). *OECD Guidelines for Micro Statistics on Household Wealth*. Paris: OECD Publishing. www.oecd.org/statistics/guidelines-for-micro-statisticson-household-wealth-9789264194878-en.htm

Pratesi M. (ed.) (2016). *Analysis of Poverty Data by Small Area Estimation*. New York: Wiley.

Qizilbash M. (2006). Philosophical accounts of vagueness fuzzy poverty measures and multidimensionality, in Lemmi A., Betti G. (eds.), *Fuzzy Set Approach to Multidimensional Poverty Measurement*. Berlin: Springer, pp. 9–28.

Ravallion M. (2011). On multi-dimensional indices of poverty, *Journal of Economic Inequality*, 9(2), 235–248.

Ravallion M. (2016). *The Economics of Poverty: History, Measurement and Policy*. New York: Oxford University Press.

Sen A.K. (1980). Equality of what? *Sen*, 1982, 353–369.

Sen, A.K. (1985). *Commodities and capabilities*. Amsterdam: North Holland.

Sen A.K. (1993). Capability and wellbeing, in Nussbaum S., Sen A.K. (eds.), *The Quality of Life*. Oxford: Clarendon Press, pp. 30–53.

Serafino P., Tonkin R.P. (2017). Comparing poverty estimates using income, expenditure and material deprivation, in Atkinson A.B., Guio A.-C., Marlier E. (eds.), *Monitoring Social Europe*. Luxembourg: Eurostat, pp. 241–258.

Stiglitz J., Fitoussi J., Durand M. (2018). *Beyond GDP: Measuring What Counts for Economic and Social Performance*. Paris: OECD Publishing. https://doi.org/10.1787/9789264307292-en.

Thorbecke E. (2013). Multidimensional poverty: Conceptual and measurement issues, in Kakwani N., Silber J. (eds.), *The Many Dimensions of Poverty*. London: Palgrave Macmillan, pp. 3–19.

Townsend P. (1979). *Poverty in the United Kingdom: A Survey of Household Resources and Standards of Living*. Leeds: Peregrine Books.

United Nations (2015). *Transforming Our World: The 2030 Agenda for Sustainable Development*. New York: United Nations.

UNECE (2017). *Guide on Poverty Measurement*. Geneva: United Nations.

Verma V., Gagliardi F., Ferretti C. (2013). Cumulation of poverty measures to meet new policy needs, in Torelli N., Pesarin F., Bar-Hen A. (eds.), *Advances in Theoretical and Applied Statistics*. Berlin: Springer, 511–522.

Voth-Gaeddert L.E., Oerther D.B. (2014). Utilizing structural equation modeling in the development of a standardized intervention assessment tool, *Procedia Engineering*, 78, 218–223.

Watts H.W. (1968). An economic definition of poverty, in D.P. Moynihan (ed.), *On Understanding Poverty*. New York: Basic Books, pp. 316–329.

Whelan C.T., Layte R., Maitre B., Nolan B. (2001). Income, deprivation and economic strain: An analysis of the european community household panel, *European Social Review*, 17(4), 357–375.

World Bank (2018). *Poverty and Shared Prosperity 2018: Piecing Together the Poverty Puzzle*. Washington, DC: World Bank. License: Creative Commons Attribution CC BY 3.0 IGO.

Zadeh L.A. (1965). Fuzzy sets. *Information and Control*, 8, 338–353.

Zheng B. (2015). Poverty: Fuzzy measurement and crisp ordering, *Social Choice and Welfare*, 45(1), 203–229.

3 Using Rippin's Approach to Estimate Multi-Dimensional Poverty in Central America

José Espinoza-Delgado and Jacques Silber

Introduction

The removal of poverty remains one of the most important aims of economic policy in many countries of the world (Chakravarty, 2018; Chakravarty & Silber, 2008); it continues to be one of the greatest global challenges and is an essential 'requirement for sustainable development' (UN, 2017, p. 1). In consequence, given that there is no meaningful development without the elimination of that source of un-freedom (Sen, 2000), Goal 1 of the Sustainable Development Goals (SDGs) calls for ending 'poverty in all its forms everywhere' (UN, 2015, p. 15). In this context, specifying how poverty is characterised, what its determinants are and finding appropriate poverty measures, our main concern in this chapter, become crucial elements for the design and assessment of policies aimed at alleviating this social problem (Ray, 1998).

As argued by Stiglitz, Sen and Fitoussi (2009a), the well-being of a population is multi-dimensional. Poverty therefore may be considered as a manifestation of the insufficiency of accomplishments in different domains of well-being; it is a multi-dimensional phenomenon characterised by deprivations in multiple dimensions of the individuals' well-being. As a result, nowadays, the multi-dimensional nature of poverty enjoys a widespread consensus (Chakravarty, 2006, 2018; Chakravarty & Lugo, 2016; Kakwani & Silber, 2008a; Stiglitz et al., 2009a, 2009b), grounded, mainly, on the capability approach proposed by Sen (1985, 1992, 1997, 2000, 2010), which is regarded as the most comprehensive approach to grasp the concept of poverty (Thorbecke, 2008). This consensus is reflected in Target 1.2 of the SDGs, which demands that by 2030 there will be a reduction 'at least by half of the proportion of men, women and children of all ages living in poverty in all its dimensions according to national definitions' (UN, 2015, p. 15).

In this regard, diverse multi-dimensional approaches to the measurement of poverty (see, for instance, Alkire & Foster, 2011; Alkire et al., 2015; Atkinson, 2003; Betti & Lemmi, 2013; Bourguignon & Chakravarty, 2003; Brandolini & Aaberge, 2014; Chakravarty, 2018; Chakravarty, Deutsch & Silber, 2008; Datt, 2019; Deutsch & Silber, 2005, 2008; Duclos, Sahn &

Younger, 2008; Kakwani & Silber, 2008b; Klasen, 2000; Lemmi & Betti, 2006, Rippin, 2013, 2016, 2017; Tsui, 2002), as well as multi-dimensional poverty indices, have become increasingly popular in recent years. Currently, the most influential and dominating methodology in developing countries is the counting approach proposed by Alkire and Foster (2011) (AF hereafter); this is a family of multi-dimensional poverty measures that employ a 'dual cut-off method' for the identification of the poor (p. 478), and it has been applied in a considerable number of studies.[1] The most famous application of the AF approach is the household-based multi-dimensional poverty index or 'global MPI' (Alkire et al., 2015, p. 177). Developed originally by the Oxford Poverty and Human Development Initiative (OPHI) in collaboration with the United Nations Development Program (UNDP) (Alkire & Santos, 2010, 2014), the global MPI has been included in the Human Development Report since 2010 (UNDP, 2010) and has become very popular (Duclos & Tiberti, 2016).

More recently, Duryea and Robles (2017), as part of the report 'Social Pulse in Latin America and the Caribbean 2017', published by the Inter-American Development Bank (IDB), and Santos and Villatoro (2018), proposed a new household-based multi-dimensional poverty index for Latin America and the Caribbean (LAC) and suggested adopting the AF method to estimate multi-dimensional poverty in LAC. Likewise, several governments, especially from LAC, for instance, Chile (Ministerio de Desarrollo Social, 2016), Colombia (DANE-DIMPE, 2014), Costa Rica (INEC, 2015), Ecuador (Castillo & Jácome, 2015), El Salvador (STPP & MINEC-DIGESTYC, 2015), Honduras (SCGG-INE, 2016), Mexico (CONEVAL, 2011) and Panama (MEF, 2017), have adopted this approach to produce their official multi-dimensional poverty index.

The AF methodology has the advantage of simplicity, flexibility and clarity, when compared to other approaches, which is indeed what makes it extremely appealing (Silber, 2011; Thorbecke, 2011); it also has a number of other attractive properties (see Alkire & Foster, 2011; Alkire et al., 2015). Yet, this approach also has some methodological shortcomings that have often been ignored in the literature (Duclos & Tiberti, 2016). Let us focus here on two of them, perhaps the most critical weaknesses of this methodology.

First, the identification method of the AF methodology assumes implicitly that up to the second cut-off (k), which is used to identify the multi-dimensionally poor (Alkire & Foster, 2011), the variables (attributes) are 'perfect substitutes', whereas the same variables are 'perfect complements' from this cut-off onwards (Rippin, 2017, p. 37), an assumption difficult to justify theoretically.[2] Choosing between substitutability and complementarity between attributes when there are more than two of them is certainly not an easy task. This issue, however, is of great significance within a dynamic framework and cannot be ignored (Thorbecke, 2008), if only because of its important policy implications (Silber, 2011; Thorbecke, 2011).[3]

Second, as emphasised by Rippin (2013, 2017), any index based on the AF approach is completely insensitive to inequality among the multi-dimensionally poor, a serious shortcoming according to Sen (1976, 1979). It should, however, be stressed that Alkire and Foster (2011) had mentioned the possibility of extending their analysis since they wrote:

> It is sometimes argued that the cross partials should be positive, reflecting a form of complementarity across dimensions; alternatively, they might be negative so as to yield a form of substitutability. Since M_α is neutral, it is a trivial matter to convert M_α into a measure that satisfies one or the other requirement: replace the individual poverty function $M_\alpha(y_i,z)$ with $[M_\alpha(y_i,z)]^\gamma$ for some $\gamma > 0$ and average across persons. The resulting poverty index regards all pairs of dimensions as substitutes when $\gamma < 1$, and as complements when $\gamma > 1$, with $\gamma = 1$ being our basic neutral case.
>
> (p. 485)

The more recent paper by Alkire and Foster (2019) emphasises this approach. Datt (2017, 2019) also underlined the need for a distribution-sensitive multi-dimensional poverty measure, but his approach did not really deal with ordinal or dichotomised variables. It is also important to stress that, as pointed by Alkire et al. (2015, ch. 2), as well as by Alkire and Foster (2019) and Seth and Santos (2019), satisfying association sensitive properties in their strict form is incompatible with a full dimensional breakdown property. Incorporating sensitivity to inequality in the poverty measure has thus a cost that should be acknowledged.

Another issue that has generally been ignored in the literature is that in the vast majority of studies empirical indices of multi-dimensional poverty have been computed at the level of the household (Bessell, 2015; Chiappori, 2016; Pogge & Wisor, 2016). In other words, these studies used the household as the unit of identification to determine who is multi-dimensionally poor and who is not, equating the poverty condition of the household with the poverty condition of all individuals belonging to the household (Espinoza-Delgado & Klasen, 2018). This assumption, however, disregards intra-household inequalities that are known to exist (see, for instance, Asfaw, Klasen & Lamanna, 2010; Bradshaw, Chant & Linneker, 2017a, 2017b; Chant, 2008; Klasen & Wink, 2002, 2003; Rodríguez, 2016), and it may also hide inequalities between different generations living in the household (Atkinson, Cantillon, Marlier, & Nolan, 2002), leading thus to biased estimates of poverty and inequality in society (Deaton, 1997; Rodríguez, 2016). Given that the ultimate objective of poverty analysis is the welfare of individuals, limiting the empirical analysis to the household level 'is simply unacceptable' (Chiappori, 2016, p. 840).

In this chapter, we adopt the general framework proposed by Silber and Yalonetzky (2014)[4] and Rippin's methodology (2013, 2017) and propose to use an inequality sensitive multi-dimensional poverty approach, with dichotomous variables, that overcomes the problems discussed previously.[5] The approach suggested is based on a 'fuzzy' identification function that specifies explicitly the kind of relationship existing between the dichotomous variables considered in the analysis. As shown in Bérenger (2016, 2017), the class of multi-dimensional poverty measures that are adopted can be decomposed into the three I's of poverty, incidence, intensity and inequality (Jenkins & Lambert, 1997). We implement such an approach by looking at poverty data in five Central American countries, namely Guatemala, El Salvador, Honduras, Nicaragua and Costa Rica. Our approach allows us to estimate multi-dimensional poverty among adults in that region and explore the determinants of multi-dimensional poverty on the basis of logit regression models.

The rest of the chapter is organised as follows. The next section explains the framework proposed; the following section introduces the data and justifies the dimensions, indicators and deprivation cut-offs, as well as the weighting structure used; the subsequent section discusses the main results and the results of the logit regression models, and the last section provides some concluding remarks.

A Framework for the Measurement of Multi-Dimensional Poverty

Notations and Definitions

Let $\mathbf{N} = \{1,\ldots,n\} \subset \mathbb{N}$ denote the set of n individuals, and let $\mathbf{D} = \{1,\ldots,d\} \subset \mathbb{N}$ represent the set of d ordinal variables measuring various aspects of individual well-being. Let $X = [x_{ij}]$ be the $n \times d$ attainments matrix, where $x_{ij} \left(\in \mathbb{N}_{++}\right)$ represents the attainment of the ith individual for the jth variable. Given that we assume that all the variables are dichotomous, x_{ij} will always be equal to either 0 or 1. In this matrix, each row vector $x_i = (x_{i1},\ldots,x_{id})$ gives the achievements of the ith individual, while each column vector $x_j = (x_{1j},\ldots,x_{nj})$ provides the distribution of the jth variable across the population. Also, let $w = (w_1,\ldots,w_d)$ be the vector of variable-specific weights with $w_j > 0 \forall j \in [1,d]$ and $\sum_{j=1}^{d} w_j = 1$. Finally, k denotes the real-valued scalar cut-off, with $0 \leq k \leq 1$. k is the minimal deprivation score an individual needs to have in order to be considered as multi-dimensionally poor ('the poverty cut-off') (Alkire & Foster, 2011, p. 478).

The Individual Multi-Dimensional Poverty Function

The construction of the individual multi-dimensional poverty function entails two steps. The first step checks for each well-being dimension j whether the individual is deprived, that is, whether x_{ij} is equal to 0 or 1. A weighted deprivations score (c_i) is then computed for each individual as the weighted sum of the deprivations suffered by each of them. This score is called the '(real-valued) counting function' (Silber & Yalonetzky, 2014, p. 11), and we write it as:

$$c_i = \sum_{j=1}^{d} w_j x_{ij}. \tag{3.1}$$

The Identification Function

The focus of the second stage of the analysis is on the identification of the multi-dimensionally poor individuals. In the AF approach, the counting function c_i is compared with the poverty cut-off k. If $c_i \geq k$, then the individual i is considered as multi-dimensionally poor. The choice of k is evidently arbitrary, and Alkire and Foster (2011) propose to use an 'intermediate cut-off' that lies somewhere between 0 and 1 (p. 478). Let $\psi^{AF}(x_{i.};w;k)$ be the identification function suggested by Alkire and Foster (2011); then, in our case of dichotomous variables, we can write that:

$$\psi^{AF}(x_{i.};w;k) = \begin{cases} 1 \, if \, c_i \geq k \\ 0 \, if \, c_i < k \end{cases} \tag{3.2}$$

Note that ψ^{AF} includes as particular cases the two conventional methods of identification introduced by Atkinson (2003) in the context of multi-dimensional poverty analysis: the union and the intersection approaches. The former assumes that the variables are perfect complements, while the latter supposes that the variables are perfect substitutes (Rippin, 2013, 2017)[6]. This is why Alkire and Foster (2011) proposed an intermediate approach as 'a natural alternative' to the two extreme methods of identification (p. 478).

In this chapter, we prefer to adopt a 'fuzzy' identification function, suggested by Rippin (2013, 2017), that makes explicit the relationship between the variables (attributes) considered in the analysis. Let γ be a parameter describing the relationship between the attributes. The function is then defined as:

$$\psi^{fuzzy}(x_{i.};w) = [c_i]^{\gamma} \tag{3.3}$$

where $[c_i]^{\gamma}$ satisfies the conditions of being non-decreasing in c_i and of having a non-decreasing marginal if the variables are assumed to be substitutes ($\gamma > 1$) and a non-increasing marginal if the variables are assumed to be complements ($\gamma < 1$).[7]

Therefore, instead of dichotomising the distribution of the weighted deprivations scores, as proposed by Alkire and Foster (2011), the fuzzy identification function distinguishes between the multi-dimensionally non-poor, on the one hand, and 'different degrees of poverty severity', on the other hand (Rippin, 2017, p. 42). Hence, it is considered to be fuzzy because unless $c_i = 1$ or $c_i = 0$, each individual is 'somewhat' multi-dimensionally poor (Silber & Yalonetzky, 2014, p. 13), depending on (i) the number of variables in which he/she is simultaneously deprived, and (ii) the type of relationship that exists among these variables. If γ is between 0 and 1, the curve describing c_i has a concave shape, while if γ is greater than 1, this curve has a convex shape. The choice between these two options depends on whether it is assumed that the variables are substitutes or complements. If the variables are perfect complements, there is no compensation and we obtain the union case; if they are perfect substitutes, there is full compensation and we get the intersection case.

The variables may be substitutes in the short term but complements in the long term (Thorbecke, 2008). In this chapter, we assume different degrees of substitutability (γ = 1.25, 1.50, 1.75, 2.00) and complementarity (γ = 0.25, 0.50, 0.75) among the variables; we test thus the robustness of our conclusions to these assumptions.

The Function Defining the Multi-Dimensional Poverty Breadth

In line with the literature, the individual multi-dimensional poverty function must not only identify the poor but also capture the intensity of the multi-dimensional poverty experience (Silber & Yalonetzky, 2014). However, with dichotomous variables the multi-dimensional poverty depth cannot be estimated as no poverty gap between the individual achievement in a given variable and the deprivation threshold for this variable may be calculated (Bérenger, 2017). To consider the poverty breadth, we make the individual multi-dimensional poverty function depend on the number of deprivations, and we define it as the product of the identification function introduced previously and a function that captures the breadth of multi-dimensional poverty (for more details, see Silber & Yalonetzky, 2014).

As multi-dimensional poverty breadth function, we adopted the one proposed by Alkire and Foster (2011):

$$g(x_i; z; w) = c_i \tag{3.4}$$

The Social Multi-Dimensional Poverty Function

In the last stage of the analysis, we derive a social multi-dimensional poverty function as the average of the individual poverty functions. We therefore end up with an index defined (for more details, see Rippin, 2017) as:

$$P^{\gamma}_{RIPPIN} = \frac{1}{n}\sum_{i=1}^{n} c_i^{\gamma+1} \tag{3.5}$$

Data Sources, Deprivation Dimensions, Indicators and Cut-Offs and Weighting Structure

Data

The data used in this chapter are the household surveys periodically performed in the countries of the Central American region, conducted by the corresponding National Institutes of Statistics. Table 3.1 shows for each country details of the nationally representative survey used. In our assessment, the unit of identification is the individual.

Dimensions, Indicators and Deprivation Cut-Offs

The choice of the dimensions and indicators for our individual-based multidimensional poverty index is grounded on the SDGs and targets (UN, 2015, 2017). Five deprivation dimensions were selected and specific indicators were chosen for each of them. The corresponding deprivation cut-offs are presented in Table 3.2.

Education

There are quite a few reasons why education should be included in a multidimensional poverty analysis (see Drèze & Sen, 2002; Robeyns, 2006).

Table 3.1 Surveys used, samples size and estimated population

Country	*Survey*	*Year*	*Sample Size* (Individuals aged 18–59)	*Estimated population* (Individuals aged 18–59)
Guatemala	Encuesta Nacional de Condiciones de Vida (GUA-ENCOVI2014)	2014	26,664	7,848,739
El Salvador	Encuesta de Hogares de Propósitos Múltiples (ELS-EHPM2016)	2016	40,842	3,553,224
Honduras	Encuesta Permanente de Hogares de Propósitos Múltiples (HON-EPHPM2013)	2013	15,760	4,070,318
Nicaragua	Encuesta Nacional de Hogares sobre Medición de Nivel de Vida (NIC-EMNV2014)	2014	15,730	3,309,715
Costa Rica	Encuesta Nacional de Hogares (CR-ENAHO2016)	2016	21,760	2,891,584
Central America	Encuestas Nacionales	Around 2015	120,756	21,673,580

Source: Authors' estimates based on GUA-ENCOVI2014, ELS-EHPM2016, HON-EPHPM2013, NIC-EMNV2014 and CR-ENAHO2016.

Table 3.2 Dimensions, indicators, weights and deprivation cut-offs

Dimensions	*Indicators*	*Weights (%)*	*Deprivation indicators: he/she is deprived if he/she ...*
1. Education (Goal 4 of the SDGs)	1.1. Schooling achievement	20.0	has not completed lower secondary school (nine years of schooling approximately).
2. Employment (Goal 8 of the SDGs)	2.1. Employment status	20.0	*Scenario 1* (does not consider domestic workers and unpaid care workers): is unemployed, employed without pay, or a discouraged worker (hidden unemployment).
		20.0	*Scenario 2* (considers Scenario 1 plus domestic workers and unpaid care workers who reported that they 'did not have a job' but were available to work): is unemployed, employed without pay, or a discouraged worker (hidden unemployment).
		20.0	*Scenario 3* (considers Scenario 2 plus domestic workers and unpaid care workers who reported that they 'did not have a job' but were not looking for and were not available to work because of unpaid care and/or domestic chores): is unemployed, employed without pay, or a discouraged worker (hidden unemployment), or is unemployed, but is not looking for a job and is not available to work because he/she has to take care of his/her children and/or a relative (s) and/or has to do domestic work.
3. Water and sanitation (Goal 6 of the SDGs)	3.1. Improved water source	12.6	does not have access to an improved water source or has access to it, but out of the house and yard/plot.
	3.2. Improved sanitation	7.4	only has access to an unimproved sanitation facility (a toilet or latrine without treatment or a toilet flushed without treatment to a river or a ravine) or to a shared toilet facility.
4. Energy and electricity (Goal 7 of the SDGs)	4.1. Type of cooking fuel	5.4	is living in a household which uses wood and/or coal and/or dung as main cooking fuel.
	4.2. Access to electricity	14.6	does not have access to electricity.
5. Quality of dwelling (Goal 11 of the SDGs)	5.1. Housing materials	4.9	is living in a house with dirt floor and/or precarious roof (waste, straw, palm and similar, other precarious material) and/or precarious wall materials (waste, cardboard, tin, cane, palm, straw, other precarious material).
	5.2. People-per-bedroom	2.9	has to share a bedroom with two or more people.
	5.3. Housing tenure	7.5	is living in an illegally occupied house or in a borrowed house.
	5.4. Assets	4.7	does not have access to more than one durable good of a list that includes: Radio, TV, Refrigerator, Motorbike, Car.

In the context of the SDGs, the inclusion of education is justified by Goal 4 that calls for ensuring 'inclusive and equitable quality education and promote lifelong learning opportunities for all' (UN, 2015, p. 17). The ordinal educational indicator selected refers to the schooling level attained by the individuals.

Employment

The inclusion of employment as a dimension is based on its instrumental significance as well as on its intrinsic importance (Atkinson et al., 2002; Klasen, 2000; Sen, 2000; Stiglitz et al., 2009a, 2009b). The SDGs call for promoting 'full and productive employment and decent work for all' (Goal 8) (UN, 2015, p. 19), which is crucial in Central American countries, where the share of informal employment in total employment is estimated to be higher than 70%, with the exception of Costa Rica (ILO, 2018, p. 18).

The ordinal indicator that we defined takes into account the employment status of the individual but also unpaid care work and domestic work. This is in line with Target 5.4 of the SDGs: 'Recognize and value unpaid care and domestic work through the provision of public services, infrastructure and social protection policies and the promotion of shared responsibility within the household and the family as nationally appropriate' (UN, 2015, p. 18). The indicator distinguishes two groups of individuals, among those who reported that they did not work the week preceding the survey: (1) individuals whose main activity was to do domestic work and/or unpaid care work (hereafter 'unpaid care and domestic workers'), and (2) individuals who were not involved in those activities. We therefore consider three scenarios (see Table 3.2).

Water and Sanitation

Water and sanitation are also of considerable instrumental and intrinsic importance (Klasen, 2000; Mara & Evans, 2018; Sorenson, Morssink & Campos, 2011). This dimension includes two indicators, improved water source and improved sanitation, which can be assumed to be related to Goal 6 of the SDGs: 'Ensure availability and sustainable management of water and sanitation for all' (UN, 2015, p. 18).

Energy and Electricity

The dimension of energy and electricity emphasises Goal 7 of the SDGs, which demands ensuring 'access to affordable, reliable, sustainable and modern energy for all' (UN, 2015, p. 19). This dimension is measured via two indicators named 'type of cooking fuel' and 'access to electricity'.

Quality of Dwelling

Finally, our index also includes a dimension that accounts for the quality of dwelling. This dimension is included in Goal 11 of the SDGs: 'Make cities and human settlements inclusive, safe, resilient and sustainable' (UN, 2015, p. 21). To measure the quality of dwelling, we use four indicators: housing materials, people-per-bedroom, housing tenure and assets.

Weighting Structure

Since all the dimensions selected are *a priori* equally important, we attach an equal weight to each of the five dimensions (20%), but for a given dimension, following Cerioli and Zani (1990), the weight of an indicator j is defined as:

$$w_j = 0.20\left(\frac{log\frac{1}{f_j}}{\sum_{j=1}^{d} log\frac{1}{f_j}}\right) \tag{3.6}$$

where f_j denotes the relative frequency of individuals deprived in the jth indicator (in this dimension), considering Central America as a whole.

Results

Estimating Multi-Dimensional Poverty Among Adults

We first illustrate empirically how the fuzzy identification function described above performs, considering Central America as a whole and only the first deprivation cut-off for employment (the first scenario). Figure 3.1 draws this function, assuming different values of γ from 0.05 to 10.0. The solid curves both at the top and at the bottom of the figure approximate the cases in which the attributes are supposed to be perfect complements (γ = 0.05) and perfect substitutes (γ = 10.00), respectively; the solid line in the middle (the 45° line) assumes, in turn, that the attributes are independent (γ = 1.00).

Figure 3.1 makes clear that the marginal increase in an individual's poverty severity is larger, the lower the substitutability between indicators (moving from γ = 10.00 to γ = 0.05), and that an individual's poverty level is higher, the harder the compensation of deprivation in one attribute. The degree of poverty of individuals depends thus not only on their weighted deprivation scores but also on the way in which these deprivations are correlated (Rippin, 2013, 2017).

The overall estimates of multi-dimensional poverty among adults in Central America as a region, as well as for each of the countries under analysis, considering the three scenarios discussed in Table 3.2 and several values of γ, are displayed graphically in Figure 3.2.[8]

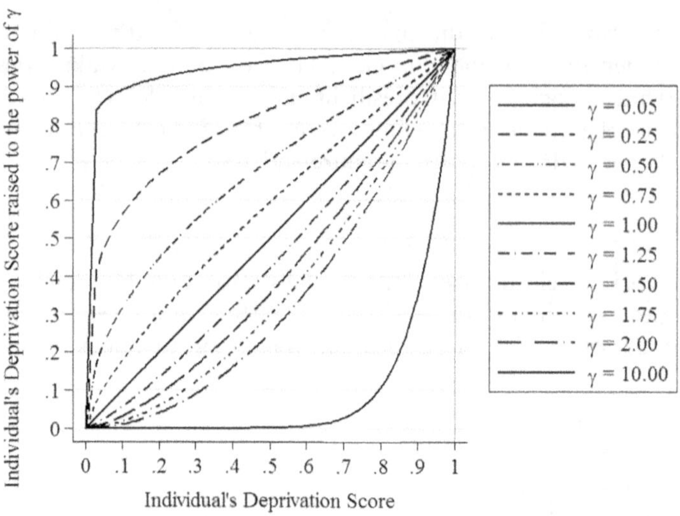

Figure 3.1 Fuzzy identification function for several values of γ. *Source:* Authors' estimates based on GUA-ENCOVI2014, ELS-EHPM2016, HON-EPHPM2013, NIC-EMNV2014 and CR-ENAHO2016.

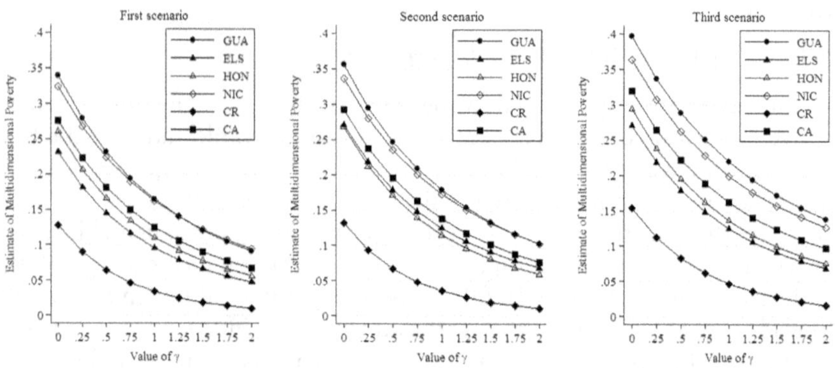

Figure 3.2 Estimates of multi-dimensional poverty in Central America (CA) as a whole and in Guatemala (GUA), El Salvador (ELS), Honduras (HON), Nicaragua (NIC) and Costa Rica (CR), considering three scenarios and several values of γ. *Source:* Authors' estimates based on GUA-ENCOVI2014, ELS-EHPM2016, HON-EPHPM2013, NIC-EMNV2014 and CR-ENAHO2016. *Note:* In the case of El Salvador, the estimates corresponding to the second and third scenarios are the same, as the deprivation rates in employment are identical. This is so because the survey does not provide the information needed to determine whether the individuals considered as 'unpaid care and domestic workers' were available to work or were not.

Figure 3.2 shows that multi-dimensional poverty is lower, the higher the degree of substitutability among the indicators. Note also that each of the resulting curves moves upwards as the threshold used to determine deprivation in employment becomes more demanding (from the first scenario to the third one). The figure also suggests that multi-dimensional poverty among adults is highest in Guatemala, followed by Nicaragua, except under the first scenario when γ takes a value of 1.50, 1.75 and 2.00, and, by contrast, it is the lowest in Costa Rica. Honduras and El Salvador appear in the middle but below the regional averages (the CA curve). Interestingly, under the third scenario, the differences in multi-dimensional poverty between Guatemala and Nicaragua become more substantial than the ones observed under the other scenarios because Guatemala has a larger percentage of unemployed adults who do unpaid care work and/or domestic work than Nicaragua.

As discussed above, the family of measures used in this chapter are sensitive to inequality among the poor and can be decomposed into the three I's of multi-dimensional poverty (Jenkins & Lambert, 1997). Therefore, to complement the previous results, Figure 3.3 presents graphically estimates of the inequality among the poor, the poverty dimension ignored by the mainstream approach, measured via the Generalised Entropy Inequality

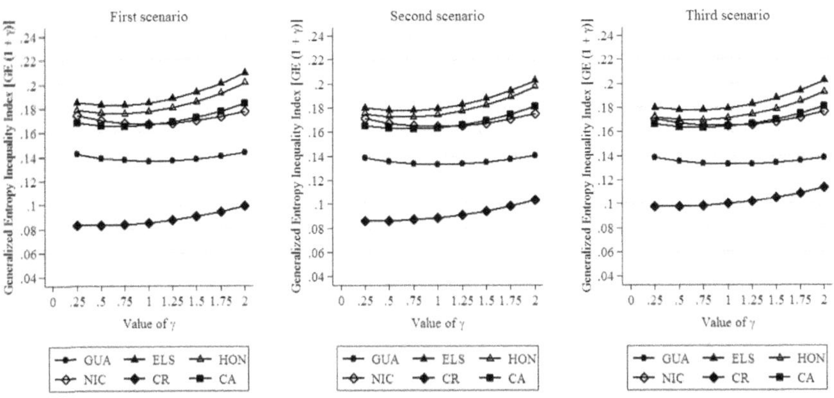

Figure 3.3 Inequality among the multi-dimensionally poor in Guatemala (GUA), El Salvador (ELS), Honduras (HON), Nicaragua (NIC) and Costa Rica (CR), as well as in Central America (CA) as a whole, considering three scenarios and several values of γ. *Source:* Authors' estimates based on GUA-ENCOVI2014, ELS-EHPM2016, HON-EPHPM2013, NIC-EMNV2014 and CR-ENAHO2016. *Note:* In the case of El Salvador, the inequality among the poor, corresponding to the second and the third scenario, is the same. This is so because the deprivation rates in employment are identical, given that the survey does not provide the information needed to determine whether the adults considered as 'unpaid care and domestic workers' were available for work or not (see Table 3.2).

Index.[9] Overall, it appears thus that the omission of inequality may lead to wrong poverty alleviation policies and programmes.

Results of Logit Regressions

As a complement to our descriptive analysis and to shed some light on the determinants of the multi-dimensional poverty of adults in Central America, in line with Wiepking and Mass (2005), we estimated logit regression models, for the region as a whole, where the endogenous variable was equal to 1 if the individual was multi-dimensionally poor, or to 0 otherwise, taking into account the three scenarios discussed previously.

As explanatory variables, we use the sex of the individuals (dummy variable equal to 1 for females), their age and the square of their age, the marital status [married, bachelor, divorced, widow(er)], the size of the household in which the individuals live and its square, the area of residence (urban, rural) and the country (Costa Rica being the country of reference), and some interaction terms between the sex of the individual and his/her marital status, as well as between the sex and the country of residence. The results are given in Table 3.3, separately for each scenario.

It seems that the pure gender effect is statistically significant, and it suggests that females are better-off than males in terms of multi-dimensional poverty; however, the final impact (size and direction) of the gender on the probability of being multi-dimensionally poor depends, *ceteris paribus*, on the marital status of the individual and the country in which he/she lives.

Table 3.3 also indicates that in Central America, regardless of the scenario considered, there is, *ceteris paribus*, a U-shaped relationship between the age of the individual and the probability that he/she will be multi-dimensionally poor. The same non-linear relationship is observed for the size of the household. It also appears that, *ceteris paribus*, adults living in rural areas have a much larger probability of being multi-dimensionally poor, this being true for all scenarios. This result was emphasised previously in the literature (see, for instance, Battiston, Cruces, López-Calva, Lugo & Santos, 2013; ECLAC, 2013; Espinoza-Delgado & Klasen, 2018; Santos & Villatoro, 2018). In other words, poverty in Central America still largely remains a rural phenomenon, an observation that has evidently important policy implications. Finally, note that the marital status of an individual and the corresponding interaction terms have a significant impact on the probability of being multi-dimensionally poor.

Concluding Remarks

The AF methodology, as the mainstream approach to the measurement of multi-dimensional poverty in the developing world, is insensitive to inequality among the poor. Additionally, the vast majority of empirical studies of multi-dimensional poverty equate the poverty status of the household with

Table 3.3 Odds ratios of being multi-dimensionally poor by sex, age, household size, area and country of residence and marital status, considering three scenarios

Poverty	*Scenario 1*		*Scenario 2*		*Scenario 3*	
Explanatory variables	*Odds Ratio*	*Robust SE*	*Odds Ratio*	*Robust SE*	*Odds Ratio*	*Robust SE*
Sex						
Male (ref.)	1.0000	...	1.0000	...	1.0000	...
Female	0.7782***	0.0296	0.7653***	0.0294	0.9152**	0.0355
Age	-0.0039***	0.0006	-0.0042***	0.0005	-0.0049***	0.0005
Age sq.	0.0001***	0.0000	0.0001***	0.0000	0.0001***	0.0000
Household size	-0.0225***	0.0025	-0.0211***	0.0023	-0.0188***	0.0021
Household size sq.	0.0038***	0.0003	0.0036***	0.0002	0.0033***	0.0002
Area of residence						
Urban (ref.)	1.0000	...	1.0000	...	1.0000	...
Rural	5.4221***	0.1124	5.3645***	0.1150	5.4571***	0.1220
Marital status						
Single (ref.)	1.0000	...	1.0000	...	1.0000	...
Married	1.1157***	0.0341	1.1286***	0.0347	1.1400***	0.0352
Unmarried	2.1083***	0.0701	2.1237***	0.0709	2.1377***	0.0717
Divorced	1.4631***	0.0758	1.4804***	0.0768	1.5146***	0.0788
Widow(er)	2.1677***	0.4273	2.1965***	0.4332	2.2030***	0.4350
Country						
Costa Rica (ref.)	1.0000	...	1.0000	...	1.0000	...
Guatemala	4.9466***	0.2034	4.9361***	0.2033	4.9443***	0.2048
El Salvador	2.9120***	0.0880	2.9070***	0.0878	2.8817***	0.0873
Honduras	2.5024***	0.0987	2.5410***	0.1006	2.5645***	0.1024
Nicaragua	3.6196***	0.1428	3.6201***	0.1431	3.6004***	0.1428
Interaction (Sex – Union status)						
Female (married)	1.3037***	0.0515	1.4877***	0.0602	1.8504***	0.0766
Female (Unmarried)	1.2327***	0.0556	1.4061***	0.0654	1.7658***	0.0851
Female (Divorced)	1.2848***	0.0786	1.3243***	0.0822	1.3685***	0.0853
Female (widow)	1.1447	0.2407	1.1988	0.2540	1.2932	0.2755
Interaction (Sex – Country)						
Female (Guatemala)	1.1221**	0.0633	1.1996***	0.0690	1.1099*	0.0665
Female (El Salvador)	1.0628	0.0442	1.4498***	0.0619	1.0923**	0.0471
Female (Honduras)	1.0290	0.0552	1.0288	0.0558	0.9509	0.0532
Female (Nicaragua)	0.8656***	0.0461	0.9013*	0.0486	0.8132***	0.0450
Constant	1.5237***	0.1507	1.7072	0.1718	2.0039***	0.2050
Observations	120756		120756		120756	
Wald chi2	16132.39		16264.02		15338.95	
Degrees of freedom	(22)		(22)		(22)	
Prob. > chi2	0.0000		0.0000		0.0000	
Pseudo R2	0.1768		0.1831		0.1821	

Notes: Survey weights used; for age and household size variables, the marginal effects are reported; outcome (Poverty): dummy equal to 1 if an individual is multi-dimensionally poor, for each of the three scenarios. *Significance levels*: *p < 0.1.; **p < 0.05; ***p < 0.01.

that of all individuals in the household, thus disregarding intra-household inequalities. In this chapter, we therefore proposed individual-based inequality sensitive multi-dimensional poverty. We applied our approach to an analysis of multi-dimensional poverty among adults (18 to 59 years old) in Guatemala, El Salvador, Honduras, Nicaragua and Costa Rica.

It appears that multi-dimensional poverty among adults is highest in Guatemala and Nicaragua and lowest in Costa Rica. We also decomposed our multi-dimensional poverty measure into the three I's of poverty and found that Guatemala and Nicaragua have the highest and Costa Rica the lowest incidence and intensity of multi-dimensional poverty in Central America.[10] El Salvador and Honduras, however, have the greatest levels of inequality.

Finally, the logit regression models corroborate the main findings of our descriptive analysis. These regressions also show that in Central America, there are country- as well as individual-specific gender differences in multi-dimensional poverty. It also seems that the total impact of gender is statistically significant, but, *ceteris paribus*, it also depends on the marital status of the individuals and on the country in which they live.

Acknowledgements

José Espinoza-Delgado would like to thank participants at workshops in Bielefeld, Goettingen, Puebla and Zaragoza for helpful comments and discussions on the topic, especially to Achille Lemmi, Stephan Klasen, Mariano Rojas and Julio López-Laborda. He also would like to thank Nicole Rippin for clarifications and useful discussions on the Correlation Sensitive Poverty Index.

This chapter was completed when José Espinoza-Delgado was a guest researcher at the German Development Institute (DIE-GDI) between September and December 2019; he is very thankful to the DIE-GDI for its warm hospitality.

Notes

1 A summary of studies that have applied the AF method can be found in Alkire et al. (2015, p. 178–181).

2 In a graph plotting on the horizontal axis the cumulative percentage of deprivations and on the vertical axis the probability of being considered as poor, the curve obtained would be identical to the horizontal axis up to the cut-off (since an individual is not poor as long as the share of his/her deprivations in the total number of possible deprivations is smaller than the cut-off) while the curve will become horizontal at height 1 as soon as the percentage of deprivations of the individual is equal to or higher than the cut-off. This special curve implies that the deprivations are perfect substitutes up to the cut-off and perfect complements beyond the cut-off.

3 'For instance, for a poverty analysis in the dimensions of education and nutritional status of children, there are production complementarities because

better-nourished children learn better. If this complementarity is strong enough, it may overcome the usual ethical judgment that favors the multiply-deprived, so that overall poverty would decline by more if we were to transfer education from poorly nourished to the better nourished, despite the fact that it increases the correlation of the two measures of well-being. Similarly, one might argue that human capital should be granted to those with a higher survival probability (because these assets would vanish following their death). Increasing the correlation of deprivations, and increasing the incidence of multiple deprivations, would then be good for poverty reduction' (Duclos, Sahn & Younger, 2006, p. 950).

4 Some of the ideas raised by Silber and Yalonetzky (2014) appear already in Yalonetzky (2012, 2014).

5 Such an approach has been used recently by Bérenger (2016, 2017), but using the household as the unit of identification.

6 Here, the concepts of 'substitutability' and 'complementarity' follow the Auspitz-Lieben-Edgeworth-Pareto (ALEP) definition and not the well-known approach proposed by Hicks and Allen (1934a, 1934b) (Silber, 2007, p. 59). The ALEP definition considers that two attributes are substitutes (complements) if their second cross-partial derivatives are larger (less) than zero and independent if they are equal to zero (Rippin, 2013, 2017). Intuitively, on the basis of the ALEP definition, if two attributes are substitutes, poverty will decrease less with a rise in attribute 1 for individuals with larger quantities of attribute 2. The contrary is evidently true when the two attributes are supposed to be complements (Silber, 2007). For instance, assuming that income and education are substitutes, the reduction in poverty due to a unit increase in income is less important for individuals who have an educational level close to the education deprivation cut-off than for individuals with very low education. Conversely, the drop in poverty would be more substantial for individuals with a larger level of education if income and education were considered to be complements (Bourguignon & Chakravarty, 2003).

7 As observed by Rippin (2017, p. 61), "A function $f(x)$ as a non-decreasing marginal if $f(x_g+1)-f(x_g) \geq f(x_h+1)-f(x_h)$ whenever $x_g \geq x_h$" The conditions that have to be satisfied by $[c_i]^{\gamma}$ are detailed in Rippin (2013, 2017).

8 Point estimates and their bootstrapped confidence intervals at 95% are available upon request from the authors.

9 Point estimates and their bootstrapped confidence intervals at 95% are available upon request from the authors.

10 These results are available upon request from the authors.

References

Alkire, S., & Foster, J. (2011). Counting and multi-dimensional poverty measurement. *Journal of Public Economics*, *95*(7–8), 476–487.

Alkire, S., & Foster, J. (2019). *The role of inequality in poverty measurement*. OPHI Working Paper, No. 126. Oxford Poverty & Human Development Initiative (OPHI), University of Oxford.

Alkire, S., Foster, J., Seth, S., Santos, M.E., Roche, J.M., & Ballón, P. (2015). *Multidimensional poverty measurement and analysis*. Oxford: Oxford University Press.

Alkire, S., & Santos, M.E. (2010). *Acute multi-dimensional poverty: A new index for developing countries*. OPHI Working Paper, 38, Oxford Poverty & Human Development Initiative (OPHI), University of Oxford.

Alkire, S., & Santos, M.E. (2014). Measuring acute poverty in the developing world: Robustness and scope of the multi-dimensional poverty index. *World Development*, *59*, 251–274.

Asfaw, A., Klasen, S., & Lamanna, F. (2009). Gender gap in parents' financing strategy for hospitalization of their children: Evidence from India. *Health Economics*, *19*(3), 265–279.

Atkinson, A.B. (2003). Multidimensional deprivation: Contrasting social welfare and counting approach. *Journal of Economic Inequality*, *1*(1), 51–65.

Atkinson, A.B., Cantillon, B., Marlier, E., & Nolan, B. (2002). *Social indicators. The EU and social inclusion*. Oxford: Oxford University Press.

Battiston, D., Cruces, G., López-Calva, L.F., Lugo, M.A., & Santos, M.E. (2013). Income and beyond: Multi-dimensional poverty in six Latin American countries. *Social Indicators Research*, *112*(2), 291–314.

Bérenger, V. (2016). Measuring multi-dimensional poverty in the three Southeast Asian countries using ordinal variables. In J. Silber & G. Wan (Eds.), *The Asian 'poverty miracle'. Impressive accomplishments or incomplete achievements?* (pp. 149–214). Cheltenham, Glos: Edward Elgar Publishing Limited.

Bérenger, V. (2017). Using ordinal variables to measure multi-dimensional poverty in Egypt and Jordan. *Journal of Economic Inequality*, *15*(2), 143–173.

Bessell, S. (2015). The individual deprivation measure: Measuring poverty as if gender and inequality matter. *Gender & Development*, *23*(2), 223–240.

Betti, G., & Lemmi, A. (2013). *Poverty and social exclusion: New methods of analysis*. Oxford: Routledge.

Bourguignon, F., & Chakravarty, S.R. (2003). The measurement of multi-dimensional poverty. *Journal of Economic Inequality*, *1*(1), 25–49.

Bradshaw, S., Chant, S., & Linneker, B. (2017a). Knowing gendered poverty in the global south: A protracted path to progress? *Spazio Filosofico*, *20*(2), 265–286.

Bradshaw, S., Chant, S., & Linneker, B. (2017b). Gender and poverty: What we know, don't know, and need to know for Agenda 2030. *Gender, Place & Culture*, *24*(12), 1667–1688.

Brandolini, A., & Aaberge, R. (2014). Multi-dimensional inequality and poverty. In A. Atkinson and F. Bourguignon (Eds.), *Handbook of income distribution*, Vol. 2A (pp. 141–216). Kidlington, Oxford: North-Holland.

Castillo, R., & Jácome, F. (2015). *Medición de la pobreza multidimensional en Ecuador*. Instituto Nacional de Estadística y Censos. http://www.ecuadorencifras.gob.ec/documentos/web-inec/Sitios/Pobreza_Multidimensional/assets/ipm-metodologia-oficial.pdf.

Cerioli, A., & Zani, S. (1990). A fuzzy approach to the measurement of poverty. In C. Dagum, & M. Zenga (Eds.), *Income and wealth distribution, inequality and poverty. Studies in contemporary economics* (pp. 272–284). Berlin, Heidelberg: Springer-Verlag.

Chakravarty, S.R. (2006). An axiomatic approach to multi-dimensional poverty measurement via fuzzy sets. In A. Lemmi & G. Betti (Eds.), *Fuzzy set approach to multi-dimensional poverty measurement* (pp. 49–72). New York: Springer.

Chakravarty, S.R. (2018). *Analyzing multi-dimensional well-being: A quantitative approach* (1st ed.). Wiley. https://www.wiley.com/en-us/Analyzing+Multidimensional+Well+Being%3A+A+Quantitative+Approach-p-9781119256953.

Chakravarty, S.R., & Lugo, M.A. (2016). Multidimensional indicators of inequality and poverty. In M. Adler & M. Fleurbaey (Eds.), *The Oxford handbook of well-being and public policy* (pp. 246–285). Oxford: Oxford University Press.

Chakravarty, S.R., & Silber, J. (2008). Measuring multi-dimensional poverty: The axiomatic approach. In N. Kakwani & J. Silber (Eds.), *Quantitative approaches to multi-dimensional poverty measurement* (pp. 192–209). New York: Palgrave Macmillan.

Chant, S. (2008). The 'feminisation of poverty' and the 'feminisation' of anti-poverty programmes: Room for revision? *Journal of Development Studies*, *44*(2), 165–197.

Chiappori, P.A. (2016). Welfare and the household. In M. Adler & M. Fleurbaey (Eds.), *The Oxford handbook of well-being and public policy* (pp. 821–843). Oxford: Oxford University Press.

CONEVAL (2011). Metodología para la medición multidimensional de la pobreza en México. Realidad, Datos y Espacio. *Revista Internacional de Estadística y Geografía*, *2*(1), 36–63.

DANE-DIMPE (2014). *Metodología. Índice de pobreza multidimensional (IPM).* Departamento Adminsitrativo Nacional de Estadística (DANE), Dirección Técnica de Metodología y Producción Estadística (DIMPE), República de Colombia. https://www.scribd.com/document/357409184/Metodologia-IPM-2.

Datt, G. (2017). *Distribution-sensitive multi-dimensional poverty measures with an application to India.* Discussion Paper, 06/17. Department of Economics, Monash University, Australia.

Datt, G. (2019). Distribution-sensitive multi-dimensional poverty measures. *The World Bank Economic Review*, *33*(3), 551–572.

Deaton, A. (1997). *The analysis of household surveys. A microeconometric approach to development policy.* Baltimore, MD: Published for the World Bank, The Johns Hopkins University Press.

Deutsch, J., & Silber, J. (2005). Measuring multi-dimensional poverty: An empirical comparison of various approaches. *Review of Income and Wealth*, *51*(1), 145–174.

Deutsch, J., & Silber, J. (2008). The order of acquisition of durable goods and the multidimensional measurement of poverty. In N. Kakwani & J. Silber (Eds.), *Quantitative approaches to multi-dimensional poverty measurement* (pp. 226–243). New York: Palgrave MacMillan.

Drèze, J., & Sen, A. (2002). *India: Development and participation* (2nd ed.). Oxford: Oxford University Press.

Duclos, J-Y., Sahn, D.E., & Younger, S.D. (2006). Robust multi-dimensional poverty comparisons. *The Economic Journal*, *116*(514), 943–968.

Duclos, J-Y., Sahn, D.E., & Younger, S.D. (2008). Using an ordinal approach to multi-dimensional poverty analysis. In N. Kakwani & J. Silber (Eds.), *Quantitative approaches to multi-dimensional poverty measurement* (pp. 244–261). New York: Palgrave MacMillan.

Duclos, J-Y., & Tiberti, L. (2016). Multidimensional poverty indices: A critical assessment. In M. Adler & M. Fleurbaey (Eds.), *The Oxford handbook of well-being and public policy* (pp. 677–708). Oxford: Oxford University Press.

Duryea, S., & Robles, M. (2017). *Social pulse in Latin America and the Caribbean 2017: Family legacy, breaking the mold or repeating patterns?* Inter-America Development Bank. http://dx.doi.org/10.18235/0000924.

ECLAC (2013). *Social panorama of Latin America, 2013 (LC/G.2580-P)*. The Economic Commission for Latin America and the Caribbean (ECLAC). Santiago de Chile: United Nations. http://repositorio.cepal.org/bitstream/handle/11362/36736/1/S2013869_en.pdf.

Espinoza-Delgado, J., & Klasen, S. (2018). Gender and multi-dimensional poverty in Nicaragua: An individual based approach. *World Development*, *118*, 466–491.

Hicks, J.R., & Allen, R.G.D. (1934a). A reconsideration of the theory of value, part I. *Economica, New Series*, *1*(1), 52–76.

Hicks, J.R., & Allen, R.G.D. (1934b). A reconsideration of the theory of value, part II. A mathematical theory of individual demand functions. *Economica, New Series*, *1*(2), 196–219.

ILO (2018). *World employment and social outlook: Trends 2018*. International Labour Organization. http://www.ilo.org/wcmsp5/groups/public/---dgreports/---dcomm/---publ/documents/publication/wcms_615594.pdf.

INEC (2015). *Índice de pobreza multidimensional (IPM): Metodología*. Costa Rica. Instituto Nacional de Estadística y Censos. http://www.inec.go.cr/sites/default/files/documentos/pobreza_y_presupuesto_de_hogares/pobreza/metodologias/mepobrezaenaho2015-01.pdf.

Jenkins, S.P., & Lambert, P.J. (1997). Three 'I's of poverty curves, with an analysis of UK poverty trends. *Oxford Economic Papers*, *49*(3), 317–327.

Kakwani, N., & Silber, J. (2008a). *The many dimensions of poverty*. London: Palgrave-Macmillan.

Kakwani, N., & Silber, J. (2008b). *Quantitative approach to multi-dimensional poverty*. London: Palgrave-Macmillan.

Klasen, S. (2000). Measuring poverty and deprivation in South Africa. *Review of Income and Wealth*, *46*(1), 33–58.

Klasen, S., & Wink, C. (2002). A turning point in gender bias in mortality? An update on the number of missing women. *Population and Development Review*, *28*(2), 285–312.

Klasen, S., & Wink, C. (2003). 'Missing women': Revisiting the debate. *Feminist Economics*, *9*(2–3), 263–299.

Lemmi, A., & Betti, G. (2006). *Fuzzy set approach to multi-dimensional poverty measurement*. New York: Springer.

Mara, D., & Evans, B. (2018). The sanitation and hygiene targets of the sustainable development goals: Scope and challenges. *Journal of Water Sanitation and Hygiene for Development*, *8*(1), 1–16.

MEF (2017). *Índice de pobreza multidimensional de Panamá – año 2017*. Ministerio de Economía y Finanzas, República de Panamá. http://www.mef.gob.pa/es/informes/Documents/Informe%20del%20Indice%20de%20Pobreza%20Multidimensional%20de%20Panama%202017.pdf.

Ministerio de Desarrollo Social (2016). *Metodología de medición de la pobreza multidimensional con entorno y redes*. Serie DocumentosMetodológicos CASEN No. 32.

Pogge, T., & Wisor, S. (2016). Measuring poverty: A proposal. In M. Adler & M. Fleurbaey (Eds.), *The Oxford handbook of well-being and public policy* (pp. 645–676). Oxford: Oxford University Press.

Ray, D. (1998). *Development economics*. Princeton, NJ: Princeton University Press.

Rippin, N. (2013). *Considerations of efficiency and distributive justice in multi-dimensional poverty measurement*. Doctoral Dissertation.

George-August-Universität Göttingen, Germany. https://www.die-gdi.de/uploads/media/Rippin_Efficiency_and_Distributive_Justice_Online_Publication.pdf.

Rippin, N. (2016). Multidimensional poverty in Germany: A capability approach. *Forum for Social Economics*, *45*(2–3), 230–255.

Rippin, N. (2017). Efficiency and distributive justice in multi-dimensional poverty issues. In R. White (Ed.), *Measuring multi-dimensional poverty and deprivation. Incidence and determinants in developed countries* (pp. 31–67). Cham: Palgrave Macmillan.

Robeyns, I. (2006). Three models of education: Rights, capabilities and human capital. *Theory and Research in Education*, *4*(1), 69–84.

Rodríguez, L. (2016). Intra-household inequalities in child rights and well-Being. A barrier to progress? *World Development*, *83*, 111–134.

Santos, M.E., & Villatoro, P. (2018). A multi-dimensional poverty index for Latin America. *Review of Income and Wealth*, *64*(1), 52–82.

SCGG-INE (2016). *Medición multidimensional de la pobreza (2016)*. Honduras. Secretaría de Coordinación General de Gobierno (SCGG) y El Instituto Nacional de Estadísticas (INE). http://www.scgg.gob.hn/ipm/assets/ipm.pdf.

Sen, A. (1976). Poverty: An ordinal approach to measurement. *Econometrica*, *44*(2), 219–231.

Sen, A. (1979). Issues in the measurement of poverty. *The Scandinavian Journal of Economics*, *81*(2), 285–307.

Sen, A. (1985). *Commodities and capabilities*. Netherlands: North-Holland.

Sen, A. (1992). *Inequality reexamined*. Cambridge, MA: Harvard University Press.

Sen, A. (1997). *On economic inequality*. Oxford: Oxford University Press.

Sen, A. (2000). *Development as freedom*. New York: First Anchor Books Edition.

Sen, A. (2010). *The idea of justice*. London: Penguin Books.

Seth, S., & Santos, M.E. (2019). On the interaction between focus and distributional properties in multi-dimensional poverty measurement. *Social Indicators Research*, *145*, 503–521.

Silber, J. (2007). Measuring poverty: Taking a multidimensional perspective. *Hacienda Pública Española/Revista de Economía Pública*, *182*(3), 29–74.

Silber, J. (2011). A comment on the MPI index. *The Journal of Economic Inequality*, *9*, 479–481.

Silber, J., & Yalonetzky, G. (2013). Measuring multi-dimensional deprivation with dichotomized and ordinal variables. In G. Betti & A. Lemmi (Eds.), *Poverty and social exclusion: New methods of analysis* (pp. 9–37). Oxford: Routledge.

Sorenson, S.B, Morssink, C., & Campos, P.A. (2011). Safe access to safe water in low income countries: Water fetching in current times. *Social Science & Medicine*, *72*(9), 1522–1526.

Stiglitz, J., Sen, A., & Fitoussi, J.-P. (2009a). *Report by the commission on the measurement of economic performance and social progress*. http://www.insee.fr/fr/publications-et-services/dossiers_web/stiglitz/doc-commission/RAPPORT_anglais.pdf.

Stiglitz, J., Sen, A., & Fitoussi, J-P (2009b). *The measurement of economic performance and social progress revisited – reflections and overview*. OFCE Working Paper, No. 2009-33, Centre de Recherche en Économie de Sciences Po.

STPP & MINEC-DIGESTYC (2015). *Medición multidimensional de la pobreza. El Salvador*. San Salvador: Secretaría Técnica y de Planificación de la Presidencia y Ministerio de Economía, a través de la Dirección de Estadística y Censos. http:

//www.secretariatecnica.gob.sv/wp-content/uploads/2015/10/Medici%C3%B3n-Multidimensional-de-la-Pobreza-El-Salvador.pdf.

Thorbecke, E. (2008). Multidimensional poverty: Conceptual and measurement issues. In N. Kakwani & J. Silber (Eds.), *The many dimensions of poverty* (pp. 3–19). New York: Palgrave Macmillan.

Thorbecke, E. (2011). A comment on multi-dimensional poverty indices. *The Journal of Economic Inequality*, *9*, 485–487.

Tsui, K.-Y. (2002). Multidimensional poverty indices. *Social Choice and Welfare*, *19*(1), 69–93.

UN (2015). *Resolution adopted by the general assembly on 25 September 2015*. United Nations General Assembly A/RES/70/1, Seventieth Session, Agenda items 15 and 116. http://www.un.org/ga/search/view:doc.asp?symbol=A/RES/70/1&Lang=E.

UN (2017). *Resolution adopted by the general assembly on 06 July 2017*. United Nations General Assembly A/RES/71/313, Seventy-first Session, Agenda items 13 and 117. http://ggim.un.org/meetings/2017-4th_Mtg_IAEG-SDG-NY/documents/A_RES_71_313.pdf.

UNDP (2010). *Human development report 2010. The real wealth of nations: Pathways to human development*. New York: United Nations Development Program.

Wiepking, P., & Maas, I. (2005). Gender differences in poverty: A cross-national study. *European Sociological Review*, *21*(3), 187–200.

Yalonetzky, G. (2012). *Conditions for the most robust multi-dimensional poverty comparisons using counting measures and ordinal variables*. ECINEQ Working Paper Series, WP 2012–257. Society for the Study of Economic Inequality (ECINEQ). http://www.ecineq.org/milano/wp/ecineq2012-257.pdf.

Yalonetzky, G. (2014). Conditions for the most robust multi-dimensional poverty comparisons using counting measures and ordinal variables. *Social Choice and Welfare*, *43*(4), 773–807. https://doi.org/10.1007/s00355-014-0810-2.

4 Can a Neighbouring Region Influence Poverty? A Fuzzy and Longitudinal Approach

Gianni Betti, Federico Crescenzi and Francesca Gagliardi

Introduction

One of the most important goals in the 2030 UN Agenda for Sustainable Development is to '*eradicate poverty, in all its forms and dimensions*' (UN, 2015). This has been particularly necessary since 2008, when the global financial crisis started, and 2015, with the failure to meet the Millennium Development Goal of halving extreme poverty in the world.

The European Union (EU) has also expressed the need to reduce poverty and launch anti-poverty programmes and policies in its Europe 2020 Strategy (European Commission, 2010), which consists of a series of policy objectives called 'headline targets' meant to be achieved by 2020. These targets include the reduction of the at-risk-of-poverty rate (ARPR, known in the literature as the headcount ratio, or FGT(0), following Foster et al., 1984) and of the at-persistent-risk-of-poverty rate in a longitudinal context to monitor poverty over time. Moreover, poverty measures are most useful to policymakers and researchers when they are finely disaggregated so that they can represent geographic units smaller than entire countries. This is the purpose of the DG Regional Policy of the European Commission, which employs sub-national/regional-level data (NUTS 2)[1] for the social indicators used for monitoring the 'headline targets' at the regional level.

To provide a comprehensive response to the needs mentioned above, in this chapter we adopt a longitudinal measure proposed by Verma et al. (2017), which is based on the fuzzy-set approach to multi-dimensional poverty: the 'fuzzy at-persistent-risk-of-poverty rate'. Then we estimate this measure at the regional level with small area estimation (SAE) techniques by introducing a spatial correlation model. In this way, we take into account whether a neighbouring region can influence poverty in all its forms and dimensions: the multi-dimensional dimension, the regional dimension and the longitudinal dimension.

The chapter is organised into six sections. Following this introduction, the second section models fuzzy measures of poverty and deprivation, covering both monetary and non-monetary aspects from cross-sectional and longitudinal perspectives. The third section presents the most important characteristics of the spatial empirical best linear unbiased predictor (SEBLUP), which is the small area technique that we believe is the most appropriate for estimating poverty at the regional level in the EU, because it includes correlations of poverty among neighbouring regions. The forth section describes the micro-dataset used and the construction of computational units for variance estimation. We briefly describe the EU survey on the statistics on income and living conditions (EU-SILC), a large-scale micro-database, from which we use a subset in our analysis. Empirical results are reported in the fifth section: fuzzy monetary and non-monetary longitudinal estimates are compared and discussed. Finally, the last section offers our concluding remarks, indicating fruitful directions for further research.

Cross-Sectional and Longitudinal Measures of Fuzzy Poverty

This section gives a mathematical description of cross-sectional and longitudinal measures of fuzzy and multi-dimensional poverty.

The fuzzy-set approach treats poverty as a matter of degree, replacing a simple dichotomy in the traditional approach in which the observations of individuals or households are divided into {0,1}. However, in principle, all individuals are liable to poverty but at varying degrees; so, each individual has a certain *propensity* towards poverty across the range [0,1].

Treating poverty as a matter of degree, applicable to all members of the population, has several advantages over using a simple 'yes–no' state. They are summarised by Verma et al. (2017) as follows:

1. Non-monetary poverty depends on barriers to access to various services or things that determine basic living conditions. An individual might have access to some of them but not others. Hence non-monetary poverty is inherently a matter of degree; therefore, a *quantitative approach* is essential.
2. The fuzzy approach provides more robust indicators of poverty in the *longitudinal* context. The conventional approach measures mobility simply in terms of movement across some designated poverty line and does not reflect the actual magnitude of the changes affecting individuals at all points in the distribution. Consequently, the degree of mobility of persons near this line tends to be over-emphasised, while that of people far from that line is largely ignored.

Apart from the various methodological choices involved in the construction of conventional poverty measures, the introduction of fuzzy measures includes *additional* factors on which choices have to be made. The fundamental factor concerns the choice of membership functions, meaning a quantitative specification of the propensity towards poverty of each person given the level and distribution of income of the population.

Cross-Sectional Fuzzy Membership Function

Betti and Verma (2008)[2] have proposed two fuzzy membership functions, based on the seminal contributions of Cerioli and Zani (1990) and Cheli and Lemmi (1995).

These are elaborated in Betti et al. (2015); in the generalised form, these membership functions are defined for any individual i as follows:

$$\mu_{i,K} = \left(\frac{\sum_{\gamma=i+1}^{n} w_\gamma \mid X_\gamma > X_i}{\sum_{\gamma=2}^{n} w_\gamma \mid X_\gamma > X_1} \right)^{\alpha_K - 1} \left(\frac{\sum_{\gamma=i+1}^{n} w_\gamma X_\gamma \mid X_\gamma > X_i}{\sum_{\gamma=2}^{n} w_\gamma X_\gamma \mid X_\gamma > X_1} \right) \tag{4.1}$$

where X is the equivalised income in monetary poverty or the overall score s in non-monetary poverty, w_γ is the sample weight of an individual with rank γ ($\gamma = 1,\ldots,n$) in the ascending distribution, and α_K ($K = 1,2$) are two parameters that correspond, respectively, to the monetary and non-monetary dimensions of poverty.

The α_K parameters are estimated such that the mean of the corresponding membership function equals the ARPR, which is calculated based on the official poverty line. Betti and Verma (2008) call the monetary-based indicator fuzzy monetary (FM) and the non-monetary indicator fuzzy supplementary (FS).

Construction of the FS Measure

Betti et al. (2015) proposed a step-by-step procedure for measuring the FS measures, as follows.

First, we identify the items to be included in the index or indices, which should be the most meaningful and useful (see Eurostat 2000, 2002). In fact, it is desirable to avoid items for which issues of choice, in terms of possession versus non-possession, cannot be satisfactorily resolved, for which possession is relatively rare (i.e. possession of a boat), or for which the degree of comparability among regions or countries is not sufficient.

Then, for each item, we determine a quantitative deprivation indicator in the range [0,1]: these indicators are used in a first exploratory factor analysis to identify the 'dimensions', which are distinct groups of items of non-monetary poverty, ideally independent of other dimensions and which describe a particular facet of living conditions. After this first exploratory factor analysis, we rearrange some items in the dimensions to create more meaningful groups: to test the goodness of fit of this final grouping, we conduct a confirmatory factor analysis, as proposed by Betti et al. (2015).

The weights to be assigned to each item are determined within each dimension; they are based on two elements: the dispersion of the item (prevalence weights) and the correlation with other items in the same dimension (correlation weights). For a detailed description of the weight construction, see Betti and Verma (2008).

Although the score $s_{i,h}$ within each dimension h is calculated as a weighted mean of items in that dimension, the overall score s_i is defined as the simple average of the dimension scores $s_{i,h}$, thus giving the same importance to all the dimensions, i.e. the several faces of non-monetary (supplementary) poverty. Finally, as explained above, the membership function FS is defined in Equation (4.1).

The positive results achieved while applying this methodology to fields other than poverty (see e.g. Aassve et al., 2007; Betti et al., 2011, 2016; Belhadj, 2015; Betti, 2017) demonstrate its applicability and robustness.

Longitudinal Measures of Fuzzy and Multi-Dimensional Poverty

In this section, we describe the construction of the fuzzy longitudinal poverty measures, which aim to estimate occasional, persistent, or chronic concepts of poverty. In the fuzzy literature, these measures are defined as: (1) anytime, for individuals who are members of fuzzy-set poverty for at least one in four years; (2) continuous, for those who have membership in all four years; and, we add a definition proposed by Verma et al. (2017), (3) the 'fuzzy at-persistent-risk-of-poverty', which refers to people who are members of the fuzzy set in the most recent year and in two or three years in the last three years. This third measure is the fuzzy counterpart of the Eurostat 'at-persistent-risk-of-poverty rate', one of the most important Laeken indicators.

From a mathematical point of view, we let μ_t be the series of T = 4 membership functions over the four periods, and then we define fuzzy measure 1 as a fuzzy union over the periods, which consists of the maximum T values:

$$\mu_{any} = \max(\mu_1, \mu_2, \mu_3, \mu_4) \tag{4.2}$$

In the same way, the continuous fuzzy measure is defined as the fuzzy intersection over the periods, which consists of the minimum T values as:

$$\mu_{cont} = \min(\mu_1, \mu_2, \mu_3, \mu_4) \tag{4.3}$$

The definition of the fuzzy at-persistent-risk-of-poverty is much more complex; for a full and detailed description, see Verma et al. (2017).

Model-Based Small Area Estimation

Sample sizes of surveys such as the EU-SILC, designed to be representative at the national level, are frequently too low to obtain efficient estimates of indicators at the small area level, such as NUTS 2. In other words, the measures calculated from such small sub-samples – called 'direct estimators' in the related literature – have variances that are too large. SAE theory is concerned with resolving these problems.

Often some additional information can be used to define estimators for small areas:[3] in some cases, they are values of the variable of interest in other, similar areas or past values of this variable in the same area or values of other variables that are related to the variable of interest. Estimation approaches based on using this information are called 'indirect or model based'. Henderson (1950) developed the best linear unbiased prediction (BLUP), which assumes that the variances associated with the model are known. In practice, of course, these variance components are unknown and have to be estimated from the data. The predictor obtained from the BLUP when unknown variance components are replaced by associated estimators is called the empirical best linear unbiased predictor (EBLUP; Fay and Herriot, 1979), defined as:

$$\hat{\theta}_i = x_i'\beta + z_i v_i + e_i \tag{4.4}$$

where θ_i ($i = 1,2,\ldots,m$) are the specific parameters of areas or domains of a population (i.e. regions), and they are assumed to be linearly related to a vector of p-area specific auxiliary variables $x_i = (x_{1i,} x_{2i},\ldots,x_{pi})^T$; where v_i are independent area-level random effects, independent of e_i; they are the sampling errors for each area, independent of one another.

This classic Fay and Herriot model in Equation (4.4) can be extended by considering that vector v follows a simultaneously autoregressive (SAR) process with spatial autoregressive coefficient ρ and proximity matrix W (Cressie, 1993). In this way, the model with spatially correlated random effects is:

$$\hat{\theta} = X\beta + Z(I - \rho W)^{-1} u + e. \tag{4.5}$$

The estimator is unknown because it depends on unknown parameters, such as ρ. By substituting them with consistent estimators, a two-stage estimator called a spatial EBLUP is obtained (for further details, see Pratesi and Salvati, 2007).

Estimating the spatial EBLUP models requires having the standard errors of the direct estimator $\hat{\theta}$. Because the poverty measures adopted in the present chapter are quite complex (e.g. the 'fuzzy at-persistent-risk-of-poverty rate')[4] and are calculated on the basis of a very complex survey, such as the EU-SILC, we estimate their standard errors with jack-knife repeated replication (JRR) as in Verma and Betti (2011).[5]

The Dataset: EU-SILC in Spain

The reference data in the present work are based on a subset of microdata from the EU-SILC survey, which is the major source of comparative statistics on income and living conditions in Europe. The survey is conducted annually in each participating country. The EU-SILC covers data and data sources of various types: cross-sectional and longitudinal, household and individual level, on income and social conditions, and from registers and interview surveys, depending on the country. A standard integrated design has been adopted by nearly all EU countries. The design recommended by Eurostat involves a rotational panel in which a new sample of households and individuals is introduced each year to replace a quarter of the existing sample. Each individual enumerated in each new sample is followed up in the survey for four years, along with that individual's entire household.

Construction of Computational Units for Variance Estimation

Variance estimation of measures from surveys such as the EU-SILC based on complex sample designs requires full information on the sample structure. Implementing practical variance computation procedures such as the one adopted here and based on JRR (Verma and Betti, 2011), requires information at a minimum including specification at the micro-level of: (1) sample weights, (2) stratum and (3) primary sampling unit (PSU). In addition, it is necessary to have a detailed description of the actual sample selection procedures used so that the micro-level information on PSUs and strata can be correctly interpreted and used to construct 'computational' PSUs and strata for variance estimation.

Although this type of information on sample structure is collected in all the EU-SILC surveys, not all of it is included in the micro-data in the public domain. This restriction on the availability of essential information results from various policy considerations, some justifiable, but not all. In any case, the absence of this information in complex samples makes it impossible to compute valid estimates of the sampling error.

Thanks to research cooperation with the Organisation for Economic Co-operation and Development (OECD) (Piacentini, 2014), we gained access to the public cross-sectional 2011 EU-SILC data (UDB) and the non-public variables concerning the sample structure on Spain: the code for regions at the NUTS 2 level (DB040), sampling strata (DB050) and PSUs (DB060).

Generally, the EU-SILC national surveys are designed with a focus on the production of reliable estimates at the national level. In fact, although the EU-SILC survey has a very large sample in Spain (13,109 households and 34,756 individuals for 2011), the regional sub-samples are very heterogeneous in size, so in some NUTS 2 regions, the estimates are not significant.

The Spain EU-SILC 2011 Intermediate Quality Report (INE, 2012) provides us with a detailed description of the sample design, which is important for understanding whether regions form independent sampling domains and for the construction of the 'computational' PSUs and strata.

DB040 and DB050 define unique strata within each region separately. The use of the sample description and of the three variables makes it possible to define the computational strata and PSUs for variance estimation.

Empirical Analysis

Using the data described above, this section analyses the direct estimates and their relative sampling errors for the poverty and deprivation variables. The results for each of the 19 regions in Spain can be entered into the Fay and Herriot (FH) and the SEBLUP models. The following statistics are considered in turn in a longitudinal context: the FM poverty rate and the FS deprivation rate. For each of these statistics, the longitudinal measures are as described above: any-time poverty, continuous poverty and the at-persistent-risk-of-poverty rate.

Table 4.1 reports the outcomes related to the FM fuzzy at-persistent-risk-of-poverty rate; the first set of values comprise direct estimates and the direct standard errors and the second set shows the FH estimates, the FH standard error and the gain of such model, reported in the percentage of reduction of direct standard errors, and the last set of measures report the values in the SEBLUP model.

Two aspects should be considered in this analysis: the substantive results at the regional level and the gain in precision using both the FH and SEBLUP models.

The highest measures of the fuzzy at-persistent-risk-of-poverty rate are found in Extremadura, Andalucía and Castilla–La Mancha, whereas Navarra, País Vasco, Madrid, Aragón, Balears and Cataluña are better off, with a fuzzy measure below 10%. Melilla has a low percentage according to the direct estimate (7%); however, because of the small sub-sample size, this measure is not significant. The results obtained by both the FH and SEBLUP models severely reduce the standard errors, but the more precise measure is much higher.

The results concerning standard errors show that both FH and SEBLUP are lower than the direct estimates. In general, we have a mean reduction in the standard error for FH of 18% and for SEBLUP of 26%. The largest reduction in standard errors is in regions with small sub-samples, such as Melilla, Ceuta and Rioja.

However, for the purpose of this chapter, it is quite interesting to observe the larger gain in spatial EBLUP over FH; the geographic information in the w matrix for vicinity clearly contributes added value, indicating that an increase in poverty in a neighbouring region affects the region under investigation as well.

Table 4.2 reports the outcomes related to the FS fuzzy at-persistent-risk-of-poverty rate; the three sets of values are the same as those in Table 4.1. The highest measures of the FS fuzzy at-persistent-risk-of-poverty rate are now in Galicia, Andalucía and Ceuta, whereas Melilla, Aragón, Asturias,

Table 4.1 FM fuzzy at-persistent-risk-of-poverty rate

	Direct	*SE*	*FH*	*SE*	*Gain FH*	*SEBLUP*	*SE*	*Gain SEBLUP*
Galicia	12.32%	1.25%	12.55%	1.19%	95.45%	12.81%	1.18%	94.40%
Asturias	10.18%	2.27%	10.57%	1.91%	84.04%	10.73%	1.62%	71.44%
Cantabria	10.87%	2.32%	10.35%	1.95%	83.79%	10.37%	1.72%	73.90%
País Vasco	7.39%	1.72%	6.85%	1.60%	93.19%	6.29%	1.48%	86.04%
Navarra	3.87%	1.39%	4.66%	1.32%	94.78%	5.37%	1.27%	91.19%
Rioja	17.33%	3.69%	13.43%	2.44%	66.19%	11.53%	1.89%	51.23%
Aragón	8.08%	1.96%	8.46%	1.73%	88.42%	8.17%	1.47%	74.98%
Madrid	8.21%	1.15%	7.67%	1.12%	98.04%	7.76%	1.17%	102.28%
Castilla y León	13.77%	2.87%	12.81%	2.19%	76.21%	13.76%	1.56%	54.25%
Castilla–La Mancha	19.83%	2.78%	17.92%	2.19%	78.80%	18.80%	1.70%	61.11%
Extremadura	24.96%	2.49%	22.58%	2.13%	85.84%	23.04%	1.92%	77.10%
Cataluña	9.06%	1.27%	9.48%	1.21%	95.19%	9.39%	1.17%	92.68%
Comunitat Valenciana	12.17%	1.54%	12.41%	1.43%	92.74%	12.37%	1.32%	86.00%
Balears	8.02%	1.53%	9.29%	1.42%	92.95%	8.65%	1.51%	98.95%
Andalucía	20.06%	1.79%	19.07%	1.63%	91.32%	19.61%	1.54%	85.95%
Murcia	15.29%	3.21%	15.61%	2.35%	73.40%	16.88%	1.89%	58.77%
Ceuta	17.05%	8.69%	18.90%	3.18%	36.55%	14.98%	2.62%	30.14%
Melilla	6.99%	6.23%	12.70%	2.79%	44.77%	9.55%	2.40%	38.44%
Canarias	12.56%	2.48%	13.77%	2.04%	82.25%	11.68%	2.01%	80.78%
					81.78%			**74.19%**

Table 4.2 FS fuzzy at-persistent-risk-of-poverty rate

	Direct	*SE*	*FH*	*SE*	*Gain FH*	*SEBLUP*	*SE*	*Gain SEBLUP*
Galicia	19.88%	2.36%	17.28%	1.98%	83.70%	17.22%	2.09%	88.62%
Asturias	7.90%	1.37%	7.80%	1.31%	95.48%	8.01%	1.34%	97.80%
Cantabria	13.21%	3.08%	11.35%	2.30%	74.60%	11.02%	2.41%	78.16%
País Vasco	8.08%	1.71%	8.75%	1.56%	90.94%	8.80%	1.60%	93.31%
Navarra	10.36%	2.87%	9.25%	2.25%	78.51%	8.70%	2.35%	81.84%
Rioja	9.07%	1.59%	9.47%	1.47%	92.21%	9.38%	1.50%	94.55%
Aragón	6.80%	1.39%	6.97%	1.32%	95.16%	7.03%	1.35%	97.67%
Madrid	8.95%	1.32%	9.94%	1.26%	95.49%	9.93%	1.28%	96.96%
Castilla y León	9.00%	1.65%	9.16%	1.51%	91.89%	9.11%	1.59%	96.63%
Castilla–La Mancha	11.73%	2.16%	11.91%	1.86%	85.79%	11.74%	1.96%	90.52%
Extremadura	12.83%	1.86%	12.10%	1.67%	89.38%	12.08%	1.72%	92.41%
Cataluña	11.00%	1.59%	10.49%	1.48%	92.78%	10.47%	1.52%	95.22%
Comunitat Valenciana	13.90%	1.78%	13.39%	1.60%	90.25%	13.45%	1.66%	93.56%
Balears	12.78%	4.35%	14.80%	2.75%	63.15%	14.75%	2.77%	63.74%
Andalucía	20.98%	2.00%	20.16%	1.87%	93.35%	20.32%	1.92%	95.82%
Murcia	14.35%	3.22%	14.19%	2.37%	73.59%	14.49%	2.46%	76.42%
Ceuta	18.75%	9.38%	13.44%	2.97%	31.70%	13.22%	2.99%	31.91%
Melilla	5.26%	0.66%	5.53%	0.65%	98.78%	5.52%	0.66%	99.16%
Canarias	17.86%	2.82%	16.57%	2.25%	79.62%	16.48%	2.27%	80.64%
					84.02%			**86.58%**

Navarra, País Vasco, Madrid, Castilla y León, Rioja and Cataluña are better off, with a fuzzy measure below or around 10%.

The results for standard errors have a smaller reduction than the corresponding FM measure: 16% for FH and 13% for SEBLUP. In this case, the effect of the geographic information in the vicinity matrix does not contribute added value.

Table 4.3 shows the results for the FM any-time poverty rates; the highest values are in Extremadura, Castilla–La Mancha and Andalucía, whereas the lowest are in Navarra, Aragón and Baleares. The average gains in standard errors for FH and SEBLUB are similar to those for the FM at-persistent-risk-of-poverty rate. Again, the largest reductions are in the smallest regions, Melilla and Ceuta.

The results for the FS any-time poverty rate are in Table 4.4, showing the highest values are in Galicia, Andalucía, Canarias and Murcia, and the lowest are in Melilla, Navarra, Aragón and País Vasco. Again, the average gains in standard errors for FH and SEBLUB are similar to those for the FS at-persistent-risk-of-poverty rate. The largest reduction is in the smallest region, Ceuta.

Table 4.5 reports the FM continuous poverty rates; the highest values are in Extremadura, Ceuta, Castilla–La Mancha, Andalucía, Murcia and Rioja, and the lowest are in Navarra, País Vasco, Asturias, Madrid and Melilla. In this case, the average gain in the standard error is larger than in all the other measures, with a mean reduction of about 20% for FH and 24% for SEBLUP.

Finally, Table 4.6 reports the FS continuous poverty rates, for which the highest values are in Ceuta, Andalucía and Galicia, and the lowest are in Melilla, Aragón and Asturias. Again, the average gains in the standard errors for FH and SEBLUB are similar to those for the other measures.

Concluding Remarks and Further Considerations

In this chapter, we propose a series of mathematical procedures to estimate longitudinal poverty and deprivation at the regional level. First, we consider direct estimates of poverty and deprivation measured by means of fuzzy-set theory. In particular, we take into account a new measure, the 'fuzzy at-persistent-risk-of-poverty rate', proposed by Verma et al. (2017); then, we employ JRR for the first time in the version of this measure in Verma and Betti (2011) to estimate the standard errors of these fuzzy direct estimates.

The primary result obtained is the extension of variance estimation to go beyond measures of monetary longitudinal poverty, specifically using a fuzzy formulation of those measures and, as a corollary, multi-dimensional measures of longitudinal deprivation, which by their nature are a matter of degree – i.e. are fuzzy. To our knowledge, no such extension has been previously presented in the literature. Moreover, we propose the use of SAE

Table 4.3 FM any-time poverty rate

	Direct	*SE*	*FH*	*SE*	*Gain FH*	*SEBLUP*	*SE*	*Gain SEBLUP*
Galicia	35.5%	2.81%	34.96%	2.60%	92.58%	33.90%	2.52%	89.67%
Asturias	23.29%	3.20%	25.12%	2.89%	90.14%	26.81%	2.67%	83.24%
Cantabria	29.50%	5.04%	28.44%	3.92%	77.81%	27.44%	3.38%	67.08%
País Vasco	25.12%	4.07%	23.53%	3.57%	87.69%	22.03%	3.19%	78.43%
Navarra	16.22%	3.12%	18.55%	2.86%	91.69%	19.61%	2.70%	86.58%
Rioja	34.03%	5.08%	31.89%	3.91%	76.99%	29.07%	3.35%	65.86%
Aragón	21.34%	3.38%	23.01%	3.03%	89.49%	24.01%	2.66%	78.54%
Madrid	27.98%	2.81%	26.00%	2.69%	95.61%	26.27%	2.81%	100.00%
Castilla y León	32.62%	4.20%	31.90%	3.50%	83.26%	33.23%	2.77%	65.86%
Castilla–La Mancha	42.09%	3.35%	40.57%	3.01%	90.10%	41.62%	2.67%	79.95%
Extremadura	46.16%	3.93%	44.76%	3.51%	89.14%	46.08%	3.19%	81.13%
Cataluña	29.56%	2.35%	29.71%	2.23%	94.90%	29.26%	2.17%	92.73%
Comunitat Valenciana	34.26%	2.99%	33.91%	2.74%	91.45%	33.79%	2.53%	84.65%
Balears	20.77%	3.28%	24.49%	2.94%	89.75%	23.59%	3.15%	95.97%
Andalucía	43.99%	2.05%	43.16%	1.99%	96.85%	43.33%	1.94%	94.74%
Murcia	36.20%	5.88%	36.61%	4.27%	72.58%	39.50%	3.40%	57.84%
Ceuta	31.50%	13.34%	40.50%	5.60%	41.96%	34.11%	5.01%	37.54%
Melilla	28.12%	25.86%	33.69%	5.32%	20.58%	27.10%	4.78%	18.48%
Canarias	35.43%	5.25%	35.78%	4.02%	76.62%	31.04%	4.01%	76.42%
					81.54%			**75.51%**

Table 4.4 FS any-time poverty rate

	Direct	*SE*	*FH*	*SE*	*Gain FH*	*SEBLUP*	*SE*	*Gain SEBLUP*
Galicia	46.54%	3.79%	41.74%	3.22%	84.89%	42.63%	3.24%	85.52%
Asturias	25.41%	3.95%	28.61%	3.30%	83.65%	27.11%	3.32%	83.95%
Cantabria	35.42%	4.64%	35.09%	3.64%	78.46%	36.61%	3.66%	78.88%
País Vasco	24.84%	2.71%	24.89%	2.55%	94.26%	24.62%	2.61%	96.23%
Navarra	24.34%	4.13%	23.79%	3.58%	86.65%	23.84%	3.68%	89.12%
Rioja	29.08%	3.76%	31.48%	3.21%	85.37%	32.39%	3.19%	84.93%
Aragón	24.44%	3.58%	27.23%	3.09%	86.44%	27.80%	3.12%	87.29%
Madrid	28.99%	2.52%	28.21%	2.39%	95.07%	28.61%	2.41%	95.88%
Castilla y León	27.74%	3.55%	30.34%	3.09%	86.85%	30.71%	3.13%	88.19%
Castilla–La Mancha	31.03%	3.92%	33.70%	3.33%	84.94%	33.36%	3.36%	85.75%
Extremadura	38.85%	4.02%	39.36%	3.44%	85.54%	39.62%	3.58%	89.00%
Cataluña	31.82%	3.15%	31.25%	2.83%	89.84%	30.82%	2.85%	90.48%
Comunitat Valenciana	39.16%	3.51%	37.80%	3.06%	87.21%	37.76%	3.07%	87.65%
Balears	30.48%	3.69%	31.49%	3.16%	85.61%	31.44%	3.15%	85.49%
Andalucía	45.55%	2.81%	43.55%	2.60%	92.56%	43.45%	2.66%	94.67%
Murcia	42.01%	5.62%	39.78%	4.07%	72.48%	37.74%	4.14%	73.72%
Ceuta	33.92%	13.36%	24.55%	5.33%	39.93%	22.43%	4.58%	34.27%
Melilla	18.95%	5.64%	21.68%	4.24%	75.22%	20.88%	4.03%	71.45%
Canarias	43.40%	3.47%	41.95%	3.08%	88.91%	41.55%	3.11%	89.63%
					83.36%			**83.79%**

Table 4.5 FM continuous poverty rate

	Direct	*SE*	*FH*	*SE*	*Gain FH*	*SEBLUP*	*SE*	*Gain SEBLUP*
Galicia	7.91%	1.14%	8.28%	1.06%	92.82%	8.10%	1.05%	91.59%
Asturias	5.11%	1.03%	5.57%	0.97%	94.00%	5.70%	0.94%	90.98%
Cantabria	7.01%	1.46%	6.72%	1.28%	88.07%	6.49%	1.21%	83.18%
País Vasco	4.43%	1.17%	4.03%	1.10%	94.32%	3.75%	1.06%	91.12%
Navarra	2.13%	0.76%	2.44%	0.74%	97.34%	2.63%	0.73%	96.64%
Rioja	11.24%	3.09%	8.61%	1.88%	60.75%	7.44%	1.58%	51.10%
Aragón	4.77%	1.02%	4.98%	0.96%	94.40%	4.86%	0.93%	91.21%
Madrid	5.59%	0.87%	5.04%	0.85%	97.78%	5.17%	0.88%	101.11%
Castilla y León	8.50%	2.07%	8.25%	1.60%	77.02%	9.04%	1.29%	62.42%
Castilla–La Mancha	13.63%	1.96%	12.55%	1.58%	80.65%	13.31%	1.37%	70.07%
Extremadura	19.49%	1.95%	17.04%	1.65%	84.45%	17.07%	1.55%	79.32%
Cataluña	6.18%	0.92%	6.44%	0.88%	95.31%	6.24%	0.87%	94.36%
Comunitat Valenciana	7.86%	1.17%	8.15%	1.08%	92.28%	8.16%	1.04%	88.80%
Balears	6.04%	1.87%	7.57%	1.51%	80.91%	6.98%	1.59%	85.02%
Andalucía	13.80%	1.58%	13.10%	1.38%	87.52%	13.82%	1.33%	83.91%
Murcia	11.08%	2.96%	11.21%	1.91%	64.37%	11.79%	1.64%	55.29%
Ceuta	14.43%	7.55%	13.95%	2.40%	31.74%	11.83%	2.26%	29.98%
Melilla	5.76%	6.01%	9.23%	2.13%	35.38%	7.68%	2.07%	34.52%
Canarias	9.19%	2.03%	9.99%	1.60%	78.97%	9.02%	1.67%	81.97%
					80.43%			**76.98%**

Table 4.6 FS continuous poverty rate

	Direct	*SE*	*FH*	*SE*	*Gain FH*	*SEBLUP*	*SE*	*Gain SEBLUP*
Galicia	13.55%	1.75%	11.52%	1.48%	84.71%	11.53%	1.55%	88.86%
Asturias	4.34%	0.93%	4.32%	0.90%	96.61%	4.53%	0.91%	98.05%
Cantabria	9.21%	2.59%	7.24%	1.84%	71.09%	6.95%	1.87%	72.30%
País Vasco	5.22%	1.68%	5.66%	1.44%	85.35%	5.81%	1.47%	87.09%
Navarra	5.64%	2.12%	5.20%	1.69%	79.80%	4.73%	1.72%	81.22%
Rioja	5.88%	1.29%	6.03%	1.17%	91.30%	5.99%	1.19%	92.86%
Aragón	3.95%	1.16%	4.06%	1.09%	94.12%	4.07%	1.10%	95.14%
Madrid	5.40%	0.82%	5.84%	0.80%	97.15%	5.85%	0.81%	98.20%
Castilla y León	5.97%	1.20%	5.92%	1.12%	92.62%	5.95%	1.14%	94.29%
Castilla–La Mancha	5.87%	1.32%	6.27%	1.20%	90.85%	6.20%	1.22%	92.45%
Extremadura	8.72%	1.62%	7.84%	1.40%	86.44%	7.73%	1.45%	89.19%
Cataluña	6.58%	1.09%	6.31%	1.02%	94.39%	6.24%	1.04%	95.81%
Comunitat Valenciana	8.14%	1.29%	7.94%	1.18%	91.19%	7.91%	1.20%	92.94%
Balears	8.58%	3.42%	9.41%	2.12%	62.07%	9.30%	2.16%	63.12%
Andalucía	14.27%	1.75%	13.25%	1.59%	90.41%	13.43%	1.61%	91.91%
Murcia	7.89%	1.56%	8.14%	1.37%	88.09%	8.27%	1.39%	89.18%
Ceuta	16.70%	8.80%	8.45%	2.31%	26.24%	7.95%	2.34%	26.63%
Melilla	1.20%	0.97%	2.03%	0.92%	95.17%	1.97%	0.94%	96.99%
Canarias	9.79%	1.90%	9.63%	1.59%	83.72%	9.52%	1.63%	85.70%
					84.28%			**85.89%**

techniques, such as spatial EBLUP, to further reduce the variability of fuzzy poverty measures at the regional level.

Overall, we conclude that both FH and SEBLUP can reduce standard errors by 20–30% on average, with a rate of 70% in regions with particular small sample sizes. Moreover, a larger gain in spatial EBLUP over FH is evident only for FM longitudinal measures, whereas little gain is achieved for FS measures, which obtain no added value from the geographic information in the w matrix of vicinity. So, in conclusion, neighbouring regions affect poverty only when we adopt a monetary measure, but it is unaffected using the multi-dimensional or non-monetary measure. Further research is necessary to understand the reasons for this outcome.

Notes

1 NUTS is an abbreviation for Nomenclature of Statistical Territorial Units. This is Eurostat's hierarchical classification of regions, from member states (NUTS 0) to smaller areas.
2 For further details on the contributions of philosophy, mathematics and economics of the fuzzy-set approach to poverty measurement, see also Lemmi and Betti (2006a, 2006b), Cheli and Betti (1999), Betti, Cheli and Cambini (2004), Belhadj (2011, 2012), Alkire and Foster (2011), Belhadj and Limam (2012) and Betti and Lemmi (2013).
3 When additional information comes from the population census, the SAE method is defined as 'poverty mapping', and the two seminal papers on it are Elbers, Lanjouw and Lanjouw (2003, 2005).
4 A 'complex measure' is an estimator which cannot be expressed in terms of average, total, or a ratio of averages. For instance, fuzzy measures in Equation (4.1), or the fuzzy APRP rate are clearly complex measures.
5 Verma and Betti (2011) demonstrate how a variant of the JRR method can fit better in the case of 'complex measures'; moreover, Betti et al. (2018) show that the JRR variant in Verma and Betti (2011) is particularly adapted for estimating variance of fuzzy poverty measures.

References

Aassve A., Betti G., Mazzuco S., Mencarini L. (2007), Marital disruption and economic well-being; a comparative analysis, *Journal of the Royal Statistical Society, Series A*, 170(3), pp. 781–799.

Alkire S., Foster J. (2011), Counting and multi-dimensional poverty measurement, *Journal of Public Economics*, 95(7–8), pp. 476–487.

Belhadj B. (2011), A new fuzzy unidimensional poverty index from an information theory perspective, *Empirical Economics*, 40(3), pp. 687–704.

Belhadj B. (2012), New weighting scheme for the dimensions in multi-dimensional poverty indices, *Economic Letters*, 116(3), pp. 304–307.

Belhadj B. (2015), Employment measure in development countries via minimum wage and poverty: new Fuzzy approach, *Opsearch*, 52(2), pp 329–339.

Belhadj B., Limam M. (2012), Unidimensional and multi-dimensional fuzzy poverty measures: New approach, *Economic Modelling*, 29(4), pp. 995–1002.

Betti G. (2017), Fuzzy measures of quality of life in Germany: a multi-dimensional and comparative approach, *Quality and Quantity*, 51(1), pp. 23–34.

Betti G., Cheli B., Cambini R. (2004), A statistical model for the dynamics between two fuzzy states: theory and application to poverty analysis, *Metron*, 62(3), pp. 391–411.

Betti G., D'Agostino A., Neri L. (2011), Educational mismatch of graduates: A multi-dimensional and fuzzy indicator, *Social Indicators Research*, 103(3), pp. 465–480.

Betti G., Gagliardi F., Lemmi A., Verma V. (2015). Comparative measures of multi-dimensional deprivation in the European Union, *Empirical Economics*, 49(3), pp. 1071–1100.

Betti G., Gagliardi F., Verma V. (2018), Simplified jackknife variance estimates for fuzzy measures of multi-dimensional poverty, *International Statistical Review*, 86(1), pp. 68–86.

Betti G., Lemmi A., eds. (2013), *Poverty and Social Exclusion: New Methods of Analysis*, London: Routledge.

Betti G., Soldi R., Talev I. (2016), Fuzzy multi-dimensional indicators of quality of life: The empirical case of Macedonia, *Social Indicators Research*, 127(1), pp. 39–53.

Betti G., Verma V. (2008), Fuzzy measures of the incidence of relative poverty and deprivation: a multi-dimensional perspective, *Statistical Methods and Applications*, 17, pp. 225–250.

Cerioli A., Zani S. (1990), A fuzzy approach to the measurement of poverty. In: Dagum C., Zenga M. (eds.), *Income and Wealth Distribution, Inequality and Poverty*, Springer, Berlin, pp. 272–284.

Cheli B., Betti G. (1999), Fuzzy analysis of poverty dynamics on an Italian pseudo panel, 1985–1994, *Metron*, 57, pp. 83–104.

Cheli B., Lemmi A. (1995), A totally fuzzy and relative approach to the multi-dimensional analysis of poverty, *Economic Notes*, 24, pp. 115–134.

Cressie N. (1993), *Statistics for Spatial Data*, New York: Wiley.

Elbers C., Lanjouw J.O., Lanjouw P. (2003), Micro-level estimation of poverty and inequality, *Econometrica*, 71(1), pp. 355–364.

Elbers C., Lanjouw J.O., Lanjouw P. (2005), Imputed welfare estimates in regression analysis, *Journal of Economic Geography*, 5(1), pp. 101–118.

European Commission (2010), *Communication from the Commission. Europe 2020. A Strategy for Smart, Sustainable and Inclusive Growth*. Brussels, 3.3.2010 COM(2010) 2020.

Eurostat (2000), *European Social Statistics: Income, Poverty and Social Exclusion*, Luxembourg: Office for Official Publications of the European Communities.

Eurostat (2002), *European Social Statistics: Income, Poverty and Social Exclusion, 2nd Report*, Luxembourg: Office for Official Publications of the European Communities.

Fay R.E., Herriot R.A. (1979), Estimates of income for small places: an application of James-Stein procedures to census data, *Journal of the American Statistical Association*, 74, pp. 269–277.

Foster J.E., Greer J., Thorbecke E. (1984), A class of decomposable poverty measures, *Econometrica*, 52, pp. 716–766.

Henderson C.R. (1950), Estimation of genetic parameters, *Annals of Mathematical Statistics*, 21, pp. 309–310.

Instituto Nacional De Estadistica (INE), (2012), Intermediate Quality Report, Survey on Income and Living Conditions Spain (Spanish ECV 2011).

Lemmi A., Betti G. eds. (2006a), *Fuzzy Set Approach to Multidimensional Poverty Measurement*, New York: Springer.

Lemmi A., Betti G. (2006b), Introduction, in Lemmi A., Betti G. (eds.), *Fuzzy Set Approach to Multidimensional Poverty Measurement*, New York: Springer, pp. 1–7.

Piacentini M. (2014), *Measuring Income Inequality and Poverty at the Regional Level in OECD Countries*, OECD Statistics Working Papers, 2014/03, OECD Publishing.

Pratesi M., Salvati N. (2007), Small area estimation: The EBLUP model based on spatially correlated random effects, *Statistical Methods and Applications*, 17(1), pp. 113–141.

United Nations (2015), *Transforming our World: The 2030 Agenda for Sustainable Development*, A/RES/70/1, United Nations.

Verma V., Betti G. (2011), Taylor linearization sampling errors and design effects for poverty measures and other complex statistics, *Journal of Applied Statistics*, 38(8), pp. 1549–1576.

Verma V., Betti G., Gagliardi F. (2017), Fuzzy measures of longitudinal poverty in a comparative perspective, *Social Indicators Research*, 130(2), pp. 435–454.

5 Multi-Dimensional and Fuzzy Poverty at the Regional Level in Iran

Hossein Khoshbakht, Francesca Gagliardi and Ali Asadi

Introduction

Over the past 30 years, many researchers have focused on the necessity of considering various aspects of deprivation simultaneously in its multiple dimensions. In fact, outstanding authors, such as Atkinson and Bourguignon (1982), Kolm (1977), Maasoumi (1986), Sen (1999) and Tsui (1985), have repeatedly stressed the need to adopt a multi-dimensional approach.

The many attempts to study poverty with a multi-dimensional perspective can be divided into two broad categories: axiomatic and non-axiomatic approaches. A non-axiomatic approach implicitly considers indicators perfectly substitutable from an economic perspective. In this approach, different indicators or items are combined in order to obtain a multi-dimensional index, and this combination can be done at the macro level (Anand and Sen, 1997) or the individual level (Klasen, 2000; Smeeding et al., 1993; Townsend, 1979). By contrast, Chakravarty, Mukherjee and Ranade (1998) and Bourguignon and Chakravarty (2003) contributed to the development of an axiomatic approach.

In this chapter, we use a non-axiomatic approach that goes beyond a conventional study of poverty based simply on a dichotomy between those who are poor and those who are not, defined in relation to a particular poverty line. By contrast, here multi-dimensional poverty is treated as a matter of degree determined in terms of the relative position of individuals in Iran, i.e. in the distribution of various aspects of their living conditions. The state of deprivation is thus seen in the form of 'fuzzy sets' to which all members of the population belong but to varying degrees. In this way, we clarify and propose a solution to one of the problems raised in the literature (Atkinson et al., 2002; Duclos, Sahn and Younger, 2001); especially Atkinson (2003): 'How can different attributes be aggregated? ... A distinction may be drowning between those who adopt a union approach and those who use an intersection measure'.

The chapter is divided into four sections. In the introduction, we describe economic conditions in Iran, which is essential for understanding the country's trends in poverty, measured using traditional approaches. The second section reviews the literature on the fuzzy-set approach to poverty measurement, from the seminal paper by Cerioli and Zani (1990) to the more recent contributions, and explains the methodology proposed. In the third section, we report our empirical analysis, which is based on the Household Budget Survey (HBS) conducted in the Solar Hijri year 1395 in Iran, which corresponds to the period 20 March 2016 to 20 March 2017; we constructed 29 indicators to examine the latent dimensions of non-monetary poverty. Finally, the last section concludes the chapter.

Overview of Iranian Economy

The Islamic Republic of Iran, the world's 18th-largest country measured by population, has the 27th-largest economy based on the gross domestic product (GDP) in current prices and the 18th-largest based on GDP in terms of purchasing power parity (PPP). Based on the 2016 Human Development Report, it ranks 69th in the world in the Human Development Index (0.774) and is considered to have high human development (UNDP, 2016). Iran's economy is characterised by over-reliance on hydrocarbons and on predominance by the state in manufacturing and finance. Using factor prices, its GDP grew 12.5% (real non-oil GDP, at a factor cost of 3.3%) in 2016 (an increase over the 0.5% average in 2013–2015) and totalled $425.4 billion, with oil as the main contributor to overall growth that year (United Nations, 2017; World Bank, 2017). Because of increasing oil production, thanks to the lifting of sanctions in January and growing oil prices, its surplus expanded from 2.3% of GDP in 2015 to 3.9% in 2016. That year, total exports increased by 41.3% as a result of the rising oil exports after the sanctions were lifted. Following five years of double-digit inflation, the data from the CBI (Central Bank of Iran) reveal that the inflation rate fell from 11.9% in 2015 to 9% in 2016, its lowest rate in a quarter of a century. This decline in inflation was driven by a stable exchange rate and food prices. Unemployment in 2016 was estimated at 12.5% by the International Labour Organisation (ILO), a slight rise in comparison with the previous year (11%). Differences between male and female unemployment indicate a large gender gap in the labour market (World Bank, 2016). Moreover, underemployment was concentrated in the youth and rural population. The official Gini coefficient of 0.38.8 in 2014 was higher than in 2013 (UNDP, 2014).

Poverty Trends in Iran

Over the past half-century, Iran implemented diverse development strategies aimed at poverty reduction. Before 1979, in the pre-revolutionary period, the dominant strategy employed to reduce poverty was growth-oriented development. But in the first decades after the revolution, the strategies changed to focus on equitable development and social justice (Assadzadeh and Paul, 2004; Salehi-Isfahani, 2009; Zonooz, 2005; Nowshirvani and Clawson, 1994). More recently, the government has implemented a major reform in its subsidy programme on key staples, replacing indirect subsidies with a direct cash transfer to Iranian households, which has raised their standard of living (World Bank, 2018).

Great attention has been paid to evolution in the extent of poverty in Iran over this period. However, until recently, to the best of our knowledge, no official information has been available regarding the precise size of the population living in poverty, which has not been measured or tracked systematically by the government (Atamanov et al., 2016; Hayati et al., 2010; Salehi-Isfahani, 2009; Assadzadeh and Paul, 2004; Zahedi-Mazandarani, 2005). Thus, it is not possible to make any definitive statement on the change in the poverty rate over time. Nevertheless, limited empirical evidence with estimates of poverty trends in Iran are available in the academic literature and documents from international organisations in English and Persian that cover the period between 1976 and 2014 (Zahedi-Mazandarani, 2005; Salehi-Isfahani, 2009; Mehran, 1975; Pesaran, 1975; Nowshirvani and Clawson, 1994; Assadzadeh and Paul, 2004; Maasoumi and Mahmoudi, 2013, Atamanov et al., 2016; Zonooz, 2005; World Bank, 2008). These poverty rates are often calculated according to either the authors' assessment of an appropriate national line or international poverty lines based on US dollars. Because they employ varying methodologies and reach widely different conclusions, they fail to present a consistent picture of poverty in Iran (Salehi-Isfahani, 2006; Zonooz, 2005). Nevertheless, to better understand trends in poverty in Iran, we review the leading studies over this period.

One prominent study, Salehi-Isfahani (2009), studied the trends in poverty and inequality for three decades after the revolution (1979–2005) finding that after the 1979 revolution and Iraq and Iran war, the welfare of the Iranian people declined and the poverty rate increased (Zonooz, 2005); between 1984 and 1989, the poverty rate overall rose from 29% to 42% but then, due to the reforms and economic reconstruction, declined to 12% in 2005. The evidence shows that the proportion of people living below the international poverty line of $2 per day ($2.90 in terms of 2005 PPP) also dropped and is about one-fourth the level before the revolution, to a level that is low by World Bank standards for developing countries. Some evidence suggests that poverty reduction in Iran is helped by having growth and pro-poor social policies, such as subsidies for food, energy and medicine, and investment in electricity, water and health and family planning services (Salehi-Isfahani, 2009). According to Assadzadeh and Paul (2004), from 1983 to 1993 the poverty rate declined in rural areas, but increased sharply in urban areas: from 1983 to 1988 it increased from about 47% to 55% in rural areas and from 24% to 51% in urban areas, and then reversed from 1988 to 1993, falling from 55% to 46% in rural areas and from 51% to 33% in urban areas.

The World Bank (2008), using the international poverty line and in local currency, examined the poverty rate in Iran for the period 1998–2005, finding that it fell in both rural and urban regions and in most provinces, regardless of the choice of poverty line. Maasoumi and Mahmoudi (2013), who conduct a robust growth-equity decomposition of change in poverty in Iran, in 2000, 2004 and 2009 (covering the country's third and fourth five-year development plans), suggest that poverty unambiguously decreased during the third development plan (1999–2004) but rose during the fourth development plan (2004–2009) in both rural and urban areas. They indicate that growth has played a more important role than redistribution in reducing poverty and vice versa (Maasoumi and Mahmoudi, 2013). This is consistent with the findings by Maasoumi and Mahmoudi (2010), who reported a drop in poverty from 2004 to 2007, and Mahmoudi (2011), who also reported an increase in poverty between 2004 and 2007. The World Bank (2017) estimated that poverty fell from 13% in 2009 to 8% in 2013 ($5.50 per day in 2011 PPP) and suggested that the decline was probably due to a direct cash transfer programme in 2010. In 2014 poverty increased to 10.5%, though this may be related to declining social assistance in real terms, according to Atamanov et al. (2016), who measured the trends in poverty in Iran from 2008 to 2014, using the international poverty line based on the USD in 2011 PPP. They indicate that poverty increased between 2008 and 2009, decreased between 2009 and 2012 and gradually increased from 2012 to 2014; this shows that poverty rates based on income are higher and more volatile than those based on expenditure per capita (Atamanov et al., 2016). The empirical evidence since the Islamic revolution indicates that in some periods the poverty rate increased; however, in general most studies agree that over the past three decades, the lower class in Iran has experienced a rising standard of living, and the poverty rate steadily declined. However, inequality has remained stable, and no empirical evidence has emerged to show otherwise (Salehi-Isfahani, 2009; Salehi-Isfahani and Majbouri, 2013).

Most of these papers fail to analyse the regional dimension of poverty; for this reason, we believe that the multi-dimensional and fuzzy-set approach proposed here, with a specific focus on Iran's 31 provinces, offer an innovative and original contribution to the literature on poverty in the country.

Fuzzy and Multi-Dimensional Approach to Poverty Measurement

In this section, we describe the basic fuzzy-set methodology for constructing monetary and non-monetary measures of deprivation. A fuzzy-set approach (Zadeh, 1965) treats poverty as a matter of degree, replacing the classical dichotomy between poor and non-poor into which statistical units (individuals or households) are traditionally divided. As stressed in Lemmi and Betti (2006), in the fuzzy conceptualisation, individuals are all subject to poverty, but in different degrees, so each individual has a certain propensity to be in poverty over the entire range [0,1]. Treating poverty as a matter of degree has several advantages, applicable to all members of the population, over simply using a 'yes–no' state, summarised by Verma et al. (2017) as follows:

1. Non-monetary poverty depends on the prevention of access to various facilities or possessions that determine basic living conditions. An individual may have access to some of them but not others. Hence, non-monetary poverty is inherently a matter of degree, and a quantitative approach (such as the one proposed here) is essential.
2. A fuzzy-set approach enables the use of more robust and stable indicators of poverty (Betti et al., 2018). Apart from the various methodological choices involved in the construction of conventional poverty measures, the use of fuzzy measures introduces additional factors about which choices have to be made. The fundamental factor concerns the choice of 'membership functions', meaning a quantitative specification of the propensity to be in poverty of each statistical unit (household/person), given the level and distribution of income of the population.

Fuzzy Membership Function

Betti et al. (2008) have proposed two fuzzy membership functions (MF, one for monetary deprivation and the other for non-monetary deprivation), based on the basic contributions of Cerioli and Zani (1990), Cheli and Lemmi (1995); these MF are further elaborated in Betti et al. (2016) and in Betti (2017) for some particular aspects of the quality of life. In the general form, these membership functions are defined for any statistical unit (household/individual) i as follows:

$$\mu_{i,K} = \left(\frac{\sum_{\gamma=i+1}^{n} w_\gamma \middle| X_\gamma > X_i}{\sum_{\gamma=2}^{n} w_\gamma \middle| X_\gamma > X_1} \right)^{\alpha_K - 1} \left(\frac{\sum_{\gamma=i+1}^{n} w_\gamma X_\gamma \middle| X_\gamma > X_i}{\sum_{\gamma=2}^{n} w_\gamma X_\gamma \middle| X_\gamma > X_1} \right) \tag{5.1}$$

$$i : 1, \ldots, n-1 \; ; \; \mu_{n,k} = 0$$

where X is equivalent income in monetary poverty or the overall score s in non-monetary poverty; w_γ is the sample weight of a unit of rank γ in the ascending distribution and α_K (K = 1,2) are two parameters corresponding, respectively, to the monetary and non-monetary dimensions of poverty. Betti et al. (2008) confirmed that this a variant of the α_K-generalised Gini index. The α_K parameters are calculated such that the mean of the corresponding membership function equals the at-risk-of-poverty rate (ARPR; Eurostat, 2002) calculated on the basis of the official poverty line. Betti et al. (2008) call the monetary-based indicator fuzzy monetary (FM) and the non-monetary indicator fuzzy supplementary (FS).

Construction of the FS Measure

The construction of the FS index follows. First, the items included in the index or indices are identified and should be those that are more meaningful and useful (see Eurostat, 2002; Betti and Lemmi, 2013). In fact, it is desirable to avoid items for which issues of choice in terms of possession versus non-possession cannot be satisfactory resolved, whose possession is relatively rare (i.e. possession of a boat), or whose degree of comparability among regions or countries is not sufficient. Then, for each item, we determine a quantitative deprivation indicator in the range [0,1]: when the item is made up of a fixed number of categories, it is transformed using the following procedure. For each item, we determine a deprivation score as follows:

$$d_{j,i} = \frac{1 - F(c_{j,i})}{1 - F(1)}; \quad j = 1,2,\ldots,k; \; i = 1,2,\ldots,n \tag{5.2}$$

where $c_{j,i}$ is the value of the category of the *j*th item for the *i*th individual, and $F(c_{j,i})$ is the value of the *j*th item cumulative function for the *i*th individual. We transform the deprivation score into a positive score as follows:

$$S_{j,i} = 1 - \frac{1 - F(c_{j,i})}{1 - F(1)} = \frac{F(c_{j,i}) - F(1)}{1 - F(1)}; \quad j = 1,2,\ldots,k; \; i = 1,2,\ldots,n \tag{5.3}$$

In particular, but also typical cases in which the indicator takes a value of either 1 or 0, the deprivation score *d* is 1 for deprivation and 0 otherwise, whereas the positive score *s* is 0 for deprivation and 1 otherwise. These indicators are used in the first exploratory factor analysis (EFA) to identify the 'dimensions' highlighted. By dimension, we mean a group of indicators to demonstrate non-monetary poverty, which ideally are independent of those in other dimensions and describe a particular facet of living conditions. After this first EFA, we rearrange some indicators into the dimensions identified to create more meaningful groups: to test the goodness of fit of this final grouping, a confirmatory factor analysis (CFA) is necessary.

To investigate the latent dimensions of non-monetary poverty, we selected 29 indicators of deprivation *in addition to total consumption expenditure.* Total consumption expenditure in 2016–2017 increased by about 11.4% over the previous year, in which the share spent on food comprised 22.9% of the total. The EFA identified seven dimensions, listed in Table 5.1, in which columns 2 and 4 report the weight of each deprivation indicator in the dimension considered.

A CFA was conducted to test the goodness of fit of the 7D model hypothesised. The results of the analysis, reported in Table 5.2, indicate that the fit is good, and all the indicators of the goodness of fit are significant.

Table 5.1 Deprivation indicators divided into seven dimensions and their weight

Dimension	*Weight*	*Dimension*	*Weight*
Dimension 1		*Dimension 3*	
Vacuum cleaner	25.43	Indoor plumbing and gas	52.69
Washing machine	20.11	Plumbing	159.41
Sewing machine	11.75	Electricity	1585.64
Dishwasher	3.42	*Dimension 4*	
Microwave oven	4.43	Central heating	6.88
Oven	128.53	Air conditioning	63.26
Refrigerator	231.56	*Dimension 5*	
Dimension 2		Bathroom	102.01
Phone	21.50	Kitchen	86.46
Computer	7.56	House tenure status	39.03
Internet	8.52	*Dimension 6*	
DVD and VCD player	10.19	Car	20.21
Mobile phone	56.92	Motorcycle	12.31
Television	114.27	Bicycle	7.31
Radio	5.18	*Dimension 7*	
Cassette player	5.59	Type of heating fuel	173.14
		Type of fuel for heating water	163.48
		Type of cooking fuel	549.51

Table 5.2 Confirmatory factor analysis results

Goodness of fit (GFI)[a]	0.9288
Adjusted GFI[b]	0.9132
Parsimonious GFI[c]	0.8167
RMSEA[d]	0.0523

a. Based on the ratio of the sum of squared discrepancies to the observed variances, it ranges from 0 to 1, with higher values indicating a good fit.
b. GFI adjusted for degrees of freedom of the model, that is, the number of fixed parameters; it ranges from 0 to 1 with higher values indicating a good fit.
c. GFI adjusted for the number of estimated parameters in the model and the number of data points.
d. The root mean squared error of approximation (RMSEA) is based on an analysis of the residuals, with low values indicating a good fit.

Then, the weights assigned to each indicator are determined within each dimension; they are based on two elements: the dispersion of the indicator (prevalence weight) and the correlation with other indicators in the same dimension (correlation weight). For a detailed description of the weight construction, see Betti et al. (2008).

The score within each dimension h, $s_{i,h}$, is calculated as the weighted mean of indicators in this dimension, and the overall score s_i is defined as the simple average of the dimension scores $s_{i,h}$. This gives the same importance to all the dimensions, each of which represents a different facet of non-monetary (supplementary) poverty. Finally, as explained above, the membership function FS is defined in Equation (5.1), which can be rewritten for every dimension h as:

$$\mu_i = FS_{hi} = \left(1 - F_{(S),hi}\right)^{\alpha-1}\left(1 - L_{(S),hi}\right)$$

$$= \left(\frac{\sum_{\gamma=i+1}^{n} w_{h\gamma} \middle| S_{h\gamma} > S_{hi}}{\sum_{\gamma=2}^{n} w_{h\gamma} \middle| S_{h\gamma} > S_{h1}}\right)^{\alpha-1}\left(\frac{\sum_{\gamma=i+1}^{n} w_{h\gamma} S_{h\gamma} \middle| S_{h\gamma} > S_{hi}}{\sum_{\gamma=2}^{n} w_{h\gamma} S_{h\gamma} \middle| S_{h\gamma} > S_{h1}}\right),$$

$$h = 1,2,\ldots,m;\ i = 1,2,\ldots,n;\ \mu_{hn} = 0$$

Methodology and Sample Selection

This methodology is used in the HBS survey in Iran, collected from 20 March 2016 to 20 March 2017. The target population of the survey consists of all households in Iran rural and urban region. According to the Central Bank of the Islamic Republic of Iran (2017), the sample households were selected in three stages

Table 5.3 reports the results of the overall and decomposed FS in all dimensions for all 31 provinces in Iran. Overall, FS ranges from 0.085 in Yazd to 0.562 in Ardabil. The most deprived regions are concentrated in the northwest and south. In general, central Iran and the capital, Tehran, are better off and the most populated areas, as it can be seen in Figure 5.1.

If we look at individual dimensions, the situation is more heterogeneous. Sistan and Baluchestan is generally the most deprived province along all dimensions, whereas Tehran has the best performance. In terms of FS1, which comprises basic consumer durables, and it is reported in Figure 5.2a, Kerman and Sistan and Baluchestan are the most deprived provinces; however, the situation is much more heterogeneous in the northwest, since provinces in that area show deprivation scores both low and high. In FS2, referring to less frequent durable goods, again Sistan and Baluchestan is the most deprived province. Central Iran and Tehran are still the better-off areas, as shown by Figure 5.2b, although the more 'reddish' provinces are less concentrated here, compared to FS overall or FS1.

In FS3, which includes residential electricity, indoor plumbing and gas, again Sistan and Baluchestan are the most deprived, and so is Hormozgan. In FS4, which comprises residential central heating or cooling, the situation is quite different, as the southern and western provinces (excluding Fars) are better off (see Figure 5.3a). FS5 takes into account housing tenure and

Table 5.3 Results of fuzzy supplementary (FS) poverty in all its dimensions

Region	*FS*	*FS1*	*FS2*	*FS3*	*FS4*	*FS5*	*FS6*	*FS7*
Markazi	0.208	0.078	0.111	0.006	0.168	0.107	0.434	0.002
Gilan	0.224	0.169	0.136	0.168	0.103	0.086	0.592	0.014
Mazandaran	0.159	0.114	0.112	0.032	0.035	0.089	0.522	0.002
East Azerbaijan	0.341	0.101	0.096	0.027	0.416	0.109	0.522	0.008
West Azerbaijan	0.395	0.107	0.157	0.104	0.449	0.118	0.543	0.001
Kermanshah	0.285	0.209	0.159	0.075	0.146	0.165	0.630	0.002
Khuzestan	0.204	0.176	0.254	0.099	0.010	0.121	0.522	0.006
Fars	0.179	0.163	0.187	0.094	0.044	0.142	0.410	0.009
Kerman	0.317	0.343	0.281	0.237	0.118	0.211	0.421	0.094
Razavi Khorasan	0.210	0.112	0.147	0.046	0.110	0.145	0.479	0.002
Isfahan	0.142	0.074	0.119	0.005	0.066	0.094	0.370	0.001
Sistan and Baluchestan	0.456	0.393	0.410	0.525	0.020	0.377	0.716	0.017
Kurdistan	0.372	0.154	0.096	0.039	0.395	0.138	0.601	0.000
Hamadan	0.341	0.163	0.169	0.012	0.381	0.083	0.482	0.001
Chaharmahal and Bakhtiari	0.224	0.132	0.110	0.032	0.165	0.123	0.468	0.011
Lorestan	0.340	0.183	0.235	0.095	0.171	0.168	0.720	0.015
Ilam	0.233	0.192	0.262	0.150	0.023	0.101	0.602	0.003
Kohgiluyeh and Bouyer-Ahmad	0.289	0.180	0.168	0.088	0.114	0.164	0.757	0.029
Bushehr	0.115	0.179	0.158	0.260	0.003	0.102	0.293	0.072
Zanjan	0.394	0.145	0.142	0.088	0.468	0.098	0.548	0.004
Semnan	0.168	0.081	0.143	0.026	0.080	0.119	0.422	0.000
Yazd	0.085	0.079	0.131	0.039	0.010	0.105	0.223	0.003
Hormozgan	0.217	0.253	0.250	0.489	0.008	0.105	0.402	0.218
Tehran	0.112	0.056	0.085	0.001	0.016	0.137	0.405	0.000
Ardabil	0.562	0.177	0.131	0.065	0.718	0.146	0.629	0.008
Qom	0.110	0.071	0.116	0.003	0.009	0.127	0.367	0.001
Qazvin	0.318	0.131	0.190	0.036	0.296	0.117	0.530	0.005
Golestan	0.221	0.205	0.200	0.035	0.025	0.148	0.544	0.002
North Khorasan	0.365	0.229	0.181	0.066	0.344	0.211	0.474	0.026
South Khorasan	0.285	0.166	0.225	0.211	0.192	0.174	0.462	0.001
Alborz	0.151	0.057	0.122	0.008	0.048	0.115	0.465	0.000

characteristics (duration of tenure and the presence of a kitchen and indoor bathroom); Sistan and Baluchestan again are the most deprived, whereas Gilan and Mazandaran are less deprived.

FS6 identifies the possession of a car, motorcycle or bike; the level of deprivation is generally very high in all regions, except for Yazd and Bushehr.

Finally, FS7 identifies the type of fuel used in the home for different purposes. In general, the level of deprivation in this dimension is very low, and even most northwestern provinces are performing quite well, as reported in Figure 5.3b.

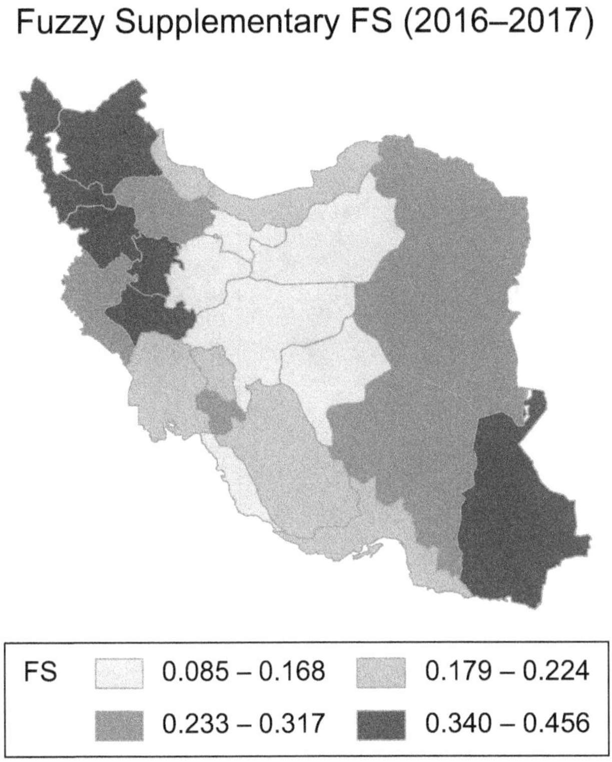

Figure 5.1 Map of Iran showing overall FS deprivation, 2016–2017.

Concluding Remarks

In this chapter, we propose a multi-dimensional and fuzzy-set approach to measuring poverty in Iran at the province level. Using this approach reveals a rather heterogeneous picture of the country, in which the most deprived regions are concentrated in the northwest and the south, and the central part of the country and Tehran are better off and the most populated areas. A more detailed analysis focused on the seven fuzzy dimensions FS1–FS7 surfaces some more finely grained results; this is because multi-dimensional poverty is treated as a matter of degree determined by the people's relative position in Iran, i.e. in the distribution of some aspects of their living conditions. These results can be summarised as follows. First, the northwestern provinces, including East and West Azerbaijan and Kurdistan, are rather heterogeneous in terms of fuzzy dimensions FS1 and FS2, but all perform quite well in terms of FS7. Second, the southern provinces, which are the worst off according to the overall FS measure and many dimensions, are surprisingly better off in terms of FS7.

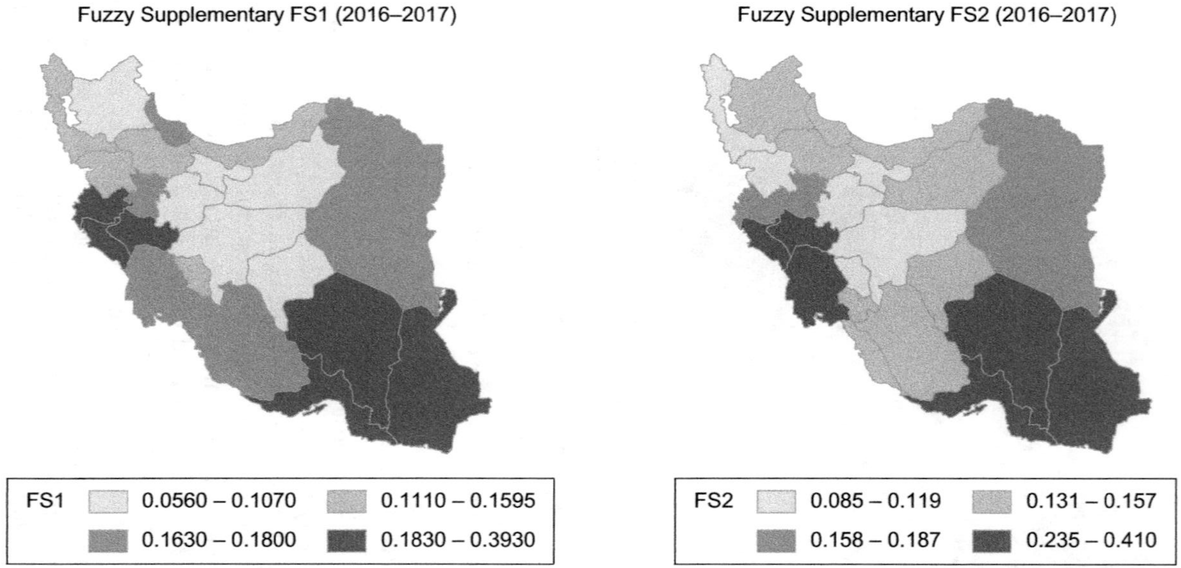

Figure 5.2 Maps of Iran showing FS1 and FS2, 2016–2017.

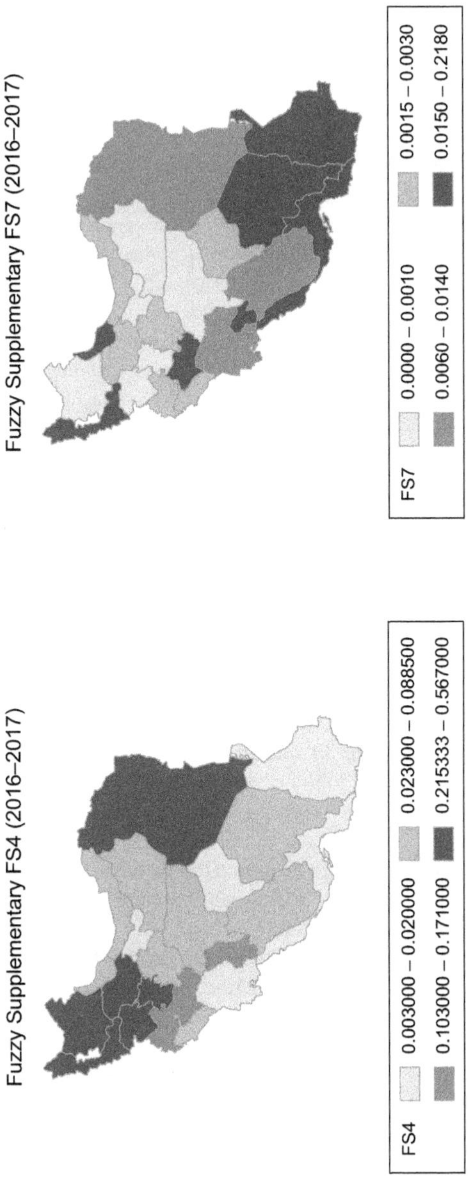

Figure 5.3 Maps of Iran showing FS4 and FS7, 2016–2017.

References

Anand S. and Sen A.K. (1997), *Concepts of human development and poverty: A multi-dimensional perspective.* Human Development Papers, United Nations Development Programme (UNDP), New York.

Assadzadeh A. and Paul S. (2004), Poverty, growth, and redistribution: A study of Iran, *Review of Development Economics*, 8(4), pp. 640–653.

Atamanov A., Mostafavi M.H., Salehi-Isfahani D. and Vishwanath T. (2016), *Constructing Robust poverty trends in the Islamic Republic of Iran: 2008–14.* World Bank, New York.

Atkinson A.B. (2003), Multidimensional deprivation: Contrasting social welfare and counting approaches, *Journal of Economic Inequality*, 1, pp. 51–65.

Atkinson A.B. and Bourguignon F. (1982), The comparison of multi-dimensional distributions of economic status, *Review of Economic Studies*, 49, pp. 183–201.

Atkinson A.B., Cantillon B., Marlier E. and Nolan B. (2002), *Social indicators: The EU and social inclusion.* Oxford University Press, Oxford.

Betti G. (2017), What impact has the economic crisis had on quality of life in Europe? A multi-dimensional and fuzzy approach, *Quality & Quantity*, 51(1), pp. 351–364.

Betti G., Cheli B., Lemmi A. and Verma V. (2008), The fuzzy approach to multi-dimensional poverty: The case of Italy in the 1990s, in Kakwani N. and Silber J. (eds.), *Quantitative approaches to multi-dimensional poverty measurement.* Palgrave Macmillan, London, pp. 30–48.

Betti G., Gagliardi F. and Verma V. (2018), Simplified Jackknife variance estimates for fuzzy measures of multi-dimensional poverty, *International Statistical Review*, 86(1), pp. 68–86.

Betti G. and Lemmi A. (2013), *Poverty and social exclusion: New methods of analysis.* Routledge/Taylor & Francis Group, London.

Betti G., Soldi R. and Talev I. (2016), Fuzzy multi-dimensional indicators of quality of life: The empirical case of Macedonia, *Social Indicators Research*, 127(1), pp. 39–53.

Bourguignon F. and Chakravarty S.R. (2003), The measurement of multi-dimensional poverty, *Journal of Economic Inequality*, 1, pp. 25–49.

Central Bank of the Islamic Republic of Iran (2017), *Household Budget Survey in Iran, 1395 (March 20, 2016–March 20, 2017).* General Directorate of Economic Statistics, September.

Cerioli A. and Zani S. (1990), A fuzzy approach to the measurement of poverty, in Dagum C. and Zenga M. (eds.), *Income and wealth distribution, inequality and poverty*, Springer, Berlin, pp. 272–284.

Chakravarty S.R., Mukherjee D. and Ranade R. (1998), On the family of subgroup and factor decomposable measures of multi-dimensional poverty, *Research on Economic Inequality*, 8, pp. 175–194.

Cheli B. and Lemmi A. (1995), A totally fuzzy and relative approach to the multi-dimensional analysis of poverty, *Economic Notes*, 24, pp. 115–134.

Duclos J.-Y., Sahn D. and Younger S.D. (2001), *Robust multi-dimensional poverty comparisons.* Université Laval, Canada.

Eurostat (2002), European social statistics Income, poverty and social exclusion: 2nd report, European Commission, Luxembourg.

Hayati D., Yazdanpanah M. and Karbalaee F. (2010), Coping with drought: The case of poor farmers of south Iran, *Psychology and Developing Societies*, 22(2), pp. 361–383.

Klasen S. (2000), Measuring poverty and deprivation in South Africa, *Review of Income and Wealth*, 46, pp. 33–58.

Kolm S.C. (1977), Multidimensional egalitarianism, *Quarterly Journal of Economics*, 91, pp. 1–13.

Lemmi A. and Betti G. (2006), Introduction, in Lemmi A., Betti G. (eds.), *Fuzzy set approach to multi-dimensional poverty measurement*. Springer, New York, pp. 1–7.

Maasoumi E. (1986), The measurement and decomposition of multi-dimensional inequality, *Econometrica*, 54, pp. 771–779.

Maasoumi E. and Mahmoudi V. (2013), Robust growth-equity decomposition of change in poverty: The case of Iran (2000–2009), *Quarterly Review of Economics and Finance*, 53(3), pp. 268–276.

Mehran, F. (1975), *Income distribution in Iran: The statistics of inequality*. International Labour Organisation, Geneve.

Nowshirvani V.F. and Clawson P. (1994), The state and social equity in post-revolutionary Iran, in Weiner M. and Banuazizi A. (eds.), *The politics of social transformation in Afghanistan*. Syracuse University Press, Iran.

Pesaran M.H. (1975), *Income distribution and its major determinants in Iran*. CBI, Tehran.

Salehi-Isfahani D. (2006), Revolution and redistribution in Iran: Poverty and inequality 25 years later, in *Third annual world bank conference on inequality*, Washington, DC. Retrieved 20 October 2018 from: https://econpapers.repec.org/paper/vpiwpaper/e06-3.htm.

Salehi-Isfahani D. (2009), Poverty, inequality, and populist politics in Iran, *Journal of Economic Inequality*, 7(1), 5–28.

Salehi-Isfahani D. and Majbouri M. (2013), Mobility and the dynamics of poverty in Iran: Evidence from the 1992–1995 panel survey, *Quarterly Review of Economics and Finance*, 53(3), pp. 257–267.

Sen A.K. (1999), Development as freedom, Oxford University Press, Oxford.

Smeeding T., et al. (1993), Poverty, inequality, and family living standards impacts across seven nations: The effect of noncash subsidies for health, education and housing, *Review Income Wealth*, 39(3), pp. 229–256.

Townsend P. (1979), *Poverty in the United Kingdom*, Allen Lane and Penguin Books, London.

Tsui K. (1985), Multidimensional generalisation of the relative and absolute inequality indices: The Atkinson-Kolm-Sen approach, Journal of Economic Theory, 67, pp. 251–265.

UNDP (2014), *The 2014 Human Development Report- Sustaining Human Progress: Reducing Vulnerabilities and Building Resilience*, United Nations Development Programme, New York.

UNDP (2016), Human development report, United Nations Development Programme, New York.

United Nations (2017), GDP and its breakdown at current prices in US dollars. United Nations Statistics Division, December.

Verma V., Lemmi A., Betti G., Gagliardi F. and Piacentini M. (2017), How precise are poverty measures estimated at the regional level? *Regional Science and Urban Economics*, 66, pp. 175–184.

World Bank (2008), *Islamic Republic of Iran. Spatial patterns of poverty and economic activity*. World Bank, Washington, DC.

World Bank (2016), *World development report 2016*. World Bank, Washington.

World Bank (2017), *Iran economic monitor*. World Bank, Washington.
Zadeh L. (1965), Fuzzy sets, *Information and Control*, 8(3), pp. 338–353.
Zahedi-Mazandarani M.J. (2005), Rural poverty in Iran: Trend and measurement, *Quarterly Journal of Social Welfare*, 17(4), pp. 289–326 (in Persian).
Zonooz B.H. (2005), Poverty and inequality of income in Iran, *Quarterly Journal of Social Welfare*, 17(4), pp. 165–206 (in Persian).

6 China's Multi-Dimensional Poverty and Trade

Elisabetta Croci Angelini and Yang Liu

Introduction

Since the late 1970s, China has achieved remarkable economic growth. According to the 2010 poverty standard, in 1978, 770.39 million people in China lived below the poverty line of RMB 366 per capita, comprising 97.5% of China's population.[1] In 2015, under the 2010 poverty standard, the poverty line was RMB 2,855 per capita, and 55.75 million people were considered to be living in poverty, corresponding to 5.7% of the population. In less than 40 years, China had lifted 714.64 million people out of poverty, with a reduction in the rate of poverty of more than 90 percentage points. Over the same period, according to data from the National Bureau of Statistics (NBS) of China, the total value of China's imports and exports rose from $20,640 million (RMB 35,500 million) in 1978 to a peak of $4,301,527 million (RMB 26,424,177 million) in 2014.

Poverty is a complex concept, and evaluating it in monetary terms neglects many aspects that are relevant to policies aimed at fighting it. Widespread agreement on the advantages of a multi-dimensional assessment of poverty has existed for many years. Multi-dimensional poverty represents a state of deprivation and has no direct impact on imports and exports. Yet the degree of deprivation expressed by each variable in an assessment of multi-dimensional poverty has a direct impact on production and consumption and affects international trade indirectly.

Evolution in China's Reduction of Poverty

The dramatic changes in China's international trade increased income and contributed to the fight against poverty. These changes can also be seen in different poverty standards. Based on China's 1978 poverty standard, between 1978 (when the poverty line was RMB 100 per capita and counted 250 million poor) and 2005 (when it was RMB 625 per capita and comprised 23.65 million), 226.35 million Chinese were lifted out of poverty, and the poverty rate dropped from 30.7% of the population to 2.5%. If this is measured in terms of the 2010 poverty standard, China achieved further progress by lifting 23.09 million people out of poverty between 2005 (when

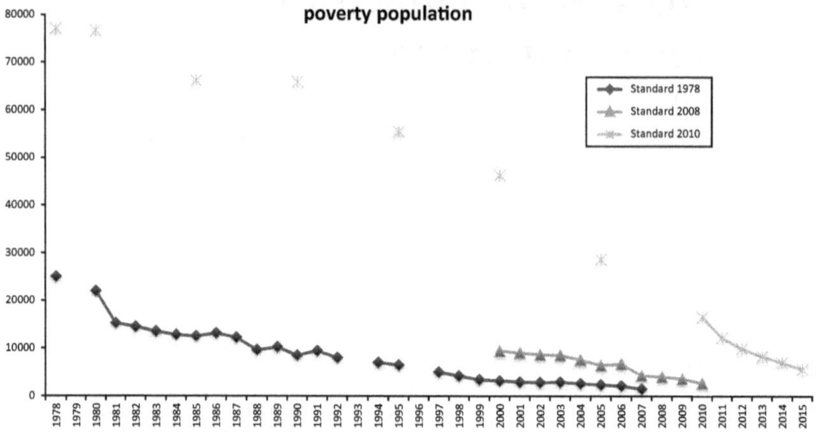

Figure 6.1 China's population living in poverty based on the standards in 1978, 2008 and 2010. *Source*: National Bureau of Statistics of China, Poverty Monitoring Report of Rural China 2016 compiled by the Department of Household Surveys, Table 1-3-1, p. 6, and Table 8-1-1, p. 182.

the poverty line was set at RMB 1,742 per capita) and 2015 (when it was RMB 2,855 per capita), as the poverty rate dropped from 30.2% of the population to 5.7%.

As China's economy developed, the poverty line, which initially targeted the rural poor, rose, too. Consequently, the poverty line raised after every adjustment, and at the same time the calculation methodology changed. The 1978 poverty standard was set up with the problem of hunger in mind, the 2008 poverty standard was meant to address the problems of hunger and clothing, and the 2010 poverty standard employed a multi-dimensional welfare approach.

Figure 6.1 shows the number of the poor (in 10,000 people on the vertical axis) calculated according to the three above-mentioned poverty lines. Some overlap exists because the NBS does not provide information about the three poverty standards for every year between 1978 and 2015.

Evolution in China's International Trade

The evolution in China's international trade can be split into three periods bounded by the economic reforms in 1978 and membership in the World Trade Organization (WTO) in 2001.

Before 1978

There is little doubt that 1978 was a turning point in China's trade history. Following the economic reforms initiated in 1978, China began to engage in trade and liberalisation on a huge scale, almost unparalleled in economic history. After Deng Xiaoping rose to power in China, he quickly abandoned most of the ideological measures and policies of the Mao era in economics and ended the country's isolation from the rest of the world. The series of reforms, labelled Reform and Opening Up, enabled the Chinese to benefit tremendously from integration into the global trade system. From this point onwards, China engaged in trade with as many countries it could and opened up its foreign trade system as much as possible. The value of imports and exports, which in 1950 was RMB 2,130 million and RMB 2,020 million, respectively, increased in 1978 to RMB 18,740 million and RMB 16,760 million, respectively; this represented great progress, as did the annual growth rate of 7.8%. Despite this high growth rate, these values were low compared with what followed.

Between 1978 and 2001

Before 1978, China's foreign trade system was fully centralised, dominated by about a dozen specialised foreign trade companies organised along product lines and based in Beijing. Since 1978, China has established special economic zones (SEZs) and successively opened coastal cities as part of opening up. State-owned enterprises and joint ventures were permitted to manage their own materials and products. In later years, some joint ventures could engage in international business as well. After 1978, trade rose slightly every year, and between 1984 and 2001 it increased sharply. The value of imports and exports increased from RMB 18,740 million and RMB 16,760 million, respectively, in 1978 to RMB 2,015,920 million and RMB 2,202,440 million in 2001. In this period, the annual growth rate was about 25%.

Between 2001 and 2016

Since China joined the WTO in 2001, as it became part of the world market economy and the multilateral trading system, it has fully engaged in bilateral trade agreements and acted as a driving force for foreign trade. China's export markets expanded by increasing supply in other countries' markets. A strong expansion in investment in China followed, and then it began its own outward foreign investment. Annual economic growth from 2001 to 2014 was 15.5%, a decline from the previous period. Nevertheless, in 2014 the value of imports and exports rose to RMB 12,035,803 and RMB 14,388,375 million, respectively, making China the world's leading exporter and second-largest importer. In 2008, because of the global financial crisis, the value of imports and exports dropped but recovered in 2010 and thereafter continued the previous growth momentum. In 2015 and 2016, the value of imports and exports fell slightly but did not change China's global trade ranking. Figure 6.2 traces the growth in the value of China's imports and exports. The figure shows China became integrated into international

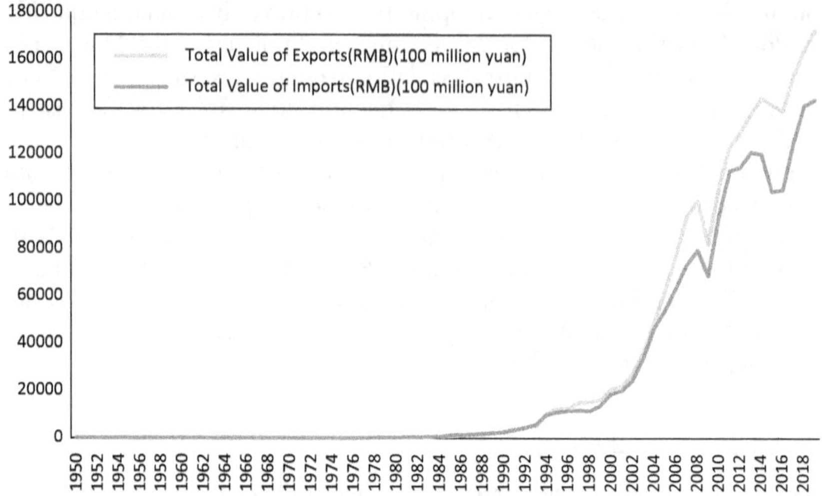

Figure 6.2 Evolution in the value of China's exports and imports, 1950–2019. *Source*: National Bureau of Statistics of China.

trade (including suffering from and reacting to two global crises), rising from a rank of 32nd in international trade in 1978 to the sixth largest importer–exporter in the world in 2001, and then to the largest exporter and second-largest importer in the world in 2009.

Multi-Dimensional Poverty

The first assessment of poverty in terms of food and non-food goods, subdivided into these two parts of poverty in a monetary variable, dates back to the book *Poverty: A Study of Town Life* (Rowntree, 1901), which identifies the budget required to afford a 'shopping basket' of 'the minimum needed to maintain physical strength'. But the actual conditions of poverty cannot be entirely captured by income alone. Then, in 1987, Hagenaars introduced leisure into the study of poverty and constructed the first multi-dimensional poverty index using the dimensions of income and leisure.

In 1990, the World Bank (1990) introduced an international poverty line of $1 a day, which was raised to $1.90 per day in 2015 (Ferreira et al., 2015).

Later, Sen (2000, 2004a, 2004b) studied poverty at the level of personal welfare, then at the level of social development. He pointed out that poverty encompasses many dimensions, some of which are objective (e.g. having clean drinking water, roads and sanitation), and others are subjective feelings of poverty.

Based on Sen's capability approach, Alkire and Foster (2011) constructed a multi-dimensional poverty index to fully reflect the multi-dimensional deprivation experienced by the poor. The index includes important indicators (e.g. environmental poverty and asset poverty) in addition to income. In 2010, based on Alkire's measurement, a multi-dimensional poverty index (MPI) was added to the Human Development Report by the United Nations Development Programme (UNDP), replacing the Human Poverty Index (HPI) and enhancing the measurement of poverty.

Multi-Dimensional Poverty in China

Few studies have been conducted on multi-dimensional poverty in China. This new concept mainly focusses on measuring the differences between urban and rural areas and in some poor areas.

Wang and Alkire (2009) measured multi-dimensional poverty in China in 2006, based on Alkire and Foster's method. They measured poverty in nine provinces along eight dimensions (housing, clean drinking water, sanitation, electricity, assets, land, education and health insurance) and concluded that multi-dimensional poverty is more serious in rural areas than urban areas, and deprivation in sanitation, electricity, education and health insurance contributes most to poverty.

Gao (2012) calculated the MPI in Chinese urban and rural areas with the education, health and living standard based on the China Health and Nutrition Survey (CHNS) dataset in 2000 and 2009. His main conclusions are that multi-dimensional poverty is more serious in rural areas than urban areas, and health insurance, sanitation, cooking fuel and housing are important dimensions of poverty reduction. Moreover, the government should pay more attention to the provinces in central and western China.

Guo and Wu (2012) measured the MPI in Shanxi Province with county-level data. They concluded that the lack of education and health care are the main reasons for multi-dimensional poverty in Shanxi, so the government should focus its efforts on improvements in those two domains. Shen and Alkire (2017) estimated MPI for China using China Family Panel Studies (CFPS). They found that deprivation in nutrition, education, safe drinking water and cooking fuel contribute most to the overall non-monetary poverty in China.

Empirical Evidence on Chinese Household Income Project (CHIP) 2013

Whereas the MPI combines health, education and living standards, we separate income and living conditions to divide information about the source of income from the employment level within a household. Therefore, multi-dimensional poverty is assessed through four dimensions (health, education, income and living standards) employing the CHIP 2013 dataset, which has the most complete information but does not cover all Chinese provinces. The four dimensions are evaluated based on three data levels of analysis:

the individual level, the household level and the provincial level. People live in a household, where the consumption of several goods is usually collective, and some income redistribution exists between earners and dependent members of the household. So, like many other studies about distributive issues, we use the household as one level of analysis. We also investigate multi-dimensional poverty at the provincial level because of its relevance to international trade.

Data and Methodology

Multi-dimensional poverty has also been investigated by Cerioli and Zani (1990), Cheli and Lemmi (1995), Betti and Verma (2008), Betti and Lemmi (2013), Betti (2017) and others employing a fuzzy-set methodology,[2] but we did not find any studies that apply this method to examine China. Here, we employ a fuzzy-set methodology, in which each level of analysis, whether a household, an individual, or a province, is evaluated based on the relevant variables related to the dimensions mentioned earlier. All variables are subsequently aggregated to assess the level of multi-dimensional poverty in a province. The fuzzy-set method introduced by Zadeh (1965) is based on the generalisation of the classical concepts of sets and the membership function.[3]

Whereas poverty at the individual and household level is evaluated with micro-data in the CHIP 2013, the provincial data prepared for the fuzzy-set method to measure multi-dimensional poverty are macro-data from the NBS.

At the individual level, the CHIP 2013 dataset offers information about the 61,162 individuals in the sample. Six variables are used to explore the four dimensions: two variables for education: the highest level of education completed and the years of formal education; one variable for health status; one for living standards in terms of employment status; and two variables for income: main job and other jobs.

At the household level, the 17,891 samples were assessed with 23 variables. The number of variables at the household level is higher because the dataset considers each household separately, and observation of each household member as an additional variable. Therefore, household income is the outcome of the following variables: household total disposable income for three years (2011, 2012 and 2013), total living expenditures by the household in 2013, the balance of financial assets (the total amount), spot cash, demand deposits, time deposits and the estimated net present value of fixed productive assets. Household education, in addition to the respondent's and spouse's education level, considers the education level of the household head's father, mother, spouse's father, spouse's mother and the siblings of the respondent. Similarly, household employment considers the employment status of the respondent, the household head's father, mother, spouse's father, spouse's mother and the employment status of siblings of the respondent. As for the standard of living, we rely upon subjective questions related to the living level: the variables refer to the amount of money needed to maintain the minimum living standard for the family, the evaluation of the living standards compared to the average, and whether the living standard is comfortable and evaluate economic conditions according to economic shocks.

At the provincial level, multi-dimensional poverty is evaluated by including 15 macro variables as follows: four variables for health: life expectancy, local government expenditure on medical and health care per capita, the number of medical personnel per capita, and the number of beds in healthcare institutions per capita; three variables for education: the ration of people with no schooling (people aged 6 and over with no schooling as a percentage of people aged 6 and over), the rate of illiteracy (illiterate population aged 15 and over as a percentage of the population aged 15 and over) and local government expenditure on education per capita; three variables for income: gross domestic product (GDP) per capita, national disposable income per capita and national expenditure per capita; and five variables for the standard of living: total national investment in fixed assets per capita, the rate of urban population with access to cooking gas, the rate of urban population with access to running water, the number of public toilets per 10,000 people and the number of public transport vehicles per 10,000 people.

Table 6.1 summarises how the four dimensions are evaluated at the three data levels with the relevant indicators.

For each of the k variables (with k = 6 for i = 61,162 individuals; k = 23 for i = 17,891 households; and k = 15 for i = 31 provinces) used as indicators (X_1, X_2 … X_k) of the four dimensions, we applied the fuzzy-set method to calculate the deprivation measure $g(x_{ij})$ of level i for the indicator j and a system of weights w_1, w_2 … w_k as follows:

$$\overline{g(x_{ij})} = \left(\sum_i g(x_{ij})\right) \Big/ n$$

$$w_j = \log\left[1 \Big/ \overline{g(x_j)}\right]$$

the membership function is therefore:

$$f(x_i) = \frac{\sum_{j=1}^{k} g(x_{ij}) w_j}{\sum_j^k w_j}$$

Thus, we evaluate poverty at three data levels (individual, household and provincial), employing the same methodology and obtaining different results to convey the complexity of deprivation in a more detailed way.

Table 6.1 Variables for each dimension (code or measurement in parentheses)

Dimensions	*Variables*		
	6 at the individual level	*23 at the household level*	*15 at the provincial level*
Education	Highest level of education completed (a13_1) Years of formal education (a13_2)	Household education level (highest for up to six people in the family: a13_1, h03_1, h03_2, h03_3, h03_4, i05_1)	Rate of no schooling at six years old (%) Illiteracy rate at 15 years old (%) Public expenditure on education (RMB)
Health	Health conditions (a16_1)	Household subjective self-evaluation of four items (p02, p06_1, p07_1, p07_2)	Life expectancy (age in 2010) Government health-care expenditure (RMB) Medical personnel (number) Beds in health-care institutions (number)
Income	Income from main job (C05_1) Income from other jobs (c11_4)	Household income (the indicator is composed of nine variables: f01_1, f01_2,_ f01_3, f02_1, f03, f03_1, f03_2, f03_3, f07_1)	Per capita GDP (RMB) National disposable income per capita (RMB) Per capita expenditure (RMB)
Living standard	Employment status (c03_1)	Household employment (for up to six family members: c03_1, h04_1, h04_2, h04_3, h04_4, i06_1)	Total national investment in fixed assets per capita (RMB) Rate of urban population with access to cooking gas (%) Rate of urban population with access to running water (%) Number of public toilets per 10,000 people (%) Number of public transport vehicles per 10,000 people (%)

Results

The variables are used to measure individual poverty and household poverty in terms of the dimensions of education, health, living standards and income and to aggregate them at the provincial level.

We defined someone as poor in education if the person has 'no schooling' or 'no more than two years of formal education'; someone as poor in health who is in a 'very poor health condition' based on self-assessment; someone as poor in employment who is a 'family worker'; and someone as poor in income who has 'less than 75% of the average income'. Then we calculated the weight of every sample of poverty according to the Neperian logarithm and average value. In the end, we determined a total multi-dimensional value for every person, and the final value was the fuzzy value that summed up all the samples for each province. A higher value meant the province had higher poverty. We processed provincial data with the same method.

Based on the individual, household and macro-data, we calculated multi-dimensional poverty (MP) values for each province to represent provincial multi-dimensional poverty. The results are presented in Table 6.2. Specifically, an MP rank of 1 means the province is the richest in multi-dimensional terms, whereas a rank of 14 means the poorest. To facilitate understanding, we ranked the provinces by their import rank in reverse order, with the top import provinces at the top of the table.

Table 6.2 shows the multi-dimensional poverty values calculated as explained above at three data levels as well as the value of provincial imports and exports; the rankings are portrayed in Figures 6.3 - 6.5. They show, with few exceptions, clustering of the highest rankings and of the lowest. The poorest provinces, in multi-dimensional terms (e.g. Gansu and Yunnan), are also the provinces with the lowest imports and exports and the richest provinces have the highest (e.g. Guangdong, Jiangsu, Shandong and Beijing).

Figure 6.4 shows that Chinese provinces' imports and exports tend to have a similar rank.

Figure 6.5 shows the individual, household and provincial ranking of multi-dimensional poverty using a fuzzy methodology.

The Effect of Multi-Dimensional Poverty on Imports and Exports

Poverty not only has a direct impact on production and consumption but also has a profound impact on trade. At the individual and the household level, poor people lack production materials and the production activities that can be carried out tend to depend on their physical ability. They engage in low-tech activities or unskilled manual labour, which are unlikely to be in a trade-oriented industry, which contributes to exports. The poor tend to have low consumption levels, mainly local low-quality products to meet subsistence needs.

Countries in poverty tend to export mostly primary goods in exchange for importing industrial manufactured products. This trade pattern creates a series of dilemmas in the global market (Williamson, 2011), including de-industrialisation, the Dutch disease, commodity price volatility and rising

Table 6.2 Value and the MP rank by individual data (AC), household data (FP), macro-data (MC), imports and exports

	MP.AC		*MP.FP*		*MP.MC*		*Imports*		*Exports*	
Province	*Value*	*Rank*	*Value*	*Rank*	*Value*	*Rank*	*Value*	*Rank*	*Value*	*Rank*
Guangdong	0.58712	3	0.82297	3	0.84373	7	549,428,183	1	731,763,406	1
Jiangsu	0.57488	2	0.81103	2	0.73258	1	259,491,086	2	333,804,198	2
Shandong	0.60286	4	0.82712	4	0.8137	3	173,395,991	3	141,546,096	3
Beijing	0.48529	1	0.80341	1	0.7405	2	98,339,383	4	33,221,397	7
Liaoning	0.61597	7	0.83917	7	0.83418	5	67,952,596	5	53,407,910	4
Henan	0.60663	5	0.8437	10	0.89681	10	24,195,796	6	38,577,788	5
Sichuan	0.65236	12	0.85051	12	0.92309	11	22,334,219	7	32,760,464	8
Chongqing	0.61597	8	0.82767	5	0.83161	4	20,573,837	8	38,211,396	6
Anhui	0.65932	14	0.85103	13	0.94285	13	16,467,306	9	22,460,220	9
Hubei	0.62098	10	0.83098	6	0.84148	6	14,649,289	10	20,985,995	10
Hunan	0.6181	9	0.84285	9	0.86693	8	9,913,099	11	14,402,966	11
Shanxi	0.6131	6	0.84237	8	0.88777	9	7,411,556	12	9,749,371	12
Yunnan	0.6524	13	0.84675	11	0.94238	12	7,055,755	13	8,768,549	13
Gansu	0.64611	11	0.86432	14	0.9569	14	5,412,130	14	1,429,426	14

Source: Authors' calculations based on CHIP 2013 for multi-dimensional poverty and NBS for trade.

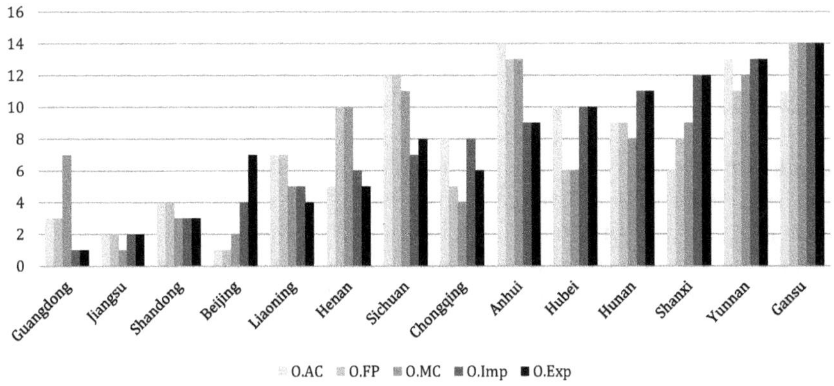

Figure 6.3 The MP rank and imports and exports.

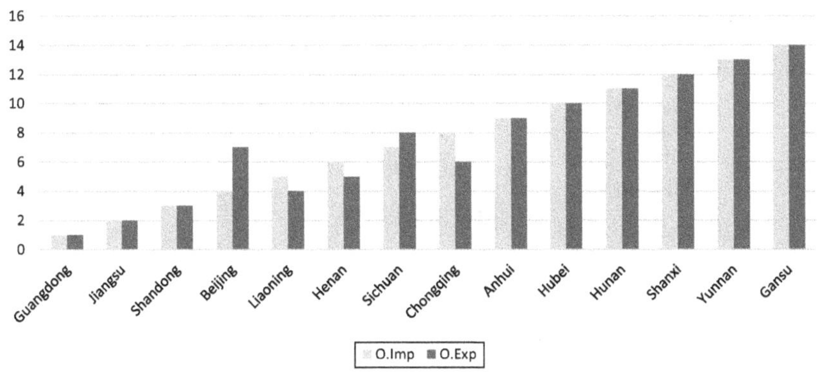

Figure 6.4 The rank of imports and exports.

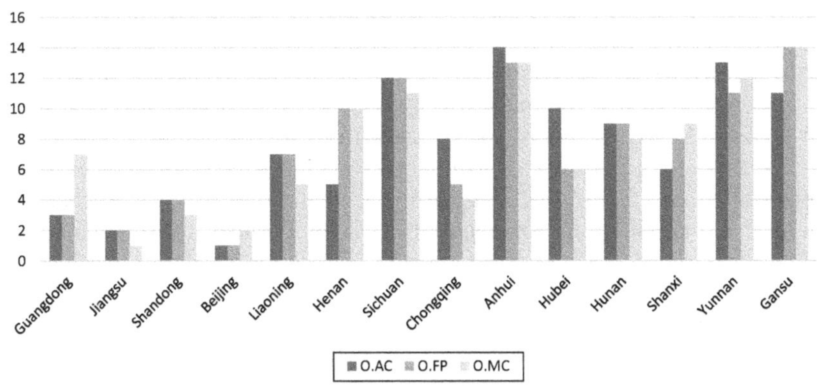

Figure 6.5 The rank of MP.

inequality, thus creating a poverty trap. The impact of living standards on production and consumption is unclear. Most research on living standards shows a significant degree of deprivation.

If we relax our hypothesis, regardless of the standard of living, we can understand that the various sub-variables of multi-dimensional poverty have an impact on production and consumption, so exports, as production surplus, and imports, as import demand, may also be affected by them. This represents only a kind of transmission, but it shows no strong link. Therefore, we cannot directly conclude whether the volume of import and export trade in a province with multi-dimensional poverty will increase or decrease. So we relax the assumption of the impact of these indicators on imports and exports and assume that if more production is produced, more surplus production is produced, and more exports are transported. The stronger domestic demand is, the greater import demand it is, and the more imports are required. In this way, we can provide a perspective with a cross-sectional data in discussing the volume of import and export trade in provinces with different levels of multi-dimensional poverty.

$$\begin{aligned}&\text{Multi-dimensional Poverty}\\&= \left\{\begin{array}{c}\text{Income}\\ \text{Education}\\ \text{Health}\\ \text{Living Standards}\end{array}\right. = \left\{\begin{array}{c}\text{Income}\\ \text{Human Capital}\\ \text{Living Standards}\end{array}\right. \rightarrow \left\{\begin{array}{c}\text{Produce}\\ \text{Consume}\end{array}\right.\\&\rightarrow \left\{\begin{array}{c}\text{Production Surplus}\\ \text{Import Demand}\end{array}\right. = \text{Import and Export}\end{aligned}$$

Concluding Remarks

We selected four dimensions based on MPI, employed CHIP data for 2013, and then measured multi-dimensional poverty using fuzzy-set theory. The results show that the top five exporters and importers in China, except Guangdong, are multi-dimensionally rich provinces. If we ignore the potential mutual causation, we could simply conclude that multi-dimensionally rich provinces have access to importing and exporting and get benefit on the top seat, even they do not rank first, and have the highest volume of imports and exports. Provinces at the mid-level in imports and exports have mid-level values of multi-dimensional poverty. Yunnan and Gansu show high levels of multi-dimensional poverty, and they are much less involved in imports and exports.

Based on the results, we do not conclude that multi-dimensional poverty reduces participation in imports and exports, and neither of them has a positive effect on multi-dimensional poverty. To some extent, they have a correlation, and the relationship should be tested with a regression model, even with panel data.

Multi-dimensional poverty was calculated based on a fuzzy-set at the provincial level. Although in recent years China has made a tremendous and successful effort to reduce poverty, it has not been eradicated, especially in rural areas. Because different observations affect production and consumption in different ways, in this chapter we assessed provincial-level poverty with three data levels of analysis, at the individual level, the household level and the provincial level. The micro-data, both individual and household data, were aggregated into a measurement of provincial multi-dimensional poverty.

We found some correlations between multi-dimensional poverty and importing/exporting, although we compared them only for 2013, which is the most recent CHIP data available. The multi-dimensionally poor provinces export and import less, while multi-dimensionally rich provinces export and import more. That means that the poor contribute less in production and consumption; therefore, they import and export less. Because the micro-data on which multi-dimensional poverty is based are cross-sectional, they do not survey all the provinces, and the CHIP data are not annual, so we could not determine whether a causal relationship exists between multi-dimensional poverty and importing/exporting.

Notes

1 In China three versions of poverty line were subsequently devised: (1) 1978 Poverty Standard (with 85% meant to be enough to buy 2,100 calories), (2) 2008 Poverty Standard (with 60% for 2,100 calories and 40% for some items of daily use) and (3) 2010 Poverty Standard (with 2,100 calories including 60 g protein, nine years of compulsory education, essential health care, basic housing). The World Bank's international poverty line was \$1 a day in 1990, \$1.08 in 1993, \$1.25 in 2005 and \$1.90 in 2015. The exchange rate per dollar was RMB 1.744 in 1990, RMB 2.271 in 1993, RMB 3.737 in 2005 and RMB 4.319 in 2015.

2 For an updated review of the method and its applications, see Betti, D'Agostino, Gagliardi and Giusti (2020).

3 In classical set theory, the membership of elements in a set is assessed in binary terms according to a crispy dichotomic condition: an element either belongs or does not belong to the set. By contrast, fuzzy-set theory permits the gradual assessment of the membership of elements in a set; this is described with the aid of a membership function valued in the real unit interval [0, 1]. Fuzzy sets generalise classical sets, since the indicator functions of classical sets are special cases of the membership functions of fuzzy sets, if the latter take only values of 0 or 1.

References

Alkire, S., Foster, J.E. (2011). Counting and multidimensional poverty measures. *Journal of Public Economics*, 95(7–8), 476–487.

Alkire, S., Shen, Y. (2017). Exploring multidimensional poverty in China: 2010 to 2014. *Research on Economic Inequality*, 25, 161–228.

Betti, G. (2017). What impact has the economic crisis had on quality of life in Europe? A multidimensional and fuzzy approach. *Quality & Quantity*, 51(1), 351–364.

Betti, G., D'Agostino, A., Gagliardi, F., Giusti, C. (2020). The integrated fuzzy and relative index for poverty analysis: A review of applications in the social sciences. *Estudios de Economìa Aplicada*, 38(1), 1–14.

Betti, G., Lemmi, A. eds. (2013). *Poverty and Social Exclusion: New Methods of Analysis*. London: Routledge.

Betti, G., Verma, V. (2008). Fuzzy measures of the incidence of relative poverty and deprivation: A multi-dimensional perspective. *Statistical Methods and Applications*, 12(2), 225–250.

Cerioli, S., Zani, S. (1990). A fuzzy approach to the measurement of poverty. In Dagum, C. Zenga, M. (eds.), *Income and Wealth Distribution, Inequality and Poverty Studies in Contemporary Economics*, 272–284. Berlin: Springer.

Cheli, B., Lemmi, A. (1995). Totally fuzzy and relative approach to the multidimensional analysis of poverty. *Economic Notes*, 24, 115–134.

Ferreira, F., Jolliffe, D.M., Prydz, E.B. (2015). The international poverty line was raised to $1.90 a day, but global poverty is basically unchanged. How is that possible? http://blogs.worldbank.org/developmenttalk/international-poverty-line-has-just-been-raised-190-day-global-poverty-basically-unchanged-how-even/.

Gao, Y.Y. (2012). The multidimensional poverty in urban and rural China: Measurement and comparison. *Statistical Research*, 29(11), 61–66.

Guo, J.Y., Wu, G.B. (2012). Jiyu butong zibiao ji quanzhong xuanzede duowei pinkun celiang: yi Shanxisheng pinkunxian weili [Multidimensional poverty measurement based on different indicators and weight selection: A case study of impoverished counties in Shanxi Province]. *Chinese Rural Economy*, 2, 12–20.

Hagenaars, A. (1987). A class of poverty indices. *International Economic Review*, 28(3), 583–607.

National Bureau of Statistics (2016). *Poverty Monitoring Report of Rural China*. Beijing: China Statistics Press.

Rowntree, B.S. (1901). *Poverty, A Study of Town Life*. London: Macmillan.

Sen, A. (2000). A decade of human development. *Journal of Human Development and Capabilities*, 1(1), 17–23.

Sen, A. (2004a). Elements of a theory of human rights. *Philosophy and Public Affairs*, 32(4), 315–356.

Sen, A. (2004b). Dialogue capabilities, lists, and public reason: Continuing the conversation. *Feminist Economics*, 10(3), 77–80.

Wang, X.L., Alkire, S. (2009). Zhongguo duowei pinkun zeliang: guji he zhengce hanyi [The measurement of multidimensional poverty in China: Estimation and policy implications]. *Chinese Rural Economy*, 12, 4–10.

Williamson, J. G. (2011). *Trade and Poverty: When the Third World Fell Behind*. Cambridge: MIT Press.

World Bank. (1990). *World Development Report 1990: Poverty*. New York: Oxford University Press.

Zadeh, L.A. (1965). Fuzzy sets. *Information and Control*, 8(3), 338–353.

7 JRR Variance Estimates for Longitudinal Fuzzy Measures of Multi-Dimensional Poverty

Gianni Betti, Francesca Gagliardi and Vijay Verma

Introduction

As highlighted in Chapter 4, one of the most important goals of the 2030 UN Agenda for Sustainable Development is to 'eradicate poverty, in all its forms and dimensions' (United Nations, 2015). Moreover, the need to reduce poverty and launch anti-poverty programmes and policies has also been expressed by the European Commission (2010) in their Europe 2020 Strategy. This consists of a series of policy objectives called 'headline targets', which should be reached by 2020. They include targets for reducing the cross-sectional at-risk-of-poverty rate (ARPR), known in the literature as the headcount ratio or as FGT(0) in the family in Foster et al. (1984), and the at-persistent-risk-of-poverty rate in a longitudinal context for monitoring poverty over time. Moreover, poverty measures are most useful to policymakers and researchers when they are finely disaggregated, at least at the level of geographic units smaller than entire countries; this is the purpose of the DG Regional Policy of the European Commission, which uses sub-national/regional-level data (NUTS 2)[1] for social indicators to monitor the 'headline targets' at the regional level.

In the framework of the Europe 2020 Strategy of the European Commission, purely monetary measures of poverty are presented together with new multi-dimensional measures of poverty. Measures of multi-dimensional poverty have been developed as well in the literature: applications are in Whelan and Maitre (2007), Betti et al. (2015) and Goedemé (2013). Betti and Verma (2008) elaborated a *fuzzy formulation* of multi-dimensional measures of deprivation. One approach to modelling fuzzy measures of multi-dimensional poverty is in the next section. The basic concept of the fuzzy approach is to treat poverty and deprivation as a matter of degree, replacing the conventional poor/non-poor dichotomy. An individual degree of poverty is determined by that person's position in the income distribution. This methodology facilitates the inclusion of other dimensions of deprivation in the analysis: by appropriately weighting indicators of deprivation to reflect their dispersion and correlation, we can construct measures of non-monetary deprivation in its various dimensions. Verma et al. (2017) extended the methodology to longitudinal fuzzy multi-dimensional measures of deprivation. The extension of cross-sections to longitudinal fuzzy measures is by no means straightforward. Fuzzy measures of multi-dimensional poverty in the cross-sectional context (e.g. those developed in the next section) need to be extended on the basis of fuzzy-set operations appropriate for the analysis of multi-dimensional poverty in the longitudinal context. This is developed in detail in the third section on fuzzy-set operations. The methodology is fairly general and can yield a variety of longitudinal measures. It provides the basis for the primary objective of this chapter: the variance estimation of longitudinal fuzzy measures of multi-dimensional poverty.

In dealing with population-based survey samples of households or persons, sampling and non-sampling errors affect the accuracy of the estimates based on these surveys, which are particularly relevant when our concern is the analysis of income poverty and inequality. These are complex statistics based on large sample surveys, normally with complex sampling designs. Unfortunately, information on sampling errors and design effects is often not obtained or at least not reported and used in the analysis of the substantive results of the surveys. It seems to be a frequent practice that poverty statistics are published without their confidence interval. Even when standard errors are published, it is not always clear whether they have been calculated accurately. These shortcomings exist even in the most developed settings: in most official publications from Eurostat on poverty indicators, for instance, standard errors are not presented, but as Goedemé (2013) notes, 'this is not a feature unique to Eurostat publications'.

In the literature, several works are devoted to the calculation of standard errors of traditional measures of monetary poverty at the national level. In the present context, when we refer to traditional measures, we mean indicators that are officially adopted by international statistical institutions such as Eurostat, for example, the ARPR, defined as the proportion of the population with an income below a certain threshold. Applications of different methods for the variance estimation of poverty measures are found in Binder (1983), Binder and Patak (1994), Binder and Kovacevic (1995), Preston (1995), Kovacevic and Yung (1997), Deville (1999), Zheng (2001), Berger and Skinner (2003), Demnati and Rao (2004), Osier (2009), Goedemé and Rottiers (2011), Muennich and Zins (2011), Verma and Betti (2011), Graf and Tillé (2014), Alper and Berger (2015) and Berger and Priam (2016). Furthermore, in recent years, the literature on the estimation of the standard errors of traditional measures of poverty at the local (sub-national, regional) level has expanded: see Verma et al. (2017) for an analysis on overall member countries of the Organisation for Economic Co-operation and Development (OECD); Verma et al. (2010a, 2010b) on survey errors and on the robustness of indicators at the regional level; Betti et al. (2012) on a methodology for constructing sub-national indicators of deprivation; Giusti et al. (2012) on small area method applications; Betti et al. (2016a) on the use of a cumulation methodology; and Elbers et al. (2003) on poverty mapping.

By contrast, relatively little attention has been paid to the standard error calculations of these multi-dimensional poverty measures. Because the scope is the estimation of these measures at the regional NUTS 2 level – at which the sample sizes are much smaller than those of corresponding country-level samples – it is essential to develop an adequate methodology for estimating standard errors. Betti et al. (2018) extended variance estimation to go beyond measures of monetary poverty, specifically fuzzy formulation of those measures and, as a corollary, to multi-dimensional measures of deprivation, which by their very nature are a matter of degree.

In this chapter, we further extend variance estimation to longitudinal multi-dimensional fuzzy poverty measures. The measures considered are based on a fuzzy representation of individuals' propensity for deprivation in monetary and diverse non-monetary dimensions and are derived from sample surveys with complex designs and fairly large samples. In particular, we describe and adopt a new longitudinal measure based on the fuzzy-set approach to multi-dimensional poverty, as proposed by Verma et al. (2017): the 'fuzzy at-persistent-risk-of-poverty rate'. The fourth section on data and variance presents a practical methodology for variance estimation – in particular, the jack-knife repeated replication (JRR) method – for multi-dimensional measures of poverty and deprivation of households and individuals in a longitudinal context. We describe and quantitatively illustrate calculation procedures and difficulties in producing reliable and robust estimates of sampling errors in such measures. Some of the problems encountered are identified, and solutions are provided in the context of actual conditions. The fifth section describes the micro-dataset used, which comes from the Spanish EU-SILC (EU Statistics on Income and Living Conditions) survey. Finally, the sixth section presents an empirical analysis, and the last section offers concluding remarks, indicating fruitful directions for further research.

Modelling Fuzzy Measures of Multi-Dimensional Poverty

This section describes the basic cross-sectional fuzzy measures of monetary and non-monetary deprivation. The fuzzy-set approach (Zadeh, 1965) treats poverty as a matter of degree, replacing the simple {0,1}, poor/non-poor, dichotomy into which individuals or households are divided in the traditional approach. In a fuzzy conceptualisation, all individuals are subject to poverty, but at varying degrees; in this way, each individual has a certain *propensity* for poverty over the entire range [0,1]. Treating poverty as a matter of degree has several advantages, applicable to all members of the population, rather than as simply a 'yes–no' state. These are summarised by Verma et al. (2017) as follows:

1. Non-monetary poverty depends on forced non-access to various facilities or possessions that determine basic living conditions. An individual might have access to some of them but not others. Hence, clearly,

non-monetary poverty is inherently a matter of degree, and a quantitative approach such as the present one is essential.

2. The fuzzy approach provides more robust indicators of poverty in a longitudinal context. The conventional approach measures income mobility simply in terms of movement across a designated poverty line and does not reflect the actual magnitude of the changes affecting individuals at all points in the income distribution. Consequently, the degree of mobility of people near this line tends to be over-emphasised, while that of people far from the line is largely ignored.

Apart from various methodological choices involved in the construction of conventional poverty measures, the introduction of fuzzy measures adds factors on which choices must be made. The fundamental factor concerns the choice of 'membership functions', a quantitative specification of the propensity for the poverty of each person, given the level and distribution of income of the population.

Cross-Sectional Fuzzy Membership Function

Betti and Verma (2008) proposed two fuzzy membership functions (MF), based on the seminal contributions of Cerioli and Zani (1990) and Cheli and Lemmi (1995), which are further elaborated in Betti et al. (2015).[2]

In the generalised form, these MF are defined for any individual i as follows:

$$\mu_{i,K} = \left(\frac{\sum_{\gamma=i+1}^{n} w_\gamma \mid X_\gamma > X_i}{\sum_{\gamma=2}^{n} w_\gamma \mid X_\gamma > X_1} \right)^{\alpha_K - 1} \left(\frac{\sum_{\gamma=i+1}^{n} w_\gamma X_\gamma \mid X_\gamma > X_i}{\sum_{\gamma=2}^{n} w_\gamma X_\gamma \mid X_\gamma > X_1} \right) \tag{7.1}$$

$$i : 1, \ldots, n-1; \mu_{n,k} = 0$$

where X is equivalised income in monetary poverty or the overall score s in non-monetary poverty; w_γ is the sample weight of individual of rank γ in the ascending distribution, and α_K ($K = 1{,}2$) are parameters corresponding, respectively, to monetary and non-monetary dimensions of poverty. α_K are estimated so that the mean of the corresponding MF is equal to the ARPR calculated on the basis of the official poverty line. Betti and Verma (2008) call the monetary-based indicator fuzzy monetary (FM) and the non-monetary indicator as fuzzy supplementary (FS).

Construction of the FS Measure

Betti et al. (2015) proposed a step-by-step procedure for measuring the FS, as follows. First, we begin by identifying the items to be included in the index or indices, which should be those that are more meaningful and useful (see

Eurostat 2000, 2002). In fact, it is desirable to avoid items for which issues of choice in terms of possession versus non-possession cannot be satisfactorily resolved, whose possession is relatively rare (i.e. possession of a boat), or whose degree of comparability among regions or countries is not sufficient. Then, for each item, we determine a quantitative deprivation indicator in the range [0,1]: these indicators are used in a first exploratory factor analysis to identify the highlighted 'dimensions'. By dimension, we mean a distinct group of items of non-monetary poverty, ideally independent of other dimensions, which describe a particular facet of living conditions. After this first exploratory factor analysis, we rearrange some items in the dimensions identified to create more meaningful groups: to test the goodness of fit of this final grouping, a confirmatory factor analysis is necessary. The weights to be assigned to each item are determined within each dimension; they are based on two elements, namely, the dispersion of the item (prevalence weights) and the correlation with other items in the same dimension (correlation weights); for a detailed description of the weight construction, see Betti and Verma (2008).

The score within each dimension h, $s_{i,h}$, is calculated as a weighted mean of the items in this dimension; the overall score s_i is defined as a simple average of the dimension scores $s_{i,h}$, thus giving the same importance to all the dimensions, each of which represents a different facet of FS poverty. Finally, as explained above, FS is defined in Equation (7.1). The positive results achieved from applying this methodology to fields other than poverty demonstrate its applicability and robustness (see e.g. Aassve et al., 2007; Betti et al., 2011, 2016b; Belhadj, 2015; Betti, 2017).

Fuzzy-Set Operations Appropriate for an Analysis of Poverty and Deprivation

In this section, we describe the rules for the manipulation of multiple fuzzy sets, which are appropriate for an analysis of deprivation longitudinally and in multiple dimensions.

Let μ_t be the propensity for the poverty of an individual at time t. In a conventional (non-fuzzy, 'crisp') analysis, it is a {0,1} dichotomy: an individual or household can have one of two possible states, 'poverty' ($\mu_t = 1$) and 'non-poverty' ($\mu_t = 0$, or its complement $\bar{\mu}_t = 1$); the two states are exhaustive and mutually exclusive, meaning $\left(\mu_t + \bar{\mu}_t = 1\right)$.

Fuzzy-set operations are a generalisation of the corresponding crisp-set operations in the sense that the former reduce to (exactly reproduce) the latter when the fuzzy membership functions, being in the whole range [0,1], are reduced to a {0,1} dichotomy. Again, at any given time t there are two possible states, 'poverty' with propensity $0 \le \mu_t \le 1$ and 'non-poverty' with propensity $0 \le \bar{\mu}_t \le 1$. In the crisp formulation, only one of the above two quantities is non-zero, and an individual belongs uniquely to one or the other of the two states. In a fuzzy formulation, generally, both the quantities are non-zero, specifying the degree to which an individual belongs to each of the two states. In common with the crisp formulation, these propensities satisfy the constraint $(\mu_t + \bar{\mu}_t = 1)$ covering the two possible states.

Operation for Two Fuzzy Sets

We start with the simple case of two fuzzy sets: they could refer to the propensity for deprivation at two points in time (e.g. for a panel of individuals) or in 2D (e.g. monetary and non-monetary). The formal treatment of the two situations is identical.[3]

Let (μ_1, μ_2) be the propensity for the poverty of an individual at times $t = (1, 2)$. The fuzzy operations of the intersection of propensities at two such time points, defining a set of four sequences or trajectories, are specified in Table 7.1.

The fourth column in Table 7.1 identifies the type of fuzzy-set operation involved, following the terminology explained by Klir and Yuan (1995).[4] Intersection (1) corresponds to the propensity for being in poverty (to be in the state 'poor') at both times $t = (1, 2)$; this is the individual propensity for being in 'continuous poverty'. Intersection (2) corresponds to the propensity for being in poverty at $t = 1$ and in non-poverty at $t = 2$; intersection (3) is just the reverse: non-poverty at $t = 1$ and poverty at $t = 2$. Together, (2) and (3) give the individuals' propensity for being in 'transient poverty'. Intersection (4) corresponds to the propensity for being in non-poverty (to be in the state 'non-poor') at both times ('never poor'). Its complement, *max* (μ_1, μ_2), corresponds to the propensity for being in poverty in at least one of the two times ('any-time poverty'). Note that this is given by standard fuzzy union, intersection (5) in Table 7.1. The fifth column in the table expresses the propensities when using the notation of an ordered set $\mu_{(1)} = max\ (\mu_1, \mu_2) \geq min\ (\mu_1, \mu_2) = \mu_{(2)}$. It clearly shows that

Table 7.1 Four sequences defined by intersection of propensities at the two points in time

Intersection	*Area in Fig. 1*	*Propensity*	*Type of fuzzy operation*	*Propensity using ordered set* $\mu_{(1)} \geq \mu_{(2)} \geq \dots$
(1) $\mu_1 \cap \mu_2$	A	$\min(\mu_1, \mu_2)$	Standard	$\mu_{(2)}$
(2) $\mu_1 \cap \bar{\mu}_2$	max(0, B)	$\max(0, \mu_1 + \bar{\mu}_2 - 1) = \max(0, \mu_1 - \mu_2)$	Bounded	Together $\mu_{(1)} - \mu_{(2)}$
(3) $\bar{\mu}_1 \cap \mu_2$	max(0, B)	$\max(0, \bar{\mu}_1 + \mu_2 - 1) = \max(0, \mu_2 - \mu_1)$	Bounded	
(4) $\bar{\mu}_1 \cap \bar{\mu}_2$	C	$\min(\bar{\mu}_1, \bar{\mu}_2) = 1 - \max(\mu_1, \mu_2)$	Standard	$1 - \mu_{(1)}$
(5) $\mu_1 \cup \mu_2$	A + B	$\max(\mu_1, \mu_2)$	Standard	$\mu_{(1)}$

μ_t = propensity for poverty at time t = (1, 2); $\bar{\mu}_t = 1 - \mu_t$. Sum of propensities (1) to (4) = 1.

the composite operation, involving standard and bounded operations in the table, satisfies the basic requirement that the propensities for the four mutually exclusive and exhaustive sequences or trajectories (1)–(4) for an individual add up to 1.

As noted, our framework for the analysis of fuzzy sets applies equally to multi-dimensional deprivation. Consider, for example, two dimensions of deprivation: monetary and non-monetary. An analysis of the occurrence of deprivation in both dimensions simultaneously parallels the analysis of continuous poverty (poverty at both times); similarly, either dimension of deprivation parallels any-time poverty.

Longitudinal Analysis of Deprivation Conceptualised as a Sequence of Fuzzy States

Now we extend the procedure presented above to an analysis of poverty over any number of time periods (or equivalently, for any number of dimensions of deprivation) in a consistent and substantively meaningful way.

Consider an individual with a propensity for poverty $\mu_t, 1 \le t \le T$ over T points in time. The corresponding propensities for non-poverty are their complements, $\bar{\mu}_t = 1 - \mu_t$. We also find it useful to order the μ_t values with the ordered set $\mu_{(1)} \ge \mu_{(2)} \ge \ldots \ge \mu_{(T)}$. Consider first a sequence of states that are 'poor' at all the T times. The fuzzy operation involved in the standard operation is:

$$\left(\mu_1 \cap \mu_2 \cap \ldots \cap \mu_T\right) = min\left(\mu_1, \mu_2, \ldots, \mu_T\right) = \mu_{(T)}.$$

This intersection is the individual's propensity for being in a state of continuous poverty during T periods. More generally, we consider the two possible states, namely being 'poor' or being 'non-poor' at each point in time. It defines 2^T distinct sequences, each of which takes a length T. For a particular sequence, let $t \in X_p$ be the set of points at which an individual's state of being poor is being considered, and $X_N = (T - X_p)$ be the set of remaining time points at which the state considered is that of being non-poor. The individual's propensity to follow that particular sequence is the intersection of the T quantities $(\mu_t, t \in X_p; \bar{\mu}_t = 1 - \mu_t, t \in X_N)$.

The result can be seen more clearly by ordering the cross-sections according to the magnitude of the propensity. With $M_N = 1 - \bar{m}_N = \max(\mu_t, t \in X_N)$, algebraically, the overlap equals:

$$\max\left(0, m_P + \bar{m}_N - 1\right) = \max\left(0, m_P - M_N\right) \qquad (7.2)$$

which is simply the bounded intersection between propensities m_p and $\bar{m}_N$.

Equation (7.2) has a non-zero value only when $m_P > M_N$. This requirement has the following noteworthy consequence: consider the sequence with P time points at which an individual's state of being poor is considered (with the state of being non-poor at the remaining time points $N = T - P$). In the set of all such sequences, only one sequence at most can have a non-zero propensity for an individual: the sequence in which P points have the highest μ_t values. Using the notation of ordered propensities $\mu_{(t)}$ introduced earlier, this means $m_P = \mu_{(P)}$ and $M_N = \mu_{(P+1)}$.

In Equation (7.2), an individual's propensity for having that particular sequence is:

$$\mu_{(P)} - \mu_{(P+1)} \tag{7.3}$$

This is an individual's propensity for being in the poor state exactly P times during the T periods. Note that these are $T + 1$ such sets, corresponding to $0 \leq P \leq T$. The sum of propensities in Equation (7.2) over these sets is 1 for any individual.[5] Summing Equation (7.3) over the series of values P, $P + 1$, ..., T gives the propensity for being in the poor state at least P times as:

$$\mu_{(P)} \tag{7.4}$$

Longitudinal Fuzzy Measures

Table 7.1 and Equations (7.2) to (7.4) provide the basis for constructing individual propensities, say μ^L, for diverse longitudinal measures of poverty. Table 7.2 shows examples of movements between the states of poverty and non-poverty.

Here are examples of the measures of persistent poverty for any T time periods.

$$\text{Poor at at least K time points } \mu^L = \mu_{(K)} \tag{7.5}$$

$$\text{Any-time poverty } \mu^L = \mu_{(1)} \tag{7.6}$$

$$\text{Continuous poverty } \mu^L = \mu_{(T)} \tag{7.7}$$

Table 7.2 Examples of movements between the states of poverty and non-poverty

T =	*pattern*[6]	*Description*	$\mu^L =$
2	pp	Continuous poverty: poor at both times	$\mu_{(2)}$
2	pn + np[7]	Transient poverty: poor at one of the two times	$\mu_{(1)} - \mu_{(2)}$
2	nn	Never poor	$1 - \mu_{(1)}$
3	pnp	Temporary exit from poverty: poor at time 1, non-poor at 2, again poor at 3	$\max(0, \min(\mu_1, \mu_3) - \mu_2)$
3	npn	Temporary fall into poverty; non-poor at time 1, poor at 2, again non-poor at 3	$\max(0, \mu_2 - \max(\mu_1, \mu_3))$
4	npnp	Constant movement between states of poverty and non-poverty	$\max(0, \min(\mu_2, \mu_4) - \max(\mu_1, \mu_3))$
etc.			

For $T = 4$ time points (say, years), persistent poverty could be defined as being in the state 'poor' for at least three of the four years, in which case:

$$\text{Persistent poverty } \mu^L = \mu_{(3)} \tag{7.8}$$

Eurostat has adopted a somewhat different definition of persistent poverty in its 'at-persistent-risk-of-poverty' rate; this rate is defined as the proportion of people who are poor in the current year (year 4) and were also poor in at least two of the preceding three years (years 1, 2 and 3). Two cases need to be considered:

(1) $\mu_4 \geq \mu_{(3)}$, in which the required propensity of EU-persistent poverty is $\mu^L = \mu_{(3)}$, as in Equation (7.8).
(2) $\mu_4 \geq \mu_{(3)}$. In this case, the propensity being considered is non-zero only for the sequence with state of poverty at all the four points, and therefore the required propensity of EU-persistent poverty is $\mu^L = \mu_4$.

Both cases are covered by:

$$\text{EU at-persistent-risk-of-poverty rate} \quad \mu^L = \min\left(\mu_4, \mu_{(3)}\right) \tag{7.9}$$

Conventional measures are usually in terms of the proportion of people with a specific pattern of poverty. Fuzzy equivalents of the conventional measures are given by the mean value of the individual propensities for the pattern concerned:

$$\text{Fuzzy estimate of a longitudinal measure L} = \sum w_i \mu_i^L \Big/ \sum w_i \tag{7.10}$$

where w_i are the appropriate sample weights.

In the section below we present estimates for Equations (7.6), (7.7) and (7.9) and of their standard errors for $T = 4$ waves of EU-SILC.

Data and Variance Estimation Procedure

Data: EU-SILC Rotational Panel Design

The data used in this chapter come from the EU-SILC survey, which is the most important source of comparable statistics on income and living conditions in Europe. The survey is conducted every year in each participating country. The EU-SILC's total sample size is about 250,000 households in 31 countries, 500,000 adults (age 16+) and 600,000 people of all ages per year. The EU-SILC collects various types of data from different sources: cross-sectional and longitudinal; at the level of households and individuals; on income and social conditions; and from registers and interview surveys depending on the country.

Nearly all EU member countries adopted a standard integrated design. The design recommended by Eurostat is developed and described in Verma and Betti (2006). It involves a rotational panel in which a new sample of households and individuals is introduced each year to replace one-quarter of the existing sample. Each person enumerated in each new sample is followed up in the survey for four years, along with that person's entire household. Every year the design yields a cross-sectional sample as well as longitudinal samples of various durations.

For each year, the cross-sectional sample is made up of four sub-samples or panels (Figure 7.1). A new panel is added each year that will remain in the survey for four years and then dropped to be replaced by another new panel. Movers from the original sample are followed up in their new location for as long as their panel remains in the survey. This scheme provides both cross-sectional and longitudinal data from the same common set of people or households. The cross-sectional sample for year *T* consists of sub-samples 1–4, with one introduced each year from (*T* – 3) to *T*. A longitudinal sample consists of those who have remained in the survey since they were first present in it. Three overlapping longitudinal samples of different durations are formed: two-year duration from sub-samples (2 + 3 + 4); three-year duration from sub-samples (3 + 4); and four-year duration from subsample (4). In this chapter, we analyse longitudinal measures over the four-year panel.

All micro-level data have been weighted for variations in selection probabilities, non-response, other shortcomings in implementation, calibration on the basis of external data and population size. For the most part, the weighting has been implemented centrally by Eurostat; the weighting procedure used is developed and described in Verma et al. (2007).

The EU-SILC survey collects comparable multi-dimensional micro-data on income, economic hardship, social exclusion, housing, labour, education and health. Information on social exclusion and housing conditions is collected mainly at the household level, whereas labour, education and health-care information is obtained for each individual aged 16 and over. The core variable, income at the very detailed component level, is collected mainly at the individual level and then it is aggregated to the household level to construct household income. The reference income is household disposable income, which is converted into the equivalised household income using a proper conversion equivalence scale. The equivalised household income is then ascribed equally to each household member.

A fundamental dimension of the EU-SILC is that both cross-sectional and longitudinal data are collected. The cross-sectional component covers

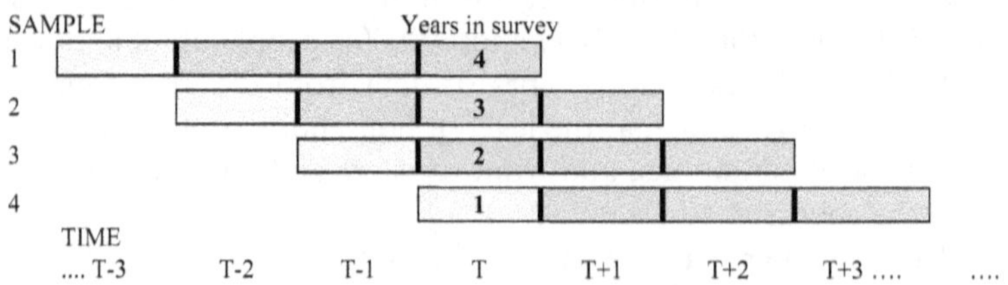

Figure 7.1 Illustration of a simple rotational design.

information pertaining to the current and recent periods, such as the preceding calendar year. It aims to provide estimates of cross-sectional levels and of net changes from one period (year) to another. The longitudinal component covers information compiled or collected through repeated enumeration of individuals and then linked over time at the micro level. It aims to measure gross (micro-level) change. Both cross-sectional and longitudinal micro-data sets are updated on an annual basis.

Data Subset Used in the Present Research

The data subset used in the EU-SILC survey is the one for Spain. For the purpose of a longitudinal analysis, we constructed a four-year panel for the years 2008–2011. In this panel, we selected only people who are present in all the four years.

Thanks to research co-operation with the OECD (Piacentini, 2014; Verma et al., 2017), we have access to the public cross-sectional and longitudinal 2011 EU-SILC data (User Data Base) for Spain and to the non-public variables concerning the sample structure, such as the code for regions at the NUTS 2 level (DB040), sampling strata (DB050) and PSUs (DB060).[8]

The EU-SILC national surveys are mainly designed with a focus on the production of reliable estimates at the national level,[9] and the EU-SILC survey for Spain has a large sample: 13,109 households and 34,756 individuals (2011 cross-sectional sample). This permits direct analysis not only at the national but also at the regional (NUTS 2) level. For our purposes, we constructed a four-year longitudinal balanced panel; this means that we consider only individuals who are present in all four years 2008–2011 of the sample. The final sample size of the panel totals 8,309.

The Spain EU-SILC 2011 Intermediate Quality Report (INE, 2012) gives us a detailed description of the sample design, which is important for understanding whether regions form independent sampling domains and for the construction of the 'computational' PSUs and strata. The sample is a two-stage design. The first-stage units are stratified census sections. In each autonomous community [self-ruling region], the first-stage units are stratified by the size of the municipality in the census section it is in.

An independent sample is designed in each autonomous community to represent it, because one of the INE's survey objectives is to provide data at this level of disaggregation. The sample is distributed across autonomous communities by allocating one part (40%) uniformly and the remainder in proportion to autonomous community size. Each section is made up of around 400 addresses. The second stage comprises principal family addresses selected for the sample in the census section; all households that usually reside in those addresses are surveyed.

The regions are treated as sampling domains. DB040, DB050 and DB060 define, respectively, the region, stratum and PSU for each individual or household in the micro-dataset. The first two variables together define unique strata within each region separately. Using the sample description and the three variables mentioned above makes it possible to define the computational strata and PSUs for variance estimation. Sample weights have been computed at the level of individuals in the sample.

JRR Variance Estimation Procedure

Practical procedures for estimating the variance in complex statistics from complex surveys require that certain basic assumptions of the sample design be met. (1) The survey is based on a probability sample. (2) The sample selection is independent between strata, with two or more primary selections (PS) drawn at random, independently and with replacement from each stratum.[10] (3) The total number of PS is large enough (say ≥ 30) for valid use of the approximations in the variance estimation methods.[11] (4) Subsampling of any complexity might involve PSUs and might differ from one PSU to another. (5) The PS at the same stratum do not differ greatly in size, i.e. in the number (more precisely the sum of sample weights) of final units selected (say $cv \leq 0.1$).

In addition, practical calculation procedures for estimating sampling errors for complex surveys: (6) must take into account the actual complex structure of the design; (7) should be flexible enough to apply to diverse designs; (8) should be suitable and convenient for large-scale application, producing results routinely for diverse statistics and sub-classes; (9) should be robust to the departure of the actual sample design from the ideal model assumed in the calculation method; (10) should have desirable statistical properties, such as small mean-square error of the variance estimator; (11) should be economical in terms of effort and cost; and (12) suitable computer software should be available to apply the method.

These assumptions are usually met or are reasonably approximated in most large-scale population-based surveys (for more details, see Verma, 1991). However, another requirement must be added, which, unlike those mentioned earlier, is often *not* met in practice. The assumption is that (13) all essential information on the sample structure is available. Sampling error calculations must take variations in the sample design into account through the definition of the sample structure. To apply the calculation procedures, it is necessary to have full access to the variables that define the structure of the sample, at least on stratification, the PSUs and weights of sample units and a detailed description of the sample design. Even when this type of information on sample structure is collected in the surveys (and in the EU-SILC surveys used in this chapter for quantitative illustration), not all of it is included in the micro-data in the public domain available to researchers. The lack of this information in complex samples makes it impossible to calculate valid estimates of the sampling error.

The calculation method used in the estimation of the standard errors of the complex statistics from the complex samples in this chapter is JRR, which is a practical method based on measures of observed variability among replications of the full sample. After the set of replications is appropriately defined for a complex design, the same variance estimation algorithm can be applied to statistics of any level of complexity. The variance estimates take into account the effect on the variance of aspects of the estimation procedure, which are repeated for each replication. In principle, this can include complex effects, such as those of imputation and weighting, though the full repetition of these procedures for each replication often is not feasible. We extended and applied JRR for estimating variances for subpopulations (including regions and other geographic divisions), longitudinal measures such as persistent poverty rates, and measures of net changes and averages over cross-sections in rotational panel designs. We use JRR in the version proposed by Verma and Betti (2011);[12] moreover, Betti et al. (2018) show that the JRR variant by Verma and Betti (2011) is particularly suitable at estimating the variance of fuzzy poverty measures.

The basic equation for JRR variance estimation is:

$$\text{var}(z) = \Sigma_h \left[(1 - f_h) \cdot \Sigma_i g_{(hi)} \left(z_{(hi)} - z_{(h)} \right)^2 \right]$$

where z is a full-sample estimate of any complexity;

subscript i indicates a sample PSU and h is its stratum; $a \geq 2$ is the number of PSUs in stratum h;

$z_{(hi)}$ is the estimate produced using the same procedure after PSU i in stratum h is eliminated and the weight of the remaining $(a_h - 1)$ units in the stratum is increased by an appropriate factor g_h;

$z_{(h)}$ is the simple average of the $z_{(hi)}$ over a_h sample units in h;

$(1 - f_h)$ is the finite population correction, usually ~1 for samples in typical social surveys; $g_{(hi)} = w_h / (w_h - w_{hi})$, where $w_h = \sum_i w_{hi}$, with $w_{hi} = \sum_j w_{hij}$ as the sum of sample weights of final units j in PSU i.

The replications are calculated by deleting one PSU at a time and appropriately increasing the weight of the remaining PSUs in the same stratum. In going from a cross-sectional to a longitudinal (panel) sample, the important point to note is that the sample structure for each final unit in the four-year panel – regions, strata, PSUs – is defined by the structure when the unit is first entered into the sample and remains fixed for the duration of the sample. A unit can move to different locations over time, but this does not affect the structure of the sample used in selecting the unit. This means that replications, once constructed, remain unchanged over the duration of the panel. Hence, each replication is itself a panel sample, so all the longitudinal measures μ^L defined above can be constructed from the cross-sectional measures μ_t in the same way. The μ_t are cross-sectional estimates for the panel sample.

Construction of Computational Strata and PSUs

This procedure enables the construction of 'computational' PSUs and strata for variance estimation. In our analysis, we imposed the sample structure, namely, regions, strata and PSUs, for each individual in the four-year panel, which are defined by the structure at the beginning of the panel and remain fixed for the duration of the panel.

(1) The strata are confined within regions. The regional and PSU codes in combination directly identify unique computational strata for estimating variances in each region in most cases. In a few cases (about 10, i.e. on average less than one per region) a stratum contains only one PSU. Because the calculation procedure requires at least two PSUs per stratum, any stratum with a single unit is merged with another stratum to provide the final computational stratum.
(2) By design, each PSU is confined to a single stratum. However, we found that, in some cases, a PSU extended across more than one stratum and occasionally even across different regions. These cases represent a misspecification of the PSU code in the rotating panel design of the survey. For each unit in the sample, the code should specify the *original* PSU where the unit was selected. It appears that these errors concern people who have changed their residence since they participated in the survey, and in error the code identifies their current rather than their original PSU. Mostly, the majority of the samples with problematic PSUs remained in the same stratum, and a very small proportion (movers) were coded as being in a different stratum. In these cases, there is no way to identify the original PSU from the information available. In each stratum, these movers were grouped to form a new, separate PSU in the stratum. In this way, the resulting computational PSUs did not cut across computational strata, as required by a design with independent sampling within regions and by the variance estimation procedure.
(3) Finally, we found some PSUs with a very small number of samples. When the number of adults in a PSU was less than six, we combined this PSU with others so that the resulting computational PSU had at least six people. In practice, this procedure was quite long and demanding, but not complex, and yielded appropriate computational PSUs and strata.

Empirical Analysis

Using the quantitative data described above, this section analyses the estimates of sampling errors for longitudinal poverty and deprivation-related variables. The results for each of the 19 regions in Spain enable analysis from a comparative perspective. Because the regions form independent sample domains, we can treat them as domains in a comparative analysis, in a way that is similar to a multi-country comparative analysis.

Tables 7.3, 7.4 and 7.5 calculate the three longitudinal measures – anytime, continuous and (EU) persistent – for the three measures of poverty: (1) conventional poverty; (2) fuzzy monetary poverty (FM); and (3) fuzzy supplementary (non-monetary) deprivation (FS).

Table 7.3 Any-time poverty measures

Region	*n*	*ANY-TIME Conventional*		*ANY-TIME FS*		*ANY-TIME FM*		*ratio est fs/conv*	*ratio est fm/conv*	*ratio CV FS/ CONV*	*ratio CV FM/ CONV*
		est	*CV*	*est*	*CV*	*est*	*CV*				
ES11	643	0.349	0.107	0.465	0.081	0.354	0.079	1.34	1.01	0.76	0.74
ES12	375	0.221	0.213	0.254	0.155	0.233	0.137	1.15	1.05	0.73	0.64
ES13	286	0.356	0.127	0.354	0.131	0.295	0.171	1.00	0.83	1.03	1.34
ES21	398	0.276	0.190	0.248	0.109	0.251	0.162	0.90	0.91	0.57	0.85
ES22	311	0.120	0.304	0.243	0.170	0.162	0.192	2.03	1.36	0.56	0.63
ES23	311	0.365	0.205	0.291	0.129	0.340	0.149	0.80	0.93	0.63	0.73
ES24	349	0.179	0.225	0.244	0.146	0.213	0.158	1.37	1.19	0.65	0.70
ES30	660	0.289	0.160	0.290	0.087	0.280	0.100	1.00	0.97	0.54	0.63
ES41	512	0.327	0.197	0.277	0.128	0.326	0.129	0.85	1.00	0.65	0.65
ES42	445	0.500	0.098	0.310	0.126	0.421	0.080	0.62	0.84	1.29	0.81
ES43	365	0.559	0.140	0.389	0.103	0.462	0.085	0.69	0.83	0.74	0.61
ES51	841	0.301	0.121	0.318	0.099	0.296	0.079	1.06	0.98	0.82	0.66
ES52	651	0.358	0.126	0.392	0.090	0.343	0.087	1.09	0.96	0.71	0.69
ES53	221	0.171	0.191	0.305	0.121	0.208	0.158	1.78	1.21	0.64	0.83
ES61	980	0.469	0.070	0.456	0.062	0.440	0.047	0.97	0.94	0.88	0.66
ES62	377	0.358	0.206	0.420	0.134	0.362	0.162	1.17	1.01	0.65	0.79
ES63	132	0.379	0.475	0.339	0.394	0.315	0.423	0.89	0.83	0.83	0.89
ES64	45	0.287	1.213	0.190	0.298	0.281	0.920	0.66	0.98	0.25	0.76
ES70	407	0.403	0.210	0.434	0.080	0.354	0.148	1.08	0.88	0.38	0.71
Mean		***0.330***	***0.241***	***0.327***	***0.139***	***0.312***	***0.183***	***0.99***	***0.95***	***0.58***	***0.76***
St. Dev./Mean		***0.338***	***1.044***	***0.244***	***0.572***	***0.255***	***1.070***	***0.72***	***0.75***	***0.55***	***1.02***

Notes: n is the number of people present in all four years of the panel. The mean and the ratio st. dev./mean for the last four columns are calculated as the ratio of the corresponding mean value across regions. The official regional codes are used, and the names of the regions are identified on the Eurostat web site.

Table 7.4 Continuous poverty measures

Region	*n*	CONTINUOUS *Conventional*		CONTINUOUS *FS*		CONTINUOUS *FM*		*ratio est fs/conv*	*ratio est fm/conv*	*ratio CV FS/CONV*	*ratio CV FM/ CONV*
		est	*CV*	*est*	*CV*	*est*	*CV*				
ES11	643	0.051	0.311	0.136	0.129	0.079	0.144	2.65	1.55	0.42	0.46
ES12	375	0.005	0.660	0.043	0.214	0.051	0.202	9.23	10.87	0.32	0.31
ES13	286	0.029	0.483	0.092	0.281	0.070	0.208	3.15	2.40	0.58	0.43
ES21	398	0.014	0.723	0.052	0.322	0.044	0.264	3.81	3.23	0.45	0.37
ES22	311	0.005	0.766	0.056	0.376	0.021	0.357	12.00	4.53	0.49	0.47
ES23	311	0.072	0.544	0.059	0.219	0.112	0.275	0.82	1.57	0.40	0.51
ES24	349	0.006	0.565	0.040	0.294	0.048	0.214	6.37	7.69	0.52	0.38
ES30	660	0.027	0.387	0.054	0.152	0.056	0.156	1.97	2.04	0.39	0.40
ES41	512	0.037	0.336	0.060	0.201	0.085	0.244	1.63	2.32	0.60	0.72
ES42	445	0.113	0.243	0.059	0.225	0.136	0.144	0.52	1.21	0.92	0.59
ES43	365	0.168	0.179	0.087	0.186	0.195	0.100	0.52	1.16	1.04	0.56
ES51	841	0.025	0.321	0.066	0.166	0.062	0.149	2.64	2.48	0.52	0.46
ES52	651	0.037	0.373	0.081	0.158	0.079	0.149	2.18	2.11	0.43	0.40
ES53	221	0.037	0.804	0.086	0.399	0.060	0.310	2.30	1.62	0.50	0.38
ES61	980	0.087	0.209	0.143	0.123	0.138	0.114	1.64	1.59	0.59	0.55
ES62	377	0.101	0.474	0.079	0.198	0.111	0.267	0.78	1.09	0.42	0.56
ES63	132	0.155	0.616	0.167	0.527	0.144	0.523	1.08	0.93	0.86	0.85
ES64	45	0.056	1.213	0.012	0.808	0.058	1.043	0.21	1.03	0.67	0.86
ES70	407	0.052	0.502	0.098	0.194	0.092	0.221	1.88	1.77	0.39	0.44
Mean		***0.057***	***0.511***	***0.077***	***0.272***	***0.086***	***0.268***	***1.36***	***1.52***	***0.53***	***0.52***
St. Dev./Mean		***0.853***	***0.493***	***0.493***	***0.610***	***0.501***	***0.795***	***0.58***	***0.59***	***1.24***	***1.61***

Notes: n is the number of people present in all four years of the panel. The mean and the ratio st. dev./mean for the last four columns are calculated as the ratio of the corresponding mean value across regions. The official regional codes are used, and the names of the regions are identified on the Eurostat web site.

Table 7.5 Persistent poverty measures

Region	*n*	*PERSISTENT Conventional*		*PERSISTENT FS*		*PERSISTENT FM*		*ratio est fs/conv*	*ratio est fm/conv*	*ratio CV FS/CONV*	*ratio CV FM/ CONV*
		est	*CV*	*est*	*CV*	*est*	*CV*				
ES11	643	0.072	0.235	0.199	0.119	0.123	0.101	2.75	1.71	0.50	0.43
ES12	375	0.074	0.397	0.079	0.173	0.102	0.223	1.06	1.37	0.44	0.56
ES13	286	0.092	0.393	0.132	0.233	0.109	0.213	1.43	1.18	0.59	0.54
ES21	398	0.034	0.471	0.081	0.212	0.074	0.233	2.35	2.15	0.45	0.49
ES22	311	0.019	0.714	0.104	0.277	0.039	0.359	5.40	2.02	0.39	0.50
ES23	311	0.164	0.343	0.091	0.175	0.173	0.213	0.55	1.06	0.51	0.62
ES24	349	0.061	0.380	0.068	0.204	0.081	0.243	1.11	1.32	0.54	0.64
ES30	660	0.048	0.353	0.090	0.147	0.082	0.140	1.86	1.71	0.42	0.40
ES41	512	0.081	0.313	0.090	0.183	0.138	0.208	1.11	1.69	0.59	0.67
ES42	445	0.198	0.234	0.117	0.184	0.198	0.140	0.59	1.00	0.79	0.60
ES43	365	0.210	0.150	0.128	0.145	0.250	0.100	0.61	1.19	0.96	0.66
ES51	841	0.055	0.250	0.110	0.145	0.091	0.140	2.02	1.66	0.58	0.56
ES52	651	0.074	0.248	0.139	0.128	0.122	0.127	1.88	1.64	0.52	0.51
ES53	221	0.043	0.719	0.128	0.340	0.080	0.191	2.97	1.86	0.47	0.27
ES61	980	0.165	0.161	0.210	0.095	0.201	0.089	1.27	1.22	0.59	0.56
ES62	377	0.145	0.370	0.144	0.224	0.153	0.210	0.99	1.05	0.61	0.57
ES63	132	0.155	0.616	0.188	0.500	0.171	0.510	1.21	1.10	0.81	0.83
ES64	45	0.056	1.213	0.053	0.125	0.070	0.891	0.94	1.25	0.10	0.74
ES70	407	0.082	0.341	0.179	0.158	0.126	0.197	2.19	1.54	0.46	0.58
Mean		***0.096***	***0.416***	***0.122***	***0.198***	***0.125***	***0.238***	***1.27***	***1.30***	***0.48***	***0.57***
St. Dev./Mean		***0.599***	***0.606***	***0.370***	***0.473***	***0.433***	***0.781***	***0.62***	***0.78***	***1.65***	***1.43***

Notes: n is the number of people present in all four years of the panel. The mean and the ratio st. dev./mean for the last four columns are calculated as the ratio of the corresponding mean value across regions. The official regional codes are used, and the names of the regions are identified on the Eurostat web site.

For each of them, standard errors are estimated using JRR. We present the estimates, their coefficient of variation, and the ratios of the estimates and the coefficients of variation (CV) of fuzzy measures over conventional measures.

The empirical analysis indicates that in general the fuzzy measures have smaller standard errors than conventional measures. This confirms the findings in Betti et al. (2018). This is particularly true for the any-time and persistent poverty measures. For continuous poverty, this is true in terms of the number of regions with smaller standard errors using fuzzy measures than with the conventional one. The values of the ratios for regions where the opposite situation (smaller standard errors for conventional measures) occurs are very large. The CV ratio offers more evidence of the stability of the fuzzy longitudinal poverty measures. For any-time poverty, the CV ratio shows a reduction of 25% in FM and 30% in FS; the FS ratio is more variable than the FM ratio. The CV ratio shows a greater reduction for continuous poverty than for any-time poverty. In this case, the reduction is about 45–50%. Again, the FS ratio is more variable than the FM ratio, but the variation is smaller than it is for any-time poverty.

The ratio of CV again shows a greater reduction for persistent poverty than for any-time poverty and is in line with the ratio for continuous poverty. The reduction is about 45%. The variation in the CV ratio for FM and FS is very similar to the one for continuous poverty.

Notes

1 NUTS is an abbreviation for Nomenclature of Statistical Territorial Units, Eurostat's hierarchical classification of regions, from member states (NUTS 0) to smaller areas.

2 See also Lemmi and Betti (2006) for further contributions on philosophy, mathematics, economics of the fuzzy-set approach to poverty measurement, and the contributions of Cheli and Betti (1999), Belhadj (2011, 2012), Alkire and Foster (2011), Belhadj and Limam (2012) and the book of Betti and Lemmi (2013).

3 We express the following arbitrarily in terms of longitudinal poverty at two points in time.

4 Fuzzy-set operations are generalisations of corresponding 'crisp' operations, however, there is more than one way to formulate the fuzzy-set operations (e.g. standard, algebraic and bounded operations), each representing an equally valid generalisation of the corresponding crisp-set operations. Klir and Yuan (1995) provide an excellent discussion of different types of fuzzy operations. The choice among alternative formulations should be made primarily on substantive grounds: some options are more appropriate (meaningful, useful, illuminating, convenient) than others, depending on the context and objectives of the application. Following Verma et al. (2017), in this chapter we present a formulation that is suitable specifically for the study of poverty and deprivation.

5 $\mu_{(0)} = 1$ and $\mu_{(T+1)} = 0$ by definition.

6 p and n are used in sequence to specify the poor and non-poor pattern referred to.

7 This is given by the sum of rows (2) and (3) in Table 7.1; at most, only one of those rows is non-zero.

8 Full information on sample structure design for other EU-SILC surveys is unavailable in the public-access data files.
9 Analysis at the regional (sub-national) level requires special procedures; see Verma et al. (2010b) on the robustness of EU-SILC-based indicators at the regional level.
10 The term 'primary selection' refers to a set of final units drawn independently from a primary sample unit (PSU).
11 This is to ensure that, although the income distribution on which the measures analysed here are based is highly skewed, the sampling distribution of the measures constructed from large enough samples tends towards a normal distribution.
12 Verma and Betti (2011) demonstrate that a variant of the JRR method can fit better in the case of 'complex measures'.

References

Aassve A., Betti G., Mazzuco S., Mencarini L. (2007), Marital disruption and economic well-being; a comparative analysis, *Journal of the Royal Statistical Society, Series A*, 170(3), pp. 781–799.

Alkire S., Foster J. (2011), Counting and multidimensional poverty measurement, *Journal of Public Economics*, 95(7–8), pp. 476–487.

Alper M.O., Berger Y.G. (2015), Variance estimation of change in poverty rates: An application to Turkish EU-SILC survey, *Journal of Official Statistics*, 31(2), pp. 155–175.

Belhadj B. (2011), A new fuzzy unidimensional poverty index from an information theory perspective, *Empirical Economics*, 40(3), pp. 687–704.

Belhadj B. (2012), New weighting scheme for the dimensions in multidimensional poverty indices, *Economic Letters*, 116(3), pp. 304–307.

Belhadj B. (2015), Employment measure in development countries via minimum wage and poverty: new Fuzzy approach, *Opsearch*, 52(2), pp 329–339.

Belhadj B., Limam M. (2012), Unidimensional and multidimensional fuzzy poverty measures: New approach, *Economic Modelling*, 29(4), pp. 995–1002.

Berger Y.G., Priam R. (2016), A simple variance estimator of change for rotating repeated surveys: An application to the EU-SILC household surveys, *Journal of the Royal Statistical Society, Series A*, 179(1), pp. 251–272.

Berger Y.G., Skinner C.J. (2003), Variance estimation of a low-income proportion, *Journal of the Royal Statistical Society, Series C*, 52, pp. 457–468.

Betti G., D'Agostino A., Neri L. (2011), Educational mismatch of graduates: A multidimensional and fuzzy indicator, *Social Indicators Research*, 103(3), pp. 465–480.

Betti G., Gagliardi F., Lemmi A., Verma V. (2012), Sub-national indicators of poverty and deprivation in Europe: methodology and applications, *Cambridge Journal of Regions, Economy and Society*, 5(1), pp. 149–162.

Betti G., Gagliardi F., Lemmi A., Verma V. (2015), Comparative measures of multidimensional deprivation in the European Union, *Empirical Economics*, 49(3), pp. 1071–1100.

Betti G., Gagliardi F., Verma V. (2016a), Variance estimation for cumulative and longitudinal poverty indicators from panel data at regional level, in Pratesi M. (ed.), *Analysis of Poverty Data by Small Area Estimation*, John Wiley, United Kingdom, pp. 129–147.

Betti G., Gagliardi F., Verma V. (2018), Simplified Jack-knife variance estimates for fuzzy measures of multidimensional poverty, *International Statistical Review*, 86(1), pp. 68–86.

Betti G., Lemmi A. eds. (2013), *Poverty and Social Exclusion: New Methods of Analysis*. London: Routledge.

Betti G., Soldi R., Talev I. (2016b), Fuzzy multidimensional indicators of quality of life: The empirical case of Macedonia, *Social Indicators Research*, 127(1), pp. 39–53.

Betti G., Verma V. (2008), Fuzzy measures of the incidence of relative poverty and deprivation: A multi-dimensional perspective, *Statistical Methods and Applications*, 17, pp. 225–250.

Binder D.A. (1983), On the variance of asymptotically normal estimators from complex surveys, *International Statistical Review*, 51, pp. 279–292.

Binder D.A., Kovacevic M.S. (1995), Estimating some measures of income inequality from survey data: An application of the estimation equation approach, *Survey Methodology*, 21, pp. 137–145.

Binder D.A., Patak Z. (1994), Use of estimation functions for interval estimation from complex surveys, *Journal of the American Statistical Association*, 89, pp. 1035–1043.

Cerioli A., Zani S. (1990), A fuzzy approach to the measurement of poverty, in Dagum C., Zenga M. (eds.), *Income and Wealth Distribution, Inequality and Poverty*, Springer, Berlin, pp. 272–284.

Cheli B., Betti G. (1999), Fuzzy analysis of poverty dynamics on an Italian pseudo panel, 1985–1994, *Metron*, 57, pp. 83–104.

Cheli B., Lemmi A. (1995), A totally fuzzy and relative approach to the multidimensional analysis of poverty, *Economic Notes*, 24, pp. 115–134.

Demnati A., Rao J.N.K. (2004), Linearization variance estimators for survey data, *Survey Methodology*, 30, pp. 17–26.

Deville J.C. (1999), Variance estimation for complex statistics and estimators: Linearization and residual techniques, *Survey Methodology*, 25, pp. 193–203.

Elbers C., Lanjouw J.O., Lanjouw P. (2003), Micro-level estimation of poverty and inequality, *Econometrica*, 71(1), pp. 355–364.

European Commission (2010), *Europe 2020 – A European strategy for smart, sustainable and inclusive growth.*

Eurostat (2000), *European Social Statistics: Income, Poverty and Social Exclusion, Detailed Tables*, Luxembourg.

Eurostat (2002), *European Social Statistics: Income, Poverty and Social Exclusion, 2nd Report,* Luxembourg.

Foster J., Greer J., Thorbecke E. (1984), A class of decomposable poverty measures, *Econometrica*, 52, pp. 761–766.

Giusti C., Marchetti S., Pratesi M., Salvati N. (2012), Robust small area estimation and oversampling in the estimation of poverty indicators, *Survey Research Methods*, 6(3), pp. 155–163.

Goedemé T., Rottiers S. (2011), Poverty in the Enlarged European Union. A discussion about definitions and reference groups, *Sociology Compass*, 5(1), pp. 77–91.

Goedemé T. (2013), How much confidence can we have in EU-SILC? Complex sample design and standard error of the Europe 2020 poverty indicators, *Social Indicators Research*, 110, pp. 89–110.

Graf E., Tillé Y. (2014), Variance estimation using linearization for poverty and social exclusion indicators, *Survey Methodology*, 40(1), pp. 61–79.

Instituto Nacional De Estadistica (INE) (2012), Intermediate Quality Report, Survey on Income and Living Conditions Spain (Spanish ECV 2011).

Klir G.J. and Yuan B. (1995), *Fuzzy Sets and Fuzzy Logic*. Englewood Cliffs, NJ: Prentice-Hall.

Kovacevic M.S., Yung W. (1997), Variance estimation for measures of income inequality and polarization – an empirical study, *Survey Methodology*, 23(1), pp. 41–52.

Lemmi A., Betti G. eds. (2006), *Fuzzy Set Approach to Multidimensional Poverty Measurement*. New York: Springer.

Muennich R., Zins S. (2011), *Variance Estimation for Indicators of Poverty and Social Exclusion*. Work package of the European project on Advanced Methodology for European Laeken Indicators (AMELI).

Osier G. (2009), Variance estimation for complex indicators of poverty and inequality using linearization techniques, *Survey Research Methods*, 3, pp. 167–195.

Piacentini M. (2014), *Measuring Income Inequality and Poverty at the Regional Level in OECD Countries*. OECD Statistics Working Papers, 2014/03, OECD.

Preston I. (1995), Sampling distributions of relative poverty statistics, *Applied Statistics*, 44, pp. 91–99.

United Nations General Assembly (2015), *Transforming Our World: The 2030 Agenda for Sustainable Development*.

Verma V. (1991), *Sampling Methods, Training Handbook*. Tokyo: Statistical Institute for Asia and the Pacific.

Verma V., Betti G. (2006), EU statistics on income and living conditions (EU-SILC): Choosing the survey structure and sample design, *Statistics in Transition*, 7(5), pp.935–970.

Verma V., Betti G. (2011), Taylor linearization sampling errors and design effects for poverty measures and other complex statistics, *Journal of Applied Statistics*, 38(8), pp. 1549–1576.

Verma V. Betti G., Gagliardi F. (2010a), *An Assessment of Survey Errors in EU-SILC*. Eurostat Methodologies and Working Papers, Luxembourg: Publications Office of the European Union.

Verma V., Betti G., Gagliardi F. (2010b), *Robustness of Some EU-SILC Based Indicators at Regional Level*. Eurostat Methodologies and Working Papers, Luxembourg: Publications Office of the European Union.

Verma V., Betti G., Gagliardi F. (2017), Fuzzy measures of longitudinal poverty in a comparative perspective, *Social Indicators Research*, 130(2), pp. 435–454.

Verma V., Betti G., Ghellini G. (2007), Cross-sectional and longitudinal weighting in a rotational household panel: applications to EU-SILC, *Statistics in Transition*, 8(1), pp. 5–50.

Verma V., Lemmi A., Betti G., Gagliardi F., Piacentini M. (2017), How precise are poverty measures estimated at the regional level?, *Regional Science and Urban Economics*, 66, pp. 175–184.

Whelan C.T., Maitre B. (2007), Measuring material deprivation in EU-Silc: Lessons from the Irish survey, *European Societies*, 9(2), pp. 147–173.

Zadeh L.A. (1965), Fuzzy sets, *Information and Control*, 8(3), 338–353.

Zheng B. (2001), Statistical inference for poverty measures with relative poverty lines, *Journal of Econometrics*, 101, pp. 337–356.

8 Overview of the Quality of Life in Europe

Antonella D'Agostino, Giulio Ghellini, María Navarro and Angeles Sánchez

Introduction

Over the past few decades, quality of life (QoL) has become a key issue in modern society and one of the most important goals for individuals. QoL implies, first, that the minimum conditions required for humans to thrive are met and, second, that opportunities and skills adequately match (Veenhoven, 2000). The process started in the more advanced democracies, replacing the search for mere material wealth and putting at the top of the public agenda new challenges for social organisation and, in particular, social policy. Within this framework, several international initiatives have been undertaken to improve the measurement of QoL (for a review, see Sánchez et al., 2018). In the context of the European Union (EU), in 2009 the European Commission initiated the project 'GDP and Beyond: Measuring Progress in a Changing World' starting with the idea that economic indicators, such as the gross domestic product (GDP), while important, do not completely indicate the effective level of well-being of a population and, consequently, how well we are operating (EU Commission, 2009).

Accordingly, the need to supplement the information provided by GDP with new data on other aspects of people's lives has become a key issue and challenge for researchers, institutions and policymakers. In this vein, a great consensus has formed about the need to develop new data sources and new surveys so as to build innovative indicators of QoL, which are useful for measuring social progress from a different perspective (Mercy, 2015). These indicators should reflect the multi-dimensionality of the concept of QoL and, therefore, cover different aspects of individuals' lives, such as living standards, social relationships, leisure and culture, good health, education and the environment (Michalos et al., 2011).

In the past few years, the relevance and the complexity of QoL measurement have driven methodological and empirical research, so, in addition to existing journals such as *Social Indicators Research* (published since 1974), new titles have emerged, including the *Journal of Happiness Studies* in 2000 and the *Applied Research in Quality of Life* in 2006 (McCrea et al., 2011). In this chapter, we focus on the measurement of QoL in Europe, considering QoL as a latent concept that can be studied as a foundational measurement model. That is, QoL is assumed to be defined by a set of indicators: (i) objective or social indicators that reflect people's objective conditions within a given cultural or geographic area, and (ii) indicators of subjective well-being that reflect individual judgements of well-being (Diener & Suh, 1997). Our main goal is to show the utility of applying a fuzzy-set approach in this framework, using micro-data collected through survey data.

The rest of this chapter is structured as follows. The second section presents a brief literature review concerning the measurement of QoL and its recent development. The third section outlines the surveys generally used in monitoring QoL in Europe, as well as the main results of some empirical studies. The fourth section briefly describes the fuzzy methodology proposed by Betti et al. (2015) for building composite indicators of QoL, showing how this approach can be a useful methodological tool in this framework. Finally, some conclusions are offered in the last section.

Measuring Quality of Life: Literature Review

Over time, the global community has moved from viewing well-being or QoL[1] as a narrow economic concept to one that encompasses people's objective conditions and their subjective evaluation of these conditions. In this section, we chronologically review the main approaches used in studying people's QoL.

In the development period since the Second World War, the dominant concept of well-being has been economic. The conditions that determined national development were defined on the basis of production in the highest possible monetary terms and the modification of productive activities when they were harmful. Economic welfare focuses on the material resources that people control, can use and dispose of, measured by income and, at the aggregate level, by national income or production per capita (Gough et al., 2007). However, since the 1950–1960s, some of the most respected economists have become aware of the limits of using GDP as a proxy for QoL – this was a criticism not only about the use of a single indicator for assessing social performance but also about the economic nature of the indicator used (see e.g. Galbraith, 1958; Mishan, 1967; Scitovsky, 1976; Sen, 1976).

In this context, from the 1970s, the social indicators movement (Andrews & Withey, 1976) argued in favour of measuring QoL more broadly, on the basis of a long list of indicators, rather than relying only on GDP per capita. At the United Nations conference 'Paris Biosphere Conference' in 1968, many official agencies focused on the development of a comprehensive system for monitoring progress with economic, social and environmental indicators. Despite its impact, the main limitation of the social indicators movement was the absence until the 1980s of a theoretical foundation, which was provided by the capability approach (Sessa, 2016).

In the 1980s, Sen (1980) introduced the capability approach as a general way to evaluate the human condition, breaking with traditional welfare economics (Gough et al., 2007; Robeyns, 2005). The capability approach is a broad normative framework for the evaluation and assessment of individual well-being or the average well-being of members of a group and the design of policies (Robeyns, 2005). The capability approach focuses on the plural or multi-dimensional aspects of development and claims that income and resources do not provide a sufficient or satisfactory indicator of well-being, as they measure the means, rather than the ends. It is necessary to take into consideration what individuals can do not only with the technology they have but also, and most importantly, with their human capital or, to be more precise, their capabilities (Nussbaum, 2011; Sen, 1980, 1992). The capability approach also provided the theoretical foundations of the human development paradigm (Fukuda-Parr & Kumar, 2004). Since 1990, the United Nations Development Programme has calculated the Human Development Index at the country level on an annual basis. However, among political decision-makers, macroeconomic indicators continued to be the most used for measuring economic and social progress and for designing policy.

In recent decades, demand has grown in the academic and political sectors, as well as the general public, for the development of better ways to measure and monitor QoL more comprehensively. The main argument is that a single economic measure does not account for the social cost of economic development, such as the cost of urbanisation or pollution, and does not consider income distribution or significant assets, such as educational opportunities, employment opportunities, personal safety and political freedom (Neumayer, 2003; Nussbaum, 2011; OECD, 2017; Stiglitz et al., 2011; Van den Bergh, 2009). Moreover, it fails to include subjective aspects that influence QoL (Diener, 2002; Frey & Sutzer, 2002). The inclusion of self-reported indicators is crucial for properly measuring QoL because they are related to the nonmaterial aspects of human well-being, such as the influence of social relations, trust in people, autonomy and self-determination (Bárcena-Martín et al., 2017; Bartolini & Sarracino, 2014; Dolan & Metcalfe, 2012; Frey & Stutzer, 2002; Stutzer & Frey, 2010). In practice, this new approach has been adopted, with several international initiatives stressing the importance of including data on self-reported well-being, as well as objective well-being, in larger-scale surveys undertaken by official statistical offices, because they all contribute to measuring QoL (see e.g. Eurofound, 2017; OECD, 2017; Stiglitz et al., 2011).

Social Indicators and Databases to Study Quality of Life in Europe

In the EU, as well as worldwide, social survey methods are the most common tool used to collect the variables needed for measuring objective and subjective indicators of QoL. In these surveys, QoL is often measured by asking respondents to report or evaluate various aspects of their lives split into QoL domains. At least four sample surveys are used in monitoring QoL in Europe: the Eurobarometer Survey, the European Values Study (EVS), the European Social Survey (ESS) and the European Quality of Life Survey (EQLS). Table 8.1 summarises the main characteristics of these surveys. The goal is to assess what these databases contain for studying QoL. Furthermore, in 2013 and 2018, Eurostat launched two ad-hoc modules of the European Union Statistics on Income and Living Conditions (EU-SILC) survey on material deprivation: well-being and housing challenges. These ad-hoc modules complement the variables permanently collected in EU-SILC by highlighting these domains of QoL. Therefore, the EU-SILC database for these two years is another useful source of information for studying QoL across Europe.

In this section, we focus on EQLS because this survey has some characteristics and advantages compared to other databases that better suit our conceptual approach to QoL. In particular, the European Foundation for the Improvement of Living and Working Conditions (Eurofound) contributes to monitoring QoL in Europe through the EQLS, which consists of nationally representative surveys conducted in several European countries, as shown in Table 8.1. It is a unique European survey that examines both the objective conditions of European inhabitants' lives and how they feel about those conditions and their lives in general. EQLS has also developed a valuable set of indicators related to environmental and social aspects of progress, which complements traditional indicators of economic growth and living standards, such as GDP and income, and they are easily integrated into the decision-making process and considered in the public debate at the EU and national levels. After Eurofound (2012, 2017, 2019), as shown in Table 8.2, QoL can be measured with a set of social indicators arranged in different domains: subjective well-being, living standards and deprivation, housing conditions and quality, health and mental well-being, employment and work-life balance, family and social life (quality of relationships), social exclusion and community involvement, local environment, public services, trust in people and institutions, and access to services. Moreover, what is more relevant is that many questions in the second EQLS were posed in the Eurobarometer Survey in 2009, which enabled the study of trends in QoL in the EU from 2003 to 2009.

In sum, the conceptual background of the EQLS (Eurofound, 2003) is based on a multi-dimensional approach that incorporates individual and societal perspectives and combines objective and subjective indicators. EQLS is also likely to be the most widely used survey by different researchers for monitoring the level and evolution of QoL in Europe following a multi-dimensional approach.

In particular, in the past few years, empirical evidence has been characterised by studies to measure the impact of the worldwide economic crisis on QoL. We present only some of the most relevant findings based on EQLS data.

Eurofound (2012) used descriptive and correlation methods to explore eight domains of QoL, taking into account the 2012 database. This report

Table 8.1 Main characteristics of surveys studying QoL in Europe

Survey	*Started*	*Frequency*	*Sample design*	*Countries(last wave)*	*Domains of QoL*
Eurobarometer	1973	Bi-annual	Repeated cross-section	European Union member countries	General life satisfaction Living conditions Social security Environment Technology Health Family issues Social exclusion
European Values Study (EVS)	1981	Every nine years	Cross-national and longitudinal	47 European countries/ regions	Family Work Environment Perceptions of life, politics and society, Religion and morality National identity
European Social Survey (ESS)	2002	Every two years	Cross-sectional	19 European countries[a]	Media and social trust Politics Subjective well-being Household Human values Others[b]
European Quality of Life Survey (EQLS)	2003	Every four years	Cross-sectional	34 countries (27 EU members in 2003, Croatia, Island, North Macedonia, Montenegro, Serbia, Turkey and Kosovo)	Employment Income Education Housing Family Health Work-life balance Happiness Life satisfaction Self-reported quality of their societies

Notes: [a] Not all the participating countries are the same in every round. [b] There are other topics, such as health care, welfare attitudes and work-life balance, but they are available in only one or two rounds.

Table 8.2 Indicators of QoL based on EQLS

Quality of life	
Subjective well-being	Life satisfaction
	Happiness
	Optimism about the future
	Optimism about children's or grandchildren's future
Living standards	Satisfaction with living standards
	Difficulty making ends meet
	Material deprivation
	Economising on food
Housing conditions	Leaks, damp, or rot in housing
	Lack of bath/shower and toilet
	Ability to pay for heating
Health and mental well-being	Self-evaluation of health
	WHO Mental Well-being
	Risk of depression
	Participation in sports or physical exercise
Work-life balance	Energy for household chores
	Difficulty fulfilling family responsibilities because of work
	Difficulty concentrating at work because of family issues
	Work hours do not fit with personal commitments
Quality of public services	
Quality ratings of public services	Health care
	Education
	Public transport
	Child care
	Long-term care
	Social housing
	State pensions
Quality of society	
Social insecurity	Job insecurity
	Housing insecurity
	Income insecurity in old age
Trust and tensions	Perceived tension between different racial or ethnic groups
	Perceived tension between poor people and rich people
	Feeling safe alone outdoors after dark
	Trust in people
	Trust in government
	Trust in local authorities
Participation and exclusion	Perceived social exclusion
	Involvement in civic and political activities
	Participation in voluntary work
	Participation in training

Note: Adapted from Eurofound (2019).

highlighted the different aspects of QoL that deteriorated during the financial and economic crisis, such as living and working conditions, with negative impacts on the everyday lives of people in several European countries. In addition, the report showed a clear division between the Nordic and Western European countries and the Southern and Eastern European countries, with a higher QoL in the former countries than in the latter countries. Betti et al. (2020a) found similar results, and we discuss it in detail in the next section.

Sommariba and Zarsosa (2019) constructed a proxy indicator for QoL using DP2 methodology using eight different dimensions with data from the 2012 EQLS. They also found a spatial pattern in which the Nordic countries, together with those in Central Europe, has a higher QoL than Eastern European countries. Specifically, their evidence showed that Bulgaria has the lowest QoL in Europe, whereas Denmark has the highest. Applying fuzzy-set theory with 2012 and 2007–2012 EQLS data, respectively, Betti (2016, 2017) found analogous results. Similar conclusions were reached by Rogge and Van Nijverseel (2019), despite using a different dataset (EU-SILC).

Eurofound (2014) examined the QoL of different types of families with children in the context of the economic crisis. The results are based on the 2007 and 2012 databases. In their report, simple statistical tools such as chi-square statistics and *t*-tests were used to identify statistically significant differences between categories and average values between different types of European families or different country groups. Eurofound (2017) used more than eight domains of QoL, the 2012 and 2016 databases, and descriptive methods. Their findings showed that QoL has improved less for Europeans in the lowest income quartile than for others, and, in general, the EU has experienced an improvement in some dimensions, such as overall health, the standard of living and the work-life balance, compared with pre-crisis levels.

Kristapsone and Bruna (2019), using eight domains of QoL from the 2012 and 2016 EQLS database, and descriptive and inferential statistical analysis, analysed changes in QoL between both years. They found that, after the economic crisis, in the EU only the indicators related to satisfaction with the present state of the economy in a country increased between 2012 and 2016, whereas the other seven indicators of QoL remained the same in both years, so satisfaction in the other domains did not change over this period. They also concluded that EQLS data show that economic growth, social and economic reforms, and the efficacy of social security in the period surveyed in the EU post-crisis have not significantly contributed to their personal assessment of QoL.

Fuzzy and Multi-dimensional Approach for Studying the Quality of Life

As we discussed previously, the empirical findings on QoL are characterised by a multiplicity of approaches because the concept varies widely and is complex because of its multifaceted nature, which is not easy to define and measure (Glatzer, 2006; Mauro et al., 2018). Thus, we concentrate on a specific methodological approach that can be used in this framework, namely, the fuzzy and multi-dimensional approach introduced by Betti et al. (2016) for studying QoL in Macedonia. This approach was later applied by Betti (2017) and Betti et al. (2020a), using a more appropriate statistical approach for measuring the effect of the economic crisis in QoL in Europe with EQLS data. Table 8.3 summarises the eight domains of QoL and the 48 social indicators described by Betti (2016, 2017), which, in turn, are based on the seminal contributions of Nussbaum and Sen (1993), Phillips (2006) and Eurofound (2003, 2010), outlined in Table 8.2.

This methodology is based on two main hypotheses:

Hypothesis 1: the theoretical concept of QoL is not directly observable; rather, it is latent, and observed social indicators can be used as partial/imperfect measures of this underlying theoretical concept

Hypothesis 2: QoL is a vague concept with different shades and degrees, rather than an attribute that is simply present or absent for individuals in society.

H1 applies this approach in a formative measurement model as well as DEA-BoD, DP2 and MPI (Jimenez-Fernandez & Ruiz-Martos, 2020). H2 is, indeed, a new feature in a formative measurement approach.

The empirical application of this approach is, obviously, strictly related to the availability of a set of social indicators organised into several QoL domains. However, the selection of meaningful and useful social indicators for the analysis is a non-trivial task. It is strictly dependent on the conceptual framework (Maggino, 2017) of the phenomenon studied and limited by data availability (see e.g. Guio & Marlier, 2017, in the framework of poverty analysis). Nevertheless, EQLS data offer a great opportunity for the empirical implementation of this approach because this survey collected several social indicators that can be organised into different domains. We briefly introduce the main steps that characterise the multi-dimensional and fuzzy approach.

In general, each social indicator is measured on a scale of 1 to a maximum (e.g. in EQLS data, the high end of the scale is generally 10) needs to be converted into the interval [0,1] according to fuzzy logic. The transformation used can be found in Betti and Lemmi (2013) and in Betti et al. (2015, 2020b).

Let I_k be the kth social indicator converted into the interval [0,1]. Explorative factor analysis (EFA) and confirmative factor analysis (CFA) are typically used to group these indicators into dimensions that represent specific aspects of QoL. Basically, each dimension s can be composed of a different number of individual indicators I_k ($k = 1, \ldots, K_s$) on the basis of the results of factor analysis. For instance, in Betti et al. (2020a), eight different dimensions were individualised (see Table 8.3). A function related to each

Table 8.3 Domains and individual social indicators of quality of life

QoL1 quality of relations	q25a	Poor and rich people
	q25b	Management and workers
	q25c	Men and women
	q25d	Old people and young people
	q25e	Different racial and ethnic groups
	q25f	Different religious groups
QoL2 trust in people and institutions	q28a	The parliament
	q28b	The legal system
	q28c	The press
	q28d	The police
	q28e	The government
	q24	In general, would you say that most people can be trusted or that you can't be too careful in dealing with people?
QoL3 access to services	q47a	Distance to doctor's office/hospital/medical centre
	q47b	Delay in getting an appointment
	q47c	Waiting time to see a doctor on the day of an appointment
	q47d	Cost of seeing the doctor
QoL4 quality of public services	q53a	Health care
	q53b	Education
	q53c	Public transport
	q53d	Child care
	q53g	State pension system
QoL5 subjective well-being	q40a	Your education
	q40c	Your present standard of living
	q40d	Your housing
	q40e	Your family life
	q40g	Your social life
	q29e	I feel left out of society
	q30	Life satisfaction
	q41	Happiness
QoL6 Housing quality	q59a	Keeping your home adequately warm
	q19b	Rot in windows, doors, or floors
	q19c	Damp or leaks in walls or roof
	q19d	Lack of indoor flush toilet
	q19e	Lack of bath or shower
	q19f	Lack of a place to sit outside (e.g. garden, balcony, terrace)
QoL7 standard of living	q19a	Shortage of space
	q59b	Paying for a week's annual holiday away from home
	q59c	Replacing any worn-out furniture

(*Continued*)

Table 8.3 Continued

	q59d	A meal with meat, chicken or fish every second day if you want it
	q59e	Buying new, rather than second-hand, clothes
	q59f	Having friends or family in for a drink or meal at least once a month
	q60a	Rent or mortgage payments for housing
	q60b	Utility bills, such as electricity, water and gas
	inc_ind	Income deciles
QoL8 health	q40f	Could you please tell me how satisfied you are with your health, on a scale of 1 to 10?
	q42_ind	In general, would you say your health is ...
	q43_44_ind	Chronic physical or mental health problems, illness or disability
	q29a_ind	I am optimistic about the future

Note: Adapted from Betti et al. (2020a).

dimension s is then calculated, called the membership function, which is a quantitative specification of the individual degree of QoL. Accordingly, the value of the membership function is 0 for the lowest level of quality of life and 1 for the highest level. Let $QoL_{(s)j}$ indicate the membership function of dimension s for individual j ($j = 1 \ldots n$) in the sample. Therefore, as the value increases from 0 to 1, the well-being of individual j for the corresponding dimension increases. $QoL_{(s)j}$ is calculated as:

$$QoL^t_{(s)j} = \sum_k w_{(s)k} I^t_{(s)kj} / \sum_k w_{(s)k} \tag{8.1}$$

where $w_{(s)k}$ is the weight of I_k in dimension s. In turn, $w_{(s)k}$ is computed as the product of two components that take into account both the dispersion of indicator I_k in the dimension s and its correlation with the other indicators in the same dimension s.

Finally, a comprehensive measure of the QoL of each individual j can be obtained as the unweighted mean over the S dimensions of the dimension-specific $QoL_{(s)j}$:

$$QoL_j = \frac{\sum_s QoL_{(s)j}}{S} \tag{8.2}$$

The outcome of this procedure allows us to obtain very simple synthesis measures. Indeed, the (sample) weighted means ($\overline{QoL_{(s)}}$, $s = 1, \ldots, S$ and $\overline{QoL}$) of Equations (8.1) and (8.2) give the measures of the degree of QoL observed in each dimension s and for all dimensions as a whole, respectively.

Following this approach, Betti et al. (2020a) found that the negative effect of the crisis on QoL was very high, especially in Greece, Malta, Ireland, Cyprus, the Czech Republic and Poland. However, they found the opposite result in Macedonia. Moreover, they pointed out the heterogeneous impacts of the economic crisis on the QoL in European countries with respect to the country and the type of dimension observed. Indeed, some dimensions seem significantly lower in many countries, whereas in others, the changes have been positive, albeit to a smaller extent. Specifically, they concluded that the economic crisis had a negative impact on the overall standard of living, on trust in institutions and on some aspects of health care, but it has led individuals to increase their connections with friends and family in order to receive some kind of help and support.

Conclusions

In this chapter, we discuss the utility of a multi-dimensional and fuzzy approach to measuring QoL, which implies measuring QoL using a formative measurement model framework. In other words, we treat QoL as a multi-dimensional latent concept that can be explained with objective and subjective social indicators arranged in different domains of QoL. Moreover, the fuzzy measure also preserves the richness of the latent concept, which is helpful because QoL is a difficult and vague concept to define. The value of the approach proposed in this chapter can be summarised in terms of at least three very interesting features, as discussed in Betti et al. (2020b).

First, the latent dimensions of QoL are not predefined *a priori*; rather, they are identified by EFA and then validated by CFA. Second, the aggregation of social indicators into a domain is performed with a statistically based weighting system that takes into account measurement errors, redundancies and other characteristics of the social indicators involved based on a 'prevalence correlation' (i.e. taking into account the dispersion of a social indicator – prevalence weights – and its correlation with the other social indicators in a given domain – correlation weights). Third, the approach has the advantage of calculating a composite indicator of QoL, simultaneously maintaining its multi-dimensionality by including different composite indicators in each domain.

However, like other formative measurement models, this methodology involves stages in which judgements must be made – for example, concerning the selection of the social indicators and the weighting system. Indeed, the notion of measuring QoL could include the measurement of practically anything of interest to anyone, and everyone could find arguments to support the selection of partially different sets of social indicators. Therefore, the empirical analysis has to be conducted with transparent steps to achieve comprehensible and meaningful results.

Note

1 Following Michalos et al. (2011) and Veenhoven (2017), in this chapter we use the terms 'well-being' and 'quality of life' interchangeably, because both terms are interpreted in the broad sense of living a good life.

References

Andrew, F.M., & Withey, S.B. (1976). *Social Indicators of Well-Being*. New York: Plenum.

Bárcena-Martín, E., Cortés-Aguilar, A., & Moro-Egido, A. (2017). Social comparisons on subjective well-being: The role of social and cultural capital. *Journal of Happiness Studies*, *18*(4), 1121–1145.

Bartolini, S., & Sarracino, F. (2014). Happy for how long? How social capital and economic growth relate to happiness over time? *Ecological Economics*, *108*, 242–256.

Betti, G. (2016). Fuzzy measures of quality of life: A multidimensional and comparative approach. *International Journal of Uncertainty, Fuzziness and Knowledge-Based Systems*, *24*(1), 25–37.

Betti, G. (2017). What impact has the economic crisis had on quality of life in Europe? A multidimensional and fuzzy approach. *Quality & Quantity*, *51*(1), 351–364.

Betti, G., D'Agostino, A., Gagliardi, F., & Giusti, C. (2020b). The integrated fuzzy and relative index for poverty analysis: A review of applications in the social sciences. *Studies of Applied Economics – Estudios de Economía Aplicada*, 38(1), pp. 1–14.

Betti, G., D'Agostino, A., Ghellini, G., & Longobardi, S. (2020a). Measuring the impact of financial crisis on quality of life in Europe. *Economics Bulletin*, *40*(1), 292–307.

Betti, G., Gagliardi, F., Lemmi, A., & Verma, V. (2015). Comparative measures of multidimensional deprivation in the European Union. *Empirical Economics*, *49*(3), 1071–1100.

Betti G., & Lemmi A. eds. (2013). *Poverty and Social Exclusion: New Methods of Analysis*. London: Routledge.

Betti, G., Soldi, R., & Talev, I. (2016). Fuzzy multidimensional indicators of quality of life: The empirical case of Macedonia. *Social Indicators Research*, *127*(1), 39–53.

Diener, E. (2002). Will money increase subjective well-being? *Social Indicators Research*, *57*, 119–169.

Diener, E., & Suh, E. (1997). Measuring quality of life: Economic, social, and subjective indicators. *Social Indicators Research*, *40*(1–2), 189–216.

Dolan, P., & Metcalfe, R. (2012). Measuring subjective well-being: Recommendations on measures for use by national governments. *Journal of Social Policy*, *41*(2), 409–427.

EU Commission (2009). *GDP and Beyond: Measuring Progress in a Changing World*. COM, 433. Brussels.

Eurofound (2003). *Monitoring Quality of Life in Europe*. Luxembourg: Office for Official Publications of the European Communities.

Eurofound (2010). *Subjective Well-Being in Europe*. Luxembourg: Office for Official Publications of the European Communities.

Eurofound (2012). *Third European Quality of Life Survey – Quality of Life in Europe: Impacts of the Crisis*. Luxembourg: Office for Official Publications of the European Communities.

Eurofound (2014). *Third European Quality of Life Survey – Quality of Life in Europe: Families in the Economic Crisis*. Luxemburg: Publications Office of the European Union.

Eurofound (2017). *European Quality of Life Survey 2016: Quality of Life, Quality of Public Services, and Quality of Society*. Luxembourg: Office for Official Publications of the European Communities.

Eurofound (2019). *European Quality of Life 2016: Life and Society in the EU Candidate Countries*. Luxembourg: Publications Office of the European Union. doi:10.2806/663872

Frey, B.S., & Stutzer, A. (2002). The economics of happiness. *World Economics*, *3*(1), 1–17.

Fukuda-Parr, S., & Kumar, A.S. (2004). *Readings in Human Development: Concepts, Measures and Policies for a Development Paradigm*. New York: Oxford University Press.

Galbraith, J.K. (1958). *The Affluent Society*. Boston: Houghton Mifflin.

Glatzer, W. (2006). Quality of life in the European Union and the United States of America: Evidence from comprehensive indices. *Applied Research in Quality of Life*, *1*(2), 169–188.

Gough, I., McGregor, A.J., & Camfield, L. (2007). Theorising wellbeing in international development. In I. Gough & A.J. McGregor (Eds.), *Wellbeing in Developing Countries: From Theory to Research* (pp. 3–44). Cambridge: Cambridge University Press.

Guio, A.C., & Marlier, E. (2017). Amending the EU material deprivation indicator: Impact on size and composition of deprived population. In A.B. Atkinson, A.-C. Guio, & E. Marlier (Eds.), *Monitoring Social Europe* (pp. 193–207). Luxembourg: Publications Office of the European Union.

Jiménez-Fernández, E., & Ruiz-Martos, M. (2020). Review of some statistical methods for constructing composite indicators. *Estudios de Economía Aplicada/Studies of Applied Economics*, *38*(1), 1–15.

Kristapsone, S., & Bruna, S. (2019, 16–18 May). Changes in the subjective assessment of quality of life in Latvia and the European Union: Results of European quality of life survey (2016). In *New Challenges of Economic and Business Development–2019: Incentives for Sustainable Economic Growth [Proceedings]*. University of Latvia, Riga, Latvia.

Maggino, F. (2017). Developing indicators and managing the complexity. In F. Maggino (ed.), *Complexity in Society: From Indicators Construction to Their Synthesis* (pp. 87–114). New York: Springer.

Mauro, V., Biggeri, M., & Maggino, F. (2018). Measuring and monitoring poverty and well-being: A new approach for the synthesis of multidimensionality. *Social Indicators Research*, *135*(1), 75–89.

McCrea, R., Marans, R.W., Stimson, R., & Western, J. (2011). Subjective measurement of quality of life using primary data collection and the analysis of survey data. In R.W. Marans & R.J. Stimson (Eds.), *Investigating Quality of Urban Life* (pp. 55–75). Dordrecht: Springer.

Mercy, J.L. (Ed.). (2015). *Quality of Life: Facts and Views*. Luxembourg: Publications Office of the European Union.

Michalos, A.C., Smale, B., Labonté, R., Muharjarine, N., Scott, K., Moore, K., Swystun, L., Holden, B., Bernardin, H., Dunning, B., Graham, P., Guhn, M., Gadermann, A.M., Zumbo, B.D., Morgan, A., Brooker, A.-S., & Hyman, I. (2011). *The Canadian Index of Wellbeing*. Technical Report 1.0. Waterloo, ON: Canadian Index of Wellbeing and the University of Waterloo.

Mishan, E.J. (1967). *The Cost of Economic Growth*. London: Staples Press.

Neumayer, E. (2003). Beyond income: Convergence in living standards, big time. *Structural Change and Economic Dynamics*, *14*, 275–296.

Nussbaum, M.C. (2011). *Creating Capabilities: The Human Development Approach*. Cambridge: Belknap Press of Harvard University Press.

Nussbaum, M.C., & Sen, A. (Eds.). (1993). *The Quality of Life*. Oxford: Oxford University Press.

OECD. (2017). *How's Life? Measuring Well-Being*. Paris: OECD.

Phillips, D. (2006). *Quality of Life: Concept, Quality, Practice*. London: Routledge.

Robeyns, I. (2005). The capability approach: A theoretical survey. *Journal of Human Development*, *6*(1), 93–114.

Rogge, N., & Van Nijverseel, I. (2019). Quality of life in the European Union: A multidimensional analysis. *Social Indicators Research*, *141*(2), 765–789.

Sánchez, A., Chica-Olmo, J., & Jiménez-Aguilera, J.D. (2018). A space-time study for mapping quality of life in Andalusia during the crisis. *Social Indicators Research*, *135*(2), 699–728.

Scitovsky, T. (1976). *The Joyless Economy*. New York: Oxford University Press.

Sen, A. (1976). Real national income. *Review of Economic Studies 43*(1), 19–39.

Sen, A. (1980). Equality of what? In S. McMurrin (Ed.), *Tanner Lectures on Human Values* (Vol. 1, pp. 197–220). Cambridge: Cambridge University Press.

Sen, A. (1992). *Inequality Re-Examined*. New York: Oxford University Press.

Sessa, M. (2016). Measuring and monitoring the achievements of the millennium development goals through dynamic composite indices. *Social Indicators Research*, *127*, 469–503.

Somarriba, N., & Zarzosa, P. (2019). Quality of life in the European Union: An econometric analysis from a gender perspective. *Social Indicators Research*, *142*, 179–200.

Stiglitz, J., Sen, A., & Fitoussi, J. (2011). *Mismeasuring Our Lives: Why GDP Doesn't Add Up*. New York: New Press.

Stutzer, A., & Frey, B.S. (2010). Recent advances in the economics of individual subjective well-being. *Social Research: An International Quarterly*, *77*(2), 679–714.

Van den Bergh, J. (2009). The GDP paradox. *Journal of Economic Psychology*, *30*(2), 117–135.

Veenhoven, R. (2000). The four qualities of life. *Journal of Happiness Studies*, *1*, 1–39.

Veenhoven, R. (2017). Greater happiness for a greater number: Did the promise of enlightenment come true? *Social Indicators Research*, *130*, 9–25.

9 A Fuzzy Approach to Financial Literacy Measurement

Albert Hizgilov and Jacques Silber

Introduction

The topic of financial literacy has become quite popular in recent years. Atkinson and Messy (2011) defined it as 'a combination of awareness, knowledge, skill, attitude and behavior to make sound financial decisions and ultimately achieve individual financial well-being'. Studies dealing with the determinants of financial literacy have shown that it is positively related to income (see Klapper et al., 2015) and education (see, for instance, Calvet et al., 2009), that women are less financially literate than men (see, for example, Lusardi and Mitchell, 2008; Bucher-Koenen et al., 2016), that employees and self-employed are more financially literate than unemployed (see Lusardi & Mitchell, 2011), that financial literacy is lower in rural than urban areas (see Klapper & Panos, 2011), that even religion (Alessie et al., 2011), political opinions (Arrondel et al., 2013) and ethnicity (Nejad & O'Connor, 2016) matter.

As far as the impact of financial literacy is concerned, it appears that financial literacy and financial management skills are correlated (see Jappeli & Padula, 2013), that people who are less financially literate use more costly forms of borrowing (see Lusardi & Scheresberg, 2013), tend to use informal sources of borrowing (Klapper et al., 2012), plan less well for their retirement (Boisclair et al., 2017), are less likely to invest in stock (Arrondel et al., 2012), and even when they participate in financial markets, they get a lower return on their investment (Chu et al., 2017). Finally, financial literacy is also associated with greater wealth accumulation (see, van Rooij et al., 2012)

Lusardi and Mitchell (2008, 2011) were among the first to attempt to estimate the extent of financial literacy. They focused their attention on three aspects of financial literacy, the notions of compound interest, inflation rates and risk diversification.

In the present chapter we take a multi-dimensional approach to financial literacy measurement. We borrow tools from the literature on multi-dimensional poverty measurement, focusing on the so-called fuzzy approach. We examine, in particular, the impact of the weighting schemes (the weights given to the different aspects or questions related to financial literacy) and emphasise the 'fuzzy approach', which is advocated by Rippin (2013) in the context of multi-dimensional poverty measurement.

The chapter is organised as follows. The second section describes the methodology adopted to deal with different weighting schemes, while the third section describes the 'fuzzy approach' of Rippin (2013). The fourth section is devoted to an empirical illustration based on Israeli data. Concluding comments are then given in the last section

A Multi-dimensional Approach to the Measurement of Financial Literacy

Let us assume a survey which includes questions on various aspects of financial literacy. We will suppose that for each question the individual can give either a correct or a wrong answer. Let then a_{ij} be a binary variable equal to 1 if individual *i* gives a correct answer to question *j*, or equal to 0 otherwise.

In this section we will focus our attention on the selection of weights for the different questions.

Giving the Same Weight to All the Questions

Looking at All the Questions Together

If, as a whole, there are *K* questions, the proportion of questions to which a correct answer was given by individual *h* will be expressed as:

$$a_h = \left(\frac{1}{K}\right)\sum_{k=1}^{K} a_{hk} \tag{9.1}$$

If *T* refers to the total number of individuals participating in the survey, the proportion of individuals having given a correct answer to question *k* will be:

$$\bar{a}_k = (1/T)\sum_{h=1}^{T} a_{hk} \tag{9.2}$$

If we now consider the whole questionnaire, the proportion $\bar{a}$ of correct answers will be:

$$\begin{aligned}\bar{a} &= \left(\frac{1}{T}\right)\left(\frac{1}{K}\right)\sum_{h=1}^{T}\sum_{k=1}^{K} a_{hk} \\ &= \left(\frac{1}{K}\right)\sum_{k=1}^{K}\left[\left(\frac{1}{T}\right)\sum_{h=1}^{T} a_{hk}\right] = \left(\frac{1}{K}\right)\sum_{k=1}^{K}\bar{a}_k \\ &= \left(\frac{1}{T}\right)\sum_{h=1}^{T}\left[\left(\frac{1}{K}\right)\sum_{k=1}^{K} a_{hk}\right] = \left(\frac{1}{T}\right)\sum_{h=1}^{T} a_h\end{aligned} \tag{9.3}$$

Taking a Separate Look at Each of the P Parts of the Questionnaire

Let us now assume that the questionnaire is divided into P parts covering different aspects of financial literacy.

Let a_{hk}^{p} be a binary variable equal to 1 if individual h gave a correct answer to question k which belongs to part p of the questionnaire, to 0 otherwise.

The proportion of individuals who gave a correct answer to question k in part p of the questionnaire will then be:

$$\overline{a}_k^p = \left(\frac{1}{T}\right)\sum_{h=1}^{T} a_{hk}^{p} \tag{9.4}$$

As a consequence, individuals will have given a correct answer to a proportion $\overline{a}^p$ of the questions included in part p of the questionnaire, with:

$$\overline{a}^p = \left(\frac{1}{T}\right)\left(\frac{1}{K^p}\right)\sum_{h=1}^{T}\sum_{k=1}^{K^p} a_{hk}^{p} \tag{9.5}$$

and where K^p refers to the total number of questions in part p of the questionnaire.

Note then that $\overline{a}$ in (9.3) may also be defined as:

$$\begin{aligned}\overline{a} &= \left(\frac{1}{T}\right)\sum_{h=1}^{T}\sum_{p=1}^{P}\left(\frac{K^p}{K}\right)\left(\frac{1}{K^p}\right)\sum_{k=1}^{K^p} a_{hk}^{p} \\ &= \sum_{p=1}^{P}\left(\frac{K^p}{K}\right)\left[\left(\frac{1}{T}\right)\left(\frac{1}{K^p}\right)\sum_{h=1}^{T}\sum_{k=1}^{K^p} a_{hk}^{p}\right] \\ &= \sum_{p=1}^{P}\left(\frac{K^p}{K}\right)\overline{a}^p\end{aligned} \tag{9.6}$$

Giving a Different Weight to Each Question

Analysing the Whole Questionnaire

Using Equation (9.2), and following Cerioli and Zani (1990), Cheli et al. (1994) and Cheli and Lemmi (1995), the weight of question k will be:

$$s_k = \frac{ln(1/\overline{a}_k)}{\sum_{k=1}^{K} ln(1/\overline{a}_k)} \tag{9.7}$$

so that the weighted proportion of questions answered correctly by individual h will be:

$$\lambda(h) = \sum_{k=1}^{K} s_k a_{hk} \tag{9.8}$$

while the weighted proportion of questions to which a correct answer was given in the whole population will be:

$$\bar{\lambda} = \left(\frac{1}{T}\right)\sum_{h=1}^{T}\lambda(h) \tag{9.9}$$

Looking at Part p of the Questionnaire

Using Equation (9.3), the weight of question k in part p of the questionnaire will be:

$$s_k^p = \frac{ln\left(1/\bar{a}_k^p\right)}{\sum_{k=1}^{K^p} ln\left(1/\bar{a}_k^p\right)} \tag{9.10}$$

so that the weighted proportion of questions to which individual h gave a correct answer in part p of the questionnaire will be:

$$\lambda^p(h) = \sum_{k=1}^{K^p} s_k^p a_{hk} \tag{9.11}$$

while the weighted proportion of questions to which individuals in the whole population gave a correct answer part p will be:

$$\bar{\lambda}^p = \left(\frac{1}{T}\right)\sum_{h=1}^{T}\lambda^p(h) \tag{9.12}$$

Aggregating All k Parts

Given $\lambda^p(h)$ as it was defined in Equation (9.11), we can now derive an alternative estimate $\lambda'(h)$ of the proportion of questions to which a correct answer was given by individual h in the whole questionnaire where:

$$\lambda'(h) = \sum_{p=1}^{P} w_p \lambda^p(h) \tag{9.13}$$

where w_p is the weight given to part p. This weight w_p may be defined, in a way similar to that in which we defined in Equation (9.10) the weight of a given question, so that we would write that:

$$w_p = \frac{ln\left(1/\bar{\lambda}^p\right)}{\sum_{p=1}^{P} ln\left(1/\bar{\lambda}^p\right)} \tag{9.14}$$

But it is also possible to assume that this weight w_p will be equal to the share of the number of questions in part p in the total number of questions in the whole questionnaire. It is also possible to give the same weight to each part p, no matter how many questions it includes, in which case we would write that $w_p = \left(\frac{1}{P}\right)$.

No matter which weight is selected, when we proceed in two stages, the alternative measure of the proportion of questions to which individuals in the population gave on average a correct answer will be expressed as:

$$\overline{\lambda'} = \left(\frac{1}{T}\right)\sum_{h=1}^{T}\lambda'(h) \tag{9.15}$$

Applying Rippin's (2012) Fuzzy Approach to Multi-dimensional Poverty to the Measurement of Financial Literacy

In this section we will ignore the case where financial literacy is measured in two stages and focus our attention on its measurement when we look at the questionnaire as a whole.

Let us start by defining the 'financial literacy counting function' flc_h of individual h as:

$$flc_h = \sum_{k=1}^{K}\tau_k a_{hk} \tag{9.16}$$

where, as before, $a_{hk} = 1$ if individual h gave a correct answer to question k, to 0 otherwise, whereas τ_k is the weight given to question k. The choice between various types of weights has been discussed above. In the specific case where the weights are the same for all questions, we would define τ_k as: $\tau_k = \left(\frac{1}{K}\right)\forall k$

One possibility is to apply Alkire and Foster's (2011) approach to multi-dimensional poverty measurement to the case of financial literacy and say that if this weighted proportion of correct answers is smaller than some threshold, the individual will be considered as financially illiterate, while if it is greater than the threshold, he/she will be considered as financially literate.

Rather than taking such a dichotomous approach, we can generalise this method (see Yalonetzky, 2012; Silber & Yalonetzky, 2013). We can, for example, apply Rippin's (2012) approach to multi-dimensional poverty measurement to financial literacy and define a 'fuzzy' identification function fli_h that requires taking into account the relationship between the various components of financial literacy (see Silber & Yalonetzky, 2013, p. 12). We then write:

$$fli_h = (flc_h)^{\beta} = \left(\sum_{k=1}^{K}\tau_k a_{hk}\right)^{\beta} \text{ with } \beta>0. \tag{9.17}$$

Note that the function fli_h is non-decreasing in flc_h. Such a fuzzy identification function fli_h makes thus a distinction between the multi-dimensionally financially literate individuals and assumes different degrees of multi-dimensional financial literacy identification (Rippin, 2017). The function fli_h is considered to be fuzzy because unless $flc_h = 1$ or $flc_h = 0$, each individual will be identified as being somewhat multi-dimensionally literate (Silber & Yalonetzky, 2013, p. 13). In other words, individuals are identified as having different degrees of multi-dimensional literacy, depending on the number of questions to which they gave a correct answer and on the type of relationship that is assumed to exist between the various components of financial literacy. The shape of the identification function fli_h depends on the value of β. If $0 < \beta < 1$, the identification function has a concave shape, while if $\beta > 1$, it has a convex shape. The choice of a specific form will depend on whether it is assumed that the components of financial literacy are assumed to be substitutes or complements. If they are considered as substitutes, we have the case of a concave function. The increase in financial literacy is marginally decreasing in flc_h. This implies that the higher the number of questions to which an individual gives a correct answer, the more he/she is identified as being financially literate, but this increase in identification becomes smaller and smaller as flc_h increases. If the components of financial literacy are perfect substitutes, we have the 'union case', so that as soon as an individual gives a correct answer to one question, he/she is considered as financially literate.

If the components of financial literacy are imperfect complements, we have the more general case approximated by a convex identification function. Then the higher the number of questions to which an individual gives a correct answer, the more he/she is identified as being financially literate, and this increase in financial literacy rises with flc_h. In the specific case where these components are perfect complements, as long as an individual did not give a correct answer to all the questions, his/her financial literacy will be equal to 0. This is the intersection case mentioned previously (Silber & Yalonetzky, 2013).

The assumption of a particular relationship among the components of financial literacy is certainly not a simple task. It is often hard enough to determine the degree of complementarity or substitutability on a pair-wise basis, let alone among combinations of *K* variables taken 3, 4, up to *n* at a time. We will therefore assume different degrees of complementarity (β = 1.25, 1.50, 1.75) and substitutability (β = 0.25, 0.50, 0.75) among the components of financial literacy.

As in the poverty measurement literature, the financial literacy identification function identifies the multi-dimensionally literate, but it also needs to take into account the intensity of the multi-dimensional literacy (Silber & Yalonetzky, 2013). However, with ordinal (binary or dichotomised) variables, the multi-dimensional literacy 'depth'[1] cannot be estimated because one cannot define a gap between the degree of literacy of an individual and some literacy threshold. We will therefore assume that the 'breadth of literacy' is measured via the number of questions to which the individual gave a correct answer. The individual multi-dimensional literacy function will then be defined as the product of the identification function defined previously and a function that captures the breadth of multi-dimensional literacy. Let $b(flc_h)$ be the function measuring the multi-dimensional literacy breadth. This function depends on the number of questions to which the individual did not give a correct answer. The degree of multi-dimensional literacy MDL_n will then be expressed as:

$$MDL_h(flc_h) = fli_h(flc_h)b(flc_h) \tag{9.18}$$

As mentioned previously, Rippin (2012) assumed that $fli_h(flc_h) = flc_h^{\beta}$. Rippin also assumed that $b(flc_h) = flc_h$. Therefore, following Rippin, the degree of multi-dimensional individual literacy MDL_h will be expressed as:

$$MDL_h = (flc_h)^{1+\beta} \tag{9.19}$$

Then, again following Rippin, the extent of multi-dimensional financial literacy MDL in the whole population will be written as:

$$MDL = \left(\frac{1}{T}\right)\sum_{h=1}^{T} MDL_h = \left(\frac{1}{T}\right)\sum_{h=1}^{T} (flc_h)^{1+\beta} \tag{9.20}$$

It is important to stress, that the measure proposed by Rippin (2012) takes into account the degree of inequality, between the individuals (households) classified as financially literate, in the number of correct answers. Such a property does not hold for the index developed by Alkire and Foster (2011).

The Empirical Analysis

The Database:

The empirical analysis uses a survey conducted by Israel's Central Bureau of Statistics (CBS) in 2012. This representative survey was part of Israel's Social Survey, which is conducted every year, and it covered 1,171 individuals who were at least 20 years old. There were 105 questions in the questionnaire and, taking into account the definition of financial literacy given by the OECD; we focused our attention on 58 questions that are shown in Appendix 1. This financial literacy survey comprises questions on financial knowledge but also on the debt, credit card and savings behaviour of the respondents. The survey also includes questions on some socio-economic characteristics of the individuals participating in the survey (e.g. age, gender, education, employment status, household income).

This database had been used previously by Meir et al. (2016) who looked at the link between financial literacy and retirement planning in Israel. Hizgilov and Silber (2019) also used this database and estimated regressions where the dependent variables were the overall degree financial literacy or the extent of financial literacy in three domains distinguished in the survey: financial behaviour, financial knowledge and financial attitude. They examined the case where an equal weight was given to the questions as well as when the questions have different weights. But in their empirical analysis they did not take into account the possibility of making a two-stage analysis, where for each of the three domains equal or different weights are given to the various questions, while in a second stage different aggregation procedures are considered to derive an overall measure of financial literacy. Moreover, when applying Rippin's approach, they did not make a distinction between the case where the different attributes of financial literacy, reflected in the various questions, are assumed to be substitutes and the case where they are supposed to be complements. In this chapter we also examine various degrees of substitutability and complementarity.

The Impact of the Weighting System on Financial Literacy by Socio-Economic Characteristics

Results When Using a One-Stage Procedure

GIVING AN EQUAL WEIGHT TO EACH QUESTION

Table 9.1 gives information on the financial literacy scores of the respondents by socio-economic characteristics and for each of the three types of questions when an equal weight is given to each question.

Financial Behaviour

This category of questions includes the largest number of questions (50 out of 58 questions). It appears that 35.4% of the individuals may be considered as financially literate, as far as financial behaviour is concerned (a score lower than for the two other categories of questions). For men, the score is 36.53%, for women 34.33% (a statistically significant difference).

Financial Knowledge

The score (39.31%) obtained is higher than that observed for the category of questions devoted to financial behaviour. Financial knowledge is higher among men (46%) than among women (33.02%), among Jews (41.57%) than among non-Jews (28.99%), this being true for both genders. As far as age is concerned, the score for financial knowledge is highest in the age group 55–59 (score of 48.06%) and 34–39 (score of 45.33%). For employment status we observe that those who are employed have the highest financial knowledge score (42.75%), while those who are not in the labour force have a sore of 31.74, with the unemployed having a score of 30.85%. The score for financial knowledge rises with the level of education, being equal to 28.22% among those who have up to 12 years of education to 37.54% among those with up to 15 years of education and to 50.04% among those with 16 or more years of education.

Table 9.1 Financial literacy scores by individual characteristics, for each of the three categories of questions, when an equal weight is given to each question

Characteristic	*Behaviour*	*Knowledge*	*Attitude*	*Number of participants*	*Share of population*
Overall sample participants	35.40	39.31	47.77	1,213	100
Gender					
Men	36.53	46.00	46.34	588	48.47
Women	34.33	33.02	49.12	625	51.53
I T-test I	(−2.9861)	(−7.3277)	(1.3007)		
Religion and minorities					
Jewish	36.94	41.57	46.63	955	82.03
Non-Jewish	28.38	28.99	52.98	218	17.97
I T-test I	(−9.1837)	(−5.4005)	(2.2883)		
Employment status					
Employed	37.49	42.75	46.61	840	69.25
Not in the labour force	31.78	31.74	50.17	299	24.65
Unemployed	26.32	30.85	51.35	74	6.10
Age					
20–24	34.01	28.24	46.67	165	13.61
25–29	35.56	34.08	50	159	13.12
30–34	37.35	41.91	51.51	132	10.89
35–39	35.85	45.53	42.28	123	10.15
40–44	33.58	39.78	46.37	124	10.23
45–49	34.38	43.46	47.19	89	7.34
50–54	35.63	38.20	44.27	96	7.92
55–59	36.98	48.06	46.28	94	7.76
60–64	36.62	43.67	43.89	90	7.43
65+	34.87	39.45	55.34	140	11.55
Education (years)				1,212	
Up to 12	29.88	28.22	46.85	397	32.75
13–15	35.16	37.65	49.43	353	29.13
16+	40.35	50.04	47.40	462	38.12

Note: The numbers of questions for each category of questions are respectively: Behaviour = 50; Knowledge = 6; Attitude = 2.

Financial Attitude

Financial attitude is the category of questions where the highest scores were achieved. However, given that this part includes only two questions, we need to be careful when interpreting the results and comparing them with those observed for the other two parts of the questionnaire. The overall score for financial attitude is 47.77%. Interestingly, women have a higher score (49.12%) than men (46.34%) (this difference is not statistically significant). Non-Jews have a higher score (52.98%) than Jews (46.63%) (statistically significant difference). Among non-Jews, Christian Arabs have the highest score (59.37%) while other non-Jewish individuals have a score of 58.75% and Muslim Arabs a score of 50.93%. As far as age is concerned, the highest scores are achieved in the age group 25–34 and among individuals who are over 65. Unemployed have a higher score (51.53%) than individuals who are not members of the labour force (50.17%) and employed individuals (46.61%). Education has no linear relationship with the score on financial attitude: the score of those who have up to 15 years of education is 49.43%, that of those with up to 12 years of education 46.85% and that of those with more than 16 years of education 47.40%.

THE CASE WHERE THE QUESTIONS HAVE DIFFERENT WEIGHTS

In what follows each question may have a different weight. The weights used are those proposed by Cerioli and Zani (1990). As was explained in above, the intuitive idea is that the less successfully answered questions should receive a higher weight while the questions to which most individuals gave a correct answer should have a lower weight. Table 9.2 shows the results obtained

Table 9.2 Financial literacy scores: the questions have different weights

Characteristic	*Financial literacy score*	*Number of participants*	*Share of population*	*|t-test|*
Overall sample participants	18.20	1,213	100	
Gender				
Men	19.60	588	48.47	4.8843
Women	16.89	625	51.53	
Religion and minorities				
Jewish	19.08	955	82.03	6.9221
Non-Jewish	14.16	218	17.97	
Employment status				
Employed	19.66	840	69.25	
Not in the labour force	15.28	299	24.65	
Unemployed	13.53	74	6.10	
Age				
20–24	16.43	165	13.61	
25–29	17.33	159	13.12	
30–34	19.23	132	10.89	
35–39	19.42	123	10.15	
40–44	17.33	124	10.23	
45–49	18.10	89	7.34	
50–54	18.56	96	7.92	
55–59	20.11	94	7.76	
60–64	19.03	90	7.43	
65+	18.00	140	11.55	
Education (years)		1212		
Up to 12	14.03	397	32.75	
13–15	17.83	353	29.13	
16+	22.08	462	38.12	

when adopting such a weighting scheme and when taking into account all the questions in the questionnaire. It then appears that the scores are lower than those observed when giving an equal eight to each question. The overall level of financial literacy then turns out to be quite low (18.2%) for the population as a whole, males having a higher score (a difference of almost 3%, in absolute terms). We observe a higher score among Jews than non-Jews, employed individuals than those unemployed or not belonging to the labour force. The highest levels of financial literacy are achieved in the age groups 30–39 and 55-64 and the score is higher, the more educated the individual is.

Results When Using a Two-Stage Procedure

In what follows we divide the questions into three categories of questions related respectively to financial behaviour, knowledge and attitude, assuming again that the questions have different weights. Table 9.3 gives the scores for each category of questions and various socio-economic and demographic characteristics of the individuals.

To derive the aggregated score obtained we proceeded in two stages, as mentioned above. First within each category of questions we applied the Cerioli and Zani procedure, using Equations (9.7) and (9.8). Then in a second stage we aggregated the three financial scores, using the weighting procedure described in expression (9.14).

It then appears that the overall aggregated financial literacy score is 28.18 when we aggregate all three parts using the Cerioli and Zani weighing system. Similar results are obtained when we use equal weights for each of the three parts (an aggregated score of 32.51%). However, the aggregated financial literacy score significantly declines (19.38%) when we use a weighting system that is based on the share of questions within each part. Whatever the aggregation method we use, men have a higher score than women. Their score is 30.27% when using the Cerioli and Zani procedure, 20.92% when using the share of questions weighting scheme and 34.55% when using equal weights. The corresponding scores for women are, respectively, 26.22%, 17.92% and 30.59%. Jews have higher scores than non-Jews: 28.94%, 20.27% and 33.01% for the three weighting schemes previously mentioned. The corresponding scores for non-Jews are 24.94%, 15.29% and 30.25%. The score is higher among employed individuals than unemployed. More educated people have higher scores. The highest level of financial literacy is observed among those belonging to the age groups 55–59 and 30–34, except for the aggregation using an equal weighting system where those individuals above the age 65 have a high financial literacy score.

Applying Rippin's Fuzzy Approach to Multi-dimensional Poverty to Financial Literacy

Table 9.4 gives the financial literacy scores by socio-economic and demographic characteristics for each category of questions separately, as well as

Table 9.3 The two-stage approach: financial literacy scores with different weighting schemes

Characteristic	*Behaviour*	*Knowledge*	*Attitude*	*Weighting scheme*	*Weighting scheme*	*Weighting scheme*	*Number of participants*	*Share of population*
				Cerioli and Zani	*Share of questions*	*Equal weights*		
Weighting scheme			45.45	28.18	19.38	32.51	1,213	100
Gender								
Men	17.41	42.66	43.59	30.27	20.92	34.55	588	48.47
Women	15.40	29.18	47.20	26.22	17.92	30.59	625	51.53
I T-test I	(3.84)	(7.76)	(1.66)	(4.73)	(5.22)	(3.79)		
Religion and minorities								
Jewish	17.20	38.04	43.79	28.94	20.27	33.01	955	82.03
Non-Jewish	12.60	25.10	53.04	24.94	15.29	30.25	218	17.97
I T-test I	(6.84)	(5.66)	(3.27)	(3.54)	(6.71)	(2.02)		
Employment status								
Employed	17.71	39.22	44.65	29.67	20.87	33.86	840	69.25
Not a member of the working force	13.71	28.15	46.84	25.01	16.35	29.57	299	24.65
Unemployed	11.87	26.58	48.94	24.10	14.67	29.13	74	6.10
Age								
20–24	15.28	24.42	45.12	24.36	17.26	28.28	165	13.61
25–29	15.79	30.21	47.83	26.85	18.39	31.28	159	13.12
30–34	17.25	38.18	49.00	30.10	20.51	34.81	132	10.89
35–39	17.28	42.56	41.03	29.62	20.72	33.63	123	10.15
40–44	15.43	36.09	44.01	27.50	18.55	31.84	124	10.23
45–49	15.99	39.82	43.75	28.79	19.42	33.19	89	7.34
50–54	16.85	35.47	42.28	27.66	19.65	31.53	96	7.92
55–59	17.81	44.47	45.60	31.41	21.52	35.96	94	7.76
60–64	17.10	39.37	40.34	28.47	20.21	32.27	90	7.43
65	16.02	36.03	51.44	29.40	19.31	34.50	140	11.55
Education (years)							1,212	
Up to 12	12.61	25.10	44.92	23.18	15.02	27.55	397	32.75
13–15	16.06	34.17	46.29	27.77	18.98	32.17	353	29.13
16+	19.86	45.98	45.36	32.81	23.44	37.07	462	38.12

Note: The numbers of questions for each category of questions are respectively: Behaviour = 50; Knowledge = 6; Attitude = 2

Table 9.4 Financial literacy scores, for each category of questions separately, as well as when no distinction is made between the various categories of questions, using Rippin's approach for the case of substitutability

Charact.	*Behav. β=0.25*	*Knowl. β=0.25*	*Attit. β=0.25*	*Tot. Fin. Lit. score β=0.25*	*Behav. β=0.5*	*Knowl. β=0.5*	*Attit. β=0.5*	*Tot. Fin. Lit. score β=0.5*	*Behav. β=0.75*	*Knowl. β=0.75*	*Attit. β=0.75*	*Tot. Fin. Lit. score β=0.75*
Gender												
Men	29.08	41.40	42.79	30.31	23.10	37.51	39.68	24.48	18.73	34.61	37.47	19.89
Women	26.87	28.23	45.53	27.13	20.99	24.40	42.40	21.38	16.69	21.59	40.16	17.01
I T-test I	(−3.15)	(−7.56)	(1.28)	(−4.37)	(−3.25)	(−7.68)	(1.26)	(−4.53)	(−3.37)	(−7.72)	(1.24)	(−4.57)
Religion and minorities												
Jewish	29.36	36.96	43.05	30.10	23.28	33.11	39.91	24.19	18.81	30.27	37.67	19.56
Muslim	20.34	21.91	47.52	20.89	15.18	18.04	44.54	15.79	11.59	15.23	42.41	12.08
Arabs												
Christian Arabs	25.81	27.31	55.87	26.37	20	23.44	52.81	20.69	15.75	20.62	50.62	16.44
Other	24.37	30.82	54.95	25.52	18.87	26.45	51.62	20.15	14.95	23.25	49.25	16.07
Non-Jew												
Employment status												
Employed	29.89	37.89	43.07	30.67	23.78	33.86	39.98	24.71	19.27	30.88	37.77	20.03
Not a member of the working force	24.49	27.41	46.31	25.02	18.85	23.89	42.94	19.52	14.81	21.31	40.53	15.39
Unemployed	19.74	26.61	48.54	20.76	14.77	23.20	46.08	15.80	11.24	20.72973	44.32	12.16
Age												
20–24	26.58	23.30	43.66	26.27	20.73	19.46	41.03	20.60	16.45	16.65	39.15	16.24
25–29	27.97	29.13	46.23	28.23	21.91	25.09	42.92	22.34	17.50	22.14	40.57	17.80
30–34	29.76	36.73	47.76	30.64	23.67	32.52	44.47	24.70	19.16	29.45	42.12	20.04
35–39	28.38	41.06	39.02	29.48	22.37	37.30	36.18	23.60	18.02	34.53	34.15	19.03
40–44	26.20	34.76	42.69	27.16	20.39	30.70	39.48	21.45	16.21	27.73	37.18	17.14
45–49	27.12	38.89	42.88	28.29	21.33	35.01	39.10	22.65	17.09	32.10	36.40	18.29
50–54	28.26	34.23	40.69	28.79	22.42	30.92	37.55	23.09	18.15	28.48	35.31	18.76
55–59	29.67	43.37	43.13	30.98	23.84	39.45	40.37	25.27	19.49	36.52	38.40	20.62
60–64	29.08	39.08	40.42	30.03	23.06	35.03	37.39	24.13	18.62	32.04	35.22	19.52
65+	27.36	35.29	51.53	28.52	21.49	31.79	48.18	22.74	17.18	29.16	45.79	18.34
Education (years)												
Up to 12	22.79	23.85	43.43	23.05	17.32	20.38	40.43	17.69	13.45	17.82	38.29	13.70
13–15	27.58	32.70	45.78	28.19	21.56	28.68	42.59	22.35	17.17	25.72	40.31	17.81
16+	32.67	45.28	43.77	33.89	26.41	41.20	40.58	27.78	21.72	38.19	38.31	22.92

Note: The numbers of questions for each category of questions are respectively: Behaviour = 50; Knowledge = 6; Attitude = 2.

the scores when no distinction is made between the categories when using Rippin's approach in the case of substitutability.

It appears that for all values of β, the overall financial literacy level of the individuals is below 30%, which is quite low. The highest scores are achieved when β is equal to 0.25 and, as expected, the scores are decreasing with β. We also observe that men outscore women when no distinction is made between the categories as well as in each category separately, except for financial behaviour. Also, those gender differences are statistically significant in all cases but financial behaviour. Furthermore, the scores are higher among Jews than among the other religious population subgroups, both when we do not make a distinction between the different categories of questions and separately for each category of questions. The only exception concerns financial behaviour where the population subgroup 'Other non-Jews' scores higher than Jews. Moreover, we observe that those individuals who are employed score higher than those who are unemployed or not members of the labour force. Additionally, we observe that the higher the educational level, the higher the scores of the participants, this being true when no distinction is made between the different categories of questions, as well as when we look separately at each of the three categories of questions. Looking at the various age groups, we observe that the highest scores are achieved by those who are between the ages of 30–39 and 55–64.

The results for the case of complementarity are very similar to those concerning the case of substitutability.[2] The highest score observed occurs when β is equal to 1.25. This score is slightly lower than 12% and declines with β. As previously, we observe that men outscore women and that Jews score higher than other population subgroups. We also see that individuals who are employed are more financially literate than those who are unemployed or those who do not belong to the labour force. Furthermore, the higher the education level of an individual, the higher his/her financial literacy score. As far as age is concerned, the highest scores are observed for the age groups 30–39 and 55–64.

Concluding Comments

In this chapter a multi-dimensional approach to financial literacy measurement was proposed, with special emphasis on the so-called 'fuzzy approach'. Particular attention was given to the possibility of using various weighting schemes (the weights given to the different aspects or questions related to financial literacy) and on their impact on the estimation of the overall degree of financial literacy. The chapter also stressed the 'fuzzy approach', that was advocated by Rippin (2013) in the context of multi-dimensional poverty measurement, in particular the fact that the various attributes of financial literacy that are supposed to be reflected in the different questions may be considered as 'substitutes' or 'complements'.

The empirical illustration was based on data collected in a survey conducted by Israel's CBS in 2012. This empirical analysis showed that, whatever the weighting scheme that was adopted, the aggregated financial literacy score was higher among males, that the relationship between age and this aggregated score was U shaped, and that married individuals had a higher aggregated financial literacy score. Other things remaining constant, Muslim Arabs generally have a lower aggregated score, this being also true for the unemployed. Finally, *ceteris paribus*, the higher the educational level, the higher the aggregated financial literacy score.

The same kind of conclusions was drawn when focusing on the Rippin approach, and these conclusions did not depend on whether the attributes of financial literacy were substitutes or complements and the degree of substitutability or complementarity did not really affect the direction of the impact of the various socio-economic variables that had been taken into account.

Notes

1 The 'depth' of poverty measures how far the poor are, on average, from the poverty line.
2 The detailed results are available upon request from the authors.

References

Alessie, R., van Rooij, M., & Lusardi, A. (2011) 'Financial literacy and retirement preparation in the Netherlands', *Journal of Pension Economics and Finance* 10(4): 527–545.

Alkire, S., & Foster, J. (2011) 'Counting and multi-dimensional poverty measurement', *Journal of Public Economics* 95(7–8): 476–487.

Arrondel, L., Debbich, M., & Savignac, F. (2012) 'Stockholding and financial literacy in the French population', *International Journal of Social Sciences and Humanity Studies* 4(2): 1309–8063.

Arrondel, L., Debbich, M., & Savignac, F. (2013) 'Literacy financial literacy and financial planning in France financial literacy and financial planning in France', *Numeracy* 6(2): Article 8.

Atkinson, A., & Messy, F.-A. (2011) 'Assessing financial literacy in 12 countries: an OECD/INFE international pilot exercise', *Journal of Pension Economics and Finance* 10(4): 657–665.

Boisclair, D., Lusardi, A., & Michaud, P.-C. (2017) 'Financial literacy and retirement planning in Canada', *Journal of Pension Economics and Finance* 16(3): 277–296.

Bucher-Koenen, T., Lusardi, A., Alessie, R., & van Rooij, M. (2016) 'How financially literate are women? An overview and new insights', *Journal of Consumer Affairs*. https://doi.org/10.1111/joca.12121

Calvet, L.E., Campbell, J.Y., & Sodini, P. (2009) 'Measuring the financial sophistication of households', *American Economic Review* 99(2): 393–398.

Cerioli, A., & Zani, S. (1990) 'A fuzzy approach to the measurement of poverty', in C. Dagum & M. Zenga (Eds.), *Income and Wealth Distribution, Inequality and Poverty: Proceedings of the Second International Conference on Income Distribution by Size: Generation, Distribution, Measurement and Applications, Held at the University of Pavia, Italy*, 28–30 September, Vol. 19 (pp. 272–284). Berlin: Springer Berlin Heidelberg.

Cheli, B., Ghellini, A., Lemmi, A, & Pannuzi, N. (1994) 'Measuring poverty in the countries in transition via the TFR method: The case of Poland In 1990–1991', *Statistics in Transition* 1(5): 585–636.

Cheli, B., & Lemmi, A. (1995) '"Totally" fuzzy and relative approach to the multi-dimensional analysis of poverty', *Economics Notes by Monte dei Paschi di Siena* 24(1): 115–134.

Chu, Z., Wang, Z., Xiao, J.J., & Zhang, W. (2017) 'Financial literacy, Portfolio choice and financial well-being', *Social Indicators Research* 132(2): 799–820.

Hizgilov, A., & Silber, J. (2019) 'On multi-dimensional approaches to financial literacy measurement', *Social Indicators Research*, forthcoming. https://doi.org/10.1007/s11205-019-02227-4

Jappelli, T., & Padula, M. (2013) 'Investment in financial literacy and saving decisions', *Journal of Banking & Finance* 37(8): 2779–2792.

Klapper, L.F., Lusardi, A., & Panos, G.A. (2012) *Financial Literacy and the Financial Crisis*. NBER Working Paper No. 17930. http://www.nber.org/papers/w17930

Klapper, L., Lusardi, A., & Van Oudheusden, P. (2015) *Financial Literacy around the World: Insights from the Standard & Poor Ratings Services Global Financial Literacy Survey*. http://gflec.org/wp-content/uploads/2015/11/Finlit_paper_16_F2_singles.pdf

Klapper, L.F., & Panos, G.A. (2011) 'Financial literacy and retirement planning: The Russian case', *Journal of Pension Economics and Finance* 10(4): 599–618.

Lusardi, A., De, C., & Scheresberg, B. (2013) *Financial Literacy and High-Cost Borrowing in the United States*. NBER Working Paper Series No. 18969. https://doi.org/10.1017/CBO9781107415324.004

Lusardi, A., & Mitchell, O.S. (2008) 'Planning and financial literacy: How do women fare?' *American Economic Review* 98(2): 413–417.

Lusardi, A., & Mitchell, O.S. (2011) 'Financial literacy and retirement planning in the United States', *Journal of Pension Economics and Finance* 10(4): 509–525.

Meir, A., Mugerman, Y., & Sade, O. (2016) 'Financial literacy and retirement planning: Evidence from Israel', *Israel Economic Review* 14(1): 75–95.

Nejad, M.G., & O'Connor, G. (2016) 'An intersectional approach to evaluating consumer financial literacy', *Journal of Financial Services Marketing* 21(4): 308–324.

Rippin, N. (2012) *Distributional Justice and Efficiency: Integrating Inequality Within and between Dimensions in Additive Poverty Indices*. Discussion Papers, 128. Courant Research Centre, 'Poverty, Equity and Growth in Developing and Transition Countries; Statistical Methods and Empirical Analysis', Georg-August-Universität Göttingen.

Rippin, N. (2013) *Considerations of Efficiency and Distributive Justice in Multidimensional Poverty Measurement*. Doctoral Dissertation. Germany: George-August-Universität Göttingen. https://www.die-gdi.de/uploads/media/Rippin_Efficiency_and_Distributive_Justice_Online_Publication.pdf.

Silber, J., & Yalonetzky, G. (2013) 'Measuring multi-dimensional deprivation with dichotomized and ordinal variables', in G. Betti & A. Lemmi (Eds.), *Poverty and Social Exclusion: New Methods of Analysis, Routledge Advances in Social Economics* (pp. 9–37). New York: Routledge.

van Rooij, M.C.J., Lusardi, A., & Alessie, R.J.M. (2012) 'Financial literacy, retirement planning and household wealth', *The Economic Journal* 122(560): 449–478.

Yalonetzky, G. (2012) 'Conditions for the most robust multi-dimensional poverty comparisons using counting measures and ordinal variables', *Social Choice and Welfare* 43(4): 773–807.

10 Multi-Dimensional Material Deprivation in the Visegrád Group

Zero-Inflated Beta Regression Modelling

Hanna Dudek and Wiesław Szczesny

Introduction

Poverty and social exclusion are complex multi-dimensional concepts. In economically advanced societies, they are often defined in terms of the inability to participate in mainstream society because they have insufficient resources. To identify these phenomena, we take various approaches, depending on the country or the purpose of the research. In the European Union (EU), we agreed on a set of indicators for monitoring poverty and social exclusion and enabling the assessment of progress in achieving the Europe 2020 Strategy targets. This indicates a shift in policy focus from one-dimensional income poverty to a multi-dimensional approach. To capture the complex nature of poverty and social exclusion in the Europe 2020 Strategy, we consider the material deprivation (MD) component in parallel with monetary poverty and exclusion from the labour market. MD in the EU conditions refers to a state of economic strain and durables defined as the enforced inability to pay unexpected expenses, afford a one-week annual holiday away from home, consume meals with meat, fish, or other sources of protein regularly, afford adequate heating of a dwelling, durable goods such a washing machine, colour television, telephone, or car and being in payment arrears (Eurostat Glossary, 2018).

Our chapter focuses on MD because analysing it has many benefits. First, it enables us to measure living standards directly by looking at the 'enforced lack' of 'necessities'. The 'enforced lack' approach means that an item is counted as lacking if people cannot afford it – distinguishing between those who choose not to obtain a specific item and those forced to forgo it because they lack the necessary economic resources (Halleröd, 1995). Thus, the lack of items is not due to lifestyle preferences and choice but, rather, is the result of the enforced lack of items, i.e. things that people would like to possess (have access to) but cannot afford (Fusco et al., 2013). Analysing MD not only provides a broad picture of living standards but also captures elements of persistent poverty because the lack of goods is usually associated with a prolonged shortage of resources (Calandrino, 2003). Moreover, an analysis of common items in the EU that captures the same aspect of deprivation enables comparability across countries (Guio, 2009).

Various approaches can be used to identify deprived households in a multi-dimensional framework (Alkire and Foster, 2011; Atkinson, 2003; Betti et al., 2015; Nasri and Belhadj, 2017; Panek, 2010; Pattanaik and Xu, 2018). The approaches most commonly used are the intersection and the union methods: the intersection method considers as deprived only those who experience a failure of functioning in every dimension, whereas the union method refers to those who are deprived at least in one dimension. However, although these approaches are intuitive and straightforward to apply, they can be ineffective at separating those who are deprived of those who are not (the non-deprived). In particular, the intersection method might consider households which evidently suffer substantial deprivation as non-deprived. In contrast, the union-based methodology might not be helpful in distinguishing and targeting the most seriously deprived (Alkire and Foster, 2011). Thus, the literature proposes the use of different intermediate approaches. In particular, the fuzzy-set approach builds on the idea of ambiguity in the identification of who is deprived. In this study, we use this approach because, like some other authors (i.e. Betti and Lemmi, 2013; Betti et al., 2015; Su et al., 2020; Wang and Wang, 2016), we think that MD should be considered a question of the degree of poverty, rather than a characteristic of households in a given population that is either present or absent. Moreover, in our opinion, the relative importance of deprivation items varies across households. Therefore, we use a system of weighting that captures the prevalence of specific deprivation items and the correlation between them. This approach, proposed by Betti and Verma (2008), is based on how common a given item is among all households in a given country and enables us to avoid double counting when the informational content of two different items partly overlaps. On the one hand, this method implies that forms of deprivation which affect only a small share of the country's population are assigned a larger weight than those that are more common in the country. On the other hand, it assesses redundancy across deprivation indicators.

Our study is conducted at the household level with cross-sectional data from the European Union Statistics on Income and Living Conditions (EU-SILC) for 2017. The analysis is based on a standard set of nine MD items adopted by all EU countries and the European Commission. In our study, we examined correlates of the risk and intensity of MD in the Visegrád Group (V4) countries – the Czech Republic, Hungary, Poland and Slovakia. These Central European countries have a lot in common in terms of their history, culture and socio-economic status. They have successfully transformed from centrally planned to market economies and joined the EU at the same time in 2004. Thus, because of their numerous common characteristics, we analyse MD across households in the V4 countries.

In the first step of our study, we used the fuzzy-set approach to construct a deprivation score, which is a composite indicator aggregating all nine MD items. Thus, for each household we obtained a score in the range [0,1], in which 0 means that a household is unambiguously non-deprived, and

1 means that a household is definitely deprived, while all intermediate values indicate partial deprivation. In the second step, to identify the correlates of MD, we conducted a regression analysis. The data analysed indicate the need to use a zero-inflated beta regression model. The application of this model in the analysis of household socio-economic conditions is relatively new, so our chapter contributes to the literature in this field.

In our study, we assumed that a score of zero on the MD scale is different from a score of at least one. Therefore, to test this hypothesis, we applied a zero-inflated beta regression model. We also hypothesised that MD profiles have significant country-specific heterogeneity. To test this hypothesis, we checked the statistical significance of country dummy variables in the model. Thus, the first goal of our chapter was to examine the methodological issues related to modelling MD. The second goal was to identify which households have a higher risk and greater intensity of MD.

The chapter contributes to the literature by providing the first econometric evidence of the factors that affect household MD in the V4 countries using a fuzzy multi-dimensional approach. Moreover, it investigates the differences between the risk and the intensity of the extent to which both indicators are subject to the same determinants. Thus, it aims to fill a gap in the literature regarding multi-dimensional MD in the V4 countries.

Literature Review

The literature on MD has expanded considerably in recent years. Important contributions in this field include Townsend (1979), Mack and Lansley (1985), Mayer and Jencks (1989), Halleröd (1995) and Nolan and Whelan (1996). Supported by these papers, the measurement of MD has been commonly used to capture the multi-dimensional character of poverty and social exclusion in developed countries. Specifically, the relevance of MD indicators in the EU has grown substantially since 2010 as a result of the adoption of the Europe 2020 Strategy on smart, sustainable, and inclusive growth (Guio et al., 2016). Currently, the set of social indicators in the EU include deprivation indicators that combine nine material and social items. They are used by all EU member states and the European Commission to monitor progress in the fight against poverty and social exclusion in individual countries and the EU (Fusco et al., 2013; Guio, 2018).

Most studies on MD in the EU specify a particular threshold to distinguish between the deprived and the non-deprived. They mainly apply logit or probit models in which the binary variable usually takes a value of 1 if MD occurs and 0 otherwise. Examples of such research include Nelson (2012), Israel (2016) and Saltkjel (2018). In contrast, studies that consider the intensity of MD include Barcena-Martin et al. (2014), Busetta et al. (2016) and Bedük (2018) – the first two of which use composite indicators that aggregate the nine deprivation items. Nonetheless, the main differences concern the scope of data and the applied models. Specifically, to model the intensity of MD in the EU, Barcena-Martin et al. (2014) applied a multi-level linear model. They showed that differences in MD across the EU can be explained from both the individual- and country-level perspectives. Busetta et al. (2016) examine the risk and intensity of MD among foreigners in Italy using a zero-inflated beta regression model, which investigates the depth of MD, and a logit regression model on to the probability of not experiencing any MD. Like Barcena-Martin et al. (2014), Bedük (2018) uses a two-part model but focuses on the number of deprivation items using zero-inflated count models. The results confirm that individuals with zero deprivation items have significantly different profiles to those who experience deprivation of at least one item (Bedük, 2018).

To some extent, these three papers have been an inspiration to us. However, unlike Bedük (2018) but in line with Barcena-Martin et al. (2014) and Busetta et al. (2016), we weighted the number of deprivation items, using a more complex weighting scheme than these last two papers. At the same time, like Bedük (2018) and Busetta et al. (2016), we employed a more sophisticated econometric methodology than Barcena-Martin et al. (2014). In our study, we modelled the risk and intensity of household MD in the V4 countries with a two-part model that simultaneously estimates both issues.

Data

The measurement of MD has been on the EU agenda regularly since at least 2010. Based on EU-SILC survey data, it focuses on enforced deprivation, including the inability to: (1) keep one's home adequately warm, (2) eat a meal with meat, chicken, fish, or a protein equivalent every two days, (3) go on a weeklong annual holiday away from home, (4) pay unexpected expenses, (5) pay the rent, mortgage and utility bills, (6) afford to have a television, (7) afford to own a washing machine, (8) afford to have a car, and (9) afford to own a telephone. The first five items are considered 'economic strain' and the last four items 'durable goods'. Our study uses a set of nine binary indicators for these items. Our calculations are based on cross-sectional data for 2017 encompassing 8,701 households in Czechia, 8,142 in Hungary, 5,602 in Slovakia and 13,057 in Poland.

Table 10.1 shows the share of households which did not experience any deprivation. We computed results for the sample and estimated results for

Table 10.1 Percentages of households without any deprivation

Share of households	*V4*	*Czechia*	*Hungary*	*Poland*	*Slovakia*
In sample	45.3%	58.5%	37.7%	43.4%	40.3%
In population (estimation)	47.5%	59.2%	42.1%	46.1%	42.9%

Source: Author's calculation

the population. In the latter case, we used sample weights for each household in order to ensure the results are representative at a national scale.

Almost half the households in the V4 countries did not exhibit any deprivation. The highest share of these households was in Czechia, and the share in the other V4 countries was similar. Moreover, we noted that the percentage of households with each of the nine deprivations in all V4 countries is infinitesimal.

To take a close look at MD in the V4 countries, we examined the impact of various household characteristics on this issue. The set of potential correlates of MD captures information on the entire household and characteristics of the household head (HH). The first group of these correlates includes disposable household income equivalent in terms of purchasing power parity (PPP), the degree of urbanisation, the presence of disabled persons and the type of household. The second group includes age, gender, education, employment, occupation and health status. Most of the explanatory variables considered are standard in MD analyses.

Methods

Material Deprivation Scores

This section describes the method used in constructing deprivation scores. Our study is based on the methodology developed by Cerioli and Zani (1990), Cheli and Lemmi (1995) and Betti and Verma (2008), according to which the state of deprivation is seen as a 'fuzzy set' to which all households of a given population belong but in varying degrees (Ciani et al., 2019).

The MD score for the *i*th household results from the weighted sum of nine deprivation items:

$$s_i = \sum_{k=1}^{9} w_k d_{ik} \tag{10.1}$$

where each d_{ik} ($k = 1,2, \ldots, 9$) is a binary indicator variable that takes a value of 1 if the *i*th household is deprived in terms of a given item or 0 if it has no deprivation, w_k is a weight for item k, in which $0 \leq w_k \leq 1$ and $\sum_{k=1}^{9} w_k = 1$.

Weights for aggregating different items can be selected using various different approaches. A common method proposed by Desai and Shah (1988) and Cerioli and Zani (1990) is to weight items in proportion to their prevalence in the population. This approach assigns a higher weight to deprivation items which are less common among households in a given population. This approach, called 'prevalence' or 'frequency-based weighting' (Fusco et al., 2013; Pi Alperin and Van Kerm, 2014), is used in MD studies by Barcena-Martin et al. (2014) and Busetta et al. (2016). It can be justified in terms of the subjective perception of MD, as the higher the proportion of households that are not deprived of a given item is, the more likely it is that a household unable to afford this item will feel deprived (Fusco et al., 2013).

Another important property that weights should satisfy is limiting the influence of indicators that are highly correlated (Betti et al., 2006). Thus, the methodology developed by Betti and Verma (2008) comprises two factors: the dispersion of the deprivation indicator and its correlation with other deprivation indicators. According to this methodology, the weights can be defined as follows:

$$W_k = W_k^a \cdot W_k^b \tag{10.2}$$

where the first factor is the coefficient of variation of the item, and the second factor is a measure which gives less weight to items that are more highly correlated with others in order to reduce the effect of redundancy. Betti and Verma (2008) give an accurate calculation of factor W^b as follows:

$$W_k^b = \left(\frac{1}{1 + \sum_{k'=1}^{9} r_{kk'} \mid r_{kk'} < r^*} \right) \cdot \left(\frac{1}{\sum_{k'=1}^{9} r_{kk'} \mid r_{kk'} \geq r^*} \right) \tag{10.3}$$

where $r_{kk'}$ is the correlation coefficient between two different indicators d_k and $d_{k'}$, and r^* is a predetermined cut-off correlation level. Finally, W_k are normalised to sum to one.

We use the Betti and Verma approach in our study because of its properties:

(1) Betti and Verma's weighting 'lets the data speak for itself'.
(2) It takes into account the problem of redundancy in information, limiting the influence of deprivation indicators that are highly correlated.
(3) In our binary indicators, W_k^a equals $\sqrt{\frac{1}{d_k} - 1}$, thus, like other frequency-based weighting, this method assigns a higher weight to deprivation items that are relatively infrequent (Pi Alperin and Van Kerm, 2014).

In other words, the Betti and Verma approach enables the calculation of data-driven weights using a sort of 'prevalence-correlation' method (Betti et al., 2016; Betti, 2017; Ciani et al., 2019). This approach has been applied across variety fields, including poverty and quality of life (Ciani et al., 2019; Dudek and Szczesny, 2017; Panek, 2010).

We compute weights using mdepriv, the Stata procedure developed by Pi Alperin and Van Kerm (2014). The weights are calculated separately for items in the 'economic strain' dimension and in the 'durables' dimension. Moreover, like Barcena-Martin et al. (2014), we use national weighting, i.e. the weight for a given item is equal across households in the same country.

In the next step, to gain deeper insights into the socio-economic and demographic correlates of the MD score, we conducted a regression analysis. The following section briefly describes the model used.

Zero-Inflated Beta Regression Model

Generally, the MD score defined by Equation (10.1) can take values in the interval [0,1]. If the number of boundary values of the unitary interval is not large, the response variable can be transformed to 'push' zeros and ones a little inwards. For example, Smithson and Verkuilen (2006) propose rescaling variable s using the transformation $s' = (s(n-1) + 0.5)/n$, where n is the sample size. Another solution is to replace a value of 0 with 0.001 or 0.005 and 1 with 0.999 or 0.995. Nonetheless, these solutions are not appropriate if the number of zeros or ones is considerable, and the boundary values of the unitary interval are values of special interest for research (Masserini et al., 2017). In this situation, to address the issue raised, Ospina and Ferrari (2012) introduced a general class of zero-or-one inflated beta regressions. Because in our study only the problem of excess zeros occurred, we focused on the zero-inflated beta regression model (ZIBRM), which assumes that the response variable has a mixed continuous-discrete distribution with a probability mass of zero. The appropriate mixture density is:

$$BI_0(s,\alpha,\mu,\psi) = \begin{cases} \alpha \text{ if } s = 0 \\ (1-\alpha)f(s,\mu,\psi) \text{ if } s \in (0,1) \end{cases} \tag{10.4}$$

where α is the probability of observing zero,
$f(s,\mu,\psi)$ is the beta distribution density function, defined as:

$$f(s,\mu,\psi) = \frac{\Gamma(\psi)}{\Gamma(\mu\psi)\Gamma((1-\mu)\psi)} s^{\mu\psi-1}(1-s)^{(1-\mu)\psi-1}, \tag{10.5}$$

Γ denotes the gamma function,
μ is the mean of the outcome variable s for $s \in (0,1)$,
Ψ is the scaling factor related to the variance of s, for $s \in (0,1)$.

Therefore, a zero-inflated beta distribution is a combination of two distributions: a beta distribution when the variable is in the interval (0,1), and another distribution function that is in effect when the variable takes a value of 0.

ZIBRM can be defined by assuming the relationships in the mixture parameter α and the conditional mean μ (Ospina and Ferrari, 2012):

$$h(\alpha_i) = z_i'\gamma \tag{10.6}$$

$$g(\mu_i) = x_i'\beta \tag{10.7}$$

where $\boldsymbol{\gamma}$ and $\boldsymbol{\beta}$ are vectors of unknown parameters to be estimated,
z_i and $\boldsymbol{x}_i$ are vectors of known covariates of the ith household, ($i = 1,2, \ldots ,n$), which may be identical or overlap in part (Masserini et al., 2017),
$h(\cdot)$: $(0,1) \rightarrow R$, $g(\cdot)$: $(0,1) \rightarrow R$, are strictly monotonic and twice continuously differentiable functions.

In our study, we estimated the parameters of ZIBRM using the Stata module zoib developed by Buis (2010), with logit link for $h(\cdot)$ and $g(\cdot)$. The ZIBRM applied consists of two sub-models:

(1) a logistic regression model for whether the MD score is 0;
(2) a beta regression model for the MD scores from the interval (0,1).

Thus, the first model estimates the probability of not experiencing any deprivations, and the second model examines the intensity of MD. The vectors of the parameters $\boldsymbol{\gamma}$ and $\boldsymbol{\beta}$ in the ZIBRM are estimated using the maximum likelihood. For a detailed description of the estimation and inference of ZIBRM, see Ospina and Ferrari (2012).

Results and Discussion

In the first stage of our study, we computed the weights assigned to each of the nine deprivation symptoms. Using the weights, we aggregated MD items to calculate a household's score, in which the score equals 1 when the household is deprived of all component indicators and equals 0 if it is not deprived of any indicator. As shown in Table 10.1, almost half the households in the V4 did not exhibit any of the nine deprivation symptoms. By contrast, we found that only six households experienced each of the symptoms considered. In these cases, we replaced an MD score of 1 with 0.999.

We surmise that the only reason for not experiencing MD is income above the poverty threshold. We decided to analyse this aspect, taking into account households that do and do not have income poverty.

Table 10.2 lists the percentage of households which did not experience any deprivation symptoms by their income level.

The results in Table 10.2 show that 18.4% of income-poor households in the V4 did not report any deprivation symptoms, whereas 52.7% of the households there who were not income poor reported not being deprived. This means that the two populations – unambiguously non-deprived and

Table 10.2 Share of households without any deprivation by income level

Income level	*V4*	*Czechia*	*Hungary*	*Poland*	*Slovakia*
Below 60% of national median equivalent income	18.4%	21.8%	22.3%	16.7%	17.6%
Above 60% of the national median equivalent income	52.7%	64.1%	45.4%	52.0%	46.3%

Source: Author calculations. The results are weighted in order to represent the structure of the population of households in each V4 country

income non-poor – do not perfectly overlap. Our findings are confirmed in the literature, showing that income poverty and MD are not closely correlated (Ayllón and Gábos, 2017). Thus, MD indicators provide more specific information on poverty than income data. These results suggest that the relationship between MD and income is complex. Two households with the same income can have different standards of living if their income does not adequately measure all their available resources or if their needs differ (Fusco et al., 2011). Therefore, after we control for income, the identification of other factors that influence households' MD is a key step. In order to assess the impact of various socio-economic and demographic factors on the risk and the intensity of MD, we estimated the ZIBRM parameters in Table 10.3.

The significance and sign of these estimates indicate the significance and direction of the partial effects. However, the estimates on the risk of deprivation are the opposite of the estimates in the second column in Table 10.3. This is because, when we analyse the risk of deprivation, we consider the probability of being deprived of at least one of the nine items, whereas the ZIBRM estimation indicates the probability of not having any deprivation. Thus, the results of ZIBRM sub-models must be interpreted in the opposite way. As the logistic regression estimates the probability that a household is unambiguously non-deprived (i.e. the probability that the MD score is zero), a negative estimate of a parameter indicates that the corresponding covariate has a positive effect on the risk of being deprived, while a positive coefficient indicates a negative effect. In the beta regression sub-model, a positive estimate indicates an increment in the incidence of MD due to growth (i.e. a change in state) in the covariate, whereas a negative coefficient shows the opposite.

As might be expected, the risk and the intensity in the V4 decline if a household's income increases. However, there is no perfect one-to-one relationship, which has already been highlighted.

When comparing results for the risk and the intensity of MD, we found that some correlates significantly affected one process but not another. Specifically, the risk of MD did not differ significantly with respect to the degree of urbanisation. However, the intensity was higher in urban areas than in rural areas. Furthermore, the risk of MD was significantly greater for households with disabled members, but there was no statistically significant difference in the intensity of MD between households without disabled members and households with those facing health challenges. This is consistent with Bedük's (2018) results, confirming that a score of zero is a qualitatively different phenomenon to a score on at least one of nine MD items.

We found that the type of household has a clear impact on the risk and intensity of MD. Specifically, we observed that one-person households and single-parent households face a difficult situation. Our results also show the importance of the characteristics of the head of household (HH), such as the

Table 10.3 Estimates of ZIBRM

Variable	*Logistic regression sub-model on the probability of not experiencing any MD*		*Beta regression sub-model on the intensity of MD*	
	Estimates of γ	*SE*	*Estimates of β*	*SE*
Constant	**–1.022**	**0.138**	**–1.777**	**0.062**
Income in thousands of PPP	**1.399**	**0.075**	**–0.367**	**0.032**
Urbanisation (Ref.: Sparse (rural) areas)				
Dense	0.083	0.047	**0.136**	**0.021**
Intermediate	0.080	0.046	**0.081**	**0.019**
Disability (Ref.: Without any disability)				
Activity limited due to health status	**–0.288**	**0.043**	0.015	0.018
Activity strongly limited due to health status	**–0.422**	**0.063**	0.016	0.023
Household type (Ref.: One-person households)				
Single parent	**–0.320**	**0.111**	–0.026	0.043
Multi-person households without children	**0.448**	**0.048**	**–0.119**	**0.022**
Two adults with one child	**0.419**	**0.080**	–0.036	0.036
Two adults with two children	**0.660**	**0.077**	**–0.152**	**0.036**
Two adults with 3+ children	**0.340**	**0.125**	–0.083	0.056
Other households with children	**0.462**	**0.083**	**–0.176**	**0.033**
Education of household head (Ref.: Higher)				
Secondary	**–0.499**	**0.053**	0.014	0.025
Primary	**–0.961**	**0.101**	**0.178**	**0.038**
Age of household head (Ref.: Below 40)				
40–60 years	**0.225**	**0.059**	**0.028**	**0.027**
More than 60 years	**0.415**	**0.088**	**–0.102**	**0.041**
Sex of household head				
Female	**–0.458**	**0.040**	0.008	0.019
Health of household head (Ref.: Very good)				
Good	**–0.265**	**0.067**	**0.097**	**0.029**
Fair	**–0.574**	**0.072**	**0.170**	**0.032**
Bad	**–0.931**	**0.091**	**0.303**	**0.037**
Very bad	**–1.194**	**0.144**	**0.352**	**0.050**
Economic activity of household head (Ref.: Retired)				
Employed	0.046	0.074	**0.097**	**0.034**
Unemployed	**–0.809**	**0.149**	**0.572**	**0.059**
Inactive	–0.151	0.091	**0.230**	**0.035**
Occupation of household head (Ref.: Intermediate)				
High skill	**0.336**	**0.049**	0.013	0.022
Unskilled	**–0.247**	**0.044**	**0.099**	**0.019**
Country (Ref.: Czechia)				
Hungary	**–0.233**	**0.049**	**0.305**	**0.022**
Poland	**–0.422**	**0.045**	**0.233**	**0.020**
Slovakia	**–0.373**	**0.052**	–0.002	0.021

Note: SE are standard errors of estimated parameters. All reported standard errors are robust to heteroscedasticity. Values in boldface are significant at the 0.05 level.

level of education, gender, economic activity, health status, occupation and age. We note that:

- when the HH has a low level of education, the risk and the intensity of MD are higher;
- the risk of MD was higher with female HH than male HH, but the intensity showed no statistical difference due to sex;
- the perceived health of the HH has a negative relationship with the risk and intensity of MD;
- households headed by unskilled persons have a higher risk and intensity of MD than households headed by persons with intermediate occupational positions;
- lower risk and intensity of MD was noted among households with an older person as the HH than those headed by people aged below 40;
- households headed by people who are unemployed were significantly more likely to report MD than those whose HH is retired. However, households headed by economically active people have a higher intensity of MD than households headed by retirees.

These results regarding HH characteristics that influence MD are largely consistent with other studies conducted in similar socio-economic contexts (Nelson, 2012; Barcena-Martin et al., 2014; Israel, 2016; Saltkjel, 2018). However, what distinguishes our study from these investigations is that we considered the risk and the intensity of MD. Furthermore, unlike other studies, we examined how the level of urbanisation affects both phenomena. Our estimates reveal that, *ceteris paribus*, households in rural areas are not more materially deprived than urban households. Moreover, the intensity of MD is lower among the former than the latter. This finding sheds new light on the issue of rural–urban disparity in the V4.

Apart from these household-level correlates, we found that the country in which households are located significantly differentiated the risk and intensity of MD after all other household-level covariates are controlled for. Specifically, Poland, Slovakia and Hungary have a higher risk of MD than Czechia. Our results show that not only is MD a problem that arises from each household characteristic, but various economic and social country-level features may also affect MD. For example, differences among countries in the risk and the intensity of MD might depend on the structure of the welfare state and the different levels of social support. Our results regarding the differences across countries are supported by the Eurostat Database (2020), revealing that in 2017 the expenditure on social protection per inhabitant was much higher in Czechia than in other V4 countries. Moreover, Czechia is a leader among V4 countries in indicators of well-being, such as the Human Development Index (UNDP, 2020) and the Better Life Index (OECD, 2020). Thus, people in countries with higher well-being in general have a lower risk of MD.

Concluding Remarks

In recent years, the European Commission has drawn attention to the need for greater emphasis on MD, which is currently measured by nine indicators related to financial stress and the enforced lack of durable goods. The MD of a household in the EU can be assessed using different approaches. In our study, we adopted the methodology proposed by Betti and Verma (2008), which enables us to simultaneously capture the multi-dimensional character of MD and its vagueness. In effect, we constructed scores in the interval [0,1], in which a higher score indicates a higher intensity of MD. Moreover, we considered the risk of MD, which in our study indicates the probability of experiencing at least one symptom of MD. We modelled the risk and intensity of households' MD by applying a two-part ZIBRM and thus jointly estimating both issues.

We focused on conditions in member countries of the Visegrád Group, which in recent years has gained the attention of the international community and analysts because it is regarded as a bloc of countries. Although many studies have been conducted on political and economic conditions in Central Europe, there is a shortage of research papers on MD in the V4 countries. Thus, by looking at these countries in terms of the potential for meeting basic material needs, we aim to fill this research gap.

We found that MD is a multi-faceted phenomenon, with risk and intensity distributed unevenly across the V4 population. It is affected by the income and health conditions, demographic composition, level of education, gender, economic activity, occupation and age of the HH. Furthermore, we showed that correlates of the risk and the intensity of MD do not fully overlap, including the degree of urbanisation and the presence of disabled members of a household. We also revealed that the country in which a household is located significantly differentiates the risk and intensity of MD after all other household-level covariates are controlled for. Various country-level features, such as the social policy, prices and the structure of the welfare state, can affect the risk as well as the intensity of MD.

We hope that our study will lead to a better understanding of the multidimensional aspects of MD in the V4 countries. By identifying the factors correlated with the risk and intensity of MD, our approach can be useful for implementing socio-economic policies to reduce MD.

References

Alkire, S., Foster, J. (2011), Counting and multidimensional poverty measurement, *Journal of Public Economics*, 95(7), pp. 476–487.

Atkinson, A.B. (2003), Multidimensional deprivation: Contrasting social welfare and counting approaches, *Journal of Economic Inequality*, 1, pp. 51–65.

Ayllón, S., Gábos, A. (2017), The interrelationships between the Europe 2020 poverty and social exclusion indicators, *Social Indicators Research*, 130(3), pp. 1025–1049.

Bárcena-Martín, E., Lacomba, B., Moro-Egido, A.I., Perez-Moreno, S. (2014), Country differences in material deprivation in Europe, *Review of Income and Wealth*, 60(4), pp. 802–820.

Bedük, S. (2018), Understanding material deprivation for 25 EU countries: Risk and level perspectives, and distinctiveness of zeros, *European Sociological Review*, 34(2), pp. 121–137.

Betti, G. (2017), What impact has the economic crisis had on quality of life in Europe? A multidimensional and fuzzy approach, *Quality & Quantity*, 51(1), pp. 351–364.

Betti, G., Cheli, B., Lemmi, A., Verma, V. (2006), Multidimensional and longitudinal poverty: An integrated fuzzy approach, in Lemmi, A., Betti, G. (eds), *Fuzzy Set Approach to Multidimensional Poverty Measurement*. New York: Springer, pp. 111–137.

Betti, G., Gagliardi, F., Lemmi, A., Verma, V. (2015), Comparative measures of multidimensional deprivation in the European Union, *Empirical Economics*, 49, pp. 1071–1100.

Betti G., Lemmi A. eds. (2013), *Poverty and Social Exclusion: New Methods of Analysis*. London: Routledge.

Betti, G., Soldi, R., Talev, I. (2016), Fuzzy multidimensional indicators of quality of life: The empirical case of Macedonia, *Social Indicators Research*, 127(1), pp. 39–53.

Betti, G., Verma, V. (2008), Fuzzy measures of the incidence of relative poverty and deprivation: A multi-dimensional perspective, *Statistical Methods and Applications*, 17(2), pp. 225–250.

Buis, M. (2010), *ZOIB: Stata Module to fit a Zero-One Inflated Beta Distribution by Maximum Likelihood. Statistical Software Components, S457156*. Boston College Department of Economics.

Busetta, A., Milito, A.M., Oliveri, A.M. (2016), The material deprivation of foreigners: Measurement and determinants, in Alleva, G., Giommi, A. (eds), *Topics in Theoretical and Applied Statistics*. New York: Springer, pp. 181–191.

Calandrino, M. (2003), *Low-Income and Deprivation in British Families*. Working Paper, No. 10. London: Department for Work and Pensions. ISBN 9781843881919.

Cerioli, A., Zani, S. (1990), A fuzzy approach to the measurement of poverty, in Dagum, C., Zenga, M. (eds.), *Income and Wealth Distribution, Inequality and Poverty, Studies in Contemporary Economics*. Berlin: Springer, pp. 272–284.

Cheli, B., Lemmi, A. (1995), A 'totally' fuzzy and relative approach to the multidimensional analysis of poverty, *Economic Notes*, 24(1), pp. 115–134.

Ciani, M., Gagliardi, F., Riccarelli, S., Betti, G. (2019), Fuzzy measures of multidimensional poverty in the Mediterranean area: A focus on financial dimension, *Sustainability*, 11(1), pp. 143, 1–13.

Desai, M., Shah, A. (1988), An econometric approach to the measurement of poverty, *Oxford Economic Papers*, 40(3), pp. 505–522.

Dudek, H. (2019), Country-level drivers of severe material deprivation rates in the EU, *Ekonomický Casopis*, 67(1), pp. 33–51.

Dudek, H., Szczesny, W. (2017), Correlates of multidimensional indicator of quality of life: Fractional outcome model approach, *Statistika: Statistics and Economy Journal*, 97(4), pp. 46–61.

Eurostat Database (2020), https://ec.europa.eu/eurostat/databrowser/view/tps00100/default/ table?lang=en, accessed 3 March 2020.

Eurostat Glossary: Material deprivation (2018), https://ec.europa.eu/eurostat/statistics-explained/index.php/Glossary:Material_deprivation, accessed 2 March 2020.

Fusco, A., Guio, A.-C., Marlier, E. (2011), *Income Poverty and Material Deprivation in European Countries*. LISER Working Paper Series 2011-04. Luxembourg: Luxembourg Institute of Socio-Economic Research.

Fusco, A., Guio, A-C., Marlier, E. (2013), Building a material deprivation index in a multinational context: Lessons from the EU experience, in Berenger, V., Bresson, F. (eds), *Poverty and Social Exclusion around the Mediterranean Sea*. New York: Springer, pp. 43–71.

Guio, A.-C. (2009), *What Can Be Learned from Deprivation Indicators in Europe?* Eurostat Methodologies and Working Papers, Luxembourg.

Guio, A.-C. (2018), Multidimensional poverty and material deprivation: Empirical findings, in D'Ambrosio, C. (eds), *Handbook of Research on Economic and Social Well-Being*. Cheltenham: Edward Elgar, pp. 171–192.

Guio, A.-C., Marlier, E., Gordon, D., Fahmy, E, Nandy, S., Pomati, M. (2016), Improving the measurement of material deprivation at the European Union level, *Journal of European Social Policy*, 26(3), pp. 219–333.

Halleröd, B. (1995), The truly poor: Direct and indirect consensual measurement of poverty in Sweden, *Journal of European Social Policy*, 5(2), pp. 111–129.

Israel, S. (2016), More than cash: Societal influences on the risk of material deprivation, *Social Indicators Research*, 129(2), pp. 619–637.

Mack, J., Landsey, S. (1985), *Poor Britain*. London: Routledge.

Masserini, L., Bini, M., Pratesi, M. (2017), Effectiveness of non-selective evaluation test scores for predicting first-year performance in university career: A zero-inflated beta regression approach, *Quality & Quantity*, 51(2), pp. 693–708.

Mayer, S.E., Jencks, C. (1989), Poverty and the distribution of material hardship, *Journal of Human Resources*, 24, pp. 88–114.

Nasri, K., Belhadj, B. (2017), Multidimensional poverty measurement in Tunisia: Distribution of deprivations across regions, *Journal of North African Studies*, 22(5), pp. 841–859.

Nelson, K. (2012), Counteracting material deprivation: The role of social assistance in Europe, *Journal of European Social Policy*, 22(2), pp. 148–163.

Nolan, B., Whelan, C.T. (1996), *Resources, Deprivation, and Poverty*. Oxford: Clarendon Press.

OECD (2020), http://www.oecdbetterlifeindex.org, accessed 3 March 2020.

Ospina, R., Ferrari S.L.P. (2012), A general class of zero-or-one inflated beta regression models, *Computational Statistics and Data Analysis*, 56, pp. 1609–1623.

Panek, T. (2010), Multidimensional approach to poverty measurement: Fuzzy measures of the incidence and the depth of poverty, *Statistics in Transition*, 11(2), pp. 361–379.

Pattanaik, P.K., Xu, Y. (2018), On measuring multidimensional deprivation. *Journal of Economic Literature*, 56, pp. 657–672.

Pi Alperin, M.N., Van Kerm, P. (2014), *MDEPRIV: Stata Module to Compute Synthetic Indicators of Multiple Deprivation. Statistical Software Components S457806*, Boston College Department of Economics.

Saltkjel, T. (2018), Welfare resources and social risks in times of social and economic change: A multilevel study of material deprivation in European countries, *European Journal of Social Work*, 21(5), pp. 639–652.

Smithson, M., Verkuilen, J. (2006), A better lemon squeezer? Maximum-likelihood regression with beta-distributed dependent variables, *Psychological Methods*, 11(1), pp. 54–71.

Su, W., Betti, G. Ucar, B. (2020), Longitudinal measures of fuzzy poverty: A focus on Czechia, Hungary and Poland after the crisis, *Quality and Quantity*, 54, pp. 27–41.

Townsend, P. (1979), *Poverty in the United Kingdom*, London: Allen Lane and Penguin Books.

UNDP (2020), http://hdr.undp.org, accessed 3 March 2020.

Wang, Y., Wang, B. (2016), Multidimensional poverty measure and analysis: A case study from Hechi City, China, *SpringerPlus*, 5(1), 642.

11 Measuring Educational Poverty in Italy

A Multi-Dimensional and Fuzzy Approach

Gaia Bertarelli, Antonella D'Agostino, Caterina Giusti and Monica Pratesi[1]

Introduction

In the past few years, educational poverty (EP) has emerged on the political agenda of several countries as a new social challenge that urgently needs to be addressed. In fact, it has been widely recognised that deprivation in education can determine a gap at a particularly vulnerable time of life that is not easy to reverse later. In its law in the 2018 budget, the Italian government introduced an experimental fund to fight EP through the removal of the economic, social and cultural obstacles that prevent the full educational achievement of minors and young adults. To provide an adequate measure of EP in Italy, the Italian National Statistical Institute (Istat) (Quattrociocchi, 2018) defined a multi-dimensional Educational Poverty Index (EPI), which measures material, relational, cultural and environmental problems that limit the ability of young people to live in a complex society. The EPI measures the overall level of EP for individuals ages 15–29, using several data sources and providing a territorial disaggregation of the Italian regions (at the NUTS 2 level). To aggregate the single indicators defining the four dimensions of the EPI – participation, resilience, standard of living and friends and skills – Istat relied on an adjusted Mazziotta-Pareto index (Mazziotta and Pareto, 2016, 2018).

Several authors have proposed alternative EP measures (Checchi, 1998; Brandolini and D'Alessio, 1998; Allmendinger, 1999; Allmendinger and Leibfried, 2003; Watkins, 2000). Checchi (1998) expressed the concept of EP within the framework of the capability approach. Brandolini and D'Alessio (1998) referred to the concept of *povertà d'istruzione* as a reference point in the discussion of education as a separate function in addition to health, social relations, labour market status, housing and economic resources. Allmendinger (1999) stressed the need to take into account the material and non-material aspects of social deprivation and referred explicitly to the living conditions approach. Watkins (2000) explored the link between educational deprivation and poverty.

In more recent empirical studies, EP has evolved into a multi-dimensional concept, linked to the idea of deprivation, for children and adolescents, of the ability to learn, experiment and develop and freely expand their skills, talents and aspirations (Save the Children, 2018). Lohman and Ferger (2014) discussed the concept of EP within the context of changes in the welfare state. Larysa and Felice (2016) applied multidimensional index of deprivation in the analysis of cognitive skills. Agasisti et al. (2020) addressed the issue of multi-dimensional poverty measures for analysing EP.

Pratesi et al. (2020) proposed the use of small area estimation methodologies to estimate the multi-dimensional index proposed by Istat, the EPI, at the sub-regional level, as local measures of EP can be crucial in tailoring policy actions in the places where people live. Specifically, the paper considered the local level, represented by the intersection between the Italian regions (NUTS 2 level) and the degree of urbanisation designated by Eurostat by the DEGURBA three-level classification (cities, towns and suburbs and rural areas). The motivating idea was to explore the potential role played by the degree of urbanisation in disentangling the EP measurement. Indeed, the work highlighted the presence in the same region of the same critical areas with high EP, together with areas with low EP.

In this chapter, we extend Pratesi et al. (2020) by providing a fuzzy multi-dimensional measure of EP based on the EPI. We limit our analysis to the previous EP dimensions, measured by the AVQ survey. Quattrociocchi (2018) included digital as well as literacy and quantitative skills in the dimension 'friends and skills'. Although we include digital skills indicators using the AVQ survey, we do not include literacy and quantitative skills in our analysis because these two skills are not collected in the AVQ survey.[2] Therefore, as explained above, in this chapter we approximate outcomes for these two education skills using the individual level of education attained.

Our first step is therefore to explore the fuzzy nature of the phenomenon as it results from the four dimensions, using only AVQ data. Indeed, as the EPI is a multi-dimensional index, the integrated fuzzy and relative (IFR) methodology can be used under the assumption that EP is a vague predicate manifested in different shades and degrees (fuzzy concept), rather than an attribute that is simply present or absent for individuals, as in the approach developed by Istat. Our aim is therefore to measure the degree of EP in the Italian regions and in the local areas at the intersection of the regions with the DEGURBA classification by defining an overall EP fuzzy measure and four EP dimension-specific measures.

The chapter is organised as follows. First, we present the data and the indicators used to define the EP multi-dimensional measure. Second, we summarise the methodology used before presenting the main findings from the analysis. Finally, we offer some concluding remarks and future extensions of our work.

Dimensions of EP and Data

The EPI defined by Istat is a multi-dimensional index that identifies four dimensions of EP for people aged 15 to 29:

- participation, meaning the lack of participation in social life;
- resilience, meaning a lack of development in an attitude of trusting oneself and one's abilities;
- standard of living, meaning a lack of opportunity to lead an inclusive, healthy and safe life with an adequate standard of living;
- friends and skills, meaning the lack of opportunity to form relationships with others and to achieve the skills (digital, literacy and quantitative skills) needed to succeed in the current fast-paced world.

The indicators currently used by Istat to measure deprivation in terms of these four dimensions come from several data sources (Quattrociocchi, 2018). In this chapter, following Pratesi et al. (2020) and due to the availability of data, we use only items from the 'aspects of everyday life' (AVQ) survey in 2016 (Istat, 2019).

Based on this source, the indicators used by Pratesi et al. (2020) to measure EP are illustrated in Figure 11.1 with rectangles, arranged in the four dimensions, which are depicted by ovals. In this framework, each indicator is a dichotomous variable defined by 53 different items in the AVQ survey.

For example, the indicator that measures the lack of 'political participation' – i.e. the percentage of people who do not engage in political activity – is binary and is defined on the basis of the following four items in the AVQ questionnaire, indicating whether an individual has taken the opportunity to:

1. attend a political rally at least once in the past 12 months;
2. participate in a political procession at least once in the past 12 months;
3. engaging in free activity for a party at least once in the past 12 months;
4. donate money to a party for either membership or support at least once in the past 12 months.

To organise our research and refine our concept of EP, we use the four dimensions articulated by Pratesi et al. (2020), but our empirical analysis is based directly on the 53 individual items arranged along these four dimensions. In this way, we preserve the richness of the data. This means that the items previously mentioned are 4 of the 53 items used in our empirical analysis.[3] Among the items we use is the educational level attained as an indicator of educational outcomes to proxy for competence scores in the 'friends and skills' dimension. Because in its Europe 2020 Strategy the European Union (EU) defines those who have an ISCED 0-2 qualification as early school leavers, we use this as a criterion in an EP threshold (Lohmann and Ferger, 2014). Nevertheless, our sample also includes individuals who

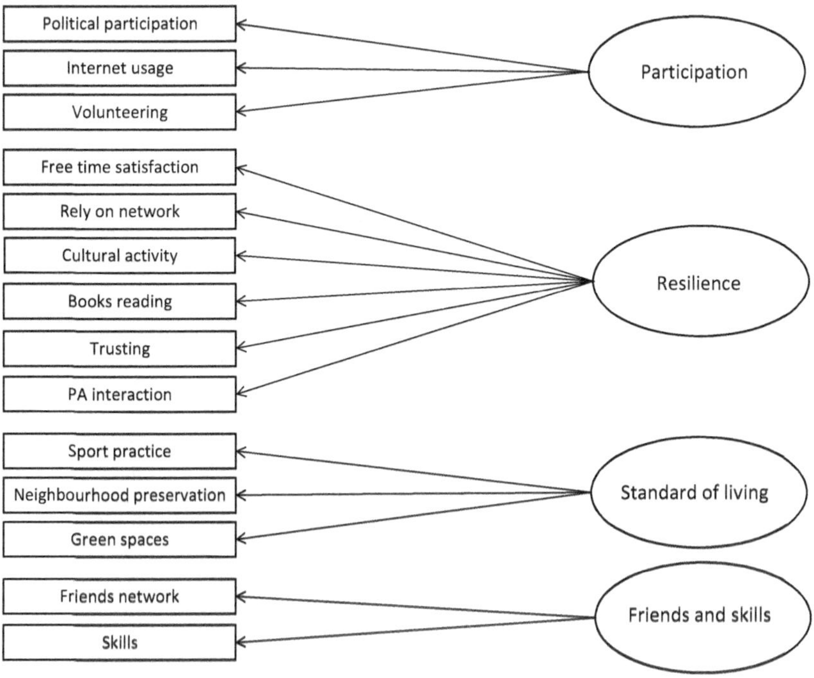

Figure 11.1 Framework adopted by Pratesi et al. (2020). *Note*: Indicators (rectangles) arranged in the four dimensions (ovals) of the EPI from the AVQ survey.

are still enrolled at compulsory school, so we consider people deprived only if they are not currently enrolled in an ISCED 3 course.

The final data set used in the empirical analysis covers 5,093 individuals aged 15–29 for whom all 53 items were available.[4] To map EP in Italy, we consider the 20 Italian regions.

For each region, Table 11.1 summarises the sample population of those aged 15–29, together with some descriptive statistics computed on this sub-sample, excluding those with missing values. The size of the sample population in the regions varies from a minimum of 106 (Valle d'Aosta) to a maximum of 537 (Campania). The gender composition is quite stable across the regions, varying from 47% males in Trentino-Alto Adige to 54% in Friuli Venezia Giulia. The other statistics considered concern the age of the sample population, namely the mean, the coefficient of variation (CV) and the percentage of people aged 20 or younger. Although the average age and the corresponding CV did not vary much across the regions, we observed more heterogeneity among people less than 20 years old, from 24% in Valle d'Aosta to 34% in Marche.

Table 11.1 Descriptive statistics across the regions, listed from north to south and then the islands

	Obs.	*% Males*	*Mean age*	*CV age*	*% age ≤ 20*
Piemonte	288	0.53	22.36	0.19	0.31
Valle d'Aosta	106	0.52	22.86	0.18	0.24
Lombardy	385	0.49	22.25	0.19	0.32
Trent. Alto Adige	316	0.47	22.27	0.19	0.32
Veneto	338	0.50	22.46	0.18	0.29
Friuli Venezia Giulia	166	0.54	22.75	0.19	0.27
Liguria	161	0.51	22.84	0.18	0.25
Emilia-Romagna	276	0.53	22.73	0.18	0.27
Tuscany	249	0.49	22.63	0.18	0.27
Umbria	134	0.51	22.11	0.18	0.31
Marche	164	0.50	22.05	0.18	0.34
Lazio	256	0.52	22.68	0.18	0.30
Abruzzo	213	0.48	22.52	0.18	0.29
Molise	181	0.53	22.86	0.18	0.25
Campania	537	0.50	22.56	0.18	0.27
Puglia	342	0.53	22.88	0.17	0.24
Basilicata	187	0.53	22.56	0.18	0.29
Calabria	299	0.51	22.85	0.18	0.26
Sicily	320	0.55	22.50	0.18	0.29
Sardinia	175	0.51	22.72	0.18	0.27

Following Pratesi et al. (2020), we also considered a finer geographic disaggregation, through the intersection of the regions with the DEGURBA degree of urbanisation, as follows:

- densely populated areas (cities, large urban areas);
- moderately densely populated areas (towns and suburbs, small urban areas);
- thinly populated areas (rural areas).

This cross-classification results in a total of 59 target areas, as Valle d'Aosta has no densely populated areas. The sample size varies from a minimum of 11 (densely populated areas in Marche) to a maximum of 365 (densely populated areas in Campania). Given the smaller sample size in several of these areas, Pratesi et al. (2020) used small area methods to obtain reliable estimates. In this chapter, we mainly aim to derive a fuzzy measure of EP in 20 regions. We also use DEGURBA areas to explore the potential differences across the regions. Nevertheless, because of the small sample size, the results of this finer geographic disaggregation require further analysis.

Methodology

As explained in the previous sections, EP is a complex phenomenon which includes different dimensions that are not usually measured directly. Its multi-dimensional nature implies that children or individuals experience a certain number of observed deprivations that can be summarised into this set of latent dimensions. Moreover, EP can be treated as a matter of degree, replacing the simple dichotomy {0,1} – presence/absence of EP – with a certain degree of EP, which varies between 0 (not deprived at all) to 1 (completely deprived) for each dimension.

In this chapter, we apply multi-dimensional and fuzzy logic (Zadeh, 1965) to study EP at the NUTS 2 (region) level and use the DEGURBA classification in Italy. In particular, we adapt the methodology called IFR (Betti et al., 2006) to this framework. See Betti et al. (2020) for an interesting literature review of this methodology. The positive results that have been achieved by applying the IFR approach to fields other than poverty (see e.g. Aassve et al., 2007; Betti et al., 2011; Betti and Lemmi, 2013; Betti et al. 2016; D'Agostino et al., 2019) demonstrate its applicability and robustness.

Let I_k be the single item associated with the observed indicator k (k = 1, ..., K, with K = 53) in the AQV survey converted into the range [0,1]. Following Quattrociocchi (2018), we define four different latent dimensions (s = 1, ..., S with S = 4). Each dimension s is composed of a different number of items I_k (k = 1, ..., K_s), as illustrated above. We calculate a function, called a membership function, for each dimension s, which is a quantitative specification of the individual degree of EP between 0 and 1, in which the lowest level of EP takes a value of 0 and the highest level takes a value of 1.

Let $EP_{(s)j}$ indicate the membership function of dimension s for individual j (j=1 ... n) in the sample, calculated as:

$$EP_{(s)j} = \sum_k w_{(s)k} I_{(s)kj} / \sum_k w_{(s)k} \tag{11.1}$$

where $w_{(s)k}$ is the weight of I_k in dimension s. In turn, $w_{(s)k}$ is calculated as the product of two components that take into account both the dispersion of I_k in dimension s and its correlation with the other indicators in the same dimension s (see Betti et al., 2006). According to Equation 11.1, as the value of EP increases from 0 to 1, the EP of individual j in the corresponding dimension increases. Finally, a comprehensive measure of EP for each individual j is calculated as the unweighted mean of the S dimensions in the dimension-specific $EP_{(s)j}$.

$$EP_j = \frac{\sum_s EP_{(s)j}}{S} \tag{11.2}$$

Finally, the weighted sample means $\overline{EP}_{(s)}$ (s = 1, ..., S) in Equation (11.1) and $\overline{EP}$ in Equation (11.2) measure the degree of EP observed at the regional level in each dimension s and for all four dimensions as a whole, respectively. In other words, $\overline{EP}$ is indeed a single composite index, which we call the Educational Poverty Fuzzy Indicator (EPFI), and each $\overline{EP}_s$ represents a single dimension-specific composite index (Betti et al., 2020). For the sake of simplicity, in the empirical analysis we call these dimension-specific indices *EPF_Participation*, *EPF_Resilience*, *EPF_Standard of living* and *EPF_Friends and skills*.

Findings: A Comparative Regional Perspective

In this section, we offer findings after using the multi-dimensional and fuzzy measures of EP discussed earlier.

The main goal of this analysis is to provide an overview of the current degree of EP from a cross-regional perspective using EPFI and the dimensional indicators *EPF_Participation*, *EPF_Resilience*, *EPF_Standard of living* and *EPF_Friends and skills*. In addition, we also outline some findings using the DEGURBA classification, even though, as stressed above, we comment on the results only if the area has a sufficient number of sample units. Figure 11.2 is a map of Italy in which the colour of each region

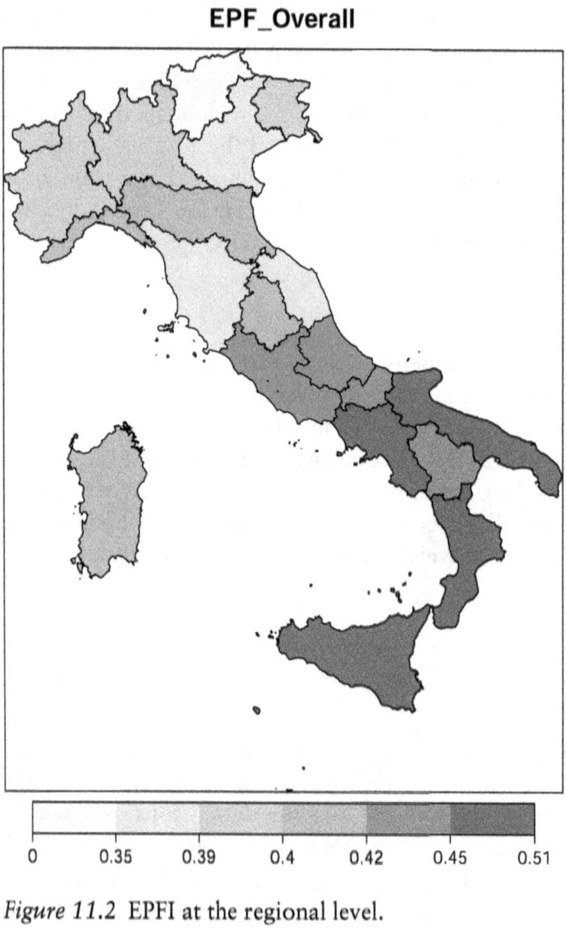

Figure 11.2 EPFI at the regional level.

depends on the degree of EP. The map shows a range of colours from white to black to indicate the degree of EP from low to high. Specifically, the value of EPFI is in the range [0,1], in which the maximum degree of EP equals 1.

The map, as expected, illustrates a clear divide between the northern/central and southern regions, in which the northern/central regions are characterised by lower levels of EP. The lowest EPFI is observed in Trentino-Alto Adige, where it is 0.36, whereas the four southern regions (Puglia, Sicilia, Calabria and Campania) have the highest levels of EPFI, with increasing intensity: the value of EPFI ranges from 0.47 in Puglia to 0.52 in Campania. Therefore, the EP issue adds to the Italian north/south divide in economic performance and living standards, which remains an unresolved issue in Italian economics and politics. A discussion on its multi-dimensional shape is certainly useful in facilitating a better understanding of EP. The maps in Figure 11.3 summarise the results obtained with respect to each of the four dimensions.

Looking at each dimension leads to further discussion. The four dimensions show some heterogeneity among them and across regions. In other words, the degree of EP in each region seems to vary in intensity across the dimensions. These findings demonstrate the importance of taking into account the multi-dimensional nature of EP. In particular, the dimension 'Participation' (see the EPF_Participation map in Figure 11.3) shows the participation of the youngest people in social life. The degree of deprivation in this dimension seems to be generally very low in Tuscany, for instance, while 'Standard of living' (see the EPF_Standard of living map in Figure 11.3) has the highest value, meaning that young people are more deprived with respect to this aspect of EP. Campania and Calabria have the highest value of the indices in each dimension and Sicily in three out of four dimensions. In these regions, therefore, young people suffer multiple types of deprivation, with a similarly high degree of intensity. The situation in Lombardy is also very interesting. Young people seem to be very deprived in terms of the dimension 'resilience', illustrating the development of an attitude of trusting oneself and one's abilities, whereas they suffer less in the 'participation' dimension. This could be a consequence of the geographic heterogeneity of the region, which may correspond with the presence of different areas according to the DEGURBA classification, as we explore below.

These findings, while highlighting numerous economic and social challenges that lie ahead, at the same time provide some guidelines on which educational policies and practices should be addressed by policymakers to reduce geographic differences in EP. The ability to further disaggregate the results using a more detailed geographic classification, namely using the DEGURBA regional classification as in Pratesi et al. (2020), is useful from a policy perspective. However, when this classification is used, the small sample size in some areas suggests the need to use small area estimation techniques, as done by Pratesi et al. (2020) in estimating the EPI index defined by Istat. Accordingly, the results obtained here using the DEGURBA

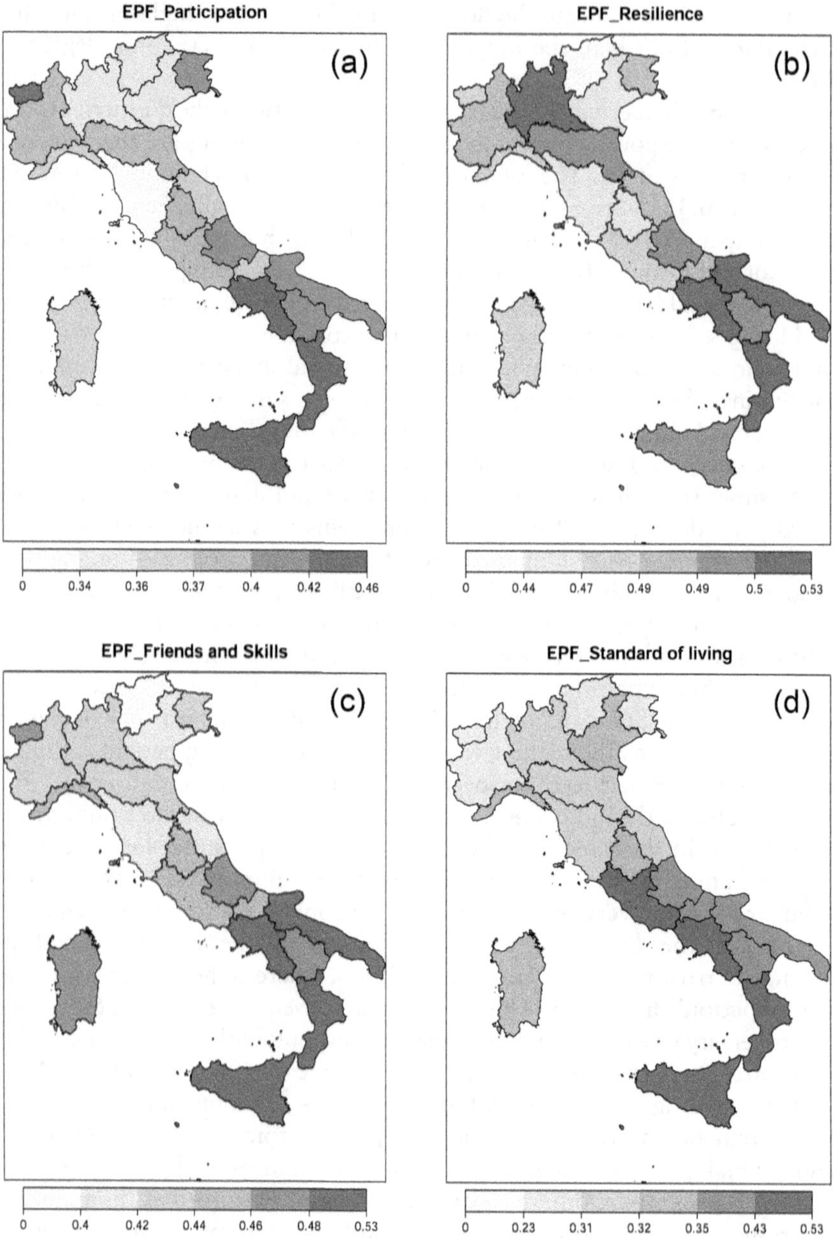

Figure 11.3 Degree of EP at the regional level in the four EPFI dimensions.

regional classification for EPFI should be interpreted as an example of the utility of a disaggregated analysis in studying EP.

The map in Figure 11.5 summarises the EPFI using the DEGURBA by regional classification. Figure 11.4 is a useful tool for representing the DEGURBA classification of Italy: cities are in dark grey, towns and suburbs in an intermediate shade of grey, and rural areas are in light grey. The regional boundaries are indicated by thick black lines.

Although some regions have no differences in EPFI values among the DEGURBA areas (e.g. in almost all southern regions), some of them, especially Emilia-Romagna, Lombardy, Marche and Friuli Venezia Giulia, have different gradations in colour, suggesting that EP varies across these areas. For instance, in Emilia-Romagna the results suggest that EP is more salient in rural areas than in the cities, and a similar conclusion can be reached about Marche.

Figure 11.4 DEGURBA regional classification of Italy: cities (dark grey), towns and suburbs (intermediate shade of grey), and rural areas (light grey). The thick black lines indicate regional boundaries.

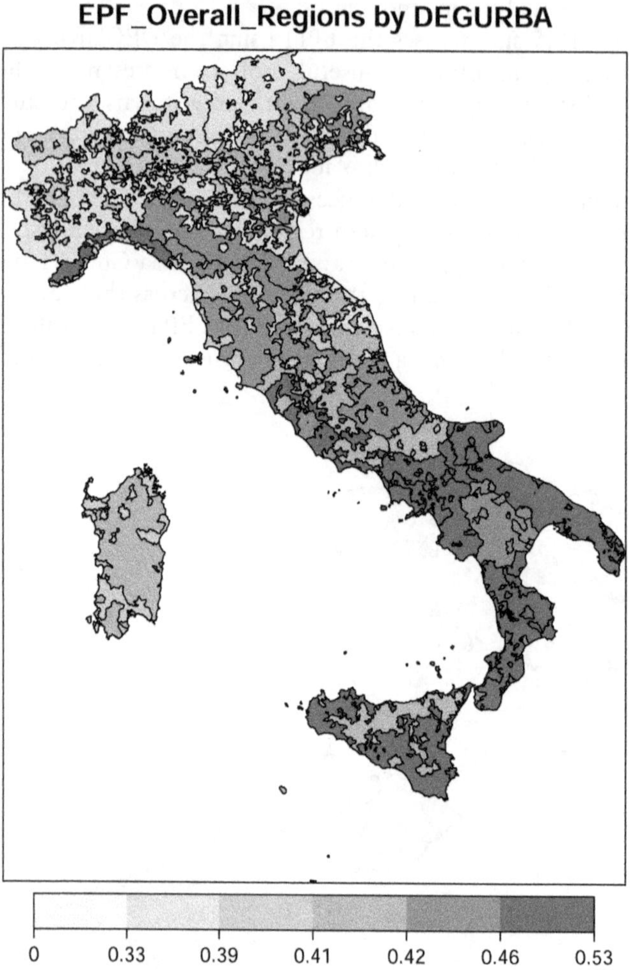

Figure 11.5 EPFI using the DEGURBA regional classification.

Some Final Remarks

In this chapter, we measure EP in Italy from a comparative perspective. First across regions and then using the DEGURBA regional classification.

We introduce a new approach for measuring EP. Indeed, we diverge from the common definition of EP as a level of education which falls below a threshold considered the minimum in a given society (Checchi, 1998; Allmendinger, 1999). In contrast, we treat EP as a multi-dimensional phenomenon composed of different dimensions, which are not directly measurable and are characterised by different degrees of intensity. That is, EP is a fuzzy measure.

For this reason, our approach also diverges from the approach used by Pratesi et al. (2020): although we use the same multi-dimensional definition of EP and the same dataset, this chapter uses a completely different methodological approach.

We computed a fuzzy index (EPFI) and 4D-specific fuzzy indices on the sample represented by individuals aged 15–29 using micro-data from the survey 'Aspects of Everyday Life' (AVQ) (Istat, 2019). Each indicator takes a value in the range [0,1], with 1 indicating the maximum degree of EP, and 0 the lowest.

Despite some limitations in the data, related to the impossibility of covering all items used by Istat (Quattrociocchi, 2018), the AVQ survey has many useful items for measuring EP in Italy. Thus, we use it to analyse EP in a multi-dimensional framework using only one source of micro-data. This is particularly important in the Italian case, where the lack of surveys on children and adolescents highly limits our ability to conduct a deep analysis on EP in a multi-dimensional framework using micro-data. Therefore, our analysis also aims to reflect the need for a useful cross-national survey to measure and monitor EP in its multi-dimensional shape. This national survey could be especially important for policymakers and practitioners and should be used to design more precise social policies. The results presented here reflect the fact that the regions and the DEGURBA areas have different degrees of EP and that even single dimensions show different levels of intensity in the same area.

From the policymaking perspective, the results of our analysis demonstrate the actual consistency and dimensions of EP at a useful local level, which in turn, suggest, for example, a revision of local governments' normal policies employed to reverse EP.

From a methodological point of view, taking a fuzzy perspective on EP attains particular significance in our multi-dimensional approach. Indeed, it overcomes the issue of transforming each single indicator used in the analysis into a simple dichotomous variable to indicate the percentage of people who are deprived with respect to each specific aspect, as implied by the approach taken by Mazziotta-Pareto (2018). In summary, the fuzzy approach preserves the richness of the original data and includes a concept of vagueness and a measurement of relative poverty; thus, it is very useful for describing the multi-faceted nature of EP.

Our approach is not intended to replace the one proposed by Quattrociocchi (2018), which uses the Mazziotta-Pareto aggregation, but aims to enrich the existing information on EP. In fact, whereas the Istat EPI index gives the distribution of EP in each area compared with the national average, our proposed fuzzy index, EPFI, provides information about the intensity of EP in each area. Our analysis has three main limitations. First, although school results by themselves do not describe the concept of EP – which is more complex and related to the individual growth – it is also true that individual skills and abilities can be considered separate potential items in the definition of EP dimensions. As this was not possible in this study, it is an interesting development to be explored in future work.

Second, our analysis does not provide standard errors of the calculated fuzzy measures. Although it is good practice to do so, this procedure requires information on the primary sampling units, rotational groups and strata, which are not available in the user database of the AVQ survey. Last, it would be useful to investigate the four EP dimensions defined by Istat and used in this chapter in order to explore other possible multi-dimensional definitions of EP under a fuzzy approach.

Notes

1 Acknowledgment: The work of Bertarelli, Giusti and Pratesi has been carried out with the support of the Project InGRID-2, European Project G.A. No. 730998.
2 The information on literacy and quantitative skills can be inferred by using the Programme for the International Assessment of Adult Competences (PIAAC) survey. But the use of this information at the micro-level implies previous probabilistic linkage between the AVQ and PIAAC surveys.
3 The full list of the items is available from the authors upon request.
4 Because some of the items have missing values, the final analysis consists of 80% of the initial sample of those aged 15–29.

References

Aassve A., Betti G., Mazzuco S., Mencarini L. (2007), Marital disruption and economic well-being: A comparative analysis, *Journal of the Royal Statistical Society Series A (Statistics in Society)*, 170(3): 781–799.

Agasisti T., Longobardi S., Prete V., Russo F. (2020, in press), The growing incidence of educational poverty in Europe: Measurement and policy implications, *Journal of Policy Modeling*.

Allmendinger J. (1999), Bildungsarmut: Zur verschrankung von bildungs-und sozialpolitik, *Soziale Welt*, 50(1): 35–50.

Allmendinger J., Leibfried, S. (2003), Education and the welfare state: The four worlds of competence production, *Journal of European Social Policy*, 13(1): 63–81.

Betti G., Cheli B., Lemmi A., Verma V. (2006), Multidimensional and longitudinal poverty: An integrated fuzzy approach. In: Lemmi A., Betti G. (eds.), *Fuzzy Set Approach to Multidimensional Poverty Measurement*. New York: Springer, pp. 111–137.

Betti G., D'Agostino A., Gagliardi F., Giusti C. (2020), The integrated fuzzy and relative index for poverty analysis: A review of applications in the social sciences, *Studies of Applied Economics – Estudios de Economía Aplicada*, 38(1), pp. 1–14.

Betti G., D'Agostino A., Neri L. (2011), Educational mismatch of graduates: A multidimensional and fuzzy indicator, *Social Indicators Research*, 103(3): 465–480.

Betti G., Lemmi A. eds. (2013), *Poverty and Social Exclusion: New Methods of Analysis*. London: Routledge.

Betti G., Soldi R., Talev I. (2016), Fuzzy multidimensional indicators of quality of life: The empirical case of Macedonia, *Social Indicators Research*, 127(1): 39–53.

Brandolini A., D'Alessio G. (1998), *Measuring Well-Being in the Functioning Space*. Rome: Banca D'Italia.

Checchi D. (1998), Povertà ed istruzione: Alcune riflessioni ed una proposta di indicatori, *Politica Economica*, 12(2): 245–282.

D'Agostino A., Gagliardi F., Giusti C., Potsi A. (2019), Investigating the impact of the economic crisis on children's wellbeing in four European countries, *Social Science Research*, 84: 1–15.

ISTAT (2019), *Aspects of Daily Life Survey*. https://www.istat.it/en/archive/129959/, accessed 24 January 2020.

Larysa M., Felice R. (2016), La misurazione multidimensionale della povertà in istruzione in Italia [Multidimensional measurement of educational poverty in Italy], *Politica Economica*, 1: 65–122.

Lohmann H., Ferger F. (2015), *Educational Poverty in a Comparative Perspective: Theoretical and Empirical Implications*, University of Bielefeld (SFB 882).

Mazziotta M., Pareto A. (2016), On a generalized non-compensatory composite index for measuring socio-economic phenomena, *Social Indicators Research*, 127(3): 983–1003.

Mazziotta, M., Pareto, A. (2018), Measuring well-being over time: The adjusted mazziotta-pareto index versus other non-compensatory indices, *Social Indicators Research*, 136(3): 967–976.

Pratesi M., Quattrociocchi L., Bertarelli G., Gemignani A., Giusti C. (2020), Spatial distribution of multidimensional educational poverty in Italy using small area estimation, *Social Indicators Research*. https://doi.org/10.1007/s11205-020-02328-5

Quattrociocchi L. (2018), *Povertà educativa: (non) finirai come tuo padre., Popolazione, istruzione, mobilità: Giornata di studio in collaborazione tra AISP, SIS, Istat e SIEDS*. https://www.slideshare.net/slideistat/lquattrociocchi-d-irezione-centrale-per-le-statistiche-sociali-e-il-censimento-della-popolazione-i-stat-povert-educativa?qid=31d4673e-0e44-45a6-a650-f1b0aa76b993&v=&b=&from_search=4/

Save The Children (2018), *Nuotare contro corrente. Povertà educativa e resilienza in Italia*. https://www.savethechildren.it/cosa-facciamo/pubblicazioni/nuotare-contro-corrente-povertà-educativa-e-resilienza-italia/

Watkins K. (2000), *The Oxfam Education Report*. Oxfam. GB.

Zadeh L.A. (1965), Fuzzy sets, *Information and Control*, 8: 338–353.

12 Fuzzy and Multi-Dimensional Measures of the Degree of Social Exclusion Risk

Evidence of Social Exclusion of the Population Aged 50+ in Poland

Tomasz Panek and Jan Zwierzchowski

Introduction

Social exclusion is a subject that attracts great interest in the social, economic and political sciences. As a concept, social exclusion is complex and multi-faceted and can be defined in various ways. It is generally understood as a process in which individuals or social groups are hindered from full participation in substantial areas of the social, cultural, economic and political life of the society in which they live (Silver, 1994, 1995). This non-participation is a result of factors that are outside individual control. The various dimensions of social exclusion often reinforce one another and consequently lead to even deeper marginalisation of individuals. Based on a comprehensive literature review, Levitas (2006) adopted the following definition of social exclusion:

> "Social exclusion is a complex and multi-dimensional process. It involves the lack or denial of resources, rights, goods and services, and the inability to participate in the normal relationships and activities, available to the majority of people in a society, whether in economic, social, cultural or political arenas. It affects both the quality of life of individuals and the equity and cohesion of society as a whole."

Social exclusion has a negative impact on the quality of human capital, limits activity, entrepreneurship and innovation and generates higher cost for the state. Hence, the goal of inclusive social policies is to counteract the threat of social exclusion. Combating social exclusion is one of the main objects of the social policy by the European Union (EU) and its member states (Maastricht Treaty). In 1989, the European Council and EU social affairs ministers adopted a resolution for combating social exclusion that outlines the different forms and shapes of social exclusion and declares it a major problem for many social groups (Commission of the European Communities, 1990). That same year, the Treaty of Amsterdam was adopted, which listed 'combating social exclusion' as one of the EU Community's objectives. A reduction in poverty and social exclusion are fundamental parts of the Lisbon Strategy. In 2010 the Council of Europe enacted policies aimed at achieving the five major goals in the Europe 2020 Strategy – one of which is to promote social inclusion (Copeland and Daly, 2012).

Because of the progressive ageing of European society, the fight against the social exclusion of older people has become an increasing challenge in EU member countries. In order to develop an environment in which people can live well into old age, we need to monitor the threat of social exclusion among the elderly and explore the factors which determine it. The main objective of this chapter is to construct a tool to help realise these goals. We propose a new methodology to measure the degree of social exclusion risk using a fuzzy multi-dimensional approach.

Social Exclusion as Capability Deprivation

The capability approach was developed and refined by Amartya Sen, after his Tanner lecture in 1979 (Sen, 1980), to describe how the well-being of an individual should be measured (Sen, 1982, 1985, 1987, 1999, 2000, 2010). It has been synthesised and applied practically by various authors in a variety of fields (Alkire, 2002; Robeyns, 2003, 2005; Kuklys, 2005; Comim, Qizilbash and Alkire, 2008; Schokkaert, 2009; Basu and López-Calva, 2011; Schlosberg, 2012; Lorgelly et al., 2015; Slabbert, 2018). This concept is based on the assumption that commodities are not crucial for achieving a high quality of life. Rather, it is their properties that enable the achievement of the desired lifestyle by individuals. Not all capabilities are generated from goods or services (Robeyns, 2005). For example, being a respected member of a community only requires the respectful behaviour of other community members. According to Nussbaum and Sen (1992, p. 27) a person's capability to live a good life can be defined:

> "in terms of the capability to achieve valuable functionings ... where functionings represent parts of the state of a person – in particular the various things that he or she manages to do or be in leading a life. Capability reflects the alternative combinations of functionings the person can achieve, and from which he or she can choose one collection."

In other words, capabilities refer to effective potential for realising goals and fulfilling expectations, whereas functioning, which represents the 'beings and doings' of a person, refer to realised goals and fulfilled expectations.

Figure 12.1 illustrates the relationship between commodities, capabilities and functioning, using the key concepts of the capability approach.

We use three sets of conversion factors – personal, social and environmental – to transform commodities into capabilities (Sen, 1992; Robeyns, 2005): personal conversion factors (personal characteristics, e.g. metabolism,

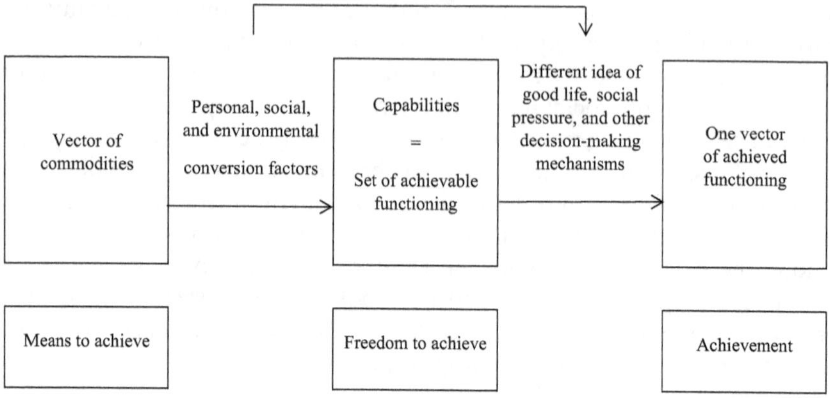

Figure 12.1 Relationship between commodities, capabilities and functioning in the capability approach. *Source*: Adapted from Robeyns (2005).

physical condition, intelligence and gender), which influence the type and degree of capabilities that a person can create with commodities; social conversion factors from the society in which one lives (the characteristics of social settings, social institutions and power structures, e.g. social norms, public policies, social hierarchies, rule of law, political rights); and environmental conversion factors from the physical or built environment in which a person lives (environmental characteristics, e.g. climate, infrastructure, institutions and public goods). The functioning achieved is the result of personal choices in selecting from among the capabilities available and subject to personal preferences, social pressure and other decision-making mechanisms. Moreover, they are constrained by personal, social and environmental characteristics (Robeyns, 2005; Crocker, 2008).

In the context of analysing inequality, people must have equal opportunity to function in the way they prefer (Sen, 1982). Only then are they free to determine their capabilities, i.e. potential ways of functioning, and to maximise their quality of life in accordance with them. Moreover, the effective freedom 'to be and to do' is essential for assessing capabilities.

In Sen's capability approach, social exclusion can be understood as the inability to achieve preferred functioning (Sen, 2000). A limited choice of capabilities can lead to deprivation and, *in extremis*, social exclusion. Thus, the *process* of social exclusion leads to a *state* of social exclusion, which can be interpreted as the deprivation of some important functioning (Poggi, 2007).

Operationalisation of the Measurement of Social Exclusion Risk in the Capabilities Approach

Despite several important advances concerning the measurement of social exclusion (e.g. Chakravarty and D'Ambrosio, 2006), there is still ongoing debate about the best analytical approach for understanding its nature and effects. The main unifying theme in the literature is that social exclusion is a multi-dimensional phenomenon.

The multi-dimensional evaluation of social exclusion under the capability approach requires consideration of several different dimensions corresponding to the relevant parts of life. Moreover, measuring social exclusion requires the determination of the social exclusion indicators in each dimension (basic indicators), the aggregation of basic indicators within dimensions, and finally the aggregation of dimension indicators into a proxy indicator for overall social exclusion. The choice of domains and basic indicators depends on both the natural complexity underlying the concept of social exclusion (criterion of reference validity) and the potential for its application in empirical assessments (criterion of usefulness).

Sen (2010, p. 148) advocated measuring latent capability, which reflects the scope of freedom, rather than observed functioning, for the purpose of assessing the quality of life. The idea is that policymakers should not attempt to design and constrain people's lives in order to optimise the value of abstract indices. They should strive to provide the population with a broad set of potential standards of living from which to choose and leave the optimisation process to individuals.

Following Sen's concept of freedom, we propose to assess social exclusion by estimating values (scores) corresponding to their latent capabilities, rather than focusing solely on observable indicators. In this way, we allow individuals to demonstrate their latent capabilities through various observable phenomena in different local settings. Therefore, we take into account the differences in individual resources, potential and preferences, as well as cultural diversity between EU member countries. That enables us to conduct a comparative empirical analysis.

In order to measure social exclusion within the framework of the capabilities approach, we apply a multi-indicator and multiple causes model (MIMIC), which is a particular version of the structural equation model (SEM) (Bollen, 1989; Brown and Moore, 2012). The MIMIC model was formulated by Hauser and Goldberger (1971) and then popularised by Jöreskog and Goldberger (1975), who presented its detailed assumptions as a special version of the SEM. Krishnakumor and Ballon (2008) considered the SEM approach the most suitable tool for estimating latent capabilities. This model allows an explanation of an individual's deprivation status and not only describe it but also assesses the impact of external determinants (individual personal, social and environmental characteristics) on latent capabilities.

The measurement of social exclusion under a MIMIC model is as follows (Krishnakumar, 2007; Krishnakumor and Ballon, 2008). The freedom of individual choice in each capability domain is represented by an unobservable latent indicator, which can be estimated based on two sets of observable indicators. First, the reflective part of the model is constructed using a set of selected basic indicators of social exclusion (signs of social exclusion). These variables can be interpreted as achieved functioning, which potentially reflects capability deprivation. The formative part of the model is constructed based on individual personal, social and environmental exogenous characteristics, which are interpreted as conversion factors that strengthen or weaken capabilities and influence the transformation of available resources into achieved functioning.

The starting point for building the MIMIC model is to define social exclusion domains as well as corresponding signs and determinants. We begin our analysis of social exclusion using the MIMIC model by defining the relationships between unobservable indicators (capabilities) and observable indicators (signs and determinants of social exclusion). The model of these relationships is presented in the form of a path diagram in Figure 12.2.

Formally, the MIMIC model equations take the following form:

$$y_k = \Lambda_{y_k} \eta_k + \varepsilon_k, \tag{12.1}$$

$$\eta_k = \Gamma_k x_k + \zeta_k \tag{12.2}$$

where

y_k is a vector of observable endogenous indicators representing the signs of social exclusion in the *k*th domain;

η_k is a vector of latent endogenous indicators representing latent capabilities in the *k*th domain;

Λ_{y_k} is a vector of factor loadings of endogenous indicators inserted into the measurement equations, i.e. relationships between observable signs of social exclusion and latent capabilities in the *k*th domain;

ε_k is a vector of random errors in the *k*th domain;

Γ_k is a vector of the coefficients of latent capabilities related to observable signs of social exclusion in the *k*th domain, defining the pattern of structural relations;

x_k is a vector of observable exogenous structural indicators representing the personal, social and environmental determinants of capabilities in the *k*th domain; and

ζ_k is a vector of random errors representing unknown omitted signs of social exclusion in the *k*th domain.

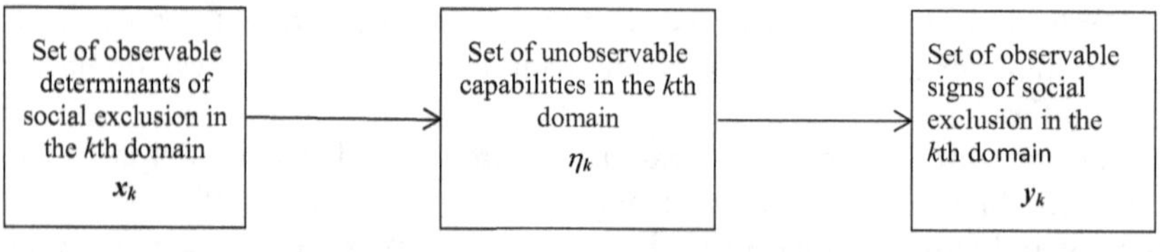

Figure 12.2 MIMIC model of individual domains of social exclusion using the capability approach

The first system of equations forms the measurement model (12.1). It describes the relationships between unobservable capabilities and their observable indicators (signs). The second system of equations describes the structural sub-model (12.2), which determines the impact of observable individual personal, social and environmental characteristics in the formation of unobservable capabilities.

The main purpose of the MIMIC analysis is an estimation of the value of latent capabilities at the individual level, which will be used in further empirical analysis as proxies for the estimation of the DSER. However, the model also allows us to assess the adequacy of the postulated theoretical model, which links the observable exogenous causes and endogenous indicators of social exclusion through latent, unobservable capabilities.

In the next step, we aggregate the resulting estimated latent capabilities into a single indicator representing overall social exclusion using classical factor analysis.

Construction of Indicators of the DSER Using a Fuzzy-Set Approach

Fuzzy-set theory (Zadeh, 1965) was used in the context of social exclusion by Cerioli and Zani (1990), who proposed the construction of indicators of the degree of poverty with survey data. That approach was further developed in a number of applications (Lemmi and Betti, 2006; Betti and Lemmi, 2013). It avoids a simplifying division of the population into groups based on whether people are socially excluded in relation to a particular threshold value. Using fuzzy-set theory, social exclusion is defined as a matter of degree of membership in the sub-set of those who are socially excluded. In addition to those who are or are not socially excluded, a set of those who feel at risk of social exclusion with varying levels of risk can be identified.

We transform both the estimated values of latent capabilities deprivation for each domain of social exclusion and the overall aggregated score of social exclusion using fuzzy-set theory.

Recent studies are dominated by a relative approach, in which all people are characterised by the degree to which one is a member of the relevant set in the range (0,1). The major drawback of this approach is that it makes assessment of the DSER totally dependent on the degree of inequality in the distribution of the exclusion risk indicator, not by the actual DSER. To avoid this shortcoming, we define the membership function using the fuzzy and absolute (FA) multi-dimensional approach (Cerioli and Zani, 1990; Panek, 2006, 2011). This approach is feasible for estimating the DSER, as the threshold values of the membership function can be defined in a natural way, because we treat individuals with the lowest values of all those signs as not being socially and those with the highest values as socially excluded.

We define the function of membership in a group of those who are socially excluded in the *k*th dimension for the *i*th individual as follows:

$$f(x_{ki}) = \begin{cases} 0 & for\, x_i \leq x_k^* \\ \dfrac{x_i - x_k^*}{x_k^{**} - x_k^*} & for\, x_k^* < x_i < x_k^{**} \\ 1 & for\, x_i \geq x_k^{**} \end{cases} \tag{12.3}$$

where:

x_{ki} is the DSER indicator's empirical value for the *i*th individual and *k*th domain;
x_k^* is the DSER indicator's lower threshold value in the *k*th domain; and
x_k^{**} is the DSER indicator's upper threshold value in the *k*th domain.

In the proposed approach, established normative thresholds x^* and x^{**} are used to determine whether people are experiencing social exclusion. Those whose value of membership functions is below the lower threshold are not considered socially excluded. Similarly, those whose value of membership functions is above the upper threshold are considered socially excluded. However, when the empirical value of the membership function is between the threshold values, the DSER is proportional to the relative distance of the indicator's value to the lower threshold.

For each domain, the lower threshold value x^* was calculated using the distribution of estimated values of the membership function among those who were not socially excluded based on the observed signs of exclusion. The 90th percentile of this distribution was adopted as the minimum threshold. The maximum threshold value x^{**} was defined in a similar way; however, this time we considered only individuals who were socially excluded based on the empirical basic indicators of social exclusion in any given domain. In this distribution, the threshold value was the 10th percentile.

This solution was adopted to provide the method with a certain degree of robustness to outliers in the data. The estimated values of the relevant social exclusion risk indicators are dependent not only on the signs of exclusion but also on the determinants of social exclusion. Among individuals who are socially excluded based on all the basic signs, the lowest values of the membership function are estimated for those who have the most favourable value of social exclusion determinants. In some extreme cases, the value of the membership function may be lower than it is for people who have no signs of exclusion but have an unfavourable value of social exclusion determinants.

In the final step, the values of the membership function with respect to the aggregated, overall social exclusion were calculated using the following equation:

$$f(x_{ki}) = \begin{cases} 0 & for\, x_i \le x^* \\ \dfrac{x_i - x^*}{x^{**} - x^*} & for\, x^* < x_i < x^{**} \\ 1 & for\, x_i \ge x^{**} \end{cases} \qquad (12.4)$$

where
x_i is the empirical value of the DSER indicator for the *i*th individual;
x^* is the lower threshold value of the DSER indicator; and
x^{**} is the upper threshold value of the DSER indicator.

The lower and upper threshold levels x^* and x^{**} are defined as estimated latent factor values for people whose calculated DSER in all five domains was considered to be 0 and 1, respectively. In this way, only these people in each domain are and are not considered socially excluded, respectively. All the others are characterised by a varying level of the DSER, represented by a value in the range (0,1), where higher values represent a higher DSER.

Comparative Analysis of the DSER for the Population Aged 50+ in Selected European Countries in 2017

Data Source

The empirical analyses in this chapter are based on data from the Survey of Health Aging and Retirement in Europe (SHARE)[1], containing international research on the European population aged 50 and over (Malter and Börsch-Supan, 2017). The eighth wave of this panel study was performed in 2017, with detailed interviews conducted with randomly drawn people aged 50 and over as well as their partners, regardless of age (Bethmann, Bergmann and Scherpenzeel, 2019). The results obtained are generalised with appropriate weighting at the national level (De Luca and Rosetti, 2018; Bethmann, Bergmann and Scherpenzeel, 2019).

The main unit of analysis was a person (the respondents or their partners). In situations where partial indicators (signs of social exclusion) apply not to persons but their households, people were assigned the value of an indicator that applied to their household.

Scope and Assumptions of the Analysis

The assessment of the DSER for Poland was carried out by voivodship. The analysis of the DSER considered the following domains of social exclusion: material conditions, economic and social activity, health and education. In addition, the DSER for all domains together was assessed. The list of domains in the analysis came from the range of data available in the SHARE study. To measure the DSER, the signs of exclusion were determined for individual areas (partial indicators, Table 12.4). All signs of social exclusion were defined as drivers: the higher the value of any given indicator, the higher the degree of exclusion. Moreover, the selected determinants of social exclusion are presented in Table 12.5 in the Appendix.

The income category used in the study was the average monthly net equivalent income in 2017. The net equivalent income was calculated by dividing disposable household income with the scale of OECD (Organisation for Economic Co-operation and Development)-modified equivalents.

Estimation of the MIMIC Model

For each domain, a MIMIC model was constructed, and its parameters were estimated. The parameters for measuring the sub-model were estimated using the maximum likelihood method with missing values using Stata 15. We began the construction of each model by defining all the signs of social exclusion for a given domain. Then, we added possible determinants one at a time, controlling for the statistical significance of the estimated parameters and overall model fit. Table 12.1 presents the estimated results and the composition of the final models.

The model fit was assessed using three measures (Hu and Bentler, 1999): NNFI, CFI and RMSEA. The NNFI and CFI measures have values in the range [0,1], where higher values indicate better fit, and values of at least 0.95 demonstrated very good fit. By contrast, for RMSEA, the lower the value, the better the model fit; values below 0.08 show an acceptable model fit.

In all the models, RMSEA and CFI met the required criteria (Table 12.6 in the Appendix). Given the complexity of the model and the richness of the underlined theoretical concepts, the models show an overall good fit.

Finally, the classical factor analysis model was proposed. It aggregates the values of the estimated group indicators of the DSER, which resulted from the five MIMIC models for each dimension of social exclusion. The purpose of the factor analysis is not only to assess the degree of overall social exclusion risk but also to determine how much each single dimension accounts for, i.e. the weight of each social exclusion domain as a share of the overall social exclusion risk determination. The models used to measure the degree of the risk of social exclusion in each domain and for all the domains are illustrated in Table 12.1.

DSER of the Population Aged 50+

The estimated DSER for every individual takes a value in the range [0,1], where 0 indicates no risk of social exclusion and 1 indicates a person who is socially excluded. These estimated values for individuals were aggregated for countries using appropriate survey weights. Therefore, values for countries should be interpreted as the average degree of risk of social exclusion in any given area for individuals aged 50 and over.

Table 12.1 MIMIC model for social exclusion domains

Dimension	*Variable*	*Coefficient*	*Std. Err.*	*z*	**P > z**	*95% Confidence Interval*	
Material conditions							
Structural part	Economic activity status	–0.051	0.010	–5.33	0	–0.070	–0.032
	Health self-assessment	0.161	0.013	12.55	0	0.136	0.186
	Place of residence	0.085	0.010	8.3	0	0.065	0.105
	Sex	0.028	0.009	3.1	0.002	0.010	0.046
Measurement part	Monetary poverty						
	Material conditions	1.000 (constrained)					
	Constant	0.085	0.018	4.79	0	0.050	0.120
	Material deprivation						
	Material conditions	0.749	0.054	13.82	0	0.643	0.855
	Constant	0.005	0.015	0.36	0.72	–0.024	0.034
	Income self-assessment						
	Material conditions	1.310	0.090	14.62	0	1.134	1.485
	Constant	0.357	0.013	26.51	0	0.331	0.384
Health							
Structural part	Age	0.231	0.012	19.99	0	0.208	**0.253**
	Education	–0.105	0.015	–7.16	0	–0.134	–0.076
	Sex	0.013	0.010	1.27	0.205	–0.007	0.034
Measurement part	Health self-assessment						
	Health	1.000 (constrained)					
	Constant	0.390	0.014	28.6	0	0.363	0.417
	Health limitations						
	Health	1.269	0.029	44.22	0	1.213	1.326
	Constant	0.310	0.015	20.4	0	0.280	0.340
	Long-term health problems						
	Health	0.970	0.023	42.61	0	0.925	1.014
	Constant	0.337	0.014	24.48	0	0.310	0.364

(*Continued*)

Table 12.1 Continued

Dimension	*Variable*	*Coefficient*	*Std. Err.*	*z*	*P > z*	*95% Confidence Interval*	
Education							
Structural part	Age	0.146	0.022	6.49	0	0.102	0.190
	Family's financial situation	0.025	0.014	1.75	0.08	–0.003	0.052
	Father's education	–0.188	0.052	–3.61	0	–0.290	–0.086
	Number of books at home	–0.259	0.020	–12.94	0	–0.298	–0.219
	Place of residence	0.100	0.015	6.85	0	0.071	0.128
	Sex	0.051	0.012	4.12	0	0.027	0.075
Measurement part	Educational attainment						
	Education	1 (constrained)					
	Constant	–0.137	0.027	–4.97	0	–0.190	–0.083
	Lifelong learning						
	Education	0.483	0.027	17.59	0	0.429	0.537
	Constant	0.097	0.017	5.7S	O	0.064	0.130
Economic and social activity							
Structural part	Age	–0.026	0.004		0	–0.034	–0.017
	Education	–0.071	0.009		0	–0.089	–0.053
	Health limitations	–0.033	0.005		0	–0.043	–0.023
	Health self-assessment	0.037	0.006		0	0.025	0.048
Measurement part	Voluntary activity						
	Economic and social activity	1 (constrained)					
	Constant	0.197	0.009	22.97	0	0.180	0.214
	Political Activity						
	Economic and social activity	0.934	0.204	4.58	0	0.535	1.333
	Constant	–0.050	0.017	–2.99	0.003	–0.083	–0.017
	Clubs activity						
	Economic and social activity	1.142	0.142	8.03	0	0.863	1.421
	Constant	0.348	0.009	39.45	0	0.331	0.365
	Economic activity						
	Economic and social activity	3.273	0.403	8.11	0	2.483	4.064
	Constant	–0.114	0.017	–6.69	0	–0.148	–0.081

Source: Author's analysis based on SHARE data.

Material Living Conditions

In 2017, in the voivodships, the DSER in the domain of material living conditions was the lowest among all the domains of social exclusion. The highest DSER in this area by far is observed in Lubelskie (Table 12.2), followed by Podkarpackie and Opolskie (the function of the degree of membership in the group of those excluded had a value of 0.460, 0.438 and

Table 12.2 DSER of the population aged 50+ in Poland by voivodship in 2017

Voivodships	*Values of the function of belonging to the socially excluded set*				
	overall social exclusion	*material living conditions*	*economic activity and social*	*health*	*education*
Łódzkie	0.631 (0.014)	0.317 (0.021)	0.739 (0.013)	0.495 (0.032)	0.745 (0.015)
Mazowieckie	0.636 (0.012)	0.384 (0.020)	0.725 (0.010)	0.479 (0.029)	0.745 (0.011)
Małopolskie	0.647 (0.019)	0.400 (0.032)	0.742 (0.015)	0.496 (0.042)	0.742 (0.017)
Śląskie	0.593 (0.011)	0.274 (0.020)	0.718 (0.011)	0.441 (0.028)	0.694 (0.011)
Lubelskie	0.677 (0.015)	0.460 (0.024)	0.766 (0.015)	0.522 (0.035)	0.762 (0.015)
Podkarpackie	0.672 (0.014)	0.438 (0.027)	0.744 (0.013)	0.429 (0.039)	0.831 (0.013)
Świę tokrzys kie	0.660 (0.015)	0.377 (0.026)	0.754 (0.013)	0.514 (0.036)	0.778 (0.017)
Podlaskie	0.623 (0.019)	0.315 (0.030)	0.722 (0.019)	0.399 (0.041)	0.783 (0.019)
Wielkopolskie	0.636 (0.013)	0.320 (0.022)	0.749 (0.011)	0.486 (0.032)	0.751 (0.013)
Zachodniopomorskie	0.613 (0.015)	0.294 (0.024)	0.737 (0.013)	0.489 (0.032)	0.703 (0.016)
Lubuskie	0.618 (0.016)	0.306 (0.028)	0.73 (0.016)	0.481 (0.038)	0.726 (0.015)
Dolnośląskie	0.618 (0.013)	0.299 (0.022)	0.739 (0.012)	0.474 (0.032)	0.720 (0.013)
Opolskie	0.657 (0.024)	0.422 (0.037)	0.739 (0.020)	0.470 (0.055)	0.777 (0.022)
Kujaws ko-pomorskie	0.631 (0.020)	0.361 (0.030)	0.734 (0.017)	0.496 (0.041)	0.724 (0.019)
Warmińs ko-mazurskie	0.605 (0.016)	0.344 (0.026)	0.696 (0.015)	0.398 (0.038)	0.739 (0.016)
Pomorskie	0.602 (0.016)	0.328 (0.026)	0.705 (0.015)	0.443 (0.037)	0.708 (0.019)
Poland	0.628 (0.004)	0.341 (0.006)	0.732 (0.003)	0.471 (0.009)	0.739 (0.004)

Source: Author's analysis based on SHARE data.

0.422, respectively) and the lowest was in Śląskie, Zachodniopomorskie and Dolnośląskie (average value of the membership function equals 0.274, 0.294 and 0.299, respectively).

Economic and Social Activity

In 2017 the DSER by voivodship was higher in economic and social activity than in other areas of social exclusion. These relatively high values reflect the fact that the majority of people in the population aged 50 and over are retired or economically inactive for other reasons. The DSER was the highest in Lubelskie and Świętokrzyskie (with a membership function value of 0.766 and 0.754, respectively) and the lowest in Warmińsko-Mazurskie and Pomorskie (value of the membership function of 0.696 and 0.705, respectively).

Health

The variations between the voivodships in the area of health were relatively high in 2017. Lubelskie and Świętokrzyskie (0.522 and 0.514, respectively) had the highest value of the function of membership in the group of those who are socially excluded. The degree of exclusion risk was the lowest in Warmińsko-Mazurskie and Podlaskie (the membership function was 0.398 and 0.399, respectively).

Education

Differences between voivodships were relatively high regarding exclusion in the domain of education as well as health. Opolskie is the most affected voivodship by the degree of social exclusion risk in this domain in 2017 (average value of the function of membership in the socially excluded group of 0.055). The DSER in this area was the lowest in Śląskie and Mazowieckie (average value of the membership function of 0.028 and 0.029, respectively).

Overall Social Exclusion

Lubelskie, Podkarpackie and Świętokrzyskie have the highest DSER for the population aged 50 and over in 2017. The membership function had a value of 0.721, 0.708 and 0.708, respectively. The lowest DSER was in Warmińsko-Mazurskie, Pomorskie and Śląskie (with an average membership function value of 0.651 and 0.656, respectively).

Symptoms and Determinants of Social Exclusion

Material Living Conditions

The DSER in the domain of material conditions (latent variable) is most strongly reflected by changes in the self-assessment of the household's income situation by the respondent, followed by changes in monetary poverty.

A low level of health self-assessment had the strongest impact on the increasing DSER in the area of material conditions. Moreover, the DSER is significantly higher for individuals living in rural areas and in small towns. In addition, reduction of this risk is influenced by people who worked in the previous week.

Economic and Social Activity

The increase in the DSER in the domain of economic and social activity is accompanied primarily by a decrease in economic activity. At the same time, the decrease in the degree of this risk is significantly and positively reflected by club activity, voluntary activity and political activity. The DSER in this domain increases significantly with a low level of education and of health self-assessment.

Health

The DSER in the area of health is most strongly reflected in the occurrence of health problems that limit paid work and health self-assessment, and the least, although significantly, by health self-assessment and by long-term or chronic health problems. The degree of exclusion risk in the health domain is significantly influenced by age. This degree of risk is also statistically significantly higher for persons with lower educational attainment.

Education

The increase in the DSER in the domain of education is accompanied by low educational attainment and, to a lesser extent, by non-participation in education. The reduction in the degree of exclusion risk in the area of education is mainly affected by having a large home library in childhood and by the father's level of higher education. At the same time, the factors that give rise to the DSER in this domain are an increase in the age of the person, being a woman and living in rural areas or small towns.

Overall Social Exclusion

The overall DSER was estimated by aggregating the values of four social exclusion domains using classical factor analysis (Table 12.3). The first factor explained over 60% of the common variance of the five dimensions of the DSER. Therefore, social exclusion risk proved to be rather unidimensional.

Factor loadings for the first factor were the highest in economic and social activity. All factor loadings were higher than 0.7, meaning that overall social exclusion represented by the first factor is highly correlated with common variance of all four dimensions. Moreover, economic and social activity have the lowest uniqueness. The uniqueness of the remaining three dimensions equalled almost 50%, meaning that almost half the variation in these domains is not shared with other domains.

Table 12.3 Factor analysis

Factors	*Eigenvalue*	*Proportion of common variance*
Factor1	2.432	60.8%
Factor2	0.736	18.4%
Factor3	0.616	15.4%
Factor4	0.215	5.4%
Variable	Factor loadings	Uniqueness
Material conditions	0.72	48.4%
Health	0.74	45.2%
Education	0.73	47.1%
Economic and social activity	0.92	16.2%

Source: Author's analysis based on SHARE data.

Conclusions

The measurement and monitoring of the risk of social exclusion for the elderly is crucial for the designers of inclusive social policies. The potential for exploring which factors determine social exclusion in its distinct dimensions is of great significance. We propose a tool that is tailored for the effective achievement of these goals. Our fuzzy multi-dimensional approach based on Sen's capability approach provides a framework for explaining the deprivation status of individuals. Under the proposed MIMIC model, the capability set of individuals is considered as a latent indicator, observed through a vector of the signs of social exclusion (deprived functioning) and influenced by external determinants (personal, social and environmental characteristics). As a result of estimation of a vector of latent indicators (factor scores), we measure the social exclusion status of individuals in its different dimensions. Next, we measure the degree of overall social exclusion risk by aggregating these scores across social exclusion domains and construct a model of these indices incorporating fuzzy-set theory.

We use this methodology to conduct a comparative analysis of the DSER of the population aged 50 and over in Poland by voivodship in 2017. In addition, we assess the impact of external determinants that strengthen or weaken the risk of social exclusion. The highest DSER among older people was recorded in voivodships with very low GDP per capita, i.e. in Lubelskie, Podkarpackie and Świętokrzyskie. The average DSER in the domain of education and economic and social activity is the higher in the voivodships studied than in other areas with social exclusion.

As shown in the results of our empirical analysis, combating social exclusion requires the individualisation of policies and programmes for each voivodship, as the levels of DSER vary significantly. Moreover, as the DSER in each of the domains is determined by different underlying factors and has a significant level of unique variance, the relevant policies should be designed specifically in order to address different dimensions of social exclusion.

Appendix

Table 12.4 Symptoms of social exclusion

Domains	*Variables*	*Description of indicators and corresponding SHARE variables*
1. Material living conditions	**1.1. Monetary poverty**	A binary indicator for a person who is a member of a household with an equivalent net income, in an average month in a year, lower than the poverty line in a given country; poverty line – 60% of the median distribution of equivalent net income [hh17]
	1.2. Material deprivation	Number of signs of material deprivation from the list: • inability to cover unexpected expenses from one's own resources (co206); • inability to afford to purchase meat, poultry, fish, or vegetarian equivalents every other day [br028 and br033]; • inability to afford to heat one's home [co209]; • arrears related to rent, mortgage, or other housing [ho010,ho022]; • declining to seek medical care for financial reasons [rh026d1, rh050d1, rh782, rh783].
	1.3. Income self-assessment	Self-assessment of the ability to make ends meet [co007].
2. Economic and social activity	**2.1. Economic activity**	The indicator includes the following aspects of economic activity: 1. being employed or self-employed [ep005] 2. being unemployed or retired [ep005] 3. long-term unemployed [ep005, ep128] 4. economically inactive [ep005]
	2.2. Voluntary activity	How often one engaged in voluntary/charity work during the past 12 months [ac036_1].
	2.3. Political activity	How often one has taken part in a political/ community-related organisation during the past 12 months [ac036_7].
	2.4. Clubs activity	How often one has gone to a sport/social/ other kind of club during the past 12 months [ac036_5]
3. Health	**3.1. Health self-assessment**	Health self-assessment [ph003].
	3.2. Health limitations	Problems in carrying out activities due to health conditions [ph005].
	3.3. Long-term health problems	Chronic or long-term physical problems [ph004].
4. Education	**4.1. Educational attainment**	Primary education or less [dn010].
	4.2. Lifelong learning	Participation in an educational course or training [ac035_d4].

Table 12.5 Determinants of social exclusion

Determinants	*Description*
1. Economic activity status	0 = the person did not work in the past four weeks; 1 = the person did paid work in the past four weeks [ep002]
2. Age	Age in years and squared age in years [age2017]
3. Sex	1 = female; 0 = male [gender]
4. Place of residence	1 = Big cities; 2 = Suburbs of big cities; 3 = Big towns; 4 = Small towns; 5 = Rural areas [areabldgi]
5. Health self-assessment	1 = Excellent; 2 = Very good; 3 = Good; 4 = Fair; 5 = Poor [ph003]
6. Health limitations	1 = lack of health problems limiting daily activities; 2 = occurrence of long-term health problems moderately limiting daily activities; 3 = occurrence of long-term health problems severely limiting daily activities [ph005]
7. Education	Respondent's highest level of education attained. 1 = ISCED code 8; 2 = ISCED codes 5, 6, and 7; 3 = ISCED code 4; 4 = ISCED code 3; 5 = ISCED code 2; 6 = ISCED code 1 and no education [isced2011_r]
8. Family's financial conditions in childhood	Family was well off financially; about average; or poor: 1 = well off; 2 = above average; 3 = poor [cc733]
9. Number of books at home in childhood	Number of books when age 10 [cc008]
10. Father's education	Father of respondent: ISCED-11 coding of education [isced2011_f]

Table 12.6 Goodness-of-fit measures of MIMIC models

Goodness-of-fit measures	*Values of goodness-of-fit measures*				
	Material living conditions	*Economic and social activity*	*Health*	*Education*	*Social relations*
RMSEA	0.036	0.068	0.046	0.045	0.051
CFI	0.962	0.952	0.964	0.916	0.956
NNFI	0.932	0.914	0.913	0.791	0.923

Source: Author's analysis based on SHARE data.

Note

1 This chapter uses data from SHARE Waves 1, 2, 3, 4, 5, 6 and 7 (DOIs: 10.6103/SHARE.w1.700, 10.6103/SHARE.w2.700, 10.6103/SHARE.w3.700, 10.6103/SHARE.w4.700, 10.6103/SHARE.w5.700, 10.6103/SHARE.w6.700, 10.6103/SHARE.w7.700), see Börsch-Supan et.al. (2013) for methodological details.

The SHARE data collection has been funded by the European Commission through FP5 (QLK6-CT-2001-00360), FP6 (SHARE-I3: RII-CT-2006-062193,

COMPARE: CIT5-CT-2005-028857, SHARELIFE: CIT4-CT-2006-028812), FP7 (SHARE-PREP: GA N°211909, SHARE-LEAP: GA N°227822, SHARE M4: GA N°261982) and Horizon 2020 (SHARE-DEV3: GA N°676536, SERISS: GA N°654221) and by DG Employment, Social Affairs & Inclusion. Additional funding from the German Ministry of Education and Research, the Max Planck Society for the Advancement of Science, the U.S. National Institute on Aging (U01_AG09740-13S2, P01_AG005842, P01_AG08291, P30_AG12815, R21_AG025169, Y1-AG-4553-01, IAG_BSR06-11, OGHA_04-064, HHSN271201300071C), and from various national funding sources is gratefully acknowledged (see www.share-project.org). The SHARE data collection for Poland and the research presented in this paper have been co-funded from the European Social Fund under the Operational Program Knowledge Education Development.

References

Alkire, S. (2002), *Valuing Freedom: Sen's Capability Approach and Poverty Reduction*, Oxford University Press, Oxford.

Basu, K. and Lopez-Calva, L.F. (2011), Functionings and Capabilities, in: K.J. Arrow, A. Sen and K. Suzumura, (eds.), *Handbook of Social Choice and Welfare*, vol. 2, Elsevier, North-Holland, 153–187.

Bethmann, A., Bergmann, M. and Scherpenzeel, A. (2019), *Sampling Guide-Wave 8. Version 9.01*, Working Paper Series, no. 33.

Betti, G., Lemmi, A. eds. (2013), *Poverty and Social Exclusion: New Methods of Analysis*, Routledge, London.

Bollen, K.A. (1989), *Structural Equations with Latent Variables*, Wiley, New York.

Börsch-Supan, A., Brandt, M., Hunkler, C., Kneip, T., Korbmacher, J., Malter, F., Schaan, B., Stuck, S., Zuber, S. (2013) Data Resource Profile: The Survey of Health, Ageing and Retirement in Europe (SHARE), *International Journal of Epidemiology*, 42(4), 992–1001.

Brown, T. and Moore, M. (2012), Confirmatory Factor Analysis, in: R.H. Hoyle (ed.), *Handbook of Structural Equation Modelling*, Guilford Press, New York, 361–379.

Cerioli, A. and Zani, S. (1990), A Fuzzy Approach to the Measurement of Poverty, in: C. Dagum and M. Zenga (eds.), *Income and Wealth Distribution, Inequality and Poverty, Studies in Contemporary Economics*, Springer, Berlin, 272–284.

Chakravarty, S. and D'Ambrosio, C. (2006), The Measurement of Social Exclusion, *Review of Income and Wealth*, 52(3), 377–398.

Comim, F., Qizilbash, M. and Alkire, S. eds. (2008), *The Capability Approach. Concepts, Measures and Applications*, Cambridge University Press, Cambridge.

Commission of the European Communities (1990), *Final Report on the Second European Poverty Programme*, COM(91)29.

Copeland, P. and Daly, M. (2012), Varieties of Poverty Reduction: Inserting the Poverty and Social Exclusion Target into Europe 2020, *Journal of European Social Policy*, 22(3), 273–287.

Crocker, D. (2008), *Ethics of Global Development: Agency, Capability and Deliberative Democracy*, Cambridge University Press, Cambridge.

De Luca, G. and Rossetti, C. (2018), *Stata Program to Compute Calibrated Weights from Scientific Usefile and Additional Database*, MEA, Max Planck Institute for Social Law and Social Policy, Munich.

Hauser, R. and Goldberger, A. (1971), The Treatment of Unobservable Variables in Path Analysis, *Sociological Methodology*, 3, 81–117.

Hu, L.T. and Bentler, P.M. (1999), Cutoff Criteria for Fit Indexes in Covariance Structure Analysis: Conventional Criteria Versus New Alternatives, *Structural Equation Modeling*, 6(1), 1–55.

Jöreskog, K.G. and Goldberger, A.S. (1975), Estimation of a Model with Multiple Indicators and Multiple Causes of a Single Latent Variable, *Journal of the American Statistical Association*, 70(351), 631–639.

Krishnakumar, J. (2007), Going Beyond Functionings to Capabilities: An Econometric Model to Explain and Estimate Capabilities, *Journal of Human Development*, 8(1), 39–63.

Krishnakumar, J. and Ballon, P. (2008), Estimating Basic Capabilities: A Structural Equation Model Applied to Bolivia, *World Development*, 36(6), 992–1009.

Kuklys, W. (2005), *Amartya Sen's Capability Approach: Theoretical Insights and Empirical Applications*, Springer, Berlin.

Lemmi, A. and Betti, G. eds. (2006), *Fuzzy Set Approach to Multidimensional Poverty Measurement*, Springer Science + Business Media, New York.

Levitas, R. (2006), The Concept and Measurement of Social Exclusion, in: C. Pantazis, D. Gordon and R. Levitas (eds.), *Poverty and Social Exclusion in Britain*, Policy Press, Bristol, 123–160.

Lorgelly, P., Lorimer, K., Fenwick, E., Briggs, A. and Anand, P. (2015), Operationalising the Capability Approach as an Outcome Measure in Public Health: The Development of the OCAP-18, *Social Science & Medicine*, 142, 68–81.

Malter, F. and Börsch-Supan, A. eds. (2017), *SHARE Wave 6: Panel Innovations and Collecting Dried Blood Spots*, MEA, Max Planck Institute for Social Law and Social Policy, Munich.

Nussbaum, M., and Sen, A. eds. (1992), *The Quality of Life*, Clarendon Press, Oxford.

Panek, T. (2006), Multidimensional Fuzzy Relative Poverty Dynamic Measures in Poland, in: A. Lemmi and G. Betti (eds.), *Fuzzy Set Approach to Multidimensional Poverty Measurement*, Springer Science + Business Media, New York, 233–256.

Panek, T. (2011), *Poverty, Social Exclusion and Inequality: Theory and Measurement*, Warsaw School of Economics Press, Warsaw (in Polish).

Poggi, A. (2007), Does Persistence of Social Exclusion Exist in Spain? *Journal of Economic Inequality*, 5, 53–72.

Robeyns, I. (2003), *The Capability Approach: An Interdisciplinary Introduction*, University of Amsterdam, Department of Political Science and Amsterdam School of Social Sciences Research, Amsterdam.

Robeyns, I. (2003), Sen's Capability Approach and Gender Inequality: Selecting Relevant Capabilities, *Feminist Economics*, 9(2/3), 61–92.

Robeyns, I. (2005), The Capability Approach: A Theoretical Survey, *Journal of Human Development*, 6(1), 93–117.

Scherpenzeel, A. (2019), *SHARE Sampling Guide – Wave 8. Version 8.0.1*, Bethmann, A., Bergmann, M. and Working Paper Series, 33.

Schlosberg, D. (2012), Climate Justice and Capabilities: A Framework for Adaptation Policy, *Ethics & International Affairs*, 26(4), 445–461.

Sen, A. (1980), Equality of What?, in S.M. McMurrin (ed.), *Tanner Lectures on Human Values*, Cambridge University Press, Cambridge, 195–220.

Sen, A. (1982), *Choice, Welfare and Measurement*, Basil Blackwell, Oxford.

Sen, A. (1985), Well-Being, Agency and Freedom: The Dewey Lectures 1984, *Journal of Philosophy*, 82(4), 169–221.

Sen, A. (1987), *The Standard of Living*, Cambridge University Press, Cambridge.

Sen, A. (1992), *Inequality Reexamined*, Oxford University Press, Oxford.

Sen, A. (1999), *Development as Freedom*, Knopf, New York.

Sen, A. (2000), *Social Exclusion: Concept, Applications, and Scrutiny, Social Development Papers, 1*, Asian Development Bank, Tokyo.

Sen, A. (2010), *The Idea of Justice*, Penguin Books, London.

Schokkaert, E. (2009), The Capabilities Approach, in: P. Anand, P. Pattanaik and C. Puppe (ed.), *The Handbook of Rational and Social Choice*, Oxford University Press, Oxford, 542–566.

Silver, H. (1994), Social Exclusion and Social Solidarity: Three Paradigms, *International Labour Review*, 5–6.

Silver, H. (1995), Reconceptualizing Social Disadvantage: Three Paradigms of Social Exclusion, in: G. Rogers, C. Gore and J.B. Figueiredo (eds.), *Social Exclusion: Rhetoric Reality Responses*, International Institute for Labour Studies, International Labour Organization, Geneva.

Slabbert, I. (2018), Applying the Capability Approach in Social Work Education, *Social Work Education*, 37(7), 867–880.

Zadeh, L.A. (1965), Fuzzy Sets, *Information and Control*, 8, 338–353.

13 Socio-economic Health Inequality Indices

A Fuzzy Approach Applied to European Countries

Stéphane Mussard and María Noel Pi Alperin

Introduction

Since the seminal work of Yaari (1987), the theory of decision has been particularly interested in the use of rank-dependent indices. This dual theory of choice under risk has led the economists to employ concentration indices (based on households' ranks in the society) because of their statistical properties and their simple interpretations – see, for instance, Kakwani et al. (1997) and Yitzhaki and Schechtman (2013). They are also commonly used as concentration indices, which are relevant for any given degree of inequality aversion supported by the decision-maker (Yitzhaki, 1983).

Makdissi et al. (2013) propose a multi-dimensional socio-economic health inequality index based on the rank-dependent approach (Yaari, 1987) and involving a parameter that accounts for the intensity of health redistribution, that is, an inequality aversion parameter. The authors employ the so-called counting approach, with categorical dimensions, in order to allow each health dimension to be gauged in proportion of the overall amount of the socio-economic health inequality index.

In this chapter, we present a multi-dimensional socio-economic health inequality index, with a rank-dependent structure, based on fuzzy-set theory. This family of indices depends on different health dimensions and on one exogenous risk factor, and reflects two very different behaviours of the social planner. First, the usual attitude towards inequality as embodied by the degree of aversion to inequality (see Yitzhaki, 1983), i.e. the willingness of the social planner to operate redistributive policies toward less healthy people in order to alleviate overall inequality in the society. Second, the degree of risk sensibility of the social planner defined by the interaction between the health dimensions and the risk factor (see Mussard and Pi Alperin, 2020). Risk factors are analysed through the prism of equality of opportunity (see e.g. Dworkin, 1981, 2000; Roemer, 1998; Fleurbaey, 2008). The literature distinguishes between fair and unfair causes of health inequalities. The origin of fair inequalities are risky behaviours which are under an individual's control (e.g. lifestyle) while unfair inequalities are associated with exogenous risks beyond the individual's control (e.g. childhood circumstances). In what follows, we will concentrate our analysis on exogenous risks factors.

The theory of fuzzy sets has been widely used to measure health. For example, Pi Alperin and Berzosa (2011) introduce a different way to measure overweight accounting for different intensities of overweight and obesity. Pi Alperin (2016) proposes a synthetic indicator of individual health, including different health dimensions evaluated by diagnosed or reported diseases and limitations on daily activities related to the mental and physical aspects of health. Finally, Mussard and Pi Alperin (2020) show that fuzzy-set theory can be applied to construct socio-economic health inequality indices. The advantage of this theory relies on the fact that each individual can be associated with a given degree of health deprivation, whereas the literature focuses on a clear state of health dimension, i.e. the individual is deprived or not. Then, fuzzy-set theory gives more flexibility to design multi-dimensional socio-economic health inequality indexes. In what follows, we employ this methodology with health dimensions constructed using fuzzy sets instead of categorical health dummy variables.

The chapter is organised as follows. The second section reviews the family of socio-economic health Gini indices based on fuzzy sets. The third section exposes how risk factors are introduced into socio-economic health Gini indexes based on fuzzy sets. A stochastic dominance criterion is also proposed to ensure a robust ranking of health deprivation matrices for a wide range of risk sensibility and inequality aversion parameters. The forth section presents the empirical strategy of the chapter. The fifth section is devoted to an application on European countries. The final section concludes the chapter.

Socio-economic Inequality Indices Based on Fuzzy Sets Health

This section summarises the rank-dependent socio-economic health inequality indices introduced by Mussard and Pi Alperin (2020) and shows how this family of indexes can be extended using the fuzzy-set theory in a multi-dimensional context.

Multi-dimensional Fuzzy Gini Indices

Let B be a fuzzy sub-set of n individuals of a population P such that any individual in B presents some degree of deprivation in at least one health dimension k, $k \in \{1,\ldots,K\}$. The K variables represent different dimensions of physical and mental aspects of health selected to measure multi-dimensional health inequality. Let y^E be an equivalent income distribution such that $F(y^E)$ is its cumulative distribution function defined over $[0,a]$, where a is the maximum conceivable equivalent income. The rank p of the individuals in B are issued from $F(y^E)$, such that $p \in [0,1]$. Instead of employing the counting approach to measure whether an individual is deprived or not in one dimension of health deprivation (e.g. Alkire and Foster, 2011; or Makdissi and Yazbeck, 2014), we adopt a fuzzy logic approach.

Let $H_B(p) = (h_1(p),\ldots,h_k(p),\ldots,h_K(p)$ be, for an individual in B at rank p of the equivalent income distribution, his/her degree of deprivation in each health dimension. The $n \times K$ health deprivation matrix is $H_B(p) = (h_1,\ldots,h_K)$, where h_k denotes the kth column of H_B and $H_B(p)$ denotes a row of $H_B(p)$ for an individual in B at rank p. If an individual at rank p is totally affected by disease k, then the individual is totally deprived in the kth dimension of health, $h_k(p) = 1$. On the contrary, if an individual at rank p is not affected by disease k, then $h_k(p) = 0$, in this case there is no deprivation in the health dimension k. If the individual at rank p is more or less affected by disease k, then $0 < h_k(p) < 1$. Thereby,

$$\mathbf{H}_B(p) := \left(h_1(p),\ldots,h_k(p),\ldots,h_K(p)\right) \in [0,1]^K, \tag{13.1}$$

represents the K-dimensional profile of deprivation of an individual in B at rank p of the equivalent income distribution.

In order to aggregate the health deprivation over the K dimensions, a generalised mean is employed:[1]

$$\bar{\mathbf{H}}_B(p,\alpha) := \sum_{k=1}^{K}\left(\theta_k h_k(p)^\alpha\right)^{\frac{1}{\alpha}}, \tag{13.2}$$

where $\theta_k \in [0,1]$ is the weight attached to dimension k (see the next subsection for the weights parametrisation).

Then, $1-\bar{H}_B(p,\alpha)$ represents the average health *achievement* for an individual at rank p (the dual part of the individual deprivation). On this basis, thanks to a rank-dependent function[2] $v(p)$, such that v: $[0,1] \to [0,1]$, which embodies the social planner's behaviour with respect to redistributive principles, the *socio-economic health achievement index based on fuzzy sets* is given by,

$$A(\mathbf{H}_B,\alpha) = \int_0^1 v(p)\left(1-\bar{\mathbf{H}}_B(p,\alpha)\right)dp \tag{13.3}$$

The fuzzy index $A(\mathbf{H}_B,\alpha)$ is a multi-dimensional extension of the health concentration index (see Erreygers et al., 2012). However, it provides the ability of society to reach a healthy state.

Then, it is possible to derive by duality a *socio-economic health inequality index based on fuzzy sets* in a multi-dimensional context:

$$I(\mathbf{H}_B,\alpha) := 1-\frac{A(\mathbf{H}_B,\alpha)}{\mu_{\varphi(\mathbf{H}_B,\alpha)}} \tag{13.4}$$

where $\mu_{\varphi(H_B,\alpha)} = \int_0^1 \left(1 - \bar{H}_B(p,\alpha)\right) dp$. Following Yitzhaki (1983), the rank-dependent function that distorts the ranks p may be chosen to provide an extended Gini index,

$$v(p) = v(1-p)^{v-1}, \forall p \in [0,1], v > 1,$$

with v the inequality aversion parameter. Therefore,

$$G(H_B,\alpha,v) := 1 - \frac{1}{\mu_{\varphi(H_B,\alpha)}} \int_0^1 v(1-p)^{v-1}\left(1 - \bar{H}_B(p,\alpha)\right) dp \qquad (13.5)$$

is a family of *socio-economic health Gini index based on fuzzy sets*, such that $v \geq 2$ outlines health inequality aversion of the social planner, whereas $v \in (1, 2)$ outlines health inequality loving (α and v will be explained in below). The intensity of the socio-economic health inequality is mainly dependent on the weights associated with each dimension.

Weight Vectors: Standard Approaches in The Fuzzy Sets Literature

In a multi-dimensional context, weights θ_k are of crucial importance to aggregate the information along dimensions (e.g. Alkire and Foster, 2011). Although one of the most used weight schemes to aggregate health achievement or health deprivation is the *equal weights* scheme, for many years now the fuzzy-set literature has tackled the problem of finding more relevant weight schemes.

In 1990, Cerioli and Zani proposed weights that take into account the distribution of the dimensions among the population. Let $\bar{h}_k \neq 0$be the arithmetic mean of the kth health dimension. The weight decreases with deprivation, that is, as far as $\bar{h}_k$ increases:

$$\theta_k^{CZ} := \log\left(\frac{1}{\bar{h}_k}\right). \qquad (13.6)$$

In 1999, Betti and Verma extended the previous weight scheme accounting for the correlation between dimensions. In other words, in the context of health measure, their weight scheme accounts for the prevalence of a given health dimension, from one side, and it limits the influence of highly correlated health dimensions on the synthetic indicator, from the other side. Therefore, Betti and Verma's weight of dimension k is built as follows:

$$\theta_k^{BV} := \theta_k^{a}\, \theta_k^{b}, \qquad (13.7)$$

where θ_k^a depends only on the distribution of h_k (coefficient of variation of h_k),

$$\theta_k^{\ a} := \frac{n\int_0^1 \left[h_k(p) - \bar{h}_k^{\ 2}\right] dp}{\left(n\bar{h}_k\right)^{1/2}}, \tag{13.8}$$

and where $\theta_k^{\ b}$ depends on the correlation between k and the other dimensions:

$$\theta_k^{\ b} := \left[1 + \sum_{k=1}^{K} \rho_{k,k'} F(\rho_{k,k'} < \rho_H)\right]^{-1} \left[1 + \sum_{k=1}^{K} \rho_{k,k'} F(\rho_{k,k'} \geq \rho_H)\right]^{-1}. \tag{13.9}$$

The index $\rho_{k,k}'$ is Pearson's correlation coefficient between dimensions k and k'. $F(\cdot)$ denotes the indicator function valued to be 1 if the expression in brackets is true and 0 otherwise, and where ρ_H is a pre-determined cut-off correlation level between the two dimensions. The weight $\theta_k^{\ b}$ is inversely linked with the intensity of the correlation between h_k and the other dimensions. Although one weight scheme must be chosen to compute multi-dimensional inequality indices, testing for different weighting schemes is important to show the robustness of this indices.

Risk Factors and Robust Ranking of Health Deprivation Matrices

The two-parameter family of the multi-dimensional Gini index based on fuzzy sets, $G(\mathbf{H}_B, \alpha, v)$, allows one to deal with a variety of parameters α and v, which represent two different behaviours of the social planner (see Mussard and Pi Alperin, 2020): the parameter α is related to the risk sensibility of the social planner, which is derived from the association between the risk dimension and the health dimensions; the parameter v reflects the fact that the social planner is more and more inclined to redistribute resources to individuals at the bottom of the income distribution y^E as far as v increases.

Risk Factors and Risk Sensibility

The parameter α should be interpreted as the risk sensibility of the social planner. However, the interpretation of this parameter is different from the usual risk aversion studied in the literature of risk and uncertainty. The social planner may focus on particular health dimensions and judge whether or not these dimensions affect his/her own view about health deprivation. For this purpose, we consider that one dimension is embodied by one specific risk factor. Indeed, the kth dimension of the health deprivation profile of an individual at rank p that is $h_K(p)$ is related to, and represents, a given exogenous risk factor.

The parametrisation of α depends on whether an individual is considered or not as totally deprived in all health dimensions. In other words, if

$1-\bar{\mathrm{H}}_B(p,\alpha)=0$, the individual is deprived in all health dimensions (non-healthy). In contrast, if, $1-\bar{\mathrm{H}}_B(p,\alpha)=1$, the individual is not deprived in any health dimension (totally healthy, i.e. the level of achievement is a maximum).

The risk sensibility properties are related to the usual union/intersection approach introduced by Atkinson (2003). The union approach is defined as follows:

$$\lim_{\alpha\to 0}\left(1-\bar{\mathrm{H}}_B(p,\alpha)\right) = 1-\prod_{k=1}^{K} h_k(p)^{\theta_k}. \tag{13.10}$$

It defines the situation where the social planner looks for only one dimension of health in which the health achievement is a maximum. For instance, if there exists one individual at rank p_1 (of the equivalent income distribution) and one dimension k, except the risk factor, $k \in\{1,\ldots,K\text{-}1\}$, such that $h_k(p_1) = 0$, then this individual is judged to be totally healthy. The result would be exactly the same for an individual at rank p_2 being healthy in all dimensions. Furthermore, whether or not those individuals are affected by the risk factor K, that is $h_K(p_i) = 1$, for $i = 1,2$, the social planner would actually judge individuals at rank p_1 and p_2 being healthy. We say in this case that the *social planner is risk-neutral*, in other terms, he/she has no sensibility towards the exogenous risk factor. Note that when an individual at rank p is not affected by the risk factor, then $h_K(p) = 0$. In addition, if this individual is non-healthy in all dimensions, then $h_k(p) = 1$ for all $k \in\{1,\ldots,K\}$. This would provide a healthy state, while the individual is non-healthy. In order to avoid this problem, risk neutrality is defined as follows:

$$\lim_{\alpha\to 0}\left(1-\bar{H}_B(p,\alpha)\right) = \begin{cases} 1-\prod_{k=1}^{K} h_k(p)^{\theta_k} \\ 0, \text{ if } h_k(p)=1\ \forall k\in\{1,\ldots,K-1\} \text{ and } h_K(p)=0 \end{cases}. \tag{13.11}$$

The risk sensibility property based on the intersection approach explains that if an individual is only deprived in risk dimension K, then the social planner judges this person as totally non-healthy, in the same manner as an individual being non-healthy in all dimensions. Let $\alpha \to \infty$, then:

$$\lim_{\alpha\to\infty}\left(1-\bar{\mathrm{H}}_B(p,\alpha)\right) = 1-max_{k=1,\ldots,K} h_k(p) \tag{13.12}$$

The risk sensibility is therefore the highest possible because the risk factor $h_K(p) = 1$ necessarily implies a non-healthy state. The α parameter allows one to deal with different types of social planners, and more precisely how they behave in accordance with the risk factor K.[3]

Stochastic Dominance

We show that the multi-dimensional socio-economic health Gini indices based on fuzzy-set theory, $G(\mathbf{H}_B, \alpha, \nu)$ are consistent with a non-ambiguous ranking between health deprivation matrices.

The willingness of the social planner to setup redistributive actions to alleviate inequality in the society is related to the intensity of the parameter ν.[4] The parametrisation $\nu = 1$ corresponds to Pen's parade: an additional income for one individual at rank p improves his/her health achievement and therefore the socio-economic health achievement index increases. The parametrisation $\nu = 2$ corresponds to a progressive transfer, from one individual at rank p_1 to another individual at rank p_2 (such that $p_1 > p_2$), which increases the socio-economic health achievement index. Those positional transfers (based on ranks rather than incomes) are generalised in such a way that the more the value of ν, the more the intensity of the income transfer towards individuals located at the lower tail of the equivalent income distribution. The class of distortions functions $v(p)$ consistent with those generalised positional transfer principles are such that,

$$(-1)^{(l)} v^{(l)}(\mathrm{p}) \geq 0, \ \forall p \in [0,1]; \forall l = 1,\ldots,\nu-1, \tag{13.13}$$

and $v^{(l)}(1) = 0$ for all $l = 1,\ldots,\nu$ (see Aaberge, 2009; Makdissi and Mussard, 2008). The socio-economic health inequality indices based on fuzzy sets satisfying the above property for $v(p)$ are included in the set Ω^{ν}.

Makdissi and Yazbeck (2014) proposed a ranking between health deprivation matrices on the basis of achievement curves. In the same spirit, we propose achievement curves, which depend on the parameter ν, and furthermore on the parameter α, the so-called (ν,α)-achievement curves. The achievement curve of order $(1,\alpha)$ is defined as, for all $\alpha > 0$:

$$A_{\mathbf{H}_B}^{1,\alpha}(p) := \frac{1-\bar{\mathbf{H}}_B(p,\alpha)}{\mu_{\varphi(\mathbf{H}_B,\alpha)}}. \tag{13.14}$$

The achievement curve of order $(1,\alpha)$ yields the health achievement of one individual at rank p of the population in proportion to the achievement mean. The (ν,α)-order achievement curve for any given $\nu \in \{2, 3,\ldots,\}$ and $\alpha > 0$ is:

$$A_{\mathbf{H}_B}^{\nu,\alpha}(p) := \int_0^p A_{\mathbf{H}_B}^{\nu-1,\alpha}(u)\,du. \tag{13.15}$$

The achievement curve of order $(2,\alpha)$ provides the proportion of the population whose health achievement is not higher than $A_{\mathbf{H}_B}^{2,\alpha}(p)$. On this basis, a robust ranking between health deprivation matrices may be proposed. Indeed, when the achievement curves do not cross, there is more (or less) inequality for all percentiles $p \in [0,1]$. This result is compatible with particular social planners being more or less inclined to perform income transfer (with respect to the value of v) and also being more or less sensitive to risk (with respect to the value of α).

Theorem 3.1in Mussard and Pi Alperin (2020) – *For all socio-economic health Gini indices based on fuzzy sets* $G(\mathbf{H}_B,\alpha,v)$ *such that* $G(\mathbf{H}_B,\alpha,v)\epsilon\ \Omega^v$ *with* $v\epsilon\{1,2,3,...\}$ *and* $\alpha > 0$, *and for two fuzzy health deprivation matrices* $\mathbf{H}_B$ *and* $\mathbf{G}_B$, *the two following statements are equivalent:*

(i) $G(\mathbf{H}_B, \alpha, v) \geq G(\mathbf{G}_B, \alpha, v)$.
(ii) $A^{v,\alpha}_{\mathbf{H}_B}(p) \leq A^{v,\alpha}_{\mathbf{G}_B}(p), \forall p \in [0,1]$.

The above result yields a non-ambiguous ranking of multi-dimensional health deprivation matrices with respect to the risk factor and to the intensity of income transfers. To be precise, socio-economic health inequalities depend on the risk insensibility of the social planner $\alpha \to 0$, on his/her risk sensibility $\alpha > 1$ and finally on his/her extreme risk sensibility $\alpha \to \infty$. In addition, as far as v increases, income transfers performed to less worthy individuals are taken into account.

Empirical Strategy

This section briefly explains the main data source used in this chapter, presents some descriptive statistics of the 13 countries included in the analysis, and describes the health dimensions selected to analyse multi-dimensional socio-economic health inequalities.

Data

This chapter uses data from waves 5 and 6 Release 7.0.0 of the Survey of Health, Ageing and Retirement in Europe (SHARE; Börsch-Supan, 2019; Malter and Börsch-Supan, 2017; Malter and Börsch-Supan, 2015; Börsch-Supan et al., 2013). SHARE is a multidisciplinary and cross-national panel database collecting micro-data on health, socio-economic status and social and family networks. The objective of the survey is to better understand the ageing process and, in particular, to examine the different ways in which people aged 50 and older live in Europe. The first wave of data was collected in 2004. Wave 5 and wave 6 were collected in 2013 and 2015, respectively. Thirteen European countries (Austria, Belgium, Czech Republic, Denmark, Estonia, France, Germany, Italy, Luxembourg, Slovenia, Spain, Sweden and Switzerland) are analysed in this chapter. In particular, all countries that collected SHARE data in both waves.

The analysis is mainly based on data from wave 6, but we also use some information from wave 5. The main reason is that wave 5 collected information on, for example, the educational level and the country of birth of an individual's parents. Hence, we matched this information about parents with information on the individual given by wave 6. This matching

Table 13.1 Descriptive statistics

Country	*Gender %*		*Age %*		*Total*
	Male	*Female*	*< 65*	*≥ 65*	
Austria	41.86	58.14	32.95	67.05	2962
Germany	46.86	53.14	45.17	54.83	4144
Sweden	45.70	54.30	26.66	73.34	3440
Spain	44.47	55.53	34.45	65.55	4850
Italy	44.48	55.52	34.48	65.52	3579
France	42.07	57.93	36.10	63.90	3069
Denmark	45.41	54.59	45.08	54.92	3312
Switzerland	44.87	55.13	37.33	62.67	2467
Belgium	44.52	55.48	42.18	57.82	4270
Czech Republic	39.56	60.44	34.30	65.70	4300
Luxembourg	45.96	54.04	49.38	50.62	1051
Slovenia	41.09	58.91	41.00	59.00	2166
Estonia	37.90	62.10	30.65	69.35	4509
Total	43.27	56.73	36.85	63.15	44,119

is possible since the information matched is not changing over the various years. Then, only individuals present in both waves are considered in the analysis. In addition, we complete the missing values using imputation techniques. The descriptive statistics of the 13 countries analysed in this chapter are present in Table 13.1.

Health Dimensions

Synthetic indicators of health are constructed following the methodology based on fuzzy sets proposed by Pi Alperin (2016). These indicators aggregate health dimensions reflecting different aspects of mental and physical health of individuals present in the SHARE survey. In particular, three dimensions belong to the mental health aspect (depression, memory and cognition) and six dimensions are part of the physical health (long-term illnesses, limitations in daily activities, limitations in instrumental activities, limitations in general activities, eyesight and hearing). Then, for each health dimension there are healthy individuals, completely non-healthy individuals and individuals characterised by different intensities of health failure.[5] More precisely, the synthetic scores are calculated as the weighted mean of the K dimensions of health. In order to determine the weights associated with each health dimension, we follow the procedure defined by Betti and Verma (2008) described previously.[6]

Socio-economic Health Inequalities by Risk Factors in European Countries

In this section, we provide for each country a ranking of health deprivation matrices by considering one risk factor at a time.

Risk Factors as Circumstances

As was explained previously, in this chapter we follow the literature on equality of opportunity. It is possible then to make a distinction between different origins of risk (Mussard et al., 2018). In our study, we deal with unfair risks related to *circumstances* beyond an individual's control. In other words, we consider variables associated with exogenous risk factors that individuals dot not control for such as the level of education of parents or their nationality. These circumstances may increase inequalities in health and, as Roemer (1995) suggests, individuals' encountering bad consequences should be compensated. Several authors investigate inequality of opportunity in health by analysing the role of circumstances during childhood such as family and social backgrounds (see, for instance, Trannoy et al., 2010; Jusot et al., 2013).

In order to perform the empirical application over European countries, we compute achievement curves over the nine dimensions of health deprivation and one risk factor. Subsequently, an achievement curve is composed of ten dimensions, the last tenth dimension being the exogenous risk factor. These dimensions are averaged using Betti and Verma's weighting scheme, Equation (13.7).[7] Subsequently, for each country we compute one achievement curve for each risk factor. In particular, four exogenous risks factors are analysed associated to the individual's parents: the nationality of parents, the educational level of parents, the economic situation of the family during childhood and the longevity of parents.[8]

The parents' nationality risk factor is valued to be 1 if both parents are immigrants and 0 otherwise. Concerning the parents' educational level, the risk factor is valued to be 1 if both parents have no education, primary or lower secondary education. In contrast, it is valued to be 0, if one of the parents studied beyond high school. Concerning the economic situation of the family during childhood, individuals were asked whether their family used to have financial difficulties when they were growing up (from birth to aged 15 inclusive). For individuals coming from low-income families or families whose financial situation varied over time, the variable is equal to 1, and 0 otherwise. Finally, the last risk factor concerns the longevity of parents. Individuals in the survey report whether the parents are still alive at the time of the survey and their age at death if applicable. With this information, the longevity risk factor was set up to be equal to 1 if at least one of the parents had short longevity (i.e. those who died younger than the life expectancy of their generation at birth) and equal to 0 for individuals with both parents enjoying longevity.

Comparing the four achievement curves issued from each risk factor, for one given country, provides the inequality of the repartition of health deprivation in such a way that it becomes possible to detect the risk factor that aggravates the level of inequality in the society. When an achievement curve, say A_N, for the risk inherent to nationality, lies

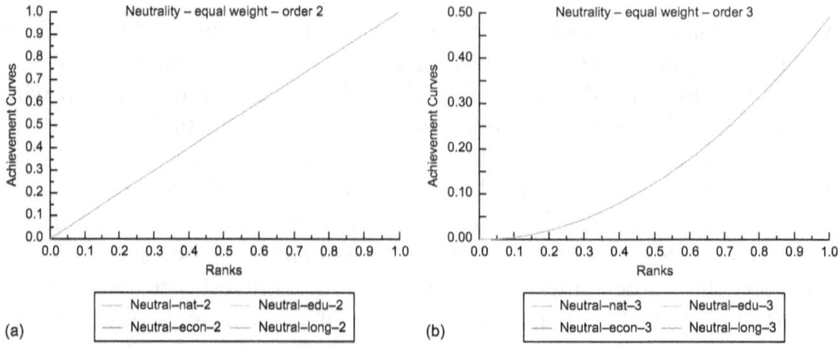

Figure 13.1 a. Order 2, $\alpha = 0$. b. Order 3, $\alpha = 0$.

nowhere above A_E being the achievement curve inherent to the risk of education, this means that the level of inequality in the society due to nationality is higher than that due to education. If the achievement curves cross, then no conclusion can be drawn for the entire society. However, if the crossing point is at rank p^*, the conclusions about inequality is only valid for individuals located before rank p^*. If the social planner has no risk sensibility ($\alpha = 0$), then, for any given type of risk dimension K, the achievement curves provide the same repartition of health deprivation among the population. As an example, for Austria (Figures 13.1a and 13.1b), considering that the social planner is inclined to perform redistributive policies (for instance $\nu = 2,3$), the four achievement curves are indistinguishable. Therefore, with regard to the four types of risk, the social planner does not make any distinction between these risk factors. Furthermore, since he/she has no risk sensibility, the repartition of health deprivation is seen to be egalitarian.

We obtain the same result for all countries. In other words, no distinction can be made about risk factors when the social planner has no risk sensibility.

Risk Sensibility

The level of risk sensibility of the social planner increases with parameter α. We suppose an intermediate value of $\alpha = 50$ ($\alpha = 100$ may be seen as a maximum). In Table 13.2 below, we expose the results of the ranking of the different risk factors for each country. We begin with the redistribution parameter $\nu = 2$. In this case, the social planner makes simple redistribution with progressive transfer from one individual at rank p to another one at rank p^1 such that $p^1 < p$ (it is a minimal requirement of redistribution). We analyse achievement curves of order ($\nu = 2$, $\alpha = 50$). If the achievement curves intersect, then no ranking is available (NR in

Table 13.2 Ranking of health inequalities by risk factors ($\nu = 2$, $\alpha = 50$)

Country	*Parent's Exogenous Risk Factors*			
	Nationality	*Education*	*Economic*	*Longevity*
Austria	NR	$p = 80\%$	NR	NR
Germany	NR	NR	NR	NR
Sweden	NR	$p = 90\%$	NR	NR
Spain	NR	NR	NR	NR
Italy	NR	1*	2*	NR
France	NR	1*	NR	NR
Denmark	NR	NR	NR	NR
Switzerland	NR	$p = 70\%$	NR	NR
Belgium	NR	$p = 75\%$	NR	NR
Czech Republic	NR	NR	NR	NR
Luxembourg	NR	$p = 67\%$	NR	NR
Slovenia	NR	NR	NR	NR
Estonia	NR	NR	NR	NR

* Possible crossing between the curves at the bottom of the income distribution

the tables below). If one achievement curve lies nowhere above the other ones, then it corresponds to the highest risk factor that aggravates the socio-economic health inequality in the society (1 in the tables below for the most important risk factor, 2 for the second more important risk factor and so on).

As can be seen in Table 13.2, the health deprivation matrices do not allow the achievement curves related to each risk factor to be fully compared (NR). However, many countries rank parents education level as the main exogenous risk factor that widens socio-economic health inequalities in society, such as in France and Italy. In other countries, the dominance of achievement curves is assessed up to a given percentile p. For instance, in Sweden, the parents education level increases the socio-economic health inequalities for all individuals below the 90th percentile of the equivalent income distribution.

In Table 13.3, the preference of the social planner who contemplates redistribution to less worthy people is increased to $\nu = 3$. In this case, the crossing between the achievement curves at the order $\nu = 2$ is less likely to be observed. This means that the socio-economic health inequalities inherent to education are, for all individuals located in the percentile interval [0,1], higher than those issued from the other risk factors for Austria, Sweden, Italy, France, Switzerland, Belgium and Luxembourg (Table 13.3).

Note that the economic situation of the family during childhood can be considered as a risk factor in Italy, although the achievement curves cross at the very bottom of the equivalent income distribution.

Table 13.3 Ranking of health inequalities by risk factors ($v = 3$, $\alpha = 50$)

Country	*Parent's Exogenous Risk Factors*			
	Nationality	*Education*	*Economic*	*Longevity*
Austria	NR	1	NR	NR
Germany	NR	NR	NR	NR
Sweden	NR	1	NR	NR
Spain	NR	NR	NR	NR
Italy	NR	1*	2*	NR
France	NR	1	NR	NR
Denmark	NR	NR	NR	NR
Switzerland	NR	1	NR	NR
Belgium	NR	1	NR	NR
Czech Republic	NR	NR	NR	NR
Luxembourg	NR	1	NR	NR
Slovenia	NR	NR	NR	NR
Estonia	NR	NR	NR	NR

Table 13.4 Ranking of health inequalities by risk factors ($v = 2$, $\alpha = \infty$)

Country	*Parent's Exogenous Risk Factors*			
	Nationality	*Education*	*Economic*	*Longevity*
Austria	NR	$p = 80\%$	NR	NR
Germany	NR	1	NR	NR
Sweden	NR	$p = 80\%$	NR	NR
Spain	NR	1	NR	NR
Italy	NR	1*	2*	NR
France	NR	1*	NR	NR
Denmark	NR	NR	NR	NR
Switzerland	NR	$p = 80\%$	NR	NR
Belgium	NR	$p = 75\%$	NR	NR
Czech Republic	NR	NR	1	NR
Luxembourg	2	1	3	4
Slovenia	NR	NR	2*	1*
Estonia	NR	NR	NR	NR

Extreme Risk Sensibility

We now suppose that the risk sensibility of the social planner is a maximum ($\alpha \to \infty$) (see Table 13.4). Results are very close to those of Table 13.3. However, new results are itemised. The economic situation of the family during childhood is the first cause of health inequalities in the Czech Republic. It is the second more important risk factor in France after education. In Luxembourg, nationality becomes the second more important risk factor after education, and the economic situation of the family during

Table 13.5 Ranking of health inequalities by risk factors ($v = 3$, $\alpha = \infty$)

Country	*Parent's Exogenous Risk Factors*			
	Nationality	*Education*	*Economic*	*Longevity*
Austria	NR	1	NR	NR
Germany	NR	NR	1	NR
Sweden	NR	1	NR	NR
Spain	NR	1	NR	NR
Italy	NR	1*	2*	NR
France	NR	1	2	NR
Denmark	NR	NR	NR	NR
Switzerland	NR	1	NR	NR
Belgium	NR	1	NR	NR
Czech Republic	NR	NR	1	NR
Luxembourg	2	1	3	4
Slovenia	NR	NR	2*	1*
Estonia	NR	NR	NR	NR

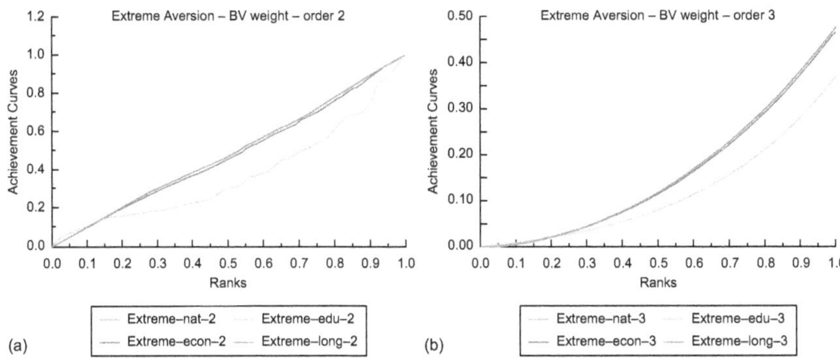

Figure 13.2 a. Order 2, $\alpha = \infty$. b. Order 3, $\alpha = \infty$.

childhood, and their longevity, appears to be ranked 3 and 4, respectively. In Slovenia, longevity is top-ranked; however, we cannot assess this result because of possible crossing between achievement curves at the bottom of the equivalent income distribution.

We obtain exactly the same results when the level of redistribution is increased by one unit $v = 3$ (Table 13.5).

For each country, the achievement curves are very close to each other, so that the dominance cannot be proven for sure. For instance, in Italy, it is apparent that the achievement curve related to education reveals concentrated inequalities (blue curves in Figures 13.2). However, a crossing between achievement curves appears at $p = 15\%$ for $v = 2$ (Figure 13.2a) and for $v = 3$ (Figure 13.2b).

Conclusion

In this chapter, a family of socio-economic health inequality indexes based on fuzzy sets has been proposed. The advantage of dealing with such a family of indexes is to simulate the behaviour of the social planner in two ways: his/her ability to perform income transfers to improve health achievement, and his/her sensibility to the exogenous risk factor. Furthermore, this family of indexes is rewritten with the aid of achievement curves that yield the ability to perform robust ranking between health deprivation matrices.

The empirical application on 13 European countries shows that the level of education of parents is the main driver of risk that aggravates the socio-economic health inequalities in society. This is particularly true, for example in Austria, Sweden, Spain, Italy, France, Switzerland, Belgium and Luxembourg.

Appendix A1: Degree of Membership of Health Dimensions

Table A.1.I Depression

*Depression scale Euro-d**	*Degree of membership*
Non-depressed (0 dimension)	0
Between 1 and 11 dimensions	$1 - (12 - X_i)/12$
Completely depressed (12 dimensions)	1

* Depression, pessimism, suicidal thought, guilty, sleep, interest, irritability, appetite, tiredness, concentration, enjoyment, tearfulness.

Table A.1.II Memory

Memory		*Degree of membership*
Four questions have been asked >regarding date, day of the week, month and year	Knows all	0
	Knows 3 of 4	0.25
	Knows 2 of 4	0.50
	Knows 1 of 4	0.75
	None of them	1

Table A.1.III Cognition

Capacity to memorise words		*Degree of membership*
How many words do you recall?*	I recall more than 15 words	0
	I recall more than 1 and less than 16	$(16 - X_i)/14$
	I recall only 1	1

* This number is the addition between the first trial and the delayed trial.

Table A.1.IV Chronic illness

Long-term illness		*Degree of membership*
Do you have any long-term health problems, illness, disability or infirmity?	No	0
	One	0.75
	More than one	1

Table A.1.V Limitation activities 1

Health and daily activities		*Degree of membership*
Because of a health problem, do you have difficulty doing any of the following daily activities?*	No	0
	Somewhat	$1 - (6 - X_i)/6$
	Yes	1

* Dressing, bathing or showering, eating, cutting up the food, walking across a room, getting in or out of bed.

Table A.1.VI Limitation activities 2

Health and instrumental activities		*Degree of membership*
Because of a health problem, do you have difficulty doing any of the following instrumental activities?*	No	0
	Somewhat	$1 - (5 - X_i)/5$
	Yes	0

* Telephone calls, taking medications, managing money, shopping for groceries, preparing a hot meal.

Table A.1.VII Limitation activities 3

Health and general activities		*Degree of membership*
Because of a health problem, do you have difficulty doing any of the following activities?*	No	0
	Somewhat	$1 - (4 - X_i)/4$
	Yes	1

* Walking 100 metres, walking across a room, climbing several flights of stairs, climbing one flight of stair.

Table A.1.VIII Eyesight

*Eyesight distance and reading**	*Degree of membership*
Both are E or VG	0
One is E or VG, the other is G or F	0.15
One is E or VG, the other is P	0.25
Both are G or F	0.30
One is G or F, the other is P	0.60
Both are P	1

*E: excellent; VG: very good; G: good; F: fair; P: poor

Table A.1.IX Hearing

Hearing		*Degree of membership*
Is your hearing*	Excellent or Very good	0
	Good	0.20
	Fair	0.50
	Poor	1

*With or without a hearing aid.

Acknowledgement

This research is part of the HEADYNAP project supported by the National Research Fund, Luxembourg (contract FNR C12/SC/3977324/HEADYNAP) and by core funding for LISER from the Ministry of Higher Education and Research of Luxembourg. This chapter uses data from SHARE Waves 5 and 6 (DOI: 10.6103/SHARE.w5.700, 10.6103/SHARE.w6.700). The SHARE data collection has been funded by the European Commission through FP5 (QLK6-CT-2001-00360), FP6 (SHARE- I3: RII-CT-2006-062193, COMPARE: CIT5-CT-2005-028857, SHARELIFE: CIT4-CT- 2006-028812), FP7 (SHARE-PREP: GA N°211909, SHARE-LEAP: GA N°227822, SHARE M4: GA N°261982) and Horizon 2020 (SHARE-DEV3: GA N°676536, SERISS: GA N°654221) and by DG Employment, Social Affairs & Inclusion. Additional funding from the German Ministry of Education and Research, the Max Planck Society for the Advancement of Science, the U.S. National Institute on Aging (U01 AG09740- 13S2, P01 AG005842, P01 AG08291, P30 AG12815, R21 AG025169, Y1-AG-4553-01,IAG BSR06-11, OGHA 04-064, HHSN271201300071C) and from various national funding sources is gratefully acknowledged (see www.share-project.org).

Notes

1 See the characterisation proposed by Blackorby et al. (1981).
2 See the seminal work of Yaari (1987).
3 See Mussard and Pi Alperin (2016) for an axiomatisation of desirable properties related to the introduction of exogenous risk factors into socio-economic health inequality indices.
4 See Aaberge (2009) for the general case of probability distortion functions .
5 See Appendix A1 for a complete description of the construction of each health dimension.
6 All the indicators of this chapter are computed using the MDEPRIV program (see Pi Alperin and Van Kerm, 2009).
7 The results are very similar with the weight scheme proposed by Cerioli and Zani.
8 These variables have been selected as they are frequently used to measure childhood conditions circumstances (see e.g. Jusot et al., 2013; Deutsch, et al., 2016).

References

Aaberge, R. (2009), Ranking intersecting Lorenz curves, *Social Choice and Welfare*, 33(2), 235–259.

Alkire, S. and J. Foster (2011), Counting and multi-dimensional poverty measurement, *Journal of Public Economics*, 95(7–8), 476–487.

Atkinson, A.B. (2003), Multi-dimensional deprivation: Contrasting social welfare and counting approach, *Journal of Economic Inequality*, 1, 51–65.

Betti, G. and V. Verma (1999), Measuring the degree of poverty in a dynamic and comparative context: A multi-dimensional approach using fuzzy set theory, *Proceedings of the Sixth Islamic Countries Conference on Statistical Science ICCS-VI, Lahore (Pakistan)*, 27–31 August, 289–301.

Betti, G. and V. Verma (2008), Fuzzy measures of the incidence of relative poverty and deprivation: A multi-dimensional perspective, *Statistical Methods and Applications*, 12(2), 225–250.

Blackorby, C., D. Donaldson and M. Auersperg (1981), A new procedure for the measurement of inequality within and among population subgroups, *Canadian Journal of Economics, Canadian Economics Association*, 14(4), 665–685.

Börsch-Supan, A. (2019), Survey of Health, Ageing and Retirement in Europe (SHARE) Wave 6. *Release Version: 7.0.0. SHARE-ERIC. Data Set*, doi:10.6103/SHARE.w6.700

Börsch-Supan, A., M. Brandt, C. Hunkler, T. Kneip, J. Korbmacher, F. Malter, B. Schaan, S. Stuck and S. Zuber (2013), Data resource profile: The Survey of Health, Ageing and Retirement in Europe (SHARE), *International Journal of Epidemiology*, doi:10.1093/ije/dyt088

Cerioli, A. and S. Zani (1990), A fuzzy approach to the measurement of poverty, in Dagum, C. and Zenga, M. (Eds.), *Income and Wealth Distribution, Inequality and Poverty*, Springer Verlag, Berlin, 272–284.

Deutsch, J., M.N. Pi Alperin and J. Silber (2016), Using the Shapley decomposition to disentangle the impact of circumstances and efforts on health inequality, *Social Indicators Research*, 138(2), 523–543.

Dworkin, R. (1981), What is equality? Part I: Equality of welfare, *Philosophy and Public Affairs*, 10, 185–246.

Dworkin, R. (2000), *Sovereign Virtue: The Theory and Practice of Equality*, Harvard University Press, Cambridge.

Erreygers, G., P. Clarke and T. Van Ourti (2012), Mirror, mirror, on the wall, who in this land is fairest of all? – Distributional sensibility in the measurement of socio-economic inequality of health, *Journal of Health Economics*, 31, 257–270.

Fleurbaey, M. (2008), *Fairness, Responsibility and Welfare*, Oxford University Press, Oxford.

Jusot, F., S. Tubeuf and A. Trannoy (2013), Circumstances and efforts: How important is their correlation for the measurement of inequality of opportunity in health? *Health Economics*, 22, 1470–1495.

Kakwani, N., A. Wagstaff and E. Van Doorseler (1997), Socioeconomic inequalities in health: Measurement, computation, and statistical inference, *Journal of Econometrics*, 77, 87–103.

Makdissi, P. and S. Mussard (2008), Analyzing the impact of indirect tax reforms on rank dependent social welfare functions: A positional dominance approach, *Social Choice and Welfare*, 30(3), 385–399.

Makdissi, P., D. Sylla and M. Yazbeck (2013), Decomposing health achievement and socio-economic health inequalities in presence of multiple categorical information, *Economic Modelling*, 35(C), 964–968.

Makdissi, P. and M. Yazbeck (2014), Measuring socio-economic health inequalities in presence of multiple categorical information, *Journal of Health Economics*, 34(C), 84–95.

Malter, F. and A. Börsch-Supan (Eds.) (2015), *SHARE Wave 5: Innovations & Methodology*, MEA, Max Planck Institute for Social Law and Social Policy, Munich.

Malter, F. and A. Börsch-Supan (Eds.) (2017), *SHARE Wave 6: Panel Innovations and Collecting Dried Blood Spots*, Munich Center for the Economics of Aging (MEA), Munich.

Mussard, S. and M.N. Pi Alperin (2020), *Accounting for risk factors on health outcomes: The case of Luxembourg, European Journal of Operational Research*, in press, https://doi.org/10.1016/j.ejor.2020.09.040.

Mussard, S., M.N. Pi Alperin and V. Thireau (2018), Health inequality indices and exogenous risk factors: An illustration on Luxembourgish workers, *The European Journal of Health Economics*, 19(9), 1285–1301.

Pi Alperin, M.N. (2016), A multi-dimensional approach to measure health, *Economics Bulletin*, 36(3), 1553–1568.

Pi Alperin, M.N. and G. Berzosa (2011), *A Fuzzy Logic Approach to Measure Obesity*, CEPS/INSTEAD Working Paper Series # 2011-55.

Pi Alperin, M.N. and P. Van Kerm (2009), MDEPRIV: Stata module to compute synthetic indicators of multiple deprivation, *Statistical Software Components S457806*, Boston College Department of Economics, revised 02 Feb 2020.

Roemer, J.E. (1995), Equality and responsibility, *Boston Review: A Political and Literary Forum*, http://bostonreview.net/BR20.2/roemer.html

Roemer, J.E. (1998), *Equality of Opportunity*, Harvard University Press, Cambridge.

Trannoy, A., S. Tubeuf, F. Jusot and M. Devaux (2010), Inequality of opportunities in health in France: A first pass, *Health Economics*, 19(8), 921–938.

Yaari, M.E. (1987), The dual theory of choice under risk, *Econometrica*, 55, 99–115.

Yitzhaki, S. (1983), On an extension of the Gini index, *International Economic Review*, 24, 617–628.

Yitzhaki, S. and E. Schechtman (2013), *The Gini Methodology. A Primer on a Statistical Methodology*, Springer Series in Statistics (SSS, volume 272), Springer.

14 The Fuzzy Perspective on Violence against Women

Challenges and Advancements

Francesca Bettio, Gianni Betti and Elisa Ticci

Overview

This chapter focuses on the application of the fuzzy-set approach for the measurement of violence against women (VAW). Although the methodology has been developed in detail elsewhere (Bettio, Ticci and Betti, 2020a), here we revisit its founding assumptions, limitations and advantages before exploring selected extensions. To do so, we often rely on concrete applications of this methodology to data from a survey conducted by the Fundamental Rights Agency (FRA) in 2012 in 28 member countries of the European Union (EU) (henceforth, FRA survey)[1]. The survey administered a detailed face-to-face questionnaire to some 40,000 women in these member states.

Gender-based violence is a complex and multi-faceted phenomenon. It is defined by the United Nations (UN) as

> any act of gender-based violence that results in, or is likely to result in, physical, sexual, or psychological harm or suffering to women, including threats of such acts, coercion or arbitrary deprivation of liberty, whether occurring in public or private life.
>
> (UN, 1994, p. 2)

The FRA survey, in line with this definition as well as with the tradition in survey-based research, distinguished three types of violence – physical, sexual and psychological – identifying several types of 'acts' with each type (9, 4 and 17, respectively). The survey investigated sexual harassment as a separate form of violence. Sexual harassment has attracted the most media attention in recent years, but it is a late-comer in terms of research and policy on VAW. That is why some uncertainty remains as to where sexual harassment is positioned with respect to the conventional trilogy of VAW types.[2] This is one reason that we leave sexual harassment out of our analysis in this chapter; a more general reason is that we primarily address methodological issues, rather than policy targets.

VAW is a universally recognised concern because it results in harm or suffering. Measuring harm is therefore central to measuring violence.

However, physical, psychological, sexual and economic harm caused by violence is bound to differ not only across acts of violence – and, therefore, across types – but also across frequencies and contexts, thus posing a formidable challenge for its measurement. Even when the victims' testimony comes from responses to a structured survey, translating their complexity into quantitative indicators is far from a trivial exercise. This explains why the most frequent quantitative measure of violence found in the literature avoids this complexity by only accounting for the prevalence of a given act or type of violence in a given population.

In this chapter, we discuss how the fuzzy-set approach advances the measurement of gender-based violence by accounting for the frequency and severity of these different acts in addition to their prevalence. Our proposal answers the call for a comprehensive indicator of violence, which has been repeatedly expressed by UN representatives. Yakin Ertürk, the special rapporteur on VAW, in her 2008 Report to the Council of Human Rights, recommended that an agreement be reached on an indicator to be used across countries, which could account for severity as well as individual frequency and prevalence in a population (UN, 2008). This reinforced the need previously emphasised by the UN Expert Group Meeting for indicators to measure VAW (2007) that the data used result in meaningful measurement of the severity of abuse. As argued elsewhere (Bettio, Ticci and Betti, 2020a), severity scales that enable going beyond prevalence measurement have long been proposed in the literature but suffer from limitations that, we believe, can be overcome using fuzzy measurement, e.g. the costly gathering of information and various selectivity biases.

Readers who are familiar with the fuzzy measurement of poverty (Cerioli and Zani, 1990; Cheli and Lemmi, 1995) know that the fuzzy approach can be used to translate a binary measure, such as the poverty headcount ratio, into a continuous measure – a fuzzy index – yielding degrees of poverty, rather than a simple binary indication of its occurrence. They are also well acquainted with the fact that fuzzy measurement can account for multiple types of deprivation. In these respects, the analogy between the fuzzy approach to poverty and to violence is straightforward. When applied to violence, the approach yields an index, which can be interpreted as degrees of violence, accounts for the multi-dimensionality of violence (different acts, different types), as well as for the frequency of violence, and allows for aggregation of acts and types of violence across individuals and groups. However, it is less straightforward to see how the fuzzy approach can capture the severity of violence, and that is the main innovation in our proposal. The basic idea is to measure perceived severity in society, rather than individually, and to proxy the former with inverse prevalence. For example, in European countries, being pushed or shoved by one's partner, an act of physical violence, occurs more frequently than being hit by the partner with a hard object, another act of physical violence, and the latter is usually considered more severe. As another example, 140 of every 100,000 European women reported having been burned at least once by their partner in the year preceding the FRA survey compared with 1,560 women who reported having been slapped. Being burned is generally considered more serious than being slapped, in line with the idea that the lower the prevalence is, the higher the social perception of severity. This is analogous to the way in which the severity of deprivation is evaluated in the fuzzy approach to poverty: the deprivation of a given item is worse when this type of deprivation is less common. In the case of violence, however, further restrictions and qualifications apply to the criterion of inverse prevalence, and we tease them out later in the chapter.

One novel dimension of violence measurement that this chapter explores is different aggregation measures. Separate fuzzy indexes for, respectively, physical, sexual and psychological violence can be aggregated into a single index by means of a simple average for the same individual and then for the chosen population sub-groups. Possible alternatives to this basic aggregation are standardising the index (with respect to the reference population group) or considering indexes of fuzzy intersections and fuzzy unions.

The rest of the chapter is structured as follows. The second section provides a step-by-step description of the way in which the basic fuzzy index and the severity scale are constructed. The third section discusses the implications, advantages and qualifying restrictions of using the fuzzy methodology to measure VAW. The forth section explores alternatives to basic aggregation and, together with the fifth section, shows how application of the fuzzy methodology to the FRA survey can resolve topical but controversial problems in the empirical analysis of violence in Europe. The concluding section wraps up the discussion.

The Steps

The procedure for constructing the fuzzy scale and the fuzzy index of VAW has five sequential steps, with steps 1 to 3 leading to the construction of the scale, step 4 developing the fuzzy index of violence for each individual and each type of violence, and step 5 aggregating the type-specific, individual indexes to obtain a single measure of violence. Step 5 is optional and features alternatives that are further examined below.

Let i denote the individual respondent, h the type of violence and j the act of violence, with $h = 1, 2, \ldots m$; $j = 1, 2 \ldots k$. The measure for the frequency of experience in classes is denoted by c and ordered from highest to lowest. The five steps are:

1. *Definition of gender 'violence' and of the reference population* (what and who). One fundamental assumption for the following procedure

is that it is applied to a sufficiently homogeneous socio-cultural context (reference population). Within this population, we need to identify types of violence and, for each of them, the different violent acts or incidents to include in the analysis.

2. *Victim status*. For each woman i and act of violence j, victim status is defined by the membership function $\mu_{j,i}$ in the interval [0,1]. The function increases as item j is experienced more frequently by women as follows:

$$\mu_{j,i} = \frac{1 - F\left(c_{j,i}\right)}{1 - F(1)}. \tag{14.1}$$

where $c_{j,i}$ is the frequency class (i.e. individual frequencies ordered from highest to lowest) of the jth act for the ith individual; $F(c_{j,i})$ is the value of the jth act cumulative function for the ith individual; $F(1)$ is the population value of the cumulative function for the highest frequency class of the jth act. In other words, for each act of violence, all the women are ordered according to whether and how frequently they have experienced that act, and the function identifies the position of each woman in this ranking of victimisation.

3. *Assessment of severity weight for each violent act: the fuzzy severity scale*. In this step, and with reference to a given type of violence h, each act of violence j is assigned a severity weight using prevalence weights (Guio, 2009). The result is a set of k weights for each type of violence h, calculated as:

$$w_{hj} = w_{hj}^{a} \cdot w_{hj}^{b}$$

This set defines the fuzzy severity scale of violence for type of violence h. Weight w_{hj} is made up of two components:

- prevalence component: w_{hj}^{a} is the coefficient of variation of item j within type h in the reference population. Because it is proportional to the inverse prevalence distribution (Betti and Verma, 2008), this component gives greater importance to items that are less widespread;
- correlation component: w_{hj}^{b} gives less weight to items that are more highly correlated with others (correlation weights). This enables us to correct possible distortions due to redundancy in the definition of overlapping or arbitrary items – for instance, when two similar questions are asked in the same questionnaire.

4. *Individual type-specific index scores*: For each individual i, membership functions are aggregated over the k items using item-specific weights (w_{hj}) to construct type-specific violence scores ($\mu_{h,i}$) or fuzzy indexes.

$$\mu_{h,i} = \frac{\sum_{j=1}^{k_h} \left(\mu_{j,i} \cdot w_{h,j} \right)}{\sum_{j=1}^{k_h} w_{h,j}}$$

We refer to $\mu_{h,i}$ as 'type-specific fuzzy index of violence', or FIV(h). In addition, weights do not necessarily sum to 1, so they are standardised by dividing them by their sum.

5. *Aggregation of individual type-specific index scores*. This is an optional step featuring several aggregation options. The basic option is to aggregate the type-specific FIV(h) indexes across types of violence by simply calculating the unweighted mean. For each individual:

$$\mu_i = \frac{\sum_{h=1}^{m} \mu_{h,i}}{m}$$

is the value of the fuzzy multi-dimensional index of all types of violence at the individual level.

Area-level values – for example, in France, the EU28, or specific sub-populations thereof – are obtained by averaging $\mu_{h,i}$ or μ_i across the chosen (sub-) population, for instance, French respondents. In the specific application to the FRA survey that we present later, the reference population is women aged 18–74 years in 28 European countries, and it is assumed to be sufficiently homogeneous in terms of legal regulations as well as socio-economic conditions. Types and acts of violence are drawn from the survey, which also asked for the frequency of abuse. To avoid standard problems with recall, we used responses related to episodes in the 12 months prior to the interview. The severity scales for the physical, sexual and psychological abuse are reported in Table A.14.1.

Strengths and Weaknesses of the Fuzzy Measurement of Violence

What are the specific advantages and limitations of employing a fuzzy measurement of VAW? We noted in the introduction that fuzzy indexes improve on the prevalence indicator by using a graduated measurement along a continuum, while, at the same time, accurately accounting for multi-dimensionality. Here, accuracy refers to the fact that different kinds of abuse (in the same type of violence) are not simply 'added on', as occurs with prevalence but, rather, are 'weighted' to account for possible redundancy (see step 3) and, crucially, for severity. The way in which severity is gauged by the proposed fuzzy indexes has some clear advantages over the existing alternatives. However, in absence of clear qualifications, fuzzy severity can be rather controversial. The following section discusses conditions and strengths.

Conditions

As mentioned earlier, the inverse prevalence criterion underpinning our severity scale (step 3) is meant to gauge socially perceived severity, namely, how a given social and economic context ranks different acts of violence in terms of their perceived severity. This is radically different from asserting that certain acts of violence should be considered or are intrinsically less serious simply because they occur more frequently. In addition, and equally important, our severity scale gauges relative severity strictly for a given type of violence while remaining intentionally silent about the comparative severity of acts of different types of violence. For instance, being hit with a hard object (physical abuse) cannot be directly compared to being prevented from seeing one's family (psychological abuse) in terms of severity. This strict separation of the scale by the type of violence is mitigated only in part when type-specific fuzzy indexes are aggregated into a single index (step 5). To repeat, however, aggregation across types is an optional step, with the strong proviso of giving the same weight to each type of violence, e.g. by simple averaging.

This relative (and compartmentalised) notion of perceived severity of harm might be considered inferior to an absolute, actual measure of harm that other violence severity scales have tried to quantify (see below). One serious counterargument, however, is that severity cannot be entirely decoupled from perception of harm, and the latter is influenced by cultural beliefs and the social context (Beck, 1976; Iacoviello et al., 2009). For instance, it has been argued that '*the negative effects of [one's partner] abuse may vary as a function of the extent to which wives believe that husbands' abusive behavior must inherently be justified*' (Do et al., 2013, p. 2). This is especially likely to apply to the emotional, psychological, mental or social consequences of violence, such as shame, embarrassment, guilt, stigmatisation, social isolation and marginalisation. And it also implies that the evaluation of the harm from the same act of violence can vary across individuals with different norms and beliefs. Although we accept this possibility, the notion of harm that we support is a kind of 'average social perception' that need not vary across individuals and enables us to carry out unbiased comparisons among groups, countries and so on, as long as the groups being compared are sufficiently homogeneous in socio-economic terms.

This brings us to the next major condition, namely that both the fuzzy scale and the fuzzy indexes refer to a fairly homogeneous socio-economic population. The importance of accounting for significant cultural differences is acknowledged in the recent kNOwVAW data initiative promoted by the United Nations Population Fund (UNFPA) and the Australian Department of Foreign Affairs and Trade to strengthen the measurement of violence against women in Asia and the Pacific. Although most of the countries in this macro region investigated violence using the survey design in the World Health Organisation (WHO) study on women's health and domestic violence as their reference point (UNFPA, 2019), in some cases the list of acts was tailored to the local context.

Lastly, the fuzzy measurement of violence that we propose is intended for interpersonal, adult violence, not armed conflict or other organised or collective forms of violence. We also suggest excluding harmful cultural practices.[3] On the one hand, harmful cultural practices are socially constructed as interpersonal violence is. On the other hand, the distinction between the two is still subject to debate (Longman and Bradley, 2015). Given that resolving these kinds of debates is beyond the scope of our proposal, we use a conservative approach, which excludes these practices from the field of application of our methodology. Unlike other forms of interpersonal VAW, the latter 'take on an aura of morality in the eyes of those practicing them' (UN, 1995, pp. 1–2).

Advantages

Adopting the fuzzy approach to measuring violence has some advantages. In our view, it has two main advantages: less risk of arbitrariness and simplicity and economy of calculation. It is easier to understand these advantages if we compare the fuzzy severity scale we propose with existing alternatives.

Less risk of arbitrariness. Two types of scales are found in the literature, which we call 'subjective' and 'objective' for convenience. Objective scales attempt to classify different acts of VAW on the basis of observed, objective harm. In doing so, they face the challenge that aggregating different types of harm – physical, emotional, economic and so on – poses serious problems of commensurability. A popular way to overcome this problem is to focus on one component of harm – often physical harm – under the implicit or explicit assumption that the measured and unmeasured components are strictly correlated. The Conflict Tactic Scale (CTS; Straus, 1979) and its revised version, the CTS-2 (Straus et al., 1996), inspired several categorisations (WHO, 2013) and questionnaires in surveys on VAW (see e.g. Black et al., 2011). This scale expresses the severity of an assault as 'the potential for producing an injury that requires medical treatment' (Straus, 1990, p. 77) and is inspired by the US legal system as shown by the fact that its distinction between severe and minor violence 'is roughly parallel to the legal distinction in the United States between "simple assault" and "aggravated assault"', with 'aggravated assault' meaning an 'attack that is likely to cause grave bodily harm' (Straus, 2007, p. 191). In other words, the claim to objective measurement is justified by anchoring the assessment of harm to an actual, existing legal system. In a similar vein, and despite being critical of CTS,

Walby and Towers (2017, p. 28) proposed a definition of violence which 'is anchored in law, which includes both action and harm' because '[T]he framework that most consistently uses this concept of "action + harm" is that of criminal law'. Therefore, these endeavours to be objective do not appear to avoid a double source of arbitrariness. First, the correlation between measured and unmeasured harm need not be strong, as Marshall (1992) argued with regard to physical and psychological harm.[4] Second, these measures of harm may be unduly influenced by specific historical and geographical legal contexts.

In our case, in contrast, the risk that the scale developed at a given time and for a given area will be applied years later on a different continent, as occurred with the CTS, is largely avoided by the qualification that the scale applies to population sub-groups that are sufficiently homogeneous in socio-economic terms. Our scale also avoids arbitrariness due to the choice of one type of harm to proxy all others. This is because inverse frequency proxies overall comparative severity, hence providing a comprehensive notion of harm. The subjective severity scales found in the literature also attempt to capture an overall perception of harm when they ask respondents to rank different acts of violence based on their comparative assessment of severity (Hudson and McIntosh, 1981; Marshall, 1992; Rodenburg and Fantuzzo, 1993). However, subjective assessment has well-known shortcomings (Uher, 2018), whereas we proxy social assessment and use objective statistical evidence (inverse prevalence) for this purpose.

Economy and simplicity of construction. Last but not least, the construction of objective or subjective scales is usually data and research-time intensive, for example, because they are based on separate questionnaires or surveys: the CTS-2, the Index of Spouse Abuse (ISA; Hudson and McIntosh, 1981), the Severity of Wife Abuse Scale (SWAS; Marshall, 1992) and the revised version of the Sexual Experiences Survey (SES; Koss et al., 2007) are all cases in point. In contrast, the fuzzy scale only exploits prevalence records from one existing survey and relies on a well-defined algorithm for its construction.

Economy, simplicity and less arbitrariness are actual advantages in favour of the fuzzy scale, provided the latter yields 'credible' results. To assess credibility, we validated our scale using both internal and external procedures, and the results are reassuring (Bettio, Ticci and Betti, 2020a). For internal validation, we used the subjective evaluation section of the FRA questionnaire and compared the ranking of the various acts of intimate partner violence that emerged from the fuzzy scale with those inferred from a 'subjective' assessment. The comparison revealed a good degree of congruence. For external validation, we compared the ranking of the fuzzy scale with that of three of the most common alternatives in the domestic violence literature: the CTS-2, the SWAS and the ISA. Again, the results showed a low incidence of misalignment between our scale and the other three.

The ultimate advantage of a novel methodology is its ability to throw new light on old problems or to open new avenues of research. The fuzzy approach to poverty has significantly advanced understanding of poverty dynamics, for instance, by reducing over-estimation of transient poverty in longitudinal studies – i.e. the spurious fluctuations of at-risk people moving in and out of poverty in successive years (Cheli and Betti, 1999). Also, the fuzzy at-persistent-risk-of-poverty indicator proposed by Verma et al. (2017) – i.e. the fuzzy counterpart of the corresponding Laeken indicator used at the EU level – has brought considerable refinement to a widely used indicator.

In VAW research, the fuzzy approach was introduced very recently but has nevertheless generated some notable results. A topical question in the VAW literature is whether women's empowerment reduces or prompts domestic violence. The empirical literature has given different answers depending on the country and empowerment indicator. In Europe, in particular, attention has been focused on the 'Nordic paradox' in which countries with the highest scores on the European Index of Gender Equality (EIGE), a comprehensive gender equality indicator, tend to report a higher prevalence of domestic violence across all types of violence (Gracia et al., 2019). Although several explanations have been offered for this finding (Davoine and Jarret, 2018; Nevala, 2017), Bettio, Ticci and Betti (2020a, 2020b) show that the paradox vanishes when fuzzy indexes of domestic violence are used, instead of simple prevalence indicators. Specifically, the correlation between the EIGE and the fuzzy index of intimate partner violence (IPV) across the 28 EU countries turns negative and significant, with more gender-equal countries showing tendentially lower levels of fuzzy IPV. In other words, the paradox is resolved by using a more accurate measurement of violence afforded by fuzzy indexes. This raises expectations that additional methodological improvements to this approach may be analytically fruitful. The next section refines the final step of our fuzzy index construction, namely, aggregation across types of violence.

Refinements: Aggregating and Intersecting Different Forms of Violence

In step 5, the three different types of violence – physical, psychological and sexual – are aggregated into the overall fuzzy index of violence (FIV) using a simple arithmetic average, giving equal weight to each type. This option has some advantages but also an important drawback: it implicitly gives more importance to dimensions with a higher prevalence, e.g. psychological violence in the European context.

The first extension to the basic methodology (steps 1–5) that we propose in this section is the rescaling or standardisation of FIVs. This is obtained by dividing each (individual) index by the corresponding mean for the reference population. For example, the standardised FIV for France is the average ratio across French women of their respective FIV and the EU28 value.

The second and third extensions that we propose are, respectively, the 'fuzzy intersection index' and the 'fuzzy union index', both of which are also standardised. The reason for introducing these new indexes is that aggregation through averaging – for the FIV or its standardised version – does not shed light on where each type of violence stands in relation to the other types. In particular, it does not indicate the degree and the ways in which the different types of violence overlap. To illustrate this point, we briefly explore the FRA source, focusing, for simplicity, only on abused women with partners. Two salient findings emerge from Table A.14.1:

1. *Overlapping between types of violence is not the rule.* In all the European countries, a small percentage of abused women with partners – i.e. women who relate at least one act of violence by an intimate partner (IPV) – report having experienced physical, sexual and psychological violence: their share ranges from 0.5% in the UK to 12.1% in Italy, with an average across Europe of less than 4%. A slightly higher frequency of women report having experienced two types of violence, with an average 10.3% of the abused women with partners in the EU28. However, the overwhelming majority of women abused by their partners report only one type of IPV: from 85% in Latvia to as much as 92.2% in Poland, with an EU average of 86%.
2. *Poly-victimisation exponentially increases violence.*[5] When overlapping occurs between types of violence, the fuzzy level of violence – encompassing frequency and severity – rises exponentially with respect to the number of types experienced, suggesting cumulative and interactive effects among the different types. This is shown in Table A.14.1 by the exponential rise in the standardised FIV between women who experienced only one type of violence and those who experienced two types, up to those who experienced all types.[6]

The implications of poly-victimisation for the measurement of violence can be explored using the (standardised) fuzzy intersection index. This index is especially useful for jointly assessing the prevalence of poly-victimisation and the level of violence suffered by women who are affected by it. The fuzzy union index might be used, instead, to infer the level of violence from the worst experiences, technically from the highest type-specific level assigned to each individual woman.

In more formal terms, and because all three types of violence have a common, 'negative' dimension,

- the most appropriate operator for the standardised fuzzy intersection index ($\mu_{\text{int},i}$) is the minimum value among the standardised indexes for the different type of violence experienced (Betti and Verma, 2008):

$$\mu_{\text{int},\,i} = \min\left(\mu_{1,i};\mu_{2,i};\mu_{3,i}\right)$$

where $\mu_{1,i}$; $\mu_{2,i}$; $\mu_{3,i}$ are, respectively, the individual fuzzy measures of sexual, physical and psychological violence. In other words, $\mu_{\text{int},i}$ gauges the overlapping of type-specific 'violence', i.e. the minimum level recorded across all the types of violence experienced by individual *i*. The standardised fuzzy intersection index takes a value of 0 for all women who did not experience all three types of violence.

- the most appropriate operator for the standardised fuzzy union index $\mu_{union,i}$ is the maximum value among the standardised indexes for the different types of violence experienced (Betti and Verma, 2008):

$$\mu_{union,i} = \max\left(\mu_{1,i};\mu_{2,i};\mu_{3,i}\right)$$

Practical Applications

How do these alternative aggregation measures – the standardised fuzzy index, the standardised fuzzy intersection index and the standardised fuzzy union index – advance analyses of violence? Again, we use country comparisons based on the FRA data source for illustration, and again we focus on IPV during the 12 months preceding the survey for convenience. In our first exercise, we gauge the extent to which the new indexes produce significantly different IPV values and rankings for European countries.

Because it picks the maximum type-specific value, the fuzzy union IPV rescales levels of violence upwards compared to the average, fuzzy IPV. In contrast, the fuzzy intersection IPV rescales downwards because it picks the minimum type-specific value (Figure 14.1). However, the fuzzy union index alters the country ranking less than the intersection alternative compared to the average index.

This is shown by the Spearman and Pearson coefficients of correlation reported in Figure 14.1. The three indexes tend to be highly correlated across countries. However, the Pearson coefficient between the average and the intersection indexes is nine percentage points lower than that between the average and the union indexes. And the decline is even more noticeable for the Spearman coefficient (about 15 points), indicating a more pronounced change in the ranking when the intersection measure is used. This is because, unlike average IPV, intersectional IPV rises exponentially, moving from low- to high-value countries. For example, Italy's IPV average score is 11 times higher than the UK's score, but its IPV intersection score is 329 times higher. Put differently, the comparison between the 'worst' and the 'best' countries is much less favourable to the former if we use the intersection than if we use the average or the union alternatives, because overall levels of violence appear to rise exponentially along with the incidence of poly-victimisation.

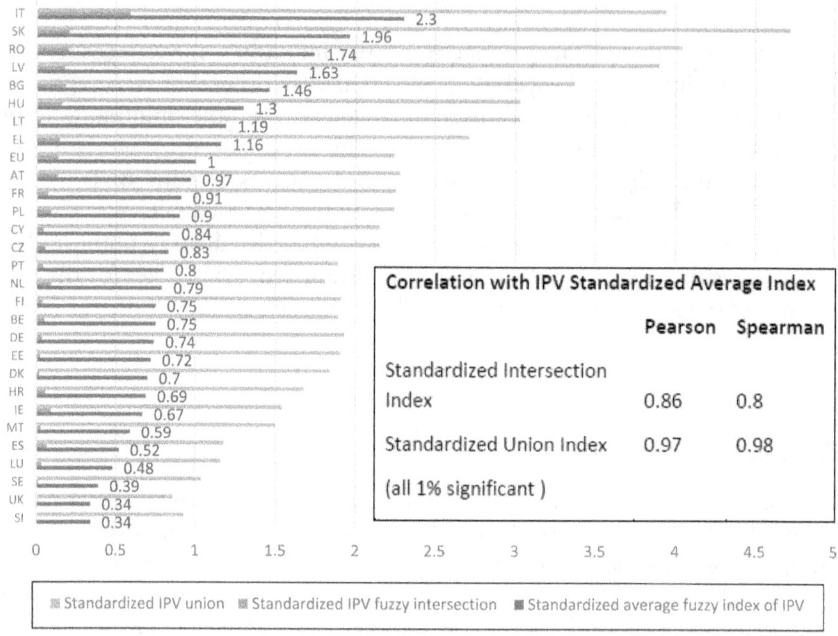

Figure 14.1 Three fuzzy indexes for IPV compared across European countries. *Source*: FRA survey, 2012.

This latter finding, combined with the evidence in Table 14.1 documenting a limited (and variable) incidence of poly-victimisation across countries, questions a widespread tenet in the literature on violence: that either different types of violence (in particular IPV) generally occur simultaneously or that one leads to another in a self-reinforcing process. This narrative is often justified by the fact that all forms of interpersonal VAW appear to share the same risk factors, such as 'growing up in a violent or broken home, substance abuse, social isolation, rigid gender roles, poverty and income inequality' (WHO, 2002, p. 19). The emphasis on co-occurrence of different types of violence probably originates in the strong selectivity of existing studies, many of which are small scale and focus on the most seriously affected female victims. For example, Rodenburg and Fantuzzo (1993) found that sexual abuse was related to severe non-sexual physical abuse in marital relationships using data on a sample of women who were receiving services from a clinic or a battered women's shelter. More recently, Basile and Hall (2011) found that, in a sample of 340 perpetrators arrested for physical assault of their female partner and court ordered to enrol in batterer intervention programmes, almost 97% of male participants reported

Table 14.1 Population share and rescaled fuzzy index of overall violence from current partner by level of poly-victimisation and by country, IPV in the previous 12 months

Country codes	*Women who experienced one type of IPV*		*Women who experienced two types of IPV*		*Women who experienced all three types of IPV*	
	Share of abused women with a partner	*Standardised, average fuzzy index for IPV*	*Share of abused women with a partner*	*Standardised, average fuzzy index for IPV*	*Share of abused women with a partner*	*Standardised average fuzzy index for IPV*
AT	90.4	0.92	5.5	18.09	4.1	55.1
BE	82.6	1.22	15.7	9.39	1.7	43.4
BG	77.0	1.79	16.6	11.32	6.3	42.0
CY	92.1	1.29	6.0	13.30	1.9	61.2
CZ	88.4	1.51	9.3	13.91	2.3	40.9
DE	87.9	1.14	11.0	12.80	1.0	56.1
DK	90.4	0.93	9.1	10.95	0.5	28.9
EE	91.7	1.07	7.5	10.73	0.8	62.8
EL	77.1	1.18	16.5	9.89	6.4	46.8
ES	91.5	1.35	5.2	10.09	3.3	37.2
FI	86.4	1.00	12.4	11.17	1.2	37.4
FR	85.0	1.11	12.5	13.78	2.4	36.2
HR	89.7	1.44	9.1	12.45	1.1	68.6
HU	83.4	1.05	12.8	14.16	3.9	48.6
IE	85.1	0.97	8.8	17.13	6.1	58.6
IT	80.5	1.23	7.4	10.10	12.1	60.3
LT	89.2	1.43	10.0	14.58	0.8	56.4
LU	91.9	1.03	7.2	7.68	0.9	61.8
LV	85.0	1.18	11.6	13.25	3.4	42.3
T	90.7	1.17	8.5	13.03	0.8	59.1
NL	87.3	0.99	10.5	8.42	2.2	56.7
PL	92.2	1.41	4.9	15.65	2.9	52.1
PT	83.0	1.25	15.6	11.30	1.3	75.5
RO	82.0	1.24	13.5	13.19	4.6	66.6
SE	92.4	1.08	7.1	8.25	0.5	68.7
SI	93.7	1.24	5.9	8.09	0.5	18.4
SK	82.1	1.16	13.2	15.88	4.7	55.6
UK	86.9	1.01	12.6	9.87	0.5	37.9

having perpetrated at least one act of physical, sexual and psychological violence. The sub-group of victims under investigation in these kinds of study often represents a strong case of intersectionality (UNWomen, 2019), i.e. women affected by multiple inequalities/oppressions (sexuality, gender identity, ethnicity, indigeneity, immigration status, disability). Guruge et al.

(2012), among others, found that it is common for immigrant and refugee women in Canada to experience various types of violence. Groups other than immigrants and refugees that are also often found to be at risk of cruel, repeated and multiple types of violence include displaced women, those with mental health problems or disabilities, some ethnic groups, and sex workers (Araujo et al., 2019; Curry et al., 2009; Deering et al., 2014).

Aggregation by means of the fuzzy union operator considerably amplifies the levels of violence measured because it selects the worst types of violence reported. In terms of country ranking, however, the union index broadly confirms the ranking yielded by a standardised arithmetic average, with few exceptions at the opposite end of the spectrum, such as Italy and Slovenia. However, whereas the (standardised) average and union fuzzy indexes appear to be largely fungible when applied to FRA data and inter-country comparisons, these results need not be replicated in analyses other than inter-country comparisons.

The second exercise we performed verifies the extent to which the negative association, which we found elsewhere between a country's gender equality and its fuzzy level of violence, continues to hold after the basic FIV above (unstandardised average across types) is replaced by the three new indicators. Tables 14.2a and 14.2b report the values and significance levels of the Pearson and the Spearman correlation coefficients between each European country gender equality score, on the one hand, and alternative fuzzy indexes of violence, on the other hand. Calculations are repeated using the gender stereotype index (GEI), instead of the EIGE. The latter is a composite indicator ranging from 1 (total inequality) to 100 (full equality) and measuring gender gaps and disparities in six core domains: work, money, knowledge, time, power and health. The GEI is based on the Special Eurobarometer 465 survey (TNS Opinion & Social Network, 2017), which conducted interviews across 28 EU countries on citizens' opinions about gender equality and stereotypes. It is computed by averaging the scores assigned to the respondents' evaluation of four statements investigating stereotypes. The EIGE and GEI are expected to move in opposite directions: the higher the EIGE indicator, the greater the degree of actual equality, whereas the perception of gender stereotypes is expected to be stronger in correspondence with higher levels of the GEI.

As shown in Table 14.2, the standardised fuzzy index of IPV confirms the negative association between the EIGE measure of gender equality and intimate partner violence found using the unstandardised version. The union index slightly strengthens the correlation, while the intersection index weakens it. The same applies, with opposite signs, to the GEI indicator of perceived stereotypes. In this exercise, therefore, alternative methods of aggregation across types of violence add little to what can be obtained with simple, unstandardised aggregation. This is unsurprising, given that we are

Table 14.2a Pearson correlation between fuzzy indexes of IPV and gender inequality/stereotype perception

	Simple average fuzzy index for IPV	*Standardised average fuzzy index for IPV*	*Standardised fuzzy IPV intersection*	*Standardised fuzzy IPV union*
EIGE	–0.6038	–0.6032	–0.4257	–0.6244
	0.0007	*0.0007*	*0.0239*	*0.0004*
GEI	0.6725	0.6033	0.3525	0.671
	0.0001	*0.0007*	0.0658	*0.0001*

Notes: p-values in italics.

Table 14.2b Spearman correlation between fuzzy indexes of IPV and gender inequality or stereotype indexes

	Simple average fuzzy index for IPV	*Standardised average fuzzy index for IPV*	*Standardised fuzzy IPV intersection*	*Standardised fuzzy IPV union*
EIGE INDEX	–0.6513	–0.6575	–0.5603	–0.6539
	0.0002	*0.0001*	*0.0019*	*0.0002*
GEI	0.6617	0.6417	0.4697	0.6786
	0.0001	*0.0002*	*0.0117*	*0.0001*

Notes: p-values in italics.

using correlation analysis, and correlation is strong across all the alternative indexes examined.

Conclusions

In this chapter, we briefly illustrated, assessed and extended the fuzzy approach to VAW measurement that we recently introduced elsewhere. The parallel to a fuzzy analysis of poverty is useful for understanding the challenges and advantages of applying this approach to VAW, but only up to a point. The specific difficulty that a fuzzy measurement of violence faces is defining severity in terms of the overall harm caused by acts of violence and constructing a severity scale which overcomes problems of commensurability in the aggregation of different types of harm – mental, physical, economic and so on. We argued that understanding severity as relative and socially perceived harm caused by a given act of violence and proxying it with the inverse prevalence of this act in the reference population meets the challenge, but only with important qualifications. From a methodological perspective, the key qualifications are that the analysis must be confined to a fairly homogeneous population in socio-economic terms, and comparisons of severity across different types of abuse must be ruled out, i.e. the severity of a given physical abuse cannot be compared to that of a psychological abuse. We also argued that meeting this challenge has some notable advantages in addition to those normally offered by the fuzzy approach, such as multi-dimensionality and the objectivity of measurement. We specifically highlighted the economy of information and simplicity of computation involved in the construction of our severity fuzzy scale, together with lower risk of arbitrariness and cultural bias, compared to existing alternatives.

The ultimate advantage of a novel methodology is its ability to reveal new findings or shed new light on existing controversies, and the fuzzy approach to VAW has already revealed its potential by disproving the Nordic paradox and showing that the most gender-equal countries report a lower, not higher, level of IPV after the severity and frequency of violence are accounted for (see Bettio, Ticci and Betti, 2020a, 2020b compared to Gracia et al., 2019). This begs the question of whether refining the basic fuzzy methodology we introduced elsewhere can further advance analysis of VAW. The refinement considered here offers three ways of aggregating type-specific indexes of violence as an alternative to the arithmetic mean: the standardised mean, aggregation by intersection and aggregation by union (as in Betti and Verma, 2008). Standardisation simply ensures that aggregation is not unduly influenced by the more widespread type of violence, whereas aggregation by intersectionality looks at the overlap between different types of VAW and identifies it with the least harmful type of violence being experienced. Finally, aggregation by union looks at and counts only the worst type of VAW being experienced. We calculated the three alternative indexes for 28 European countries and confirmed that only aggregation by intersection alters the ranking of countries to a noticeable extent compared with aggregation by arithmetic mean. The intersection index therefore is suitable when the analysis targets sub-groups of women at risk of the worst combination of different types of violence. We also checked whether using the three newly defined indexes alters our previous finding of a negative and significant association between fuzzy measures of IPV and indicators of gender equality across European countries. We found that all the indexes are broadly fungible in the latter respect, resulting in limited differences in the strength of the correlation with gender equality indicators. However, fungibility need not be confirmed by analyses focusing on, say, interpersonal or group comparisons instead of country-level comparisons. Hence, this latter result warrants further investigation.

Appendix

Table A.14.1 Fuzzy violence scale: Severity weights by act and type of violence based on FRA survey data

Violence type	*Acts (items of violence)*	*Severity weight*
Psychological violence	*How often has your current partner...*	
	Belittled or humiliated you in private?	0.616
	Got angry if you speak with another man/woman?	0.666
	Insisted on knowing where you are in a way that goes beyond general concern?	0.703
	Belittled or humiliated you in front of other people?	0.739
	Become suspicious that you are unfaithful?	0.747
	Done things to scare or intimidate you on purpose, for example, by yelling and smashing things?	0.754
	Tried to keep you from seeing your friends?	0.774
	Prevented you from making decisions about family finances and from shopping independently?	0.854
	Tried to restrict your contact with your family of birth or relatives?	0.915
	Threatened to hurt you physically?	1.084
	Forbidden you to work outside the home?	1.141
	Threatened to take the children away from you?	1.208
	Forbidden you to leave the house, taken away your car keys, or locked you up?	1.279
	Threatened to hurt or kill someone else/someone you care about?	1.355
	Hurt your children?	1.355
	Threatened to hurt your children?	1.392
Physical violence	*How often has something like this happened to you? Your current partner/Someone has ...*	
	Pushed you or shoved you?	0.712
	Slapped you?	0.751
	Grabbed you or pulled your hair?	0.795
	Thrown a hard object at you?	0.798
	Beaten you with a fist or a hard object or kicked you?	0.874
	Beaten your head against something?	1.003
	Tried to suffocate you or strangle you?	1.089
	Burned you?	1.401
	Cut or stabbed you or shot at you?	1.576
Sexual violence	Have you consented to sexual activity because you were afraid of what your current partner might do if you refused?/of what might happen if you refused?	0.944
	Has your current partner/someone: Made you take part in any form of sexual activity when you did not want to or you were unable to refuse?	1.003
	Attempted to force you into sexual intercourse by holding you down or hurting you in some way?	1.008
	Forced you into sexual intercourse by holding you down or hurting you in some way?	1.046

Source: Authors' computation using FRA survey microdata (entire sample for 28 European countries).

Notes: Psychological violence refers to abuse by current partner. Sexual and physical violence refer to episodes in the prior 12 months by the current partner or non-partners. Answer options for psychological violence are: *never*, *sometimes*, *often*, *all the time*, *I don't know*, *No answer*, *Refused*. Answers options for sexual and physical violence: *never*, *once*, *2–5 times*, *six or more times*, *I don't know*, *No answer*, *Refused*.

Notes

1. Individual, anonymised records from the FRA survey are currently handled by the UK DATA SERVICE and are available upon request.
2. The International Labour Organisation (ILO), in the Violence and Harassment Convention No. 190, issued in June 2019 at its 108th session of the International Labour Conference, took a pragmatic approach in defining violence and harassment at work worldwide: 'Definitions vary and lines are often blurred. For example, sexual "harassment" is often classified as a form of gender-based "violence"'. The Conference defined violence and harassment as 'a range of unacceptable behaviours and practices' that 'aim at, result in, or are likely to result in physical, psychological, sexual or economic harm' (answer to FAQ: https://www.ilo.org/global/about-the-ilo/newsroom/news/WCMS_711891/lang--en/index.htm; accessed July 2020).
3. Examples include female genital mutilation, early marriage and pregnancy, practices which prevent women from controlling their own fertility, traditional birth practices, and female infanticide.
4. To cite a more recent example, in a case study on the Philippines, Antai et al. (2014) find that psychological abuse was a stronger predictor of suicide attempts than physical abuse.
5. We borrow and adapt to our context the term 'poly-victimization' introduced by Finkelhor et al. (2007) to describe children's exposure to multiple types of victimization.
6. Violence by non-partners takes a similar pattern in Europe (evidence not reported here) though, in this case, poly-victimization is reduced to experiencing two types of violence, sexual and physical, because the FRA survey did not gather information on psychological abuse by non-partners.

References

Antai, D., Oke, A., Braithwaite, P., Lopez, G.B. (2014) The effect of economic, physical, and psychological abuse on mental health: A population-based study of women in the Philippines. *International Journal of Family Medicine*, Article ID 852317.

Araujo, J. O., Souza, F. M., Proença, R., Bastos, M. L., Trajman, A., Faerstein, E. (2019) Prevalence of sexual violence among refugees: A systematic review. *Revista de Saude Publica*, 53, 78.

Basile, K.C., Hall, J.E. (2011) Intimate partner violence perpetration by court-ordered men: Distinctions and intersections among physical violence, sexual violence, psychological abuse, and stalking. *Journal of Interpersonal Violence*, 26(2), 230–253.

Beck, A.T. (1976) *Cognitive Therapy and the Emotional Disorders*. International Universities Press, Oxford.

Betti, G., Verma, V. (2008) Fuzzy measures of the incidence of relative poverty and deprivation: A multi-dimensional perspective. *Statistical Methods and Applications*, 17(2), 225–250.

Bettio, F., Ticci, E., Betti, G. (2020a) A fuzzy index and severity scale to measure violence against women, *Social Indicators Research*, 148(1), 225–249.

Bettio, F., Ticci, E., Betti, G. (2020b) Does gender equality reduce violence against women? [L'eguaglianza di genere riduce la violenza sulle donne?]. *Rassegna Italiana di Sociologia*, 61(1), 29–58.

Black, M.C., Basile, K.C., Breiding, M.J., Smith, S.G., Walters, M.L., Merrick, M.T., Chen, J., Stevens, M.R. (2011) *The National Intimate Partner and Sexual Violence Survey (NISVS): 2010 Summary Report*. National Center for Injury Prevention and Control, Centers for Disease Control and Prevention, Atlanta, GA.

Cerioli, A., Zani, S. (1990) A fuzzy approach to the measurement of poverty. In: Dagum, C., Zenga, M. (eds.), *Income and Wealth Distribution, Inequality and Poverty*. Springer Verlag, Berlin, 272–284.

Cheli, B., Betti, G. (1999) Fuzzy analysis of poverty dynamics on an Italian pseudo panel, 1985–1994. *Metron*, 57, 83–104.

Cheli, B., Lemmi, A. (1995) A totally fuzzy and relative approach to the multidimensional analysis of poverty. *Economic Notes*, 24, 115–134.

Curry, M.A., Renker, P., Hughes, R.B., Robinson-Whelen, S., Oschwald, M., Swank, P.R., Powers, L.E. (2009) Development of measures of abuse among women with disabilities and the characteristics of their perpetrators. *Violence Against Women*, 15(9), 1001–1025.

Davoine, L., Jarrett, E. (2018) *Uncovering Possible Causes of Violence Against Women to Explain Country Differences Across the EU, Manuscript*. European Commission, Brussels.

Deering, K.N., Amin, A., Shoveller, J., Nesbitt, A., Garcia-Moreno, C., Duff, P., Argento, E., Shannon, K. (2014) A systematic review of the correlates of violence against sex workers. *American Journal of Public Health*, 104(5), e42–e54.

Do, K.N., Weiss, B., Pollack, A. (2013) Cultural beliefs, intimate partner violence and mental health functioning among vietnamese women. *International Perspectives in Psychology: Research, Practice, Consultation*, 2(3), doi:10.1037/ipp0000004.

Gracia, E., Martín Fernández, M., Lila, M., Merlo, J., Ivert, A.K. (2019) Prevalence of intimate partner violence against women in Sweden and Spain: A psychometric study of the Nordic paradox. *PLoS ONE*, 14(5), e0217015.

Guio, A.C. (2009) *What Can Be Learned from Deprivation Indicators in Europe? Eurostat Methodologies and Working Paper*. Eurostat, Luxembourg.

Guruge, S., Roche, B., Catallo, C. (2012), Violence against women: An exploration of the physical and mental health trends among immigrant and refugee women in Canada. *Nursing Research and Practice*, Article ID 434592.

Hudson, W.W., McIntosh, S.R. (1981) The assessment of spouse abuse: Two quantifiable dimensions. *Journal of Marriage and Family*, 43(4), 873–885.

Iacovello, B.M., Grant, D.A., Alloy, L.B., Abramson, L.Y. (2009) Cognitive personality characteristics impact the course of depression: A prospective test of sociotropy, autonomy and domain-specific life events. *Cognitive Therapy and Research*, 33, 187–198. doi:10.1007/s10608-008-9197-7

Koss, M.P., Abbey, A., Campbell, R., Cook, S., Norris, J., Testa, M., Ullman, S., West, C., White, J. (2007) Revising the SES: A collaborative process to improve assessment of sexual aggression and victimization. *Psychology of Women Quarterly*, 31(4), 357–370.

Longman, C., Bradley, T. (2015) *Interrogating Harmful Cultural Practices. Gender, Culture and Coercion*. Routledge, London.

Marshall, L.L. (1992) Development of the severity of violence against women scales. *Journal of Family Violence*, 7(2), 103–121.

Nevala, S. (2017) Coercive control and its impact on intimate partner violence through the lens of an EU-wide survey on violence against women. *Journal of Interpersonal Violence*, 32(12), 1792–1820.

Rodenburg, F.A., Fantuzzo, J.W. (1993) The measure of wife abuse: Steps toward the development of a comprehensive assessment technique. *Journal of Family Violence*, 8, 203–228.

Straus, M.A. (1979) Measuring intrafamily conflict and violence: The Conflict Tactics (CT) scales. *Journal of Marriage and Family*, 41(1), 75–88.

Straus, M.A. (1990) Injury and frequency of assault and the 'Representative Sample Fallacy' in measuring wife beating and child abuse. In Murray, M.A., Gelles, R.J. (eds.), *Physical Violence in American Families: Risk Factors and Adaptations to Violence in 8,145 Families*. Transaction Publishers, New Brunswick, NJ, pp. 75–91.

Straus, M.A. (2007) *Conflict Tactics Scales, in Encyclopedia of Domestic Violence, N. A. Jackson*. Routledge: Taylor & Francis Group, New York, 190–197.

Straus, M.A., Hamby, S. L., Boney-McCoy, S., Sugarman, D.B. (1996) The revised Conflict Tactics Scales (CTS2): Development and preliminary psychometrics data. *Journal of Family Issues*, 17(3), 283–316.

TNS Opinion & Social Network (2017) *Special Eurobarometer 465. Gender Equality 2017*. European Union, http://ibdigital.uib.es/greenstone/collect/portal_social/index/assoc/coeuro01/47.dir/coeuro0147.pdf.

Uher, J. (2018) Quantitative data from rating scales. An epistemological and methodological enquiry. *Frontiers in Psychology*, 9, Article 2599, doi:10.3389/fpsyg.2018.02599.

UN (1994) *Declaration on the Elimination of Violence Against Women*. United Nations, New York, 23 February, Resolution No. A/RES/48/104.

UN (1995) *UN Fact Sheet No.23, Harmful Traditional Practices Affecting the Health of Women and Children*. United Nations, New York.

UN Human Rights Council (2008) *Report of the Special Rapporteur on Violence Against Women, Its Causes and Consequences, Yakin Ertürk: Indicators on Violence Against Women and State Response*, 29 January, A/HRC/7/6, http://www.refworld.org/docid/47cd6c442.html, accessed 17 April 2018.

UNFPA (2019) *Violence Against Women. Regional Snapshot (2019). kNOwVAWdata*. https://asiapacific.unfpa.org/en/resources/violence-against-women-regional-snapshot-2019-knowvawdata/.

UNWomen (2019) *The Value of Intersectionality in Understanding Violence Against Women and Girls, (VAWG) JULY 2019*. United Nations, New York.

Verma, V., Betti, G., Gagliardi, F. (2017) Fuzzy measures of longitudinal poverty in a comparative perspective. *Social Indicators Research*, 130(2), 435–454.

Walby, S., Towers, J. (2017) Measuring violence to end violence: Mainstreaming gender. *Journal of Gender-Based Violence*, 1(1), 11–31.

Wang, D. Fuzzy fault tree analysis for fire and explosion of crude oil tanks. *Journal of Loss Prevention in the Process Industries*, 26, 6 (2013), 1390–1398.

WHO (2002) *World Report on Violence and Health: Summary*. World Health Organization, Geneva.

WHO (2013) *Global and Regional Estimates of Violence Against Women. Prevalence and Health Effects of Intimate Partner Violence and Non-Partner Sexual Violence*. World Health Organization, Geneva.

15 System Safety Analysis of Industrial Processes Using Fuzzy Methodology

Tony Venditti, Nguyen Duy Phuong Tran and Anh Dung Ngo

Introduction

The operation of industrial machines involves various risks, particularly for the operators. In most jurisdictions, employers must take the necessary measures to protect the health, safety and physical integrity of the workers [1]. Among these measures, performing a risk assessment is paramount [1]. The importance of risk assessment appears clearly, for instance, in the European Machinery Directive, which requires a risk assessment to be performed and be documented during the machine design phase.

By the same token, engineers who design machines are required by their Professional Code of Practice to know and follow recognised safety standards which are published by various institutions around the world such as CSA, ISO, ANSI and others. These standards demand that a risk assessment is performed. Risk assessment more specifically requires identification of the hazards as well as an estimation (qualitative, as it is often seen in practice, or quantitative) of the probability of occurrence of the events associated with these hazards and of the gravity of the consequences following the event.

Risk and Uncertainty

By definition, risk analysis deals with uncertain situations, that is, with situations in which we do not have complete and accurate knowledge about the state of the system [2]. It is therefore very important to be able to represent uncertainty in risk analysis as adequately as possible.

Three types of uncertainties can be distinguished:

1. completeness uncertainty;
2. modelling uncertainty;
3. parameter uncertainty.

The completeness of uncertainty refers to the question of whether all significant phenomena and all relationships have been considered. This uncertainty is difficult to quantify, but this type is a major contributor in a qualitative hazard analysis, especially with the identification of RAS.

Modelling uncertainty refers to the inadequacies and deficiencies in various models used to assess accident scenario probabilities and consequences. Availability and validity of these models may enable the assessment of different degrees of belief in each model. This is a major type of uncertainty in consequence assessment. This is a subjective type of uncertainty of knowledge elicited from experts, which is often incomplete, imprecise and fragmentary.

The imprecision and inaccuracies in the parameters which are used as an input to risk assessment models are called parameter uncertainty.

In addition, as we have seen, risk assessment is a complex subject shrouded in uncertainty and vagueness. Vague terms are unavoidable, since safety professionals often assess risks in qualitative linguistic terms.

Modelling Uncertainty With Fuzzy Sets

Under these circumstances, conventional approaches may not be able to model safety effectively. These safety assessment approaches, such as probabilistic risk assessment, have been widely utilised; but they may be difficult to use under circumstances where there is a lack of information about past experience. For these cases, fuzzy sets are a useful tool.

A fundamental idea behind the concept of a fuzzy number is that it may belong to more than one set [3].

This multiple membership to many sets concept provides not only a useful representation of uncertainties, but also a meaningful representation of vague concepts expressed in natural language [4]. Thus, fuzzy variables can reflect and express uncertainties in measurements, observations or knowledge. Traditional variables, which we may refer to as crisp variables, do not have this capability. Although the definition of states by crisp sets is mathematically correct, it is unrealistic in the face of unavoidable uncertainty for certain applications.

Applications of Fuzzy Concepts to Risk and Safety

Fuzzy logic has been used in various contexts related to work and safety [5], such as:

> Oil drilling risk, safety and ergonomics in oil and gas refineries, construction site safety, safety in chemical process plants and many others.

Chemical Safety

Here is now an example of the use of fuzzy numbers in the context of chemical safety [6], compared the behaviour of an interval-based safety index and the fuzzy-logic approach for a simplified chemical reaction involved in the industrial production of acetic acid. The reaction takes place around the proposed pressure range (25–50 bar) and temperature range (150–300 °C). At a pressure of 24 bar and temperature of 149°C, the interval-based index indicates an inherent safety score of 27, while the fuzzy-logic-based index provides a score of 9.95. When conditions change to 25 bar and temperature to 150°C, the interval-based index yields an inherent safety score of 29, and the fuzzy-logic index a score of 10.04. When the conditions are changed to the upper limits of the temperature and pressure intervals (300°C and 50 bar), the interval-based index is not sensitive, resulting in a score of 29, while the fuzzy-logic index presents 10.83. These results show that the fuzzy approach is more sensitive to changes in index due to the smooth transitions between sub-ranges provided by the overlap of the fuzzy sets [6].

However, some others use fuzzy sets (distributions) that do not overlap for *ease of analysis* [7].

Fuzzy Risk Scale in Occupational Health and Safety

Risk indices are often used to estimate the risk levels associated with various industrial work situations [8]. The following example from [8] illustrates the concept.

Risk can be defined conveniently as:

$$\begin{aligned}\text{Risk} &= \text{Probability of Occurrence} \times \text{Severity} \times \text{Current Safety Level}\\ &= \text{AL} \times \text{AS} \times \text{CSL}.\end{aligned}$$

Each parameter can be characterised by a score between say 0 and 10, which can be represented on a fuzzy scale. As explained previously, the idea of a fuzzy number is that it can belong to more than one set.

For instance, consider a potentially hazardous situation to which workers can be exposed. Experts have estimated that the probability of occurrence AL of an injury in such a situation as 7.69 on 10 (based on an accepted risk estimation scheme).

Fuzzy-logic based risk calculation shows that AL = 7.69 belongs at a 46.2% degree to the set 'Reasonably Low' and at a 53.8% degree to the fuzzy set 'Average'. The same procedure is applied to the two other parameters AS and CSL. These fuzzy values can then be 'aggregated' so as to obtain a final value, expressed as a numerical value. Ultimately, the value of the Risk index can then be found by multiplication.

Risk Matrices

Risk matrices are another well-known technique used in occupational health and safety used to express risk levels [9].

The concept of a fuzzy number belonging to many sets can generate a risk matrix with more precise, nuanced risk levels. An example from reference [10], will illustrate the point.

Consider the following 'traditional' risk matrix, reported in Table 15.1.

Consider a particular risk for which the risk index is calculated to be equal to 2 corresponding to a risk level TA which is tolerable–acceptable. A fuzzy risk assessment, on the other hand, yields a value of 1.35 belonging to a 0.75 extent to the TA fuzzy set and to a 0.25 extent to the A fuzzy set, Acceptable. Thus, the fuzzy assessment is more nuanced.

Fuzzy Concepts in Human Reliability Analyses.

Human error is a component of all industrial machines whenever human operation and interaction is necessary. Various techniques have been developed to analyse human reliability and estimate the probability of occurrence of a human error. Two such techniques are known by the acronyms HEART and CREAM (see [11] and [12]).

Fuzzy HEART

The HEART technique is based on the principle that any task performance is influenced by Error Promoting Conditions (EPCs), also called Performance Shaping Factors (PSFs) [11]. Nine generic tasks have been identified and for them, human (un)reliability values have been proposed.

The human error probability for a given task is calculated with the help of the expression:

$$P = P_0 \left\{ \prod [EPC_i - 1] A_{P_i} + 1 \right\} \tag{15.1}$$

Where P_0 is the failure probability value associated with a generic identified task taken from a list of nine tasks. The factors, A_{P_i} are assigned to each EPC_i by experts and are used to modify the influence of the EPC_i on the

Table 15.1 An example of a standard risk matrix

	I	*II*	*III*	*IV*	*V*
G	TNA	TNA	NA	NA	NA
F	TA	TNA	TNA	NA	NA
E	TA	TA	TNA	TNA	NA
D	A	TA	TA	TA	TNA
C	A	A	TA	TA	TNA
B	A	A	A	A	TA
A	A	A	A	A	TA

Key: Frequency categories: A: remote, B: unlikely, C: very low, L: low, M: medium, H: high, G: very high; Severity categories: I: negligible, II: low, III: moderate, IV: high, V: catastrophic; risk categories: A: acceptable, TA: tolerable–acceptable, TNA: tolerable–unacceptable, NA: unacceptable.

probability of occurrence of the actual task being considered. These factors can be expressed as fuzzy numbers reflecting the experts' opinions.

Fuzzy CREAM

The basis CREAM model assumes that the probability of human failure depends on the level of control and knowledge of the operator regarding the task which he is requested to perform [12].

Nine so-called Contextual Control Modes are defined, which are considered to determine four types of human actions that can be followed for a given task. These are defined as 'scrambled', 'opportunistic', 'tactical' and 'strategic'. For each, human error probability is assumed according to Table 15.2.

For a given scenario in which the task is performed, the control mode is determined by nine Common Performance Conditions (CPCs) that qualify the context in terms of linguistic descriptors. For example, regarding 'Adequacy of Organisation' the descriptors are: 'deficient', 'inefficient', 'efficient' and 'very efficient', depending on whether the organisation reduces or improves human performance levels.

To estimate the probability of human error, the procedure applies 'if-then-else' fuzzy rules (fuzzy inference) following the logic of CREAM, as described above. The input parameters are the fuzzy CPCs sets, and the output values are the fuzzy action failure probabilities, in accordance with Table 15.2. An example will make the process clearer (from the same reference).

> If the adequacy of organization (CPC number 1) is inefficient AND the working conditions (CPC number 2) are compatible AND the availability of procedures and plans (CPC number 4) is acceptable AND the adequacy of man machine interface and operational support (CPC number 3) is tolerable AND the number of simultaneous goals (CPC number 5) is more than actual capacity AND the available time (CPC number 6) is adequate AND the time of the day (CPC number 7) is day AND the adequacy of training and experience (CPC number 8) is highly accurate AND the crew collaboration quality (CPC number 9) is efficient, THEN the operator would act in a OPPORTUNISTIC way.

Table 15.2 Human action failure probability in CREAM method

Control Mode	*Action Failure Probability*
Strategic	$5 \times 10^{-6} < p < 0.01$
Tactical	$0.001 < p < 0.1$
Opportunistic	$0.01 < p < 0.5$
Scrambled	$0.1 < p < 1.0$

This fuzzy probability output is then defuzzified by one of the methods in use in fuzzy logic such as, for instance, the centroid method, thus yielding the crisp human failure probability value for the task being analysed.

These probability intervals quite naturally lend themselves to a triangular fuzzy number representation

Fuzzy Numbers

In safety analyses like the ones we just surveyed, then, we often do not know the precise values of the probabilities of occurrence or of failure of the systems or of its components. So one way to deal with this problem is to consider that the variables of interest follow a normal probability distribution with a mean value and a standard deviation. However, another approach to the problem is to use a fuzzy triangular number.

Definition of a Fuzzy Number

A fuzzy number is represented by three numbers $< a_1, a_2, a_3 >$. This representation is interpreted as a membership function, such as:

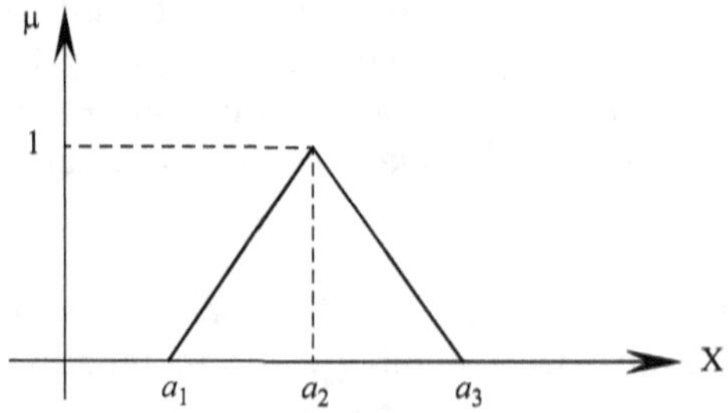

$$\mu_A(x) = \begin{cases} 0 & x < a_1 \\ \dfrac{X - a_1}{a_2 - a_1} & \text{for } a_1 \le x \le a_2 \\ \dfrac{a_3 - X}{a_3 - a_2} & \text{for } a_2 \le x \le a_3 \\ 0 & x > a_3 \end{cases} \tag{15.2}$$

In this representation, a_2 corresponds to a membership value of 1 meaning that we think that the most probable value of the variable under consideration is a_2. So a_2 is akin to the mean value in a normal probability distribution. In this representation, we mean also that the variable under interest lies between the values a_1 and a_3, which have 'membership values' of 0. In other words, a_1 and a_3 are akin to the 3σ values from the mean in a standard normal probability distribution.

Introduction to Fuzzy Operations and Operators

In order to perform calculations on fuzzy fault trees, arithmetic operations on fuzzy numbers have to be introduced.

Basic Arithmetical Operations with Fuzzy Numbers for Ease of Computation

The following are the four operations that can be performed on fuzzy triangular numbers [13]:

Let $\mu_A = < a_1, a_2, a_3 >$ and $\mu_B = < b_1, b_2, b_3 >$ where a_i and b_i are positive numbers, then we have:

(i) Addition: $\mu_{A+}\mu_B = < a_1 + b_1, a_2 + b_2, a_3 + b_3 >$
(ii) Subtraction: $\mu_{A-}\mu_B = < a_1 - b_3, a_2 - b_2, a_3 - b_1 >$
(iii) Multiplication: $\mu_A \times \mu_B = < a_1\, b_1, a_2\, b_2, a_3\, b_3 >$
(iv) Division: $\mu_A / \mu_B = < a_1/b_3, a_2/b_2, a_3/b_1 >$

A problem with triangular fuzzy numbers is that addition and subtraction as well as multiplication and division are not reciprocal operations. To overcome this difficulty, subtraction and division operations definitions have to be modified.

Thus, subtraction can be performed as $< a_1 - b_1, a_2 - b_2, a_3 - b_3 >$ if the following condition is satisfied [14]:

$$\mathrm{DP}(\mu_A) \geq \mathrm{DP}(\mu_B)$$

Where

$$\mathrm{DP}(\mu_A) = \frac{a_3 - a_1}{2} \text{ and } \mathrm{DP}(\mu_B) = \frac{b_3 - b_1}{2} \tag{15.3}$$

If this condition is not met, then the definition given above in (ii) applies.

As for division, this operation can be written as: $\mu_A / \mu_B = < a_1/b_1, a_2/b_2, a_3/b_3 >$ if the following condition is satisfied:

$$\frac{\mathrm{DP}(\mu_A)}{\mathrm{MP}(\mu_A)} \geq \frac{\mathrm{DP}(\mu_B)}{\mathrm{MP}(\mu_B)} \tag{15.4}$$

Where

$$\mathrm{MP}(\mu_A) = \frac{a_3 + a_1}{2} \text{ and } \mathrm{MP}(\mu_B) = \frac{b_3 + b_1}{2} \tag{15.5}$$

If this condition is false, then definition (iv) above applies.

Fuzzy Operators

In order to calculate probabilities in a fuzzy fault tree, we need the ANF, ORF and NEGF operators. In a fuzzy fault tree, the probability of occurrence μ of the top event in the ANF case is evaluated as follows:

$$\mu_{\text{ANF}} = \prod \mu_1 \tag{15.6}$$

As for the ORF case,

$$\mu_{\text{ORF}} = 1 - \prod(1 - \mu_1) \tag{15.7}$$

As for the negation operator, NEGF, it is simply

$$\mu_{\text{NEGF}} = 1 - \mu_1 \tag{15.8}$$

Fuzzy Fault Tree Analysis

In order to illustrate these concepts, we will consider the case of a press brake used in many parts of industry. Our goal will be to evaluate a fuzzy fault tree whose top event is an accident such as: 'an operator gets his hand caught between the closing dies of the press'.

Fuzzy Fault Tree (FSFT)

As the methodology that will be followed uses a fault tree, let us review this concept. A fault tree is a logical diagram that attempts to identify the ways that the various causes can combine to lead to an accident. Once this causal chain of events is established, the probability of occurrence of the accident can be calculated [15].

The situation under consideration will be that of an operator faced with an industrial machine such as a metal bending press (also often called a brake press). In such machines, a crushing zone exists due to the closing of mating parts. In order to do a more quantitative analysis, the probabilities of occurrence of the contributing (bottom) events must be determined or at least estimated. A press brake is a machine commonly found in the metal manufacturing industry. It is used to bend sheet metal in different shapes. A typical press brake is illustrated in Figure 15.1.

The machine is composed of two main structural components, a top beam mounted on a plate and a bottom table. Dies are clamped on the top and bottom parts. Either the top or the bottom half of the press then closes in (via a hydraulically-powered mechanism) on the stationary part. The operator holds the piece-part and actuates the closing motion with a foot pedal, in most applications. A hazardous situation is thus created from the proximity of the workers' hands to the press closing motion. A possible undesirable event (often called a hazardous event) in such a situation is then that the worker gets his hands caught between the closing dies (the hazardous zone of the machine).

Figure 15.1 Press brake. *Source*: CSST Revue Prévention au travail. Québec. Automne 2008.

These are indicated in the fault tree:

In this diagram, the boxes labelled E_1 and E_2 represent events (causes) which can contribute to the occurrence of the accident.

Safety regulations and standards require that such machines be equipped with protective devices which either prevent entry of the operator in the hazardous zone or stop the hazardous motion when parts of the workers' body are in the hazardous zone. The protective device often utilised with press brake takes the form of a light (laser) sensor beam which spans the length of the press and is mounted between the two dies. Such a device is shown in the above picture of a press brake (1 is the sensor beam and 2 refers to the emitting and receiving components of the device).

An accident can occur when the operator gets his hands caught between the closing dies. The contributing events that can lead to such an accident can then be represented in a fault tree and are:

- an equipment failure event such as the protective device fails while a worker is bending, E_1;
- the human factor event, hands in danger zone due to wrong handling part, E_2.

The top event is then the result of the conjunction of events E_1 and E_2 and its probability is therefore evaluated using an AND gate, as reported in Figure 15.2.

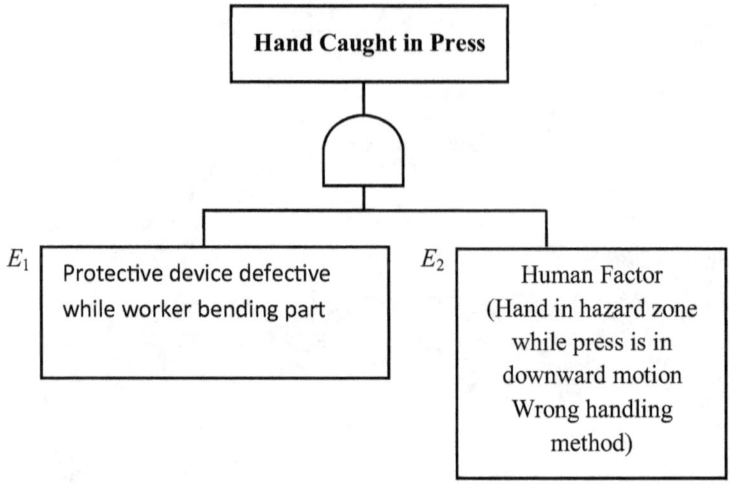

Figure 15.2 Fault tree.

Expert Elicitation

The data needed for the probability calculation were obtained from participants who were solicited for this purpose. These were eight bending press operators in a large manufacturing plant. The health and safety coordinator as well as the workers' supervisor were also solicited.

A questionnaire was handed to them which consisted of a set of brief instructions followed by three questions which were provided with multiple possible answers to choose from. The three questions posed were the following:

1. A bending sequence requires the worker to turn off a protective device in order to complete a certain bend due to the complexity of the shape. The worker must then turn the protective device back on to resume the bending sequence. What is your estimate of the probability that a worker forgets to re-activate the protective device?
2. What is your estimate of the probability that the protective device fails while the worker is bending a part?
3. What is the probability that a worker has his hands between the dies of the press while operating the machine?

The participants were given a choice of answers phrased in this manner:

(1) Very probable
(2) Probable

(3) Not too probable
(4) Improbable
(5) Very improbable

The questionnaire also contained examples corresponding to each of these probability statements to serve as comparison points.

A general introduction was given by the analyst to the participants in a group meeting on the shop floor, which consisted of presenting the thesis and its purpose. The questions and the choice of answers were read to the group. The questionnaire was then handed to them. The whole process took little time to complete.

The following Table 15.3 shows partial results of an expert elicitation conducted by the authors at one industrial establishment.

The aggregation is then taken as a weighted average of the experts' opinions, the weighing method taking into account various factors.

Since linguistic terms are not mathematically operable, to cope with that difficulty, each linguistic term is associated with a fuzzy number, which represents the meaning of each generic verbal term.

The principle of this system is to pick a scale that matches all the linguistic terms in a row (attribute) of the decision matrix and use the fuzzy numbers on that scale to represent the meaning of these linguistic terms.

In this work, we thus adopted a scale which combines the direct fuzzy number translation approach with a probability level from recognised safety standards such as [16].

Opinion Aggregation

The final aggregated fuzzy estimate of the probabilities is obtained by simply taking the average of the experts' estimates for each of the three components of the fuzzy numbers corresponding to the expert's linguistic probability estimate, as given in the scale. No weighing has been done for the following reasons. All workers have extensive experience except for one worker who had 2.5 years' experience. However, all workers get thorough technical training on all aspects of press brake operation. In addition, specific health and safety training sessions are periodically given to all workers. The company in question is a large, unionised, well-structured enterprise which performs extensive, on-going, health and safety monitoring and preventive activities.

First, the (fuzzy) probability of events E_1 and E_2 will be taken as being equal to:

For E_1 we get $< 0.4125, 0.5000, 0.6125 > * 10^{-6}$
For E_2 we get: $< 0.225, 0.325, 0.450 > * 10^{-6}$

Table 15.3 Partial results from expert elicitation experiment

Participant #	*Title/Function*	*Years of experience*	*Questions #*		
			1 Worker forgets to turn the laser back on	*2 Protective device defective while worker bending part*	*3 Hands in die while operating press*
1	Brake Press Operator	23	Probable	Very improbable	Very improbable
2	Id.	30	Improbable	Very probable	Improbable
3	Id.	37	Very probable	Very improbable	Improbable
4	Id.	36	Probable	Very probable	Improbable
5	Id.	28	Probable	Probable	Improbable
6	Id.	2,5	Not too Probable	Not too Improbable	Not too Probable
7	EHS Coordinator	20	Improbable	Very improbable	Improbable
8	Supervisor	10	Probable	Probable	Not too probable

These estimates represent the experts' estimates of the probability of occurrence of the events in question, expressed in linguistic, qualitative terms. **In order for us to solve the fault tree for the top event probability**, we need to first transform these qualitative statements into quantitative, fuzzy numbers. Then, the fuzzy estimates must be aggregated in order to obtain one final fuzzy probability estimate.

Table 15.4 Linguistic estimate to fuzzy number conversion

Very improbable	$< 0, 0.1, 0.2 > \times 10^{-4}$
Improbable	$< 0.2, 0.3, 0.4 > \times 10^{-4}$
Not too probable	$< 0.4, 0.5, 0.7 > \times 10^{-4}$
Probable	$< 0.7, 0.8, 0.90 > \times 10^{-4}$
Very probable	$< 0.90, 0.95, 1 > \times 10^{-4}$

We are now in a position to finally calculate the fuzzy probability associated with the top event, according to the rules explained earlier:

$$< 0.9281, 1.625, 2.756 > *10^{-12}$$

Optimisation of a Fault Tree

The problem we wish to tackle is the following. We want to first define a cost function which is related to the accidents that can occur on an industrial process or machine. A legitimate objective is to minimise this cost function, given the constraints that must be faced. These constraints can be, typically, a maximum failure or accident rate imposed by safety or company or industry standards. This constraint might correspond to the probability of occurrence of the top event in a fault tree. In addition, the failure rates and occurrence probabilities must necessarily be numbers (in our case, triangular fuzzy ones) between 0 and 1.

The cost function can logically be thought to depend on the contributing (bottom) events in a fault tree. In such a fault tree, some of these factors can be taken as variables which can then be designed to achieve the required minimisation. These variables can be determined, in particular, in two ways. First, we may use a FFMEA approach. In this method, the contributing events are ranked by calculating the product fuzzy risk priority number (FRPN) of the probabilities of occurrence times the severity of each event and the detection capability of the system for each failure or accident event. We can then choose as design variables the ones with the highest rankings. The second way is to choose as variables, the ones that can be controlled.

Nonlinear Inequality Constraints Fuzzy Optimisation

The Problem

The problem just stated when formulated in mathematical terms will lead to a minimisation problem with many nonlinear inequality constraints (all in terms of fuzzy numbers) of the following general form:

$$\min f(\mu_X) \quad \text{such that } h_i(\mu_X) \leq 0 \text{ for } = 1 \ldots p \qquad (15.9)$$

where f and the functions h_i are differentiable.

Karush-Kuhn-Tucker (KKT) Conditions

The stated problem can be solved using an extension of the Lagrange multipliers method

$$\text{which can be expressed as:}\begin{cases} \nabla f(\mu_X)+\sum_{i=1}^{p}\lambda_i \nabla h_i(\mu_X)=0 \\ \lambda_i h_i(\mu_X)=0 \\ h_i(\mu_X)\le 0 \\ \lambda_i \ge 0 \end{cases} \tag{15.10}$$

Method for Solving Fuzzy Nonlinear Equations

Once the satisfying conditions above have been determined, the final result will be a nonlinear equation in one of the unknown variables equal to zero.

The solution could be solved by the above method involving the Lagrange multipliers. However, the solution can also be found using the fmincon Matlab function, applied to the three members of the given fuzzy numbers at hand. This is the approach that will be taken here.

The design variables which will have been found can then be used to determine the minimised cost function, thus achieving our goal.

Example for a Press Brake

In order to perform the mathematical analysis, the example of the press brake. This problem statement will then lend itself to a mathematical representation as follows.

Referring to the fault tree presented in above, we will choose as design variables, a human factor variable and a method-related variable which we will denote by μ_{X_1} and μ_{X_2}. These are variables which can be controlled, for instance, by training and selection of experienced personnel. For this case, the probability associated with the top event will be taken as a given constraint μ_{SF}.

The cost function is composed of two components. The first reflects the cost of achieving a given level of reliability while the second part reflects the costs of accidents or failures, which can still occur. Thus the cost function is chosen to be of the following general form:

$$\mathrm{CF}=\sum\left(\mu_{pc_i}\left(1-\mu_{x_i}\right)^{kp_i}+\left(\mu_{fc_i}\mu_{x_i}\right)^{kf_i}\right) \tag{15.11}$$

This expression reflects the fact that higher reliability (less accident) involves higher costs; hence the factors $(1-\mu_{X_i})$ which express reliability are used instead of just μ_{X_i} which represent failure probabilities.

The coefficients μ_{C_i} are fuzzy numbers as well. The reason for this is that the cost of obtaining a certain component of required reliability varies with the supplier or, in the case of a human factor, it might vary with the person.

We will consider a quadratic cost function for calculation purposes.

So, our optimisation model will take the following form

Minimise the Cost Function:

$$\mu_{pc_1}\left(1-\mu_{x_1}\right)^2+\mu_{pc_2}\left(1-\mu_{x_2}\right)^2+\mu_{fC_1}\mu_{x_1}^2+\mu_{fC_2}\mu_{x_2}^2 \tag{15.12}$$

subject to:

$$\begin{cases} (\mu_{SS})(\mu_{X_1})(\mu_{X_2}) \le \mu_{SF} \\ \mu_{X_1}-1\le 0 \\ \mu_{X_2}-1\le 0 \\ -\mu_{X_1}\le 0 \\ -\mu_{X_2}\le 0 \end{cases} \tag{15.13}$$

μ_{SS} is a variable introduced because of the < sign in the first condition.

The values of the coefficients will be taken, purely for demonstration purposes, as:

μ_{pc_1} = < 90, 100, 110 >
μ_{pc_2} = < 100, 110, 120 >
μ_{fC_1} = < 95, 105, 115 >
μ_{fC_2} = < 105, 115, 125 >
μ_{SS} = < 1, 1, 1 >
μ_{SF} = < 0.3, 0.4, 0. 5 >
μ_{C_1} will be taken as < 90, 100, 110 > and μ_{C_2} = < 100, 110, 120 >

This problem was solved, with Matlab, using Lagrange multipliers and Newton's root solving method. The algorithm checked the conditions on the fuzzy numbers stated in section 3.2.2.1 and used the appropriate arithmetic operations.

With this method, we obtained the following results:

μ_{x1} = < 0.4865, 0.4878, 0.4889 >
μ_{x2} = < 0.4878, 0.4889, 0.4898 >

To test the validity of our results, we plotted the cost function (Figure 15.3) and found indeed a zero in the vicinity of 0.5.

The corresponding cost function value (as defined in Equation (1)) was CF = < 9.7022, 17.9457, 41.7209 > should be middle value 107.

We may conclude that this is a global minimum because λ_1 is calculated from Equation (a), inserting the found values of μ_{x1} and of μ_{x2}, is found to be positive, as necessary from the Kuhn-Tucker conditions. To the knowledge of the authors, similar results have not been previously published.

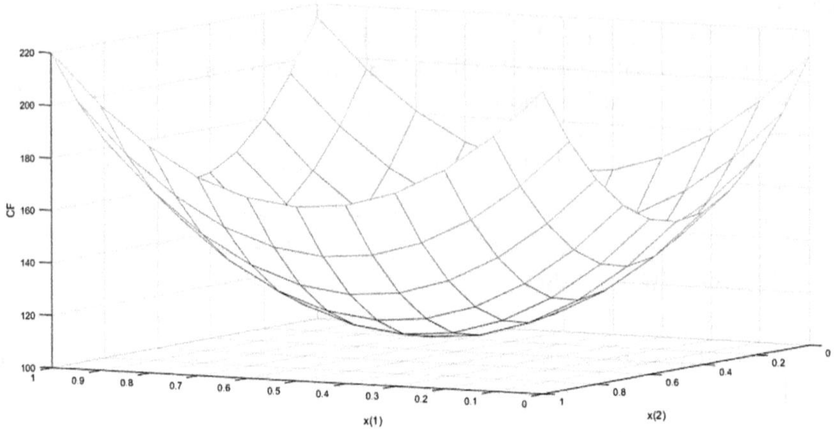

Figure 15.3 Plot of a cost function.

Conclusion

In this chapter we presented a survey of applications of fuzzy methodology to occupational risk analysis. A safety analysis of an industrial bending press was analysed based on fuzzy fault tree analysis. The probabilities associated with the bottom events have been assumed in this chapter. These probabilities were assumed to possess a normal probability distribution which was converted into triangular fuzzy numbers. These fuzzy numbers possess particular algebra rules which were discussed and which will be used later on in this research. The fuzzy probability of occurrence of the top event, which represented a worker accident, was then calculated.

We also addressed a so-called inverse problem in static fuzzy fault tree analysis in which a cost function reflecting work accidents is minimised subject to the constraint that the accident probability of occurrence is specified, by regulation or standard. The problem was expressed mathematically as an optimisation problem and solved using a Matlab algorithm with fuzzy numbers as arguments. The optimised variables corresponding to the contributing events probabilities of occurrence were calculated as well as the cost. This gives the analyst target values to reach for the variables that are under his/her control.

References

Hietikko, Marita et al. Risk estimation studies in the context of a machine control function. *Reliability Engineering and System Safety*, 96 (2011), 767–774.

Markowski, A.S. et al. Uncertainty aspects in process safety analysis. *Journal of Loss Prevention in the Process Industries*, 23 (2010), 446–454.

Markowski, A.S. et al. Fuzzy logic for process safety analysis. *Journal of Loss Prevention in the Process Industries*, 22 (2009), 695–702.

Kentel. Probabilistic-fuzzy health risk modeling. *Stochastic Environmental Research and Risk Assessment*, 18 (2004), 324–338.

Jamshidi et al. Developing a new fuzzy inference system for pipeline. *Journal of Loss Prevention in the Process Industries*, 26 (2013), 197–208.

Gentile et al. Development of a fuzzy logic-based inherent safety index. *Trans IChemE*, 81, Part B (2003), 444–456.

Murè et al. Fuzzy Application Procedure (FAP) for the risk assessment of occupational accidents. *Journal of Loss Prevention in the Process Industries*, 22 (2009), 593–599.

Gurcanli et al. An occupational safety risk analysis method at construction sites using fuzzy sets. *International Journal of Industrial Ergonomics*, 39 (2009), 371–387.

Markowski, A. et al. Fuzzy logic for piping risk assessment (pfLOPA). *Journal of Loss Prevention in the Process Industries*, 22 (2009), 921–927.

Markowski, A., M.S. Mannan. Fuzzy risk matrix. *Journal of Hazardous Materials*, 159 (2008), 152–157.

Akyuz, E. et al. A practical application of human reliability assessment for operating procedures of the emergency fire pump at ship. *Ship and Offshore Structures*, 13 (2008), 208–216.

Castiglia, F. et al. Analysis of operator human errors in hydrogen refueling stations: Comparison between human rate assessment techniques. *International Journal of Hydrogen Energy*, 38 (2013), 1166–1176.

Gani, A.N. A new operation on triangular fuzzy numbers for solving fuzzy linear programming problems. *Applied Mathematical Sciences*, 6, 11 (2012), 525–532.

Rogers, F., J. Younbae Fuzzy nonlinear optimization for the linear fuzzy real number system. *International Mathematical Forum*, 4, 12 (2009), 587–596.

Yiu, T.W. Fuzzy fault tree framework of construction dispute negotiation failure. *IEEE Transactions on Engineering Management*, 62, 2 (2015), 171–183.

Department of Defense USA. *MIL-STD-882D Standard Practice for System Safety*, 1993.

16 A Fuzzy Approach to the Measurement of Employment and Unemployment

Bruno Cheli, Alessandra Coli and Andrea Regoli

Introduction

Analyses of the labour force are traditionally based on a clear-cut distinction between those who are employed and those who are unemployed, which form complementary sets. However, this distinction appears too rigid because it obscures all the nuances between people who are fully employed and those who work only occasionally but need to, or wish to, work more. Furthermore, this way of proceeding involves a significant loss of statistical information which could be used for portraying and measuring the phenomenon more accurately.

In our view, employment should be considered not as a simple condition that is either present or absent but, rather, as a matter of degree. In logical terms, this implies moving from a Boolean conception to a 'fuzzy' one.

Fuzzy-set theory (Zadeh, 1965) has been applied in a wide variety of research fields. For what concerns socio-economic studies, it has been successfully used in the measurement and analysis of poverty (Cerioli and Zani, 1990; Cheli and Lemmi, 1995; Betti et al., 2008; Betti and Lemmi, 2013). To date, however, it has not been applied to analyses of the labour force.

The goal of this chapter is to define fuzzy measures of employment and unemployment using available information on the weekly number of hours worked and on the desire or need of workers to work more hours.

Employment and Unemployment in Official Statistics

According to the International Labour Organisation directives (ILO, 1982), the population of working age (people aged 15 and older) can be divided into three mutually exclusive groups: those who are employed, those who are unemployed and those who are inactive (those who are retired, unable to work and for whatever reason are not seeking work). The first two groups constitute the labour force.

These three groups are identified on the basis of information collected in surveys of the labour force in a hierarchical process, which first identifies the employed, then the unemployed and then those considered inactive.

According to the European Union Labour Force Survey (EU-LFS), those who are employed are at least 15 years old and meet one of the following conditions: (1) over the course of a week, they perform some work – even if for just one hour – for pay, profit or family gain; or (2) if they were not at work during that week, they had a job or business from which they were temporarily absent.

Those who are unemployed are of working age and: (1) did not work during the survey period; (2) are currently available for work and have taken concrete actions over that period to seek paid employment or self-employment. Finally, those who are considered inactive are of working age and have not been classified as either employed or unemployed.

The way in which the employed, unemployed and inactive population groups are identified affects the value of employment and unemployment rates. The unemployment rate is defined as the share of the total labour force that is unemployed, whereas the employment rate is the share of the working age population that is employed.

Fuzzy Measures of Employment and Unemployment: A Methodological Proposal

The fuzzy measure of employment is intended to avoid the sharp distinction between the employed and the unemployed. The application of fuzzy-set theory (Zadeh, 1965) to employment rejects the binary division between these two labels, which considers the employed to designate every individual who performed some work during a particular week, regardless of the number of hours worked. Instead, we define a membership function (MF) μ_E in the fuzzy subset E of the employed, which is measured on a scale from 0 to 1, in which 1 means full membership in the set of the employed and 0 means full non-membership.

A fuzzy measure of employment reflects the unmet need among the employed for working additional hours, thus accounting for labour under-utilisation. The concept of labour under-utilisation encompasses both time-related underemployment and involuntary part-time employment. These categories refer to people who share some characteristics with the unemployed even though they are officially considered to be employed. In the fuzzy approach that we propose, we treat them as employed to a certain degree: the less the time they work, the lower their degree of employment.

Contextually, we define MF μ_U in the fuzzy subset U of the unemployed. Among those in the labour force, we assume that the fuzzy set U of the unemployed is complementary to the fuzzy set E of the employed: therefore, the MF in the fuzzy set U is given by $\mu_U = 1 - \mu_E$. According to the ILO/EU employment categories, those who are inactive are not considered to be in the labour force; therefore, they are assigned a value of MF μ_E and μ_U that equals 0. For those who are employed (according to ILO/EU employment categories), we calculate the value of the MF μ_E following the assumptions illustrated in Figure 16.1.

The value of μ_E depends on the number of hours worked by a person and on whether that person is satisfied with it. We define an upper bound (threshold) for the number of hours worked weekly. This threshold acts as a limit set by statutory or collectively agreed standards and approximately corresponds to the number of hours worked on average by full-time workers. Obviously, the threshold takes different values in different countries.

MF $\mu_E = 1$ (and therefore $\mu_U = 0$) for: (1) full-time workers with a number of hours worked that is not lower than the threshold; (2) full-time workers who do not wish to work more, even if they are employed for less than the specified threshold; and (3) people working part-time voluntarily.

The value of μ_E is greater than 0 and less than 1 for underemployed workers, which are made up of: (1) involuntary part-time workers, i.e. people who could not find a full-time job; (2) full-time workers who work less than the threshold number of hours and are willing to work additional hours. For both categories of underemployed workers, the MF is defined as the ratio of the hours actually worked to the threshold value. Finally, individuals classified as unemployed based on ILO/EU criteria are assigned the values $\mu_E = 0$ and $\mu_U = 1$.

Empirical Application Based on Italian Labour Force Data

We used the fuzzy approach to measure employment and unemployment using 2018 annual Italian data from the EU-LFS (Eurostat, 2019),[1] focusing

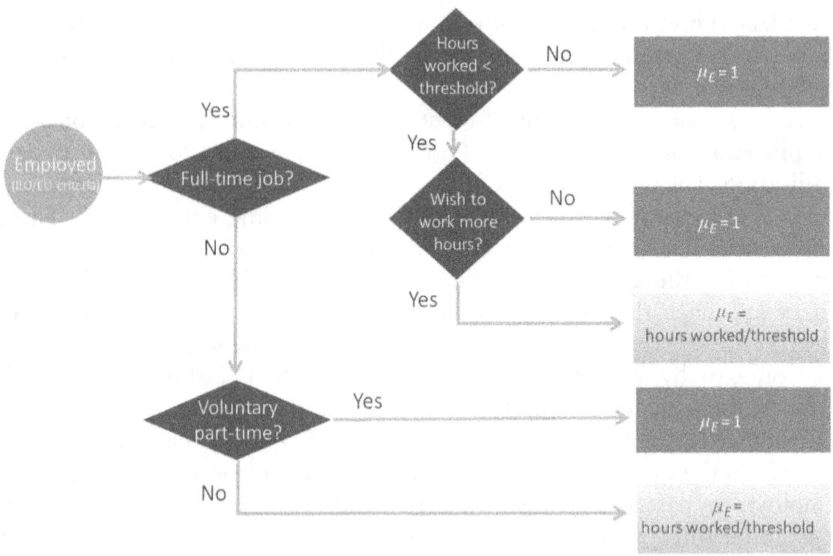

Figure 16.1 Specification of the membership function μ_E for individuals who are employed according to ILO/EU criteria.

on people between 15 and 64 years old. The upper bound of hours worked is set at 40 weekly hours for full-time workers in the private sector (employees, self-employed and family workers) and at 36 weekly hours for full-time public sector employees. These values coincide with the modes of the corresponding distributions in the Italian LFS data. Because the modes and medians are about equal in the two groups, we consider the mode a suitable measure of the central tendency.

Table 16.1 shows the composition of people who are employed according to the five categories described above and referred to in Figure 16.1. More than two-thirds (67.88%) are employed full-time, with the number of hours worked not less than the fixed upper bound. By contrast, about 13.38% are employed full-time, work less than the fixed threshold and declare themselves satisfied with this situation. The percentage of those who work less than the threshold and wish to work more is negligible (0.42%). Finally, voluntarily part-time workers account for 6.29%, which is approximately half the share of involuntary part-time workers (12.02%).

In summary, people who have full membership in the employed fuzzy set are about 88% of the employed.

Analysing the differences in the values of the MF μ_E by occupational criteria (Table 16.2a), we find that the share of people who have full membership in the employed fuzzy set is close to 90% for self-employed, family workers and employees with a permanent job. On the other hand, it shrinks to about 75% for employees with a temporary job. The share of the employed with μ_E values of less than 2/3 ranges from 6.34% for the self-employed to 19.29% for temporary employees.

Our analysis by the type of occupation (ISCO code, see Table 16.2b) shows that the share of people who partially belong to the fuzzy set of the employed ($0 < \mu_E < 1$) ranges from about 6% for high-skilled non-manual occupations to approximately 30% for basic occupations.

The fuzzy rate of employment is calculated as the arithmetic mean of the individual MF μ_E using survey sample weights across all the individuals of working age (between 15 and 64 years old).[2] As such, it can be compared

Table 16.1 Composition of employed based on the criteria in Figure 16.1

Employment Category	*Composition (%)*
Full-time workers whose hours worked are not lower than the threshold	67.88
Full-time workers whose hours worked are lower than the threshold, but do not want to work more hours	13.38
People working part-time voluntarily	6.29
People working part-time involuntarily	12.02
Full-time workers whose hours worked are lower than the threshold and are willing to work more hours	0.42
Total	100.00

Table 16.2a Distribution of ILO/EU employed by membership values and professional status (15–64 years) (in %)

Membership function μ_E	*Self-employed*	*Employees with a permanent job*	*Employees with a temporary job*	*Working for a Family business*	*Total employment*
$0 < \mu_E < 1/3$	2.25	1.13	3.98	1.34	1.74
$1/3 \leq \mu_E < 2/3$	4.09	6.47	15.31	5.94	7.16
$2/3 \leq \mu_E < 1$	2.05	3.16	7.09	1.98	3.45
$\mu_E = 1$	91.62	89.24	73.62	90.74	87.65
Total	100.00	100.00	100.00	100.00	100.00

Table 16.2b Distribution of ILO/EU employed by membership values and ISCO code (15–64 years) (in %)

Membership function μ_E	*High-skill non-manual occupations (ISCO codes 1 to 3)*	*Low-skill non-manual occupations (ISCO codes 4 to 8)*	*Basic occupations (ISCO code 9)*	*Total employment*
$0 < \mu_E < 1/3$	1.09	1.26	6.24	1.74
$1/3 \leq \mu_E < 2/3$	3.20	7.94	17.03	7.16
$2/3 \leq \mu_E < 1$	2.09	3.93	5.93	3.45
$\mu_E = 1$	93.62	86.87	70.80	87.65
Total	100.00	100.00	100.00	100.00

with the traditional employment rate (Table 16.3). The results show that, among the total population between 15 and 64 years old, the fuzzy employment rate is 55.2%, which is 5.6% less than the official rate (T = 58.5%). The downward correction (calculated as (F/T)*100 – 100) is more marked among females (9.3%) than males (2.8%), meaning that the unmet need for working more hours is greater by far among female workers than male workers. Young adults (less than 35 years old), foreign-born individuals and workers with a low education level are the groups of workers who are the most severely affected by labour under-utilisation. In terms of the geographic area of residence, the downward correction of the fuzzy measure is slightly above average in southern Italy and the Islands and slightly below average in northern Italy. In contrast, no substantial difference emerges in terms of the degree of urbanisation.

Now let us shift our attention to unemployment. The weighted mean of the MF μ_U across individuals in the labour force provides the fuzzy rate of unemployment, which is compared with the conventional measure in Table 16.4. For all the people in the labour force aged 15 to 64, the fuzzy

Table 16.3 Comparison of traditional and fuzzy employment rates (workers 15–64 years old) (%)

		Traditional measure (T)	*Fuzzy measure (F)*	*(F/T)*100*
Total		58.5	55.2	94.4
By gender	Male	67.6	65.7	97.2
	Female	49.5	44.9	90.7
By age group	15–24 years	17.7	15.8	89.3
	25–34 years	61.7	57.3	92.9
	35–44 years	73.4	69.4	94.6
	45–54 years	72.3	68.6	94.9
	55–64 years	53.7	51.4	95.7
By country of birth	Native born	58.1	55.2	95.0
	Foreign born	60.9	55.5	91.1
By education level	Lower secondary	43.8	40.7	89.3
	Upper secondary	64.3	60.9	92.9
	Third secondary	78.7	75.4	95.8
By regional group (NUTS 1 code)	North-West	66.8	63.5	95.1
	North-East	68.1	65.0	95.4
	Central	63.2	59.0	87.0
	South	44.9	41.9	93.3
	Islands	43.7	40.3	92.2
By degree of urbanisation	Cities	58.9	55.3	93.9
	Towns and suburbs	58.2	55.2	94.8
	Rural areas	58.5	55.3	94.5

measure is 15.8%, 46.3% higher than the traditional rate (T = 10.8%). The fuzzy approach reveals that the gender gap in the unemployment rate is wider than is shown by the traditional approach. The gap between those born in Italy and foreign-born migrants also increases when the unemployment rate is derived through the fuzzy method. As for other classifications, we find that the largest upward corrections are in the categories that are less affected by unemployment, namely, the highest age groups, highly educated individuals and those who live in the Northeast or in rural areas. Moreover, we can observe that the gap in the unemployment rate shrinks slightly when we use a fuzzy measurement rather than the traditional one. For example, the unemployment rate for the age group 15–24 is 5.6 times higher than that of the age group 55–64 using the traditional approach and four times higher using the fuzzy approach.

Conclusions

The division of the working-age population into three mutually exclusive and exhaustive groups of those who are employed, unemployed and

Table 16.4 Unemployment rates (15–64 years) (%)

		Traditional measure (T)	*Fuzzy measure (F)*	*(F/T)*100*
Total	Total	10.8	15.8	146.3
By gender	Male	10.0	12.6	126.0
	Female	11.9	20.1	168.9
By age group	15–24 years	32.2	39.2	121.7
	25–34 years	15.9	21.9	137.7
	35–44 years	9.3	14.2	152.7
	45–54 years	7.7	12.4	161.0
	55–64 years	5.7	9.7	170.2
By country of birth	Italian born	10.3	14.8	143.7
	Foreign born	13.7	21.4	156.2
By education level	Lower secondary	14.9	21.0	140.9
	Upper secondary	10.2	15.0	147.1
	Third secondary	6.1	10.1	165.6
By regional group (NUTS 1 code)	North-West	7.1	11.7	164.8
	North-East	6.1	10.3	168.9
	Centre	9.6	15.1	157.3
	South	18.1	23.4	129.3
	Islands	20.1	26.3	130.8
By degree of urbanisation	Cities	11.6	17.0	146.6
	Towns and suburbs	10.5	15.2	144.8
	Rural area	10.1	15.0	148.5

Note: For definitions, see Table 16.3.

economically inactive conceals relevant grey areas among them, such as underemployment and marginal labour force attachment, which deserve special attention.

In this chapter, we focused on people in between employment and unemployment. Using a fuzzy approach, we introduced the concept of being 'employed to a certain degree'. Our methodological proposal considers both the number of hours actually worked and the fact that a person might wish/need to work more.

The results of our empirical application to 2018 data on the Italian labour force reveal to what extent our fuzzy measures of employment and unemployment differ from the traditional ones. The fuzzy employment rate of the total population is 55.2%, which is 5.6% lower than the official rate. We observe the largest downward correction for female workers, young workers, foreign-born workers and workers living in central Italy.

The fuzzy measurement of unemployment is 15.8%, which is 46.3% higher than the traditional rate. The largest upward correction is seen among female workers, workers between 55 and 64 years old, foreign-born workers, third-secondary educated and those living in the North.

Moreover, the fuzzy approach amplifies the disadvantages of female and foreign-born workers with respect to both employment and unemployment.

Notes

1 All conclusions drawn from the data are entirely those of the authors.
2 As specified, inactive people are assigned a μ_E value of 0.

References

Betti G., Cheli B., Lemmi A., Verma V. (2008) The fuzzy set approach to multidimensional poverty: the case of Italy in the 1990s, in N. Kakwani, J. Silber (eds.), *Quantitative Approaches to Multidimensional Poverty Measurement*, Palgrave MacMillan, London, pp. 30–48.

Betti G., Lemmi A. eds. (2013) *Poverty and Social Exclusion: New Methods of Analysis*, Routledge, London.

Cerioli A., Zani S. (1990) A fuzzy approach to the measurement of poverty, in C. Dagum, M. Zenga (eds.), *Income and Wealth Distribution, Inequality and Poverty*, Springer, Berlin, pp. 272–284.

Cheli B., Lemmi A. (1995) A 'totally' fuzzy and relative approach to the multidimensional analysis of poverty. *Economic Notes* 24, 115–134.

Eurostat (2019) *EU Labour Force Survey Database UserGuide*, November, Publications Office of the European Union, Luxembourg.

ILO (1982) *Statistics of Labour Force, Employment, Unemployment and Underemployment*, Report II of the 13th International Conference of Labour Statisticians, Geneva.

Zadeh L.A. (1965) Fuzzy sets. *Information and Control* 8, 338–353.

17 The Relationship Between Employment and Poverty Using Fuzzy Regression

Besma Belhadj and Firas Kaabi

Introduction

Poverty has many causes, first among them is unemployment or low-wage employment. Because of their income, or its absence, the poor cannot afford health care, making them more susceptible to disease and less likely to work full- or even part-time.

The eradication of extreme poverty requires addressing its root causes. Therefore, information on the characteristics of the population living in poverty is essential. In particular, data on their employment status (i.e. whether they are employed, unemployed or not part of the labour force) can provide insights into the factors that create poverty. For those who are employed yet still live in poverty, also called the working poor, it is likely that low earnings and, more generally, sub-standard working conditions, are to blame. Conversely, for the poor who are either unemployed or uncounted for in the labour force, poverty may be driven by a lack of employment opportunities and insufficient social protections.

Data on employment broken down by economic class, especially the share of the employed who are poor (the working poverty rate) conveys information on the link between employment and poverty, which is highly relevant for the formulation of effective policies. Employment should be a vector to lift people out of poverty, but this is true only if job quality is sufficient, including adequate earnings, job security and a safe working environment. The relationship between employment and poverty depends greatly on the extent to which decent work is ensured for the labour market.

To express this relationship, we use a classical statistical linear regression binder the poverty rate at the unemployment rate. In this statistical regression, problems can occur in the following situations: the number of observations is inadequate (small data set); difficulties arise in verifying distribution assumptions; the relationship between input and output variables is vague; the events or the degree to which they occur are ambiguous; and linearisation introduces some inaccuracy and distortion.

Thus, this statistical regression is problematic because of vagueness in the relationship between the independent and dependent variables and ambiguity associated with the event. This is the kind of situation that fuzzy regression is meant to address.

This chapter is structured as follows: The second section estimates the poverty rate based on the unemployment rate and explains the results and limitations of this estimation. The third section outlines an alternative estimation method called fuzzy regression. In this section, estimators of a linear fuzzy regression model are constructed, and the consistency of these estimators is established. The last section concludes.

The Poverty Rate as a Function of the Unemployment Rate

We start with the observation that poor people derive most of their income from work. This basic fact means that employment and the access which the poor have to decent earnings opportunities are crucial determinants in the reduction of poverty.

This observation leads us to estimate the relationship between the poverty rate P_i and the unemployment rate U_i in the period 2000–2015 for a group of developing countries for which the unemployment rate and the poverty rate are available, as follows:

$$P_i = 17.37 - 0.81U_i$$

$$(2.89)(-1.94) \tag{17.1}$$

$$\left(R^2 = 0.201; N = 23; t \text{ values in parentheses}\right)$$

This relationship depends on national income: the unemployment rate is generally higher in developing middle-income countries, and the poverty rate is higher in developing low-income countries. These two facts make the relationship negative.

Equation (17.1) is only illustrative, however, because unemployment data generally include not only the long-term unemployed but also the short-term unemployed, some of whom may be poor. However, the assumption made here is that the majority are long-term unemployed.

Fuzzy Linear Regression Models

Tanaka et al. (1982) were the first to introduce a fuzzy linear regression model. They constructed a linear regression model with fuzzy response data, crisp prediction data and fuzzy parameters as a mathematical programming problem. Their approach was later improved in many other studies, which can be roughly divided into two approaches: linear programming-based methods, called the possibilistic approach (e.g. Tanaka, 1987; Tanaka and Ishibuchi, 1991; Diamond and Tanaka, 1999; Hong and Yi, 2003; Hong et al., 2004), and fuzzy least-squares methods (e.g. Diamond, 1988; D'Urso and Gastaldi, 2000; D'Urso, 2003; Yang and Liu (2003).

Classical Statistical Regression and Fuzzy Regression Analysis

In many situations, the observations cannot be described accurately, for instance, when they depend on individual responses, as in the case of poverty. In this case, we can provide only an approximate description of them or an interval in which to enclose them. Here, we are concerned with a kind of uncertainty which is different from randomness, sometimes referred to as vagueness.

In ordinary regression analysis, deviations between the observed values and the estimates are assumed to be due to random errors. However, these deviations are sometimes due to the indefiniteness of the structure of the system or imprecise observations. The uncertainty in this type of regression model then becomes fuzziness, not randomness.

In fact, randomness and fuzziness are two different kinds of uncertainty (Chang and Ayyub, 2001). In ordinary regression analysis, the performance and validity of the least-squares method are reduced if its assumptions, such as independence and homogeneity of error terms, are violated. Fuzzy linear regression aims to model vague and imprecise phenomena using fuzzy model parameters. Fuzzy regression is different from ordinary least squares in the sense that it is not a statistical method (Kim and Chen, 1997).

The functional form of regression model (1) is as follows:

$$P_i = a_1 + a_2 U_i + \varepsilon_i \tag{17.2}$$

In some cases, we may need to consider that the relationship expressed in Equation (17.2) may be fuzzy. Indeed, three cases are possible when the predictor variable is fuzzy, but the parameters are crisp,

$$\vec{P}_i = a_1 + a_2 \vec{U}_i + \vec{\varepsilon}_i \tag{17.3}$$

the predictors are crisp and the parameters are fuzzy,

$$\vec{P}_i = \vec{a}_1 + \vec{a}_2 U_i + \vec{\varepsilon}_i \tag{17.4}$$

and when both the predictor and parameters are fuzzy,

$$\vec{P}_i = \vec{a}_1 + \vec{a}_2 \vec{U}_i + \vec{\varepsilon}_i \tag{17.5}$$

where $\vec{P}_i$ are the fuzzy responses.

Fuzzy Least-Squares Method

In this section, we estimate the parameters of model (17.4) in which the predictor or unknown parameters are trapezoidal fuzzy numbers.

$\vec{E} = (e_l, e_m, e_n, e_p)$ is a trapezoidal fuzzy number in which e_l and e_p are the left and right endpoints of the corresponding trapezoid, and e_m and e_n are the left and right midpoints (Figure 17.1).

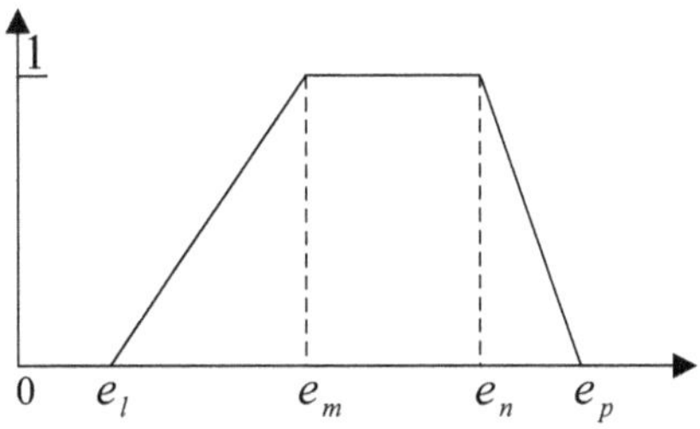

Figure 17.1 Trapezoidal fuzzy number.

In model (17.4), if $\vec{a}_1$ and $\vec{a}_2$ are trapezoidal fuzzy numbers, where $\vec{a}_1 = (a_{1l}, a_{1m}, a_{1n}, a_{1p})$ and $\vec{a}_2 = (a_{2l}, a_{2m}, a_{2n}, a_{2p})$, then, for $U_i > 0$, $\vec{a}_1 + \vec{a}_2 U_i$ is the trapezoidal fuzzy number:

$$\left(a_{1l} + a_{2l}U_i, a_{1m} + a_{2m}U_i, a_{1n} + a_{2n}U_i, a_{1p} + a_{2p}U_i\right)$$

To find an estimate for a_1 and a_2 we minimise the sum of the squared distances (Arabpour and Tata, 2008):

$$\begin{aligned} L(a_1, a_2) &= \sum_{i=1}^{n} d^2\left(\vec{P}_i, \vec{a}_1 + \vec{a}_2 U_i\right) \\ &= \sum_{i=1}^{n} \Big\{ \left(P_i - a_{1l} - a_{2l}U_i\right)^2 + 0.5\left(P_i - a_{1m} - a_{2m}U_i\right)^2 \\ &\quad + 0.5\left(P_i - a_{1n} - a_{2n}U_i\right)^2 + \left(P_i - a_{1p} - a_{2p}U_i\right)^2 \Big\} \end{aligned} \tag{17.6}$$

Differentiating with respect to a_{1l}, a_{1m}, a_{1n}, a_{1p} and a_{2l}, a_{2m}, a_{2n}, a_{2p}, we obtain the estimates of $\vec{a}_1$ and $\vec{a}_2$ as follows:

$$\hat{\vec{a}}_1 = \left(\hat{a}_{1l}, \hat{a}_{1m}, \hat{a}_{1n}, \hat{a}_{1p}\right) \text{ and } \hat{\vec{a}}_2 = \left(\hat{a}_{2l}, \hat{a}_{2m}, \hat{a}_{2n}, \hat{a}_{2p}\right)$$

where $\hat{a}_{2l} = \dfrac{\sum_{i=1}^{n} U_i P_{il} - n\bar{U}\bar{P}_{il}}{\sum_{i=1}^{n} U_i^2 - n\bar{U}^2}$, and $\hat{a}_{1l} = \bar{P}_l - \hat{a}_{2l}\bar{U}$,

$$\hat{a}_{2m} = \frac{\sum_{i=1}^{n} U_i P_{im} - n\bar{U}\bar{P}_{im}}{\sum_{i=1}^{n} U_i^2 - n\bar{U}^2}, \text{ and } \hat{a}_{1m} = \bar{P}_l - \hat{a}_{2m}\bar{U},$$

$$\hat{a}_{2n} = \frac{\sum_{i=1}^{n} U_i P_{in} - n\bar{U}\bar{P}_{in}}{\sum_{i=1}^{n} U_i^2 - n\bar{U}^2}, \text{ and } \hat{a}_{1n} = \bar{P}_l - \hat{a}_{2n}\bar{U},$$

$$\hat{a}_{2p} = \frac{\sum_{i=1}^{n} U_i P_{ip} - n\bar{U}\bar{P}_{ip}}{\sum_{i=1}^{n} U_i^2 - n\bar{U}^2}, \text{ and } \hat{a}_{1p} = \bar{P}_l - \hat{a}_{2p}\bar{U},$$

$$\text{and } \bar{U} = \frac{\sum_{i=1}^{n} U_i}{n}, \bar{P}_l = \frac{\sum_{i=1}^{n} P_{il}}{n}, \bar{P}_m = \frac{\sum_{i=1}^{n} P_{im}}{n}, \bar{P}_n = \frac{\sum_{i=1}^{n} P_{in}}{n}, \bar{P}_p = \frac{\sum_{i=1}^{n} P_{ip}}{n}$$

In the following sections, we propose two alternative methods to the least-squares method. These are, respectively, the error's membership function method and the dissemblance index method.

The Error's Membership Function Method

Beginning with model (17.4), we can write:

$$\mu_{\tilde{\varepsilon}_i}(\varepsilon_i) = \mu_{\tilde{P}_i(-)\tilde{a}_1 + \tilde{a}_2 U_i}(\varepsilon_i),\ \varepsilon_i = P_i - a_1 - a_2 U_i \tag{17.7}$$

The term on the right-hand side of Equation (17.7) shows subtraction of fuzzy numbers as follows:

$$\begin{aligned} \mu_{\tilde{\varepsilon}_i}(\varepsilon_i) &= \mu_{\tilde{P}_i(-)\tilde{a}_1 + \tilde{a}_2 U_i}(\varepsilon_i) \\ &= \bigvee_{\varepsilon_i} \left(\mu_{\tilde{a}_1 + \tilde{a}_2 U_i}(a_1 + a_2 U_i) \wedge \mu_{\tilde{P}_i}(P_i) \right) \end{aligned} \tag{17.8}$$

The estimate of a_1 and a_2 in model (17.4) involves solving the following minimisation problem:

$$\min \mu_{\tilde{\varepsilon}_i}(\vec{a}_1, \vec{a}_2) \tag{17.9}$$

Suppose that $\mu_{\tilde{P}_i}(P_i)$ and $\mu_{\tilde{a}_1 + \tilde{a}_2 U_i}(a_1 + a_2 U_i)$ are represented as in Figure 17.2; they are expressed, respectively, in Equations (17.10) and (17.11).

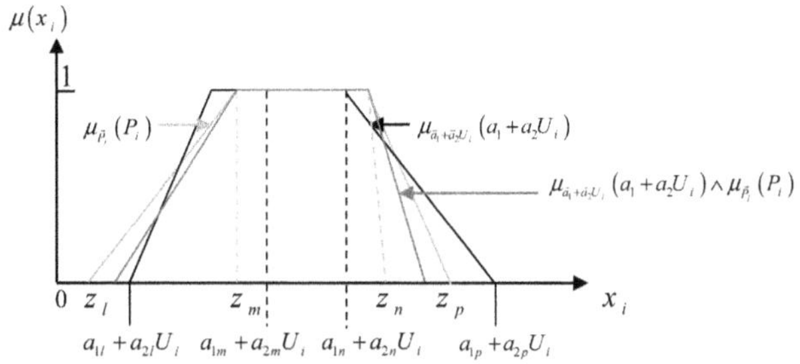

Figure 17.2 Error's membership function.

Let

$$\mu_{\tilde{P}_i}(x_i)=\begin{cases} 0 & x_i < z_l \\ \dfrac{x_i - z_l}{z_m - z_l} & z_l \le x_i < z_m \\ 1 & z_m \le x_i < z_n \\ \dfrac{x_i - z_p}{z_n - z_p} & z_n \le x_i < z_p \\ 0 & x_i \ge z_p \end{cases}, \tag{17.10}$$

and

$$\mu_{\tilde{a}_1+\tilde{a}_2U_i}(x_i)=\begin{cases} 0 & x_i < a_{1l}+a_{2l}U_i \\ \dfrac{x_i - a_{1l} - a_{2l}U_i}{(a_{1m}-a_{1l})+(a_{2m}-a_{2l})U_i} & a_{1l}+a_{2l}U_i \le x_i < a_{1m}+a_{2m}U_i \\ 1 & a_{1m}+a_{2m}U_i \le x_i < a_{1n}+a_{2n}U_i \\ \dfrac{x_i - a_{1p} - a_{2p}U_i}{(a_{1n}-a_{1p})+(a_{2n}-a_{2p})U_i} & a_{1n}+a_{2n}U_i \le x_i < a_{1p}+a_{2p}U_i \\ 0 & x_i \ge a_{1p}+a_{2p}U_i \end{cases} \tag{17.11}$$

$\mu_{\tilde{a}_1+\tilde{a}_2U_i}(a_1+a_2U_i)\wedge\mu_{\tilde{P}_i}(P_i)$ in Equation (17.8) is represented in Figure 17.2 and expressed in Equation (17.12).

Now using Equation (17.10), let $\forall\alpha\in[0,1]\quad \alpha=\dfrac{z_l^{(\alpha)}-z_l}{z_m-z_l}$

$$\alpha = z_m^{(\alpha)}$$

$$\alpha = z_n^{(\alpha)}$$

$$\alpha = \frac{z_p^{(\alpha)}-z_p}{z_n-z_p}$$

From which $\vec{P}_\alpha=\left(z_l^{(\alpha)},z_m^{(\alpha)},z_n^{(\alpha)},z_p^{(\alpha)}\right)$

$$=\left[\alpha\left(z_m-z_l\right)+z_l,z_m,z_n,\alpha\left(z_n-z_p\right)+z_p\right]$$

Now using Equation (17.11), we obtain $\alpha=\dfrac{b_{il}^{(\alpha)}-b_{il}}{b_{im}-b_{il}}$

$$\alpha = b_{im}^{(\alpha)}$$

$$\alpha = b_{in}^{(\alpha)}$$

$$\alpha = \frac{b_{ip}^{(\alpha)}-b_{ip}}{b_{in}-b_{ip}}$$

From which $\left(\vec{a}_1+\vec{a}_2U\right)_\alpha=\left(b_{il}^{(\alpha)},b_{im}^{(\alpha)},b_{in}^{(\alpha)},b_{ip}^{(\alpha)}\right)$

$$=\left[\alpha\left(b_{im}-b_{il}\right)+b_{il},b_{im},b_{in},\alpha\left(b_{in}-b_{ip}\right)+b_{ip}\right]$$

We must then have

$$\vec{P}_\alpha(-)\left(\vec{a}_1+\vec{a}_2U\right)_\alpha=\left(z_l^{(\alpha)},z_m^{(\alpha)},z_n^{(\alpha)},z_p^{(\alpha)}\right)(-)\left(b_{il}^{(\alpha)},b_{im}^{(\alpha)},b_{in}^{(\alpha)},b_{ip}^{(\alpha)}\right)$$

$$=\left[z_l^{(\alpha)}-b_{ip}^{(\alpha)},z_m^{(\alpha)}-b_{in}^{(\alpha)},z_{in}^{(\alpha)}-b_{im}^{(\alpha)},z_p^{(\alpha)}-b_{il}^{(\alpha)}\right]$$

Thus, if we define $z_l^{(\alpha)}-b_{ip}^{(\alpha)}=z_l-\alpha\left(b_{im}-b_{il}\right)-b_{il}$

$$z_p^{(\alpha)}-b_{il}^{(\alpha)}=z_p-\alpha\left(b_{in}-b_{ip}\right)-b_{ip}$$

$$\alpha = \frac{z_l^{(\alpha)}-b_{ip}^{(\alpha)}-z_l+b_{il}}{b_{im}-b_{il}}$$

$$\alpha = \frac{z_p^{(\alpha)}-b_{il}^{(\alpha)}-z_p+b_{ip}}{b_{in}-b_{ip}}$$

Then,

$$\mu_{\tilde{P}_i(-)(\vec{a}_1+\vec{a}_2U_i)}(x_i)=\begin{cases}0 & x_i<-b_{il}+z_l\\ \dfrac{x_i+b_{il}-z_l}{b_{im}-b_{il}} & -b_{il}+z_l\le x_i<b_{im}-2b_{il}+z_l\\ 1 & b_{im}-2b_{il}+z_l\le x_i<b_{in}-2b_{ip}+z_p\\ \dfrac{x_i+b_{ip}-z_p}{b_{in}-b_{ip}} & b_{in}-2b_{ip}+z_p\le x_i<-b_{ip}+z_p\\ 0 & x_i\ge -b_{ip}+z_p\end{cases} \quad (17.12)$$

where $b_{ij}=a_{1j}+a_{2j}U_i \quad j=l,m,n,p \quad i=1,..,n.$

We note that the graph for Equation (17.12) can be visualised as in Figure 17.2.

We show that to solve Equation (17.9) is to solve the system

$$\begin{cases}b_{im}-b_{il}=0\\ b_{in}-b_{ip}=0\end{cases} \quad \forall i=1,..,n.$$

This proves that the error's membership function, $\mu_{\vec{\varepsilon}_i}(\vec{a}_1,\vec{a}_2)$, is also the hatched area of Figure 17.3 given by the difference between the membership function of the observed value $\mu_{\tilde{P}_i}(P_i)$ and the membership function of the estimated value $\mu_{\vec{a}_1+\vec{a}_2U_i}(a_1+a_2U_i)$ of P_i. Therefore, the solution to Equation (17.9) is equivalent and it amounts to minimising the hatched areas, hence the following method.

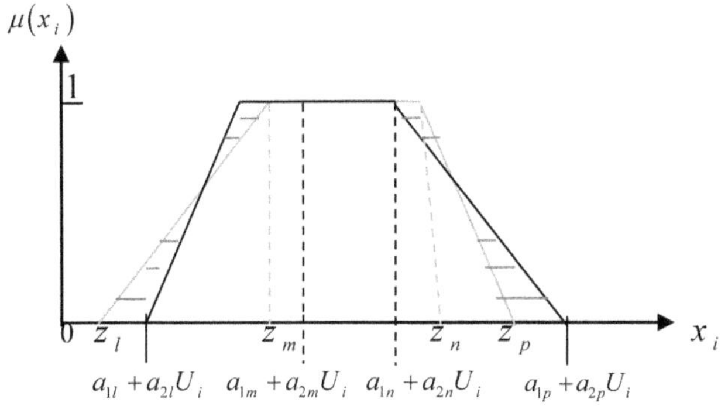

Figure 17.3 Distance $\delta(A,B)$ (using the area method)

The Dissemblance Index Method

Starting with Equation (17.10), we define $A = [z_l, z_m, z_n, z_p]$

$$\text{or } \forall \alpha \in [0,1] \alpha = \frac{x - z_l}{z_m - z_l} \Rightarrow x = \alpha(z_m - z_l) + z_l$$

$$\alpha = \frac{x - z_p}{z_n - z_p} \Rightarrow x = \alpha(z_n - z_p) + z_p$$

$$A_\alpha = [z_l + \alpha(z_m - z_l), z_p + \alpha(z_n - z_p)],$$

and starting with Equation (17.11), $B_\alpha = [b_{il} + \alpha(b_{im} - b_{il}), b_{ip} + \alpha(b_{in} - b_{ip})]$

where $b_{ij} = a_{1j} + a_{2j}U_i \qquad j = l, m, n, p.$

Note that $A = [z_l, z_m, z_n, z_p]$ and $B = [b_{il}, b_{im}, b_{in}, b_{ip}]$ intersect at the following two points: $z_l + \alpha(z_m - z_l) = b_{il} + \alpha(b_{im} - b_{il})$ yields

$$\alpha_1 = \frac{b_{il} - z_l}{z_m - z_l - b_{im} + b_{il}} \tag{17.13}$$

$z_p + \alpha(z_n - z_p) = b_{ip} + \alpha(b_{in} - b_{ip})$ yields

$$\alpha_2 = \frac{b_{ip} - z_p}{z_n - z_p - b_{in} + b_{ip}} \tag{17.14}$$

We then have

$$\begin{aligned} z_l^{(\alpha)} - b_{il}^{(\alpha)} &= z_l + \alpha(z_m - z_l) - b_{il} - \alpha(b_{im} - b_{il}) \\ &= z_l - b_{il} + \alpha(z_m - z_l - b_{im} + b_{il}), \end{aligned}$$

$$\begin{aligned} \text{and } z_p^{(\alpha)} - b_{ip}^{(\alpha)} &= z_p + \alpha(z_n - z_p) - b_{ip} - \alpha(b_{in} - b_{ip}) \\ &= z_p - b_{ip} + \alpha(z_n - z_p - b_{in} + b_{ip}) \end{aligned}$$

If we proceed to integrate from $\alpha = 0$ to $\alpha = 1$, we obtain a distance $\delta(A,B)$ by summing the distances $\delta(A,B) = \int_{\alpha=0}^{1} \delta(A_\alpha, B_\alpha) d\alpha$, which is called the dissemblance index of A and B. $\delta(A,B)$ is a distance between the fuzzy numbers A and B.

$$
\begin{aligned}
\delta(A,B) = & \int_{\alpha=0}^{\alpha_1} \left[z_l - b_{il} + \alpha\left(z_m - z_l - b_{im} + b_{il}\right)\right] d\alpha \\
& + \int_{\alpha_1}^{1} \left[z_l - b_{il} + \alpha\left(z_m - z_l - b_{im} + b_{il}\right)\right] d\alpha \\
& + \int_{\alpha=0}^{\alpha_2} \left[z_p - b_{ip} + \alpha\left(z_n - z_p - b_{in} + b_{ip}\right)\right] d\alpha \\
& + \int_{\alpha_2}^{1} \left[z_p - b_{ip} + \alpha\left(z_n - z_p - b_{in} + b_{ip}\right)\right] d\alpha
\end{aligned} \tag{17.15}
$$

The calculation of Equation (17.15) shows that:

$$
\begin{aligned}
\delta(A,B) = & \frac{1}{2}\left(z_l - b_{il} + z_m - b_{im}\right) \\
& + \frac{1}{2}\left(z_p - b_{ip} + z_n - b_{in}\right)
\end{aligned} \tag{17.16}
$$

where $b_{ij} = a_{1j} + a_{2j}U_i \qquad j = l,m,n,p \quad i = 1,\ldots,n.$

With trapezoidal fuzzy numbers, the distance $\delta(A,B)$ is the sum of the hatched areas in Figure 17.3.

The estimate of a_1 and a_2 in model (17.4) consists of solving the following minimisation problem:

$$
\min \sum_i \delta^2(A,B) = \min \sum_i \delta^2(\vec{a}_1, \vec{a}_2) \tag{17.17}
$$

The solution to Equation (17.17) consists of solving Equation (17.18).

$$
\begin{cases}
\dfrac{\partial \delta^2(\vec{a}_1,\vec{a}_2)}{\partial a_{1j}} = 0 \\
\dfrac{\partial \delta^2(\vec{a}_1,\vec{a}_2)}{\partial a_{2j}} = 0
\end{cases} \qquad \forall j = l,m,n,p \tag{17.18}
$$

The solution to Equation (17.18) for $n \to \infty$ is:

$$
a_{1l} = z_n / \sum_j z_j + \frac{2\bar{U}^2}{U^2 - \bar{U}^2} z_n, a_{2l} = \frac{-2\bar{U}}{U^2 - \bar{U}^2} z_n \tag{17.19}
$$

$$
a_{1p} = z_m / \sum_j z_j + \frac{2\bar{U}^2}{U^2 - \bar{U}^2} z_m, a_{2l} = \frac{-2\bar{U}}{U^2 - \bar{U}^2} z_m \tag{17.20}
$$

Based on Equations (17.19) and (17.20), in developing countries, the relationship between the poverty rate and the unemployment rate is always negative.

One explanation for this finding is that in developing countries, the poor are forced to work without receiving real social assistance. In these countries, it also appears that the long-term unemployed, for the most part, cannot be considered poor. The reason for these two facts is illustrated by the potential for a negative relationship between the unemployment rate and the poverty rate.

The nature of the relationship between poverty and unemployment has recently been unclear. Although this topic has received more extensive scholarly attention worldwide, no studies have examined this negative relationship in developing countries. This is because policymakers approach the general notion of the labour market according to the conditions in a developed market economy. In these economies, which have systems of social insurance, the problem of poverty is rightly captured in the unemployment rate.

Conclusion

In this chapter we use a new method to estimate the parameters of a fuzzy regression model with a crisp predictor and fuzzy parameters. This method is especially attractive because it is based on an integral abstraction of reality while retaining the same process as a classical linear regression. Moreover, in this method, the method of calculation is related to the form of the membership functions and therefore to the reality considered. In a future work, we extend our methodology to the case of a fuzzy predictor and fuzzy parameters.

References

Arabpour A.R., Tata M. (2008), Estimating the parameters of a fuzzy linear regression model, *Iranian Journal of Fuzzy Systems*, 5(2): 1–19.

Chang Y., Ayyub B. (2001), Fuzzy regression methods: A comparative assessment, *Fuzzy Sets and Systems*, 119: 187–203.

Diamond P. (1988), Fuzzy least squares. *Information Sciences: An International Journal*, 46(3): 141–157.

Diamond P., Tanaka H. (1999), Fuzzy regression analysis. In Roman Słowiński (Ed.), Fuzzy Sets in Decision Analysis, *Operations Research and Statistics*, p. 387. Kluwer Academic.

D'Urso P. (2003), Linear regression analysis for fuzzy/crisp input and fuzzy/crisp output data, *Computational Statistics and Data Analysis*, 42(1–2): 47–72.

D'Urso P., Gastaldi T. (2000), A least-squares approach to fuzzy linear regression analysis, *Computational Statistics and Data Analysis*, 34(4): 427–440.

Hong D., Hwang C., Ahn C. (2004), Ridge estimation for regression models with crisp inputs and Gaussian fuzzy output, *Fuzzy Sets and Systems*, 142(2): 307–319.

Hong D., Yi H. (2003), A note on fuzzy regression model with fuzzy input and output data for manpower forecasting, *Fuzzy Sets and Systems*, 138(2): 301–305.

Kim K.J., Chen H. (1997), A comparison of fuzzy and nonparametric linear regression, *Computers & Operations Research*, 44: 505–519.

Tanaka H. (1987), Fuzzy data analysis by possibilistic linear models, *Fuzzy Sets and Systems*, 24: 363–375.

Tanaka H., Ishibuchi H. (1991), Identification of possibilistic linear systems by quadratic membership functions of fuzzy parameters, *Fuzzy Sets and Systems*, 41(2): 145–160.

Tanaka H., Uejima S., Asai K. (1982), Linear regression analysis with fuzzy model, *IEEE Transactions Systems Man and Cybernetics*, 12(6): 903–907.

Yang M., Liu H. (2003), Fuzzy least-squares algorithms for interactive fuzzy linear regression models, *Fuzzy Sets and Systems*, 135: 305–316.

18 Geo-Marketing, a New Approach Using Fuzzy Clustering

Lorenzo Mori and Duccio Stefano Gazzei

Introduction

Constant economic evolution, the discovery of new technologies and the increasing importance of the customer in recent decades have led to rapid developments in marketing. Marketing is not a new science. As Jones and Shaw (2002) wrote, it has existed since ancient times but has become a great global challenge for companies that spend millions every year on advertising. The paradigm has also changed, as the priority today is not selling but, rather, understanding what clients want and creating custom products for everyone. From this perspective, a lot of work has recently been done.

Marketing techniques encompass many subjects. Neuroscience yielded neuro-marketing (see Lee, Broderick and Chamberlain, 2007), which focuses on channels for emotional communication. Out of digitisation grew digital marketing, which played a decisive role in the development of e-commerce. Others include relationship marketing, buzz marketing and guerrilla marketing.

In this chapter, we are mainly interested in geo-marketing, which uses geo-location to plan and implement marketing activities (see Cliquet, 2006). Interest has grown in techniques to determinate the particular geographic zone where potential consumers live, work or do something else. Among the most important is the Voronoi cell, also known as Thiessen polygons, which contain all the points closest (in terms of distance) to a particular place. Recently, Azri, Ujang and Abdul-Rahman et al. (2016, 2020) have addressed the use of 3D geo-marketing segmentation with 3D Voronoi cells to deal with the locations of vertical components in high-rise and multi-storey buildings, specifically cluster urban areas from a new multi-dimensional perspective – for example, the placement of a shop within a multi-level marketplace. Another well-known way to determine the basin of gravitation by people is an isochrone map, which is generally used to define accessibility to a certain location in terms of time; for an example, see Baltyzhakova and Bryzhataya (2019). This is a critical point for highly competitive shops.

Table 18.1 Eurisko groups

Cluster number	*Education*	*Wealth*	*Age*	*ID*
1	1	1	1	Tycoon
2	1	1	0	Cultural élite
3	1	0	1	Disillusioned
4	1	0	0	Young innovator
5	0	1	1	Affluent
6	0	1	0	Functional
7	0	0	1	Distant
8	0	0	0	Disengaged

It is also possible to find fuzzy applications for geo-marketing. Hsu, Chu and Chan (2000), trying to solve the problem of traditional segmentation, which assigns a single membership, presented an application of *c*-means fuzzy clustering to determine market segments. In India, Jain and Krishnapuram (2001) used fuzzy sets for the personalisation of e-commerce and demonstrated the advantages of employing a fuzzy approach to marketing, especially in determining targets. Grekousis and Hatzichristos (2013) applied unsupervised fuzzy clustering with a Gustafson-Kessel algorithm (1978) for the delineation of geo-marketing regions in the metropolitan region of Athens, Greece.

In this chapter, we use consumer data from a big Italian bank with a simple but efficient technique to divide customers into different clusters. Eurisko segmentation logic[1] is a method that enables us to cluster the population using socio-demographic information. Many different subdivisions can be used, but with respect to banks we are interested in clustering the population based on only three dimensions: wealth (IW), education (IE) and age (IA). For example, tycoons are rich, older and highly educated. In this way, it is possible to determine what consumers want and how they want to be approached. This logic allows us to define these dimensions for each consumer, such that it equals 1 if it is high, and 0 if it is low. We obtain eight groups, as seen in Table 18.1.

In the following discussion, we suggest an alternative approach to geo-marketing. We try to design a method which does not dichotomise the population and has more flexible definitions of wealth, education and age. In particular, our goal is a predictive model for an area about which we do not know very much or in which we do not already have many customers.

A Fuzzy Approach to Geo-Marketing

Several steps are necessary to obtain the three dimensions presented in the Eurisko segmentation using a fuzzy method (Betti and Verma, 2008; Betti and Lemmi, 2013; Betti et al., 2015; Betti et al., 2016; Betti, 2017; Bettio et al., 2020).

1. identification of the variables to include in the analysis;
2. transformation of the variables into the interval [0,1];
3. exploratory and confirmatory factor analysis;
4. calculation of weights within each dimension (each group);
5. construction of the three fuzzy measures.

Identification of the Variables

To define the three dimensions, we begin with data from the census division of Rome. We restrict our study to the census area within the square built around the Grande Raccordo Anulare, the A90 (literally, the Great Ring Junction).

We selected 15 variables for the dimension of wealth, 11 for the dimension of education and 5 for the dimension of age. Some of the variables are continuous and others are discrete. All these variables are in terms of the average in a household in the census area.[2]

Transformation of the Variables into the Interval [0,1]

Calculating a fuzzy index requires the determination of a membership function to transform each variable into the interval [0,1]. For continuous variables, the membership function is a cumulative distribution function, in which j is the category of the variable x for individual i, and $F_{j,i}(x)$ is the value of a cumulative function of j for i. In order to transform the positive score to a deprivation score we consider the complement to one that is, 1- $F_{j,i}(x)$

Discrete variables are divided into classes (categorical value), and the membership function is as follows:

$$d_{j,i} = \frac{1 - F(c_{j,i})}{1 - F(1)} \tag{18.1}$$

where $C_{j,i}$ is the value of category j for i, and $F(c_{j,i})$ is the value of the cumulative function of j for i and $F(1)$ is the value assumed for the highest category. To obtain the deprivation score from the positive ones, we use the following equation:

$$s_{j,i} = 1 - \frac{1 - F(c_{j,i})}{1 - F(1)} \tag{18.2}$$

Commonly, if the variable is dichotomous, the deprivation index d is 1 for deprivation and 0 otherwise, whereas a positive score s is 0 for deprivation and 1 otherwise.

Table 18.2 List of variables

Dimension		*Variable*
Wealth	1	Square metres
	2	Income
	3	Consumption
	4	Postal savings
	5	Bank accounts
	6	Bank deposits
	7	Securities accounts
	8	Funds
	9	Asset administration
	10	Insurance policies
	11	Asset management
	12	Deposit and savings accounts
	13	Current bank accounts
	14	Debit card
	15	Credit card
Education	1	Degree*
	2	High school*
	3	*Junior high school**
	4	*Elementary school* *
	5	EET (employed-educated-trained)*
	6	Housewife/Husband
	7	*Looking for work*
	8	*Looking for a first job*
	9	*NEET (not-employed-educated-trained)* *
	10	Employed*
	11	Students
Age	1	Number of members*
	2	Unmarried*
	3	*Widowed**
	4	*Divorced**
	5	Average age of members*

*Discrete variables. **Variables in italics have a negative score.

Some variables that should be discrete (e.g. debit and credit cards) are considered continuous here because we are using an average value, so the choice as to whether to bring back them in class is determined by their distribution. It is also important to stress that the negative or positive score was assumed and then confirmed using factor analysis.

In Table 18.2, we report all the variables to clarify which are assumed to have a positive or negative score.

Exploratory and Confirmatory Factor Analysis

To construct a summary index, we first have to identify and investigate the latent group of geographical variables. To achieve this objective, we

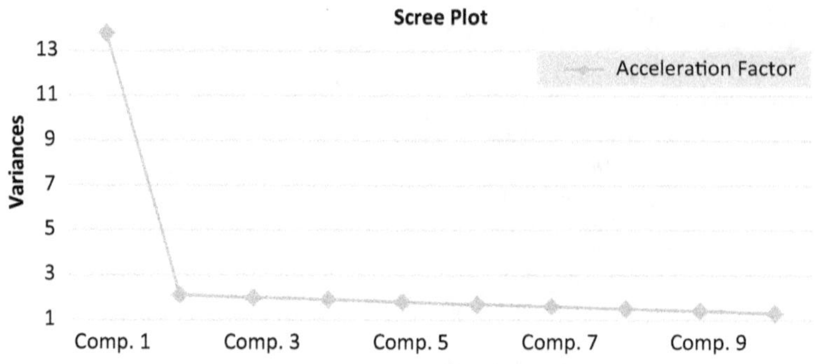

Figure 18.1 Scree plot.

use exploratory and confirmatory analysis. Figure 18.1 shows how many groups were 'suggested' by the exploratory analysis.

The method in the acceleration factor, which is a mathematical method for determining where the slope of the curve changes most, suggests that the number of groups might be only one.

It is also possible to use other criteria to choose the number of groups.

- *Parallel analysis*: also known as Horn's parallel analysis (1965), it compares the eigenvalues generated from the data matrix to the eigenvalues generated from a Monte-Carlo simulated matrix of the same size. It suggests six groups;
- *Optimal coordinates*: this method determines the location of the scree by measuring the gradients associated with eigenvalues and their preceding coordinates. It suggests six groups;
- *Eigenvalues*: the number of groups, if this is the method followed, equals the number of eigenvalues greater than their mean. It suggests seven groups.

The solution could be very different if we consider one method instead of another. Nevertheless, the standardised loadings (pattern matrix) based upon the correlation matrix show that many variables do not clearly belong to a unique group.

In order to achieve our goal of reproducing the three Eurisko indicators in a fuzzy way, we evaluate a confirmatory factor analysis (CFA) with the parameter in which the number of clusters was three. We summarise the results of this procedure.

Table 18.3 reports the following index:

- the comparative fit index (CFI) analyses the model fit by comparing the discrepancy between the data and the hypothesised model, which has a range between 0 and 1, with larger value indicating a better fit;

Table 18.3 Confirmatory factor analysis

Estimator:	ML
Optimisation method	NLMINB
Number of free parameters	65
Number of observations	7156
User model versus baseline:	
Comparative fit index (CFI)	0.616
Tucker-Lewis index (TLI)	0.586
Root mean square error of approximation:	
RMSEA	0.242
P-Value RMSEA < = 0.05	0.000
Standardised root mean square residual:	
SRMR	0.095

- The Tucker-Lewis index (TLI), also known as a non-normed fit index, analyses the discrepancy between the chi-square value of the hypothesised model and the chi-square value of the null model, which has a range between 0 and 1. A value of $k\%$ indicates that the model of interest improves the fit by $k\%$ relative to the null model;
- Root mean square error of approximation (RMSEA) is based on an analysis of the residual, and a good fit is indicated by a low value;
- Standardised root mean square residual (SRMR) is the square root of the difference between the residuals of the sample covariance matrix and the hypothesised model, with low value indicating a good fit.

Obtaining a good fit enables us to continue our analysis with a hypothesis on three groups, as defined in the first paragraph.

Calculation of Weights Within Each Group

To obtain the final three indicators, we have to calculate weights. To do this, we adopted the approach proposed by Betti and Verma (2008), in which the weights are given by the product of two factors: the dispersion of variables and their correlation with other variables in each index.

$$w = w_a * w_b \tag{18.3}$$

In particular, for the dimension of wealth, we use the inverse of variable coefficients to give greater importance to rare things (Table 18.4).

Construction of the Three Fuzzy Measures

Step 5 uses the weights found in step 4, so we use the following equation to obtain the three indicators.

Table 18.4 Weight of variables

Dimension	N	*Variable*	W_a	W_b	W
Wealth	1	Square metre	1.486	0.120	1.493
	2	Income	1.510	0.077	0.969
	3	Consumption	1.512	0.077	0.973
	4	Postal savings	1.533	0.078	1.000
	5	Bank accounts	1.499	0.074	0.926
	6	Bank deposits	0.763	0.183	1.166
	7	Securities	1.472	0.076	0.938
	8	Cash	1.466	0.076	0.925
	9	Asset administration	1.484	0.075	0.928
	10	Insurance policies	1.480	0.075	0.922
	11	Asset management	1.481	0.074	0.920
	12	Deposits and savings accounts	1.526	0.080	1.022
	13	Bank accounts	1.502	0.074	0.928
	14	Debit card	1.509	0.077	0.964
	15	Credit card	1.484	0.075	0.926
Education	1	Degree	0.206	0.243	0.134
	2	High school	0.386	0.289	0.301
	3	Junior high school	0.210	0.226	0.127
	4	Elementary school	0.077	0.222	0.046
	5	EET (employed-educated-trained)	1.063	0.279	0.799
	6	Housewife/Husband	2.117	0.276	1.573
	7	Looking for employment	2.829	0.286	2.175
	8	Looking for a first job	2.963	0.349	2.783
	9	NEET (not-employed-educated-trained)	3.001	0.305	2.646
	10	Employed	0.710	0.290	0.555
	11	Students	1.233	0.315	1.043
Age	1	Number of members	4.848	0.712	1.811
	2	Unmarried	1.334	0.731	0.511
	3	Widowers	4.258	0.756	0.168
	4	Divorced	0.374	0.781	0.153
	5	Average age of members	2.141	0.744	0.835

$$\hat{I}_{h,i} = \frac{\sum_{J=1}^{k_h} v_{j,i} \cdot w_{h,j}}{\sum_{J=1}^{k_h} w_{h,j}} \quad (18.4)$$

where $\hat{I}_{h,i}$ is the estimation of the index in one of the h = 1,2,3 dimension (in our dimensions for wealth, education and age) for zone i, while $v_{j,i}$ is the value of variable j for zone i, and $w_{h,j}$ is the weight.

A graphical analysis[3] of the indicators could be helpful in understanding what we have done. In Figure 18.2, we plot three different maps of Rome, in which every dot is the centre of a census zone, and a darker colour (as detailed in the legends) means the index is closer to one. In the wealth dimension in particular, the red dots mark the richest districts and yellow dots indicate the poorest. For the other two dimensions, obtaining similar

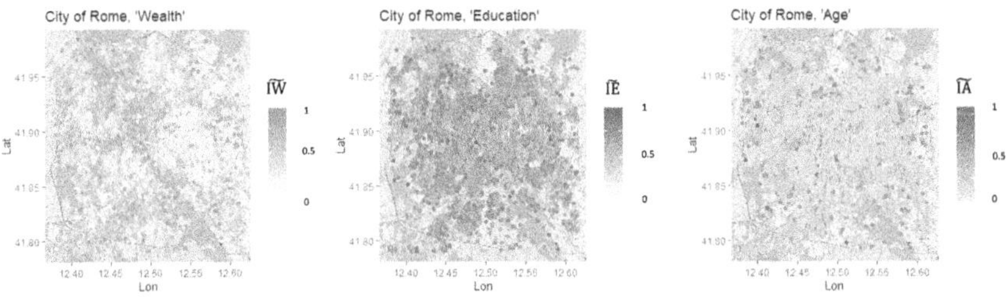

Figure 18.2 A graphical illustration of the dimensions (scale: 1: 500,000 cm).

confirmation is more complex where there is less variability, and it is also difficult to know which districts have a high value.

Estimation of Parameters

In order to estimate the three fuzzy dimensions for very small areas (we subdivided the area considered before into 90,000 sub-areas), we selected a sample of 10,000 geo-referenced bank customers, for whom we have the value of the three dichotomous dimensions. We use the membership function described above to transform the variables into the interval [0,1]. The consumers extracted were added to the census zone data obtained earlier.

We stress two points in estimating the value. The first law of geography is: '*Everything is related to everything else, but near things are more related than distant things*' (Tobler, 1970). Taking this into account and applying it to the economy, we assume that the closer people live to one another, the more similar they are. Each of the 90,000 cells is delimited with geo-referenced coordinates, and, when they form a rectangular cell, we use their centre as the point from which we perform the estimation.

Borrowing the inverse distance weighting (IDW) interpolation from geostatistics,[4] we obtained the estimation. To apply this model, we formed a hypothesis: the maximum distance (d_i) beyond which no similarities are found between the points is 2 kilometres. The weights (λ_i) we use are inversely proportional to the distance and scaled so that they add up to one.

$$\tilde{I}_h = \sum_{i=1}^{n} \lambda_i \cdot \hat{I}_i \text{ with } \lambda_i = \frac{1/d_i}{\sum_{i=1}^{n} \frac{1}{d_i}} \lambda_i = \begin{cases} \dfrac{1/d_i}{\sum_{i=0}^{n} \frac{1}{d_i}}, & d_i \le 2 \\ 0, & d_i > 2 \end{cases}, \sum_{i=1}^{n} \lambda_i = 1 \quad (18.5)$$

This method enables us to obtain a good estimation of the three dimensions. To confirm the estimation, we sample 10,000 other consumers in the bank dataset ten times, and to compare the data, we assign a value of

1 if the estimation is equal to or higher than the third quartile of the distribution of the estimates, and 0 otherwise. In Table 18.5, we summarise the results.

It is also interesting to focus on one area (e.g. the area around the Vatican City) and see the data illustrated in a map (see Figure 18.3).

These maps contain 5,400 of the 90,000 cells that we have created and for which we have estimated the value. We can see from them how the value changes from one part of the city to another even in a small zone.

Although the individual estimations are not far from the real value, we are also interested in obtaining a good degree of accuracy in the composition of the three dimensions, in such a way as to reproduce the Eurisko model. If we try to do that with the same approach as described above, we obtain the results reported in Table 18.6.

Clearly, that is not very good. Anyway, it was impossible to expect a different result from the moment that not only the single estimation has to have a good accuracy but also the triad of the three indicators must. To solve this problem, we seek an alternative method for achieving Eurisko segmentation and use *c*-means clustering (Dunne, 1973; Bezdek, 1981). Also known as *k*-means fuzzy clustering, it similar to classical *k*-means clustering except that fuzzy clustering does not give a unique group for each unit but, rather, the degree of its membership in all groups. Using a method that is not different from Eurisko's, we use eight clusters; however, some methods enable us to determine the number of optimal clusters (Xie and Beni index, Fuzzy silhouette index, etc.).

This procedure yields the following Centers for the clusters (see Table 18.7), where N is the number of cells with a larger membership function for that cluster.

It is obvious that it is impossible to link these centres to the Eurisko ones, but if each of the 90,000 cells has not a single person but, rather, a set of

Table 18.5 Accuracy of the estimations

	$\widetilde{IW}$	$\widetilde{IE}$	$\widetilde{IA}$
1	0.6755	0.5632	0.5286
2	0.6823	0.5523	0.5387
3	0.6774	0.5488	0.5337
4	0.6748	0.5558	0.5323
5	0.6784	0.5610	0.5305
6	0.6862	0.5572	0.5334
7	0.6752	0.5546	0.5347
8	0.6826	0.5571	0.5328
9	0.6764	0.5607	0.5327
10	0.6819	0.5589	0.5342
Mean	0.6791	0.5570	0.5332

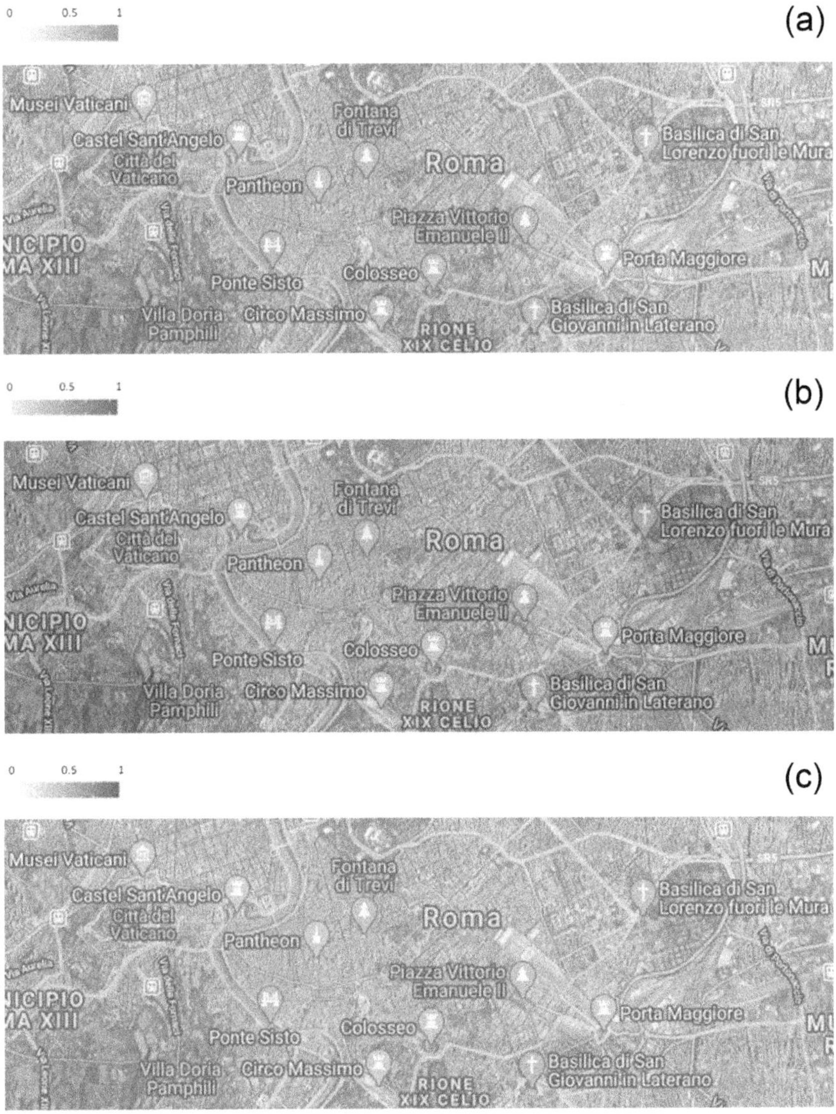

Figure 18.3 Map of Rome with cells.

them, it is difficult for all of them to be part of a single segmentation group. In this sense, *c*-means is more flexible and, in our opinion, more appropriate when we are talking about a set of subjects.

Figure 18.4 shows an example of how the results can be interpreted. In particular, we sample 3 of the 90,000 cells and obtain the results in Table 18.8.

Table 18.6 Matches of the tern

	Tern
1	0.2141
2	0.2139
3	0.2081
4	0.2096
5	0.2094
6	0.2220
7	0.2150
8	0.2188
9	0.2167
10	0.2167
Mean	0.2144

Table 18.7 Centres of clusters

Cluster	$\widetilde{IW}$	$\widetilde{IE}$	$\widetilde{IA}$	N
1	0.302	0.494	0.249	11,185
2	0.269	0.471	0.276	12,908
3	0.235	0.479	0.237	14,998
4	0.530	0.565	0.174	3,388
5	0.202	0.425	0.265	11,731
6	0.336	0.496	0.190	7,595
7	0.173	0.380	0.334	13,788
8	0.227	0.437	0.308	14,407

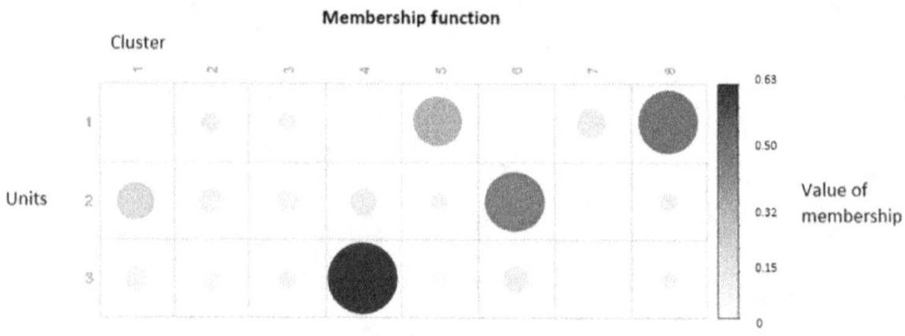

Figure 18.4 Membership function.

In Figure 18.4, the higher the value of membership, the larger and darker the dot is. It is easy to conclude that cell 3 is highly linked to cluster 4, which (looking at the centre of the cluster) can be summarised as composed of young people with a high education and wealth. Cell 2 seems to be mainly part of cluster 6, in which people are still young and have a high education

Table 18.8 Estimated value of variables

	Cell	*Long.*	*Lat.*	$\widetilde{IW}$	$\widetilde{IE}$	$\widetilde{IA}$
1	33505	12.53995	41.86196	0.207	0.418	0.304
2	15210	12.5435	41.82267	0.391	0.538	0.204
3	11022	12.55295	41.81325	0.507	0.560	0.246

Note: The coordinates refer to the centre of the cell.

but less rich than the previous one. Lastly, cell 1 does not have a value of membership greater than the others but, rather, has values very close to those of clusters 5 and 8, so we conclude that both these groups have low wealth. Now, it is clear that if you want to promote a new type of bank card for young and rich people, you should first go to cell 3, where the right customers for our product will surely be found.

Conclusion

In this chapter, we try to identify an alternative method, not to substitute for the Eurisko segmentation of customers, but to cluster new potential consumers who are in a specific cell using fuzzy clustering, which enables us to improve on it.

First, defining fuzzy indicators means we do not have to find a point where the population is dichotomised. This might be a minor detail, but it is easy to understand the importance if we think about the variations, especially of wealth, in a country. If a company wishes to open a new branch in a city where it does not yet have any customers, it could be very difficult to define the point from which it should dichotomise hypothetical new customers, so it could be an error to use the same point as is used in another city that is far away.

Furthermore, IDW interpolation enables us to follow the law that people with similar characteristics live nearby (e.g. neighbourhoods), and we obtained good results with low estimated error for the 90,000 small areas into which Rome was subdivided. A graphical analysis of the map confirmed and demonstrated the accuracy of our estimates.

Finally, using *c*-means clustering, for each cell we assign a membership degree to a cluster, which can help us to understand the characteristics of potential customers within this zone and therefore guide decisions in our business activities.

Notes

1 Eurisko is an Italian research institute founded by G. Calvi in 1972, which began to develop Eurisko segmentation in 1976.

2 To clarify: if a specific area has 20 households, whose total income is 1 million euros and did not have enough average household values for the zone, which we consider half a million euros per household.
3 For more on this issue, see Tyner (2010), Iliffe (2008) and Lovelace, Nowosad and Münchow (2019).
4 For an overview of this method, see Babak and Deutsch (2009).

References

Azri, S.A., Ujang, U., and Rahman, A.A. (2020), 'Voronoi Classified and Clustered Data Constellation: A New 3D Data Structure for Geomarketing Strategies'. *ISPRS Journal of Photogrammetry and Remote Sensing* 162: 1–16.

Azri, S.A., Ujang, U., Rahman, A., Anton, F., and Mioc, D. (2016), '3D Geomarketing Segmentation: A Higher Spatial Dimension Planning Perspective'. *ISPRS-International Archives of the Photogrammetry, Remote Sensing and Spatial Information Sciences* XLII-4/W: 1–7. doi:10.5194/isprs-archives-XLII-4-W1-1-2016.

Babak, O., and Deutsch, C.V. (2009), 'Statistical Approach to Inverse Distance Interpolation'. *Stochastic Environmental Research and Risk Assessment* 23, no. 5: 543–53.

Baltyzhakova, T.I., and Bryzhataya, E.S. (2019), 'Analysis of Urban Territory in Terms of Accessibility to Social Objects'. *Journal of Physics: Conference Series* 1333: 032005. https://doi.org/10.1088/1742-6596/1333/3/032005.

Betti, G. (2017). 'What Impact Has the Economic Crisis Had on Quality of Life in Europe? A Multidimensional and Fuzzy Approach'. *Quality & Quantity* 51(1): 351–364.

Betti, G., Gagliardi, F., Lemmi, A., and Verma, V. (2015), 'Comparative Measures of Multidimensional Deprivation in the European Union'. *Empirical Economics* 49, no. 3: 1071–1100.

Betti, G., and Lemmi, A. eds. (2013), *Poverty and Social Exclusion: New Methods of Analysis*. London: Routledge.

Betti, G., Soldi, R., and Talev, I. (2016), 'Fuzzy Multidimensional Indicators of Quality of Life: The Empirical Case of Macedonia'. *Social Indicators Research* 127, no. 1: 39–53.

Betti, G., and Verma, V. (2008), 'Fuzzy Measures of the Incidence of Relative Poverty and Deprivation: A Multi-Dimensional Perspective'. *Statistical Methods and Applications* 17, no. 2: 225–250.

Bettio, F., Ticci, E., and Betti, G. (2020), 'A Fuzzy Index and Severity Scale to Measure Violence against Women'. *Social Indicators Research*, 148, no. 1: 225–249.

Bezdek, J.C. (1981), *Pattern Recognition with Fuzzy Objective Function Algorithms*. Boston: Springer.

Cliquet, G. (2006), *Geomarketing: Methods and Strategies in Spatial Marketing*. Geographical Information Systems Series. Newport Beach, CA: ISTE USA.

Dunn, J.C. (1973), 'A Fuzzy Relative of the ISODATA Process and Its Use in Detecting Compact Well-Separated Clusters'. *Journal of Cybernetics* 3, no. 3: 32–57.

Grekousis, G., and Hatzichristos, T. (2013), 'Fuzzy Clustering Analysis in Geomarketing Research'. *Environment and Planning B: Planning and Design* 40, no. 1: 95–116.

Gustafson, D., and Kessel, W. (1978), 'Fuzzy Clustering with a Fuzzy Covariance Matrix'. In *1978 IEEE Conference on Decision and Control Including the 17th Symposium on Adaptive Processes*, 761–766. San Diego: IEEE.

Horn, J.L. (1965), 'A Rationale and Test for the Number of Factors in Factor Analysis'. *Psychometrika* 30, no. 2: 179–185.

Hsu, T.H., Chu, K.M., and Chan, H.C. (2000), 'The Fuzzy Clustering on Market Segment'. In *Ninth IEEE International Conference on Fuzzy Systems. FUZZ-IEEE 2000 (Cat. No. 00CH37063)*, 2, 621–626. San Antonio, TX: IEEE.

Iliffe, J. (2008), *Datums and Map Projections for Remote Sensing, GIS, and Surveying*. Boca Raton: CRC Press.

Jain, V., and Krishnapuram, R. (2001), 'Applications of Fuzzy Sets in Personalization for E-Commerce'. In *Proceedings Joint 9th IFSA World Congress and 20th NAFIPS International Conference (Cat. No. 01TH8569)*, 1, 263–268. Vancouver, BC: IEEE.

Jones, B.D.G., and Shaw, E.H. (2002), 'A History of Marketing Thought'. In *Handbook of Marketing*, edited by Weitz, B.A., and Wensley, R., 39–64. London: SAGE.

Lee, N., Broderick, A.J., and Chamberlain, L. (2007), 'What Is "Neuromarketing"? A Discussion and Agenda for Future Research'. *International Journal of Psychophysiology: Official Journal of the International Organization of Psychophysiology* 63, no. 2: 199–204.

Lovelace, R., Nowosad, J., and Münchow, J. (2019), *Geocomputation with R*. Boca Raton: Taylor & Francis.

Tobler, W.R. (1970), 'A Computer Movie Simulating Urban Growth in the Detroit Region'. *Economic Geography* 46: 234.

Tyner, J.A. (2010), *Principles of Map Design*. New York: Guilford Press.

19 Satisfaction in Higher Education

A Multi-Dimensional and Fuzzy Approach

Francesca Gagliardi, Laura Neri, Edmira Shahu and Aurora Hoxha

Introduction

The dynamics of higher education in the western Balkan region remain on the margins of studies on contemporary higher education. Regional higher education has never been the subject of systemic research, and both data and prior studies are lacking.

In Albania, institutions of higher education (HEIs) are both public and private. The first university there was founded in 1957, and until 1990 it was the only university, though some new institutes or branches were established in this period.

Reforms outlined in 'On Higher Education and Scientific Research in Higher Education Institutions in the Republic of Albania' were approved in 2015. These reforms aim to create a sustainable mechanism of quality assurance at HEIs that align with European standards. This framework measures and evaluates the performance of everyone involved in academic life based on those standards. They are intended to better integrate teaching with scientific research and to ensure that the system of higher education is oriented towards the needs of the labour market.

Against this background, the Graduates Advancement and Development of University Capacities in Albania (GRADUA) project in Albania aims to construct an innovative IT-based platform for tracking graduates and their employability with the support of policymaking and reform in higher education. Unlike the current experience, which involves databases and job intermediaries, this platform is an integrated system with a model based on an online database of Albanian graduates that matches supply and demand and is easily replicable across universities, creating concrete synergy between universities and the labour market by providing unified and innovative recruitment tools.

Our analysis of the GRADUA project database and the quantitative indicators built employ a fuzzy methodology. The goal of the analysis is to evaluate student satisfaction with the system of higher education in Albania. Student satisfaction is evaluated based on a multi-dimensional approach, using fuzzy indicators. For this purpose, we identified a set of variables in a GRADUA survey of students grouped into three dimensions.

The remainder of this chapter is organised as follows. The literature on student satisfaction is reviewed in the second section. The empirical strategy is presented in the third section. The dataset and variables used in the empirical analysis are described in the forth section. In the fifth section, the main results are provided. Finally, the last section concludes the analysis.

Literature Review on Student Satisfaction With University Education

The literature on customer satisfaction is based on ideas such as perceived value, quality of service, experience, expectations and consequently service evaluation (Joseph et al., 2015). Indeed, satisfaction is the state in which an individual feels that an experience meets his/her expectations (Lagrosen et al., 2014). Therefore, satisfaction is a perception of pleasurable fulfilment of a service (Oliver, 1997). In the university education context, students are the customers, and student satisfaction is the only sign of the performance of quality of service for suppliers of higher education (Parameswaran and Glowacka, 2015).

Student satisfaction is a multi-dimensional concept which is influenced by different factors. Several explanations exist for the dimensions of student satisfaction.

Student satisfaction in higher education is affected mainly by two groups of factors: personal and institutional factors (Marzo-Navarro et al., 2005; Appleton-Knapp and Krentler, 2006). The personal factors include age, gender, employment status, a student's grade point average (GPA) and the preferred teaching system, whereas the institutional factors are the quality of instruction, the timeliness of feedback, clarity of the expected results and the teaching style. Wilkins and Balakrishnan (2013) identified the following determinants of student satisfaction: teacher quality, quality of physical facilities and the use of technology. Other researchers list the quality of classrooms, the quality of feedback, the teacher-student relationship, interaction with fellow students, course content, learning equipment available, library facilities and learning materials (García-Aracil, 2009; Kuh and Hu, 2001). Teaching ability, university status and prestige, independence, flexible curriculum, student growth and development, student centrality, campus climate and institutional effectiveness have also been identified as significant factors in student satisfaction in higher education (Palacio et al., 2002). Finally, Walker-Marshall and Hudson (1999) claim that the student's GPA is the most influential factor in that person's satisfaction.

Methodology

In the international literature, student satisfaction is considered a multi-dimensional concept. From a methodological perspective, it can be treated in a manner similar to those used for concepts of poverty (Betti and Verma,

2008) or educational mismatch (Betti et al., 2011). All these concepts are very complex issues in which many reasons converge, and a definition based on a univariate measure simplifies the phenomenon too much. Moreover, defining the concept by dividing it into two distinct groups (poor vs. not poor or matching vs. mismatching, satisfied vs. not satisfied in our study) can create a misleading impression, as a dichotomous indicator cannot take into account the different degrees of this phenomenon (i.e. of satisfaction) that might be experienced.

In this chapter, we use a multi-dimensional approach for defining student satisfaction and, at the same time, fuzzy-set theory (Zadeh, 1965; Dubois and Prade, 1980) to create fuzzy indicators that overcome the division of satisfaction into two exclusive groups.

In describing a given phenomenon, the fuzzy set approach (Zadeh, 1965) treats measures as a matter of degree, replacing a simple dichotomy {0,1} (i.e. poverty/non-poverty, satisfied/non-satisfied) into which individuals or households are divided in the traditional approach. In the fuzzy approach, individuals who are subject to a phenomenon experience it in varying degrees; that is, everyone has a certain degree of *propensity* to experience a phenomenon, defined in the range [0,1].

Betti et al. (2015) proposed a step-by-step procedure for constructing a fuzzy multi-dimensional index, as follows. First, the items to be included in the index or indices, which should be those that are the most meaningful and useful, need to be identified. Then, for each item, a quantitative indicator is defined in terms of the range [0,1]: the set of indicators defined for the set of items, are used in a preliminary exploratory factor analysis to identify underlined unobserved 'dimensions'. By 'dimension', they mean a distinct group of items that describe the phenomenon under analysis, ideally independent of the other dimensions, and which should describe a facet of it. After this exploratory factor analysis, they rearrange some items in the dimensions identified, to create more meaningful groups: a confirmatory factor analysis is necessary to test the goodness of fit of the final grouping. The weights assigned to each item are determined within each dimension; they are based on two elements: the dispersion of the item (prevalence weights) and the correlation weights, which show the correlation with other items in the same dimension (Betti and Verma, 2008). The score assigned within each dimension h to each student i ($s_{i,h}$), is calculated as a weighted mean of items in this dimension, whereas the 'overall score' of each student i (s_i) is defined based on the simple average:

$$s_i = \frac{\sum_{h=1}^{m} s_{i,h}}{m} \tag{19.1}$$

thus, giving the same importance to all dimensions, each represents a different facet of the phenomenon. The positive results achieved from applying this methodology to different fields demonstrate its applicability and robustness (see e.g. Aassve et al., 2007; Betti et al., 2011, 2016; Belhadj, 2015; Betti, 2017).

The Dataset

Our empirical analysis is based on the GRADUA project database. The project aims to set up an innovative IT-based platform for graduates in Albania in order to track their employability with the support of policymaking. The platform has a twofold scope: enhance university-enterprise cooperation and the employability of graduates using data aggregation, strengthening both the effectiveness/efficiency of the higher education system with IT-based practices and methodology.

To collect qualitative data, the working group organised some dissemination activities with the university representatives who were responsible for informing students about the platform and a questionnaire that they had to complete, in order to be registered on this platform. The survey's purpose was to collect data on students' university experience and their future prospects according to a set of variables that emerged from six online surveys of students who were going to graduate in the academic year 2019. Specifically, the questionnaire consists of the following sections: 1. Personal information, 2. Education and training, 3. Information on the course that graduate is completing, 4. Evaluation of the course that graduate is completing, 5. Information about the graduate's family and 6. Future intentions and prospects.

The survey database contains the full set of responses from 2,635 graduating students at Albanian universities. In particular, data come from nine universities: University of Tirana, Polytechnic University of Tirana, Agricultural University of Tirana, University of Arts, University of Medicine, European University of Tirana, Polis University, Catholic University Our Lady of Good Counsel and Albanian University.

The goal of this chapter is to construct the fuzzy multi-dimensional indicators of student satisfaction with the degree programme they are concluding and their university experience. For this purpose, we identified a set of variables in the questionnaire that could be grouped into three dimensions, based on their satisfaction with the course, the teachers and the university's facilities. In Figure 19.1, we summarise the variables identified for each dimension.

Empirical Results

The fuzzy methodology described in below is applied to the variables regarding the GRADUA database (see Figure 19.1). For this purpose, only observations with complete information are used, yielding a sample for analysis made up of 2,480 students.

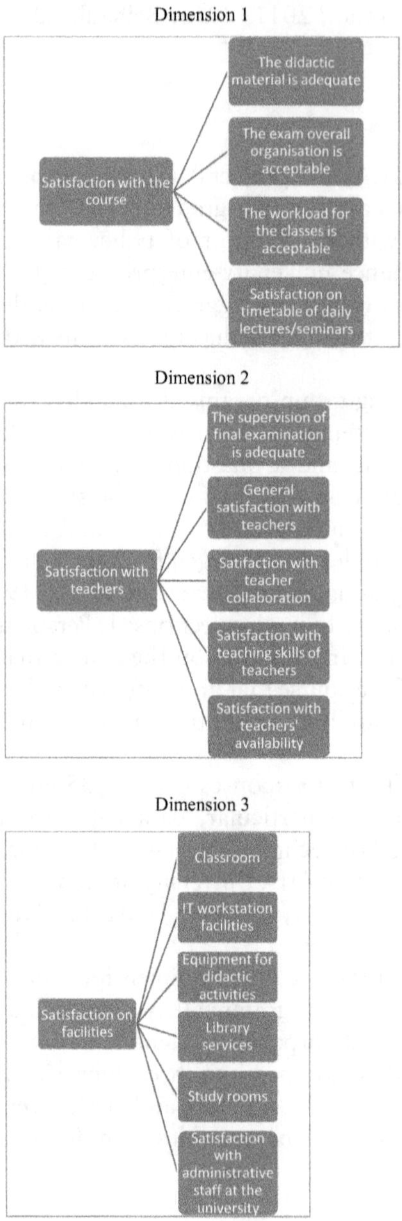

Figure 19.1 The three dimensions of satisfaction.

For each of the three dimensions, we calculated a score as well as an overall score on general satisfaction, in which s is the score of overall satisfaction concerning all aspects of the degree programme, s_1 is the score for satisfaction with the courses, s_2 is the score for satisfaction with the teachers and s_3 is the score for satisfaction with the facilities. These scores range between 0 and 1, where 1 means completely satisfied and 0 means totally unsatisfied. Table 19.1 reports a descriptive analysis of overall satisfaction in terms of these four scores.

Students are particularly satisfied with the courses (the average value of s_1 is about 0.72) and with their teachers (the average value of s_2 is about 0.72), but they are slightly less satisfied with the facilities (the mean of s_3 is about 0.67). Overall, they are satisfied: the average degree of overall student satisfaction (s) is about 0.70.

The coefficient of variation for all scores is quite low, meaning that the students' answers show strong convergence; however, the scores on satisfaction with teachers and facilities are a bit more heterogeneous than the others; thus s_2 and s_3 are the most informative in the empirical analysis.

The scores on the three dimensions and overall student satisfaction (s) are cross analysed with the GRADUA survey question on 'general satisfaction'. The respondents could choose a value from among four Likert-scale items, from 1 (not satisfied at all) to 4 (completely satisfied). Table 19.2 and Figure 19.2 show that, as the Likert-scale value increases, so does the mean value of all the scores. This is additional proof of the robustness of the measures obtained with multi-dimensional analysis.

For Likert-scale values between 2 and 4, the score means are similar and constant. This is not the case for the lowest value for general satisfaction

Table 19.1 Mean and coefficient of variation (%) of the satisfaction measures

	n	*Mean*	*Coeff. of variation*
s	2480	0.699	30.10
s1	2480	0.717	29.97
s2	2480	0.707	37.01
s3	2480	0.672	35.98

Table 19.2 Satisfaction scores by 'general satisfaction' with the degree programme

General satisfaction	s	s_1	s_2	s_3
1	0.384	0.583	0.297	0.272
2	0.401	0.465	0.353	0.387
3	0.596	0.630	0.580	0.578
4	0.823	0.822	0.860	0.789

Likert scale: 1 (not satisfied at all) to 4 (completely satisfied)

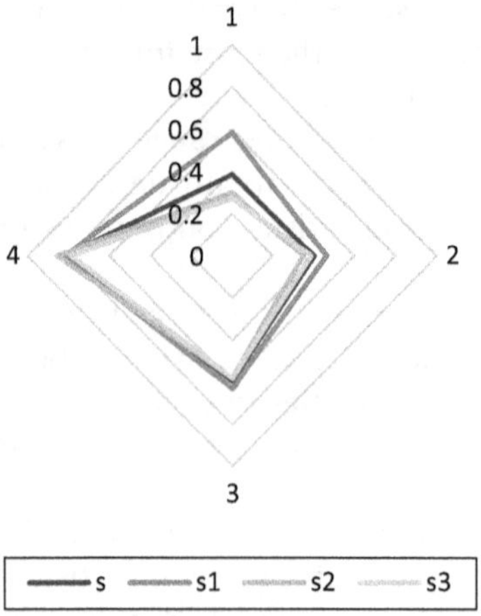

Figure 19.2 Satisfaction scores by 'general satisfaction' with the degree programme.

Table 19.3 Satisfaction scores by university

University	s	s_1	s_2	s_3
University of Tirana	0.567	0.610	0.545	0.545
Polytechnic University of Tirana	0.597	0.626	0.614	0.552
Agricultural University of Tirana	0.704	0.735	0.718	0.658
University of Arts	0.645	0.584	0.710	0.643
University of Medicine	0.598	0.630	0.591	0.572
European University of Tirana	0.781	0.765	0.773	0.803
Polis University	0.868	0.853	0.858	0.894
Catholic University Our Lady of Good Counsel	0.810	0.757	0.833	0.841
Albanian University	0.835	0.834	0.866	0.804

('not satisfied at all'): students who are not satisfied at all with the degree programme are not satisfied with teachers and facilities, but are much more satisfied with the courses. Students who are completely satisfied with the degree programme have the highest level of satisfaction with teachers.

The four multi-dimensional satisfaction scores are disaggregated by university in Table 19.3 and Figure 19.3. Based on the results, the scores are much higher at private universities than public universities. Polis University has the best performance (overall satisfaction score of about 0.87), followed by Albanian University (overall satisfaction score of about 0.84). Both universities are private and have a very high degree of satisfaction with all aspects of the degree programme. Among the public universities, the Agricultural University of Tirana received the highest scores. Public universities appear to perform very poorly in satisfaction with the facilities,

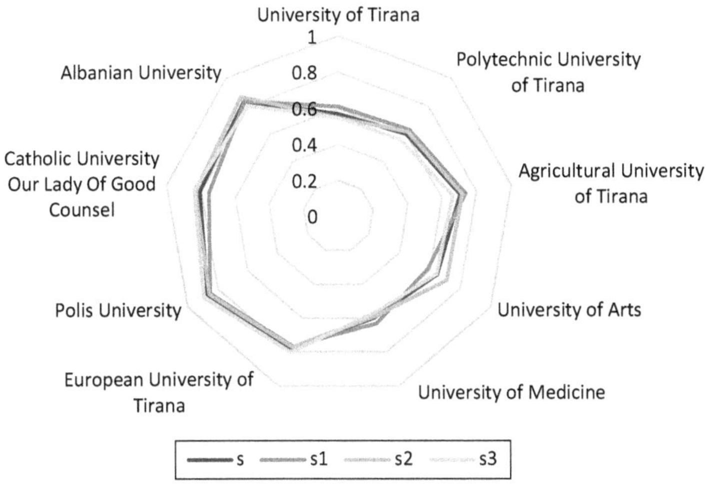

Figure 19.3 Satisfaction scores.

which reflects the low level of investment and financing for facilities. The University of Tirana has the lowest degree of satisfaction overall and with teachers and facilities.

The variation in the four scores among universities is low, the coefficient of variation is around 0.14 for s_1 and around 0.16 for s and s_2; however, it is 0.19 for s_3 (satisfaction with facilities), meaning that this aspect could be positive at some universities and negative at others.

All the scores are disaggregated by the gender of respondents (see Figure 19.4). Differences between male and female students are negligible, but in general satisfaction is higher among male than female respondents in all dimensions of satisfaction and overall.

The degree of satisfaction is also analysed by the student's place of birth (Figure 19.5). Albania has few foreign students; few university programmes are offered in foreign languages and attended by foreign students. However, the number of returning migrants whose children were born abroad (e.g. Greece) is growing. Based on the results, satisfaction is higher among students born in other countries than among those born in Albania. There may be an explanation: students who are born outside the country, especially those who do not speak Albanian, are expected to select programmes offered in foreign languages, which are given by private universities, which score higher on satisfaction overall.

In the questionnaire, the respondents were also required to mention the country where they attended high school. The degree of satisfaction is also disaggregated by this variable (Figure 19.6). Like students born in other countries, students who attended high school elsewhere (many of whom

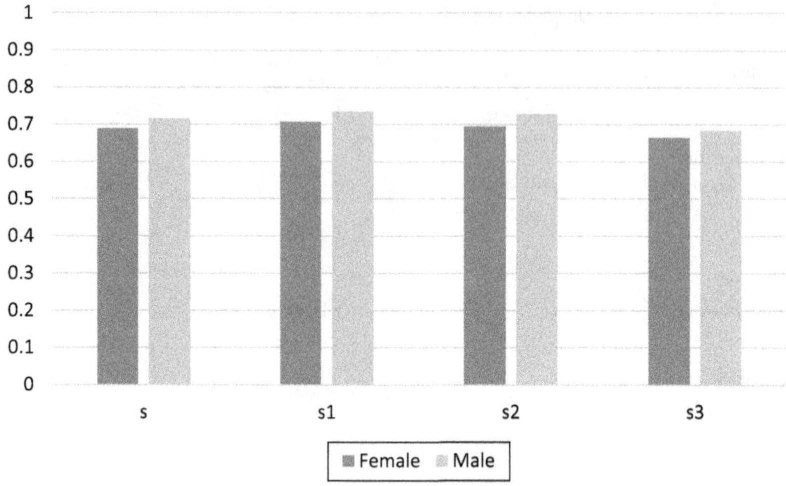

Figure 19.4 Satisfaction scores by gender by university.

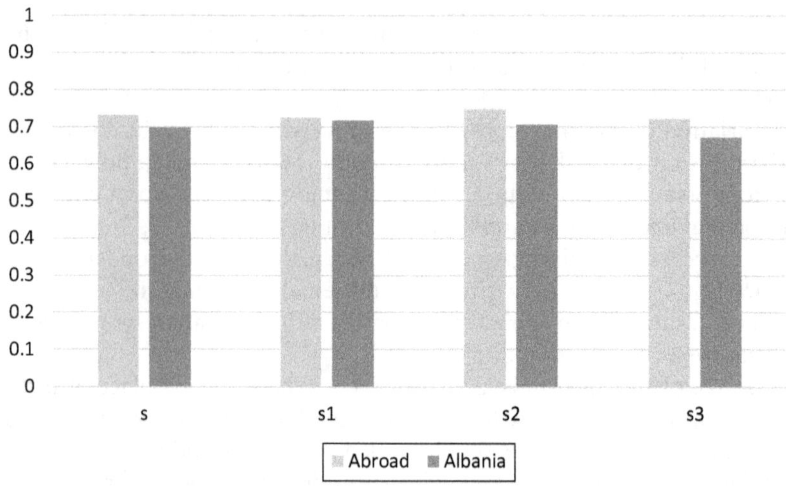

Figure 19.5 Satisfaction scores by place of birth.

were very likely to have been born elsewhere) also have a higher level of satisfaction than those who attended high school in Albania. The differences in this variable are larger. The largest gap in the scores are for satisfaction with facilities and with teachers.

The degree of satisfaction is also cross analysed with the degree of education of the students' parents (Table 19.4 and Figure 19.7), based on the parents' highest level of education. The parents' education appears to be

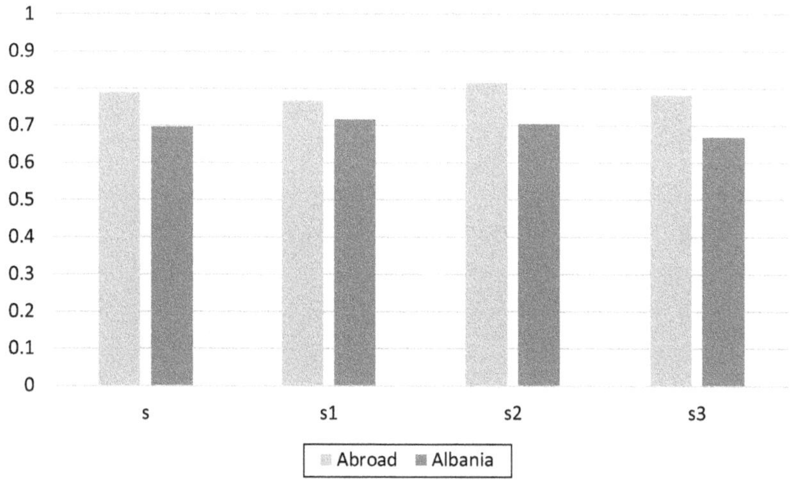

Figure 19.6 Satisfaction scores by the location (country) of the high school attended.

Table 19.4 Satisfaction scores by the highest education level of the students' parents

	s	s_1	s_2	s_3
No qualification	0.793	0.809	0.806	0.763
Primary school	0.716	0.672	0.736	0.740
Middle school	0.716	0.734	0.737	0.677
Secondary school	0.690	0.712	0.699	0.658
University degree	0.701	0.717	0.706	0.681

inversely related to the overall satisfaction index. Thus, the higher the level of education of students' parents is, the lower the degree of overall satisfaction for students is. In particular, respondents whose parents have the lowest education level had the highest level of satisfaction on all three scores and the overall score. Probably students from families with a high level of education have higher expectations, not just with respect to the facilities but also the courses and teachers.

Conclusions

This chapter is based on an assumption that student satisfaction is a multi-dimensional and fuzzy concept. This perspective aligns with the literature on this topic, which holds that student satisfaction is a complex issue influenced by many factors. The added value of our research is the use of a multi-dimensional approach for defining satisfaction, employing fuzzy-set theory to measure satisfaction according to the degree of membership in a set, instead of dichotomous indicators. Our main findings about student

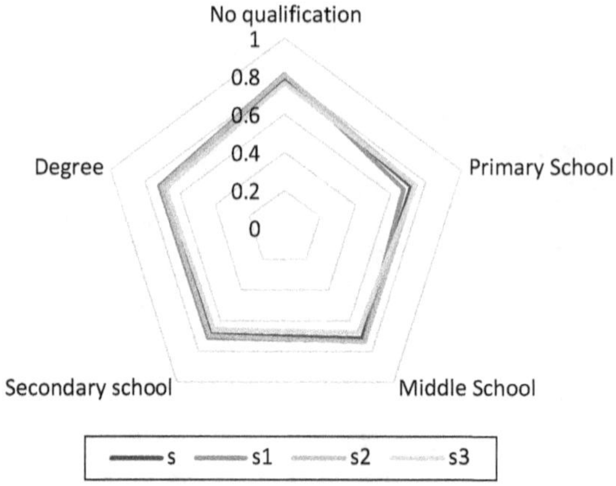

Figure 19.7 Satisfaction scores by the highest education level of the students' parents.

satisfaction regarding the system of higher education in Albania can be summarised as follows.

The use of this methodology in different research fields has had good results, which is also the case in our study of student satisfaction. We find a strong relationship between overall student satisfaction, calculated as a simple average of the satisfaction scores for the three dimensions identified, and the general satisfaction indicator, on the basis of the sample data.

The satisfaction scores for each dimension reveal new evidence on student satisfaction. This issue is crucial in terms of policy implications. It is, of course, important to know that students are more or less satisfied, but it is much more important to understand which aspects (dimensions) of higher education make students feel more or less satisfied. For example, it is important for universities to find out that they have the highest heterogeneity in terms of satisfaction with facilities: this finding should concern the management of the universities with the lowest scores in this dimension.

Future research on this topic could construct an econometric model using the indicators proposed here as dependent variables. Then, the inferences from the model could be used to evaluate the net effect of student characteristics on the different dimensions of satisfaction and general satisfaction.

References

Aassve, A., Betti, G., Mazzuco, S., Mencarini, L. (2007). Marital disruption and economic well-being; A comparative analysis. *Journal of the Royal Statistical Society, Series A*, 170(3), pp. 781–799.

Appleton-Knapp, S., Krentler, K. (2006). Measuring student expectations and their effects on satisfaction: The importance of managing student expectations. *Journal of Marketing Education*, 28(3), pp. 254–264.

Belhadj, B. (2015). Employment measure in development countries via minimum wage and poverty: New fuzzy approach. *Opsearch*, 52(2), pp. 329–339.

Betti, G. (2017). What impact has the economic crisis had on quality of life in Europe? A multidimensional and fuzzy approach. *Quality and Quantity*, 51(1), pp. 351–364.

Betti, G., D'Agostino, A., Neri, L. (2011). Educational mismatch of graduates: A multidimensional and fuzzy indicator. *Social Indicators Research*, 103(3), pp. 465–480.

Betti, G., Gagliardi, F., Lemmi, A., Verma, V. (2015). Comparative measures of multidimensional deprivation in the European Union. *Empirical Economics*, 49(3), pp. 1071–1100.

Betti, G., Soldi, R., Talev, I. (2016). Fuzzy multidimensional indicators of quality of life: The empirical case of Macedonia. *Social Indicators Research*, 127(1), pp. 39–53.

Betti, G., Verma, V. (2008). Fuzzy measures of the incidence of relative poverty and deprivation: A multi-dimensional perspective. *Statistical Methods and Applications*, 17(2), pp. 225–250.

Dubois, D., Prade, H. (1980). *Fuzzy Sets and Systems: Theory and Applications*. New York: Academic Press.

García-Aracil, A. (2009). European graduates' level of satisfaction with higher education. *Journal of Higher Education*, 57(1), pp. 1–21.

Joseph, M., Yakhou, M., Stone, G. (2015). An educational institution's quest for service quality: Customers' perspective. *Quality Assurance in Education*, 13(1), pp. 66–82.

Kuh, G., Hu, S. (2001). The effects of student-faculty interaction in the 1990s. *Review of Higher Education*, 24(3), pp. 309–332.

Lagrosen, S., Seyyed-Hashemi, R., Leitner, M. (2014). Examination of the dimensions of quality in higher education. *Quality Assurance in Education*, 12(2), pp. 61–69.

Marzo-Navarro, M., Iglesias, M., Torres, M. (2005). A new management element for universities: satisfaction with the offered courses. *International Journal of Educational Management*, 19(6), pp. 505–526.

Oliver, R. (1997). *Satisfaction: A Behavioral Perspective on the Consumer*. New York: McGraw-Hill.

Palacio, A., Meneses, G., Perez, P. (2002). The configuration of the university image and its relationship with the satisfaction of students. *Journal of Educational Administration*, 40(5), pp. 486–505.

Parameswaran, R., Glowacka, A.E. (2015). University image: An information processing perspective. *Journal of Marketing for Higher Education*, 6(2), pp. 41–56.

Walker-Marshall, A., Hudson, C.M. (1999). *Student Satisfaction and Student Success in the University System of Georgia*. AIR 1999 Annual Forum Paper.

Wilkins, S., Balakrishnan, M.S., (2013). Assessing student satisfaction in transnational higher education. *International Journal of Educational Management*, 27(2), pp. 146–153.

Zadeh, L.A. (1965). Fuzzy sets. *Information and Control*, 8, pp. 338–353.

20 A Multi-dimensional Clustering on Fuzzy Metrics to Classify CPG Pricing and Price Promotion Strategies

The Case of Pasta in Italy

Luigi Palumbo, Tiziana Laureti and Ilaria Benedetti

Introduction

Price promotions, which are temporary price changes offered by a seller, play a crucial role in retail, especially in consumer packaged goods (CPG) (Gómez, Rao & McLaughlin, 2007; Besanko, Dubé & Gupta, 2005; Gedenk, Neslin & Ailawadi, 2010). Their importance for CPG manufacturers is indicated by the share of total revenue allocated for trade promotions,[1] which varies between 10% and 25% (Boston Consulting Group, 2012; Gartner, 2015) and by the long-term impact of price promotions on consumer habits (Mela, Gupta & Lehmann, 1997).

Discounted products are generally in the minority on store shelves compared to those at regular prices (McShane, Chen, Anderson & Simester, 2016), but they comprise a proportionally larger share of sales. According to different sources and definitions, the share of sales for goods on promotion over total grocery sales varies across countries. For example, in the UK the share of products on promotion accounted for 32% in 2009 (Nielsen, 2009a) and 51.5% in 2015 (IRI, 2016), whereas in the US it accounted for 42.8% in 2009 (Nielsen, 2009b) and 34.9% in 2015 (IRI, 2016). The share of turnover for products on price promotion in Australia was 40.6% in 2015 (IRI, 2016) and 40% in 2017 (Nielsen, 2018a), whereas in New Zealand, it accounted for 55.8% in 2015 (IRI, 2016) and almost 60% in 2017 (Nielsen, 2018b). Finally, in Italy, the share of sales for goods on price promotion accounted for 27.9% in 2015 (IRI, 2016).[2]

Empirical evidence regarding the profitability of price promotion is controversial. Several studies reveal that promotions not only influence retailers' revenue (Jedidi, Mela & Gupta, 1999; Drèze & Bell, 2003) but also have a positive impact on key intangible assets, such as brand equity (Buil, de Chernatony & Martínez, 2012) and brand loyalty (Gedenk & Neslin, 1999). However, other studies demonstrate that price promotions tend to have little long-term effects (Srinivasan, Pauwels, Hanssens & Dikempe, 2004). A recent study by Nielsen shows that 67% of trade promotions in the US in 2014 had a negative return for the manufacturer (Nielsen, 2015a). In addition, the positive impact on sales sometimes comes with negative effects for brands (Zoellner & Schaefers, 2015; DelVecchio, Henard & Freling, 2006).

Yet, retailers use various types of price promotion to increase sales and undertake complex managerial decision-making processes to define them (Bogomolova, Szabo & Kennedy, 2017). To shed light on the pricing strategies most widely adopted in Italy, we use fuzzy metrics, which allow us to better identify and understand the different commercial strategies used by retailers and brands. Given its importance in Italy and its complex competitive landscape, we focus on pasta (Cacchiarelli & Sorrentino, 2019).

Retailers are likely to have different pricing strategies for different category-brand combinations. By focusing on a single product category, i.e. pasta (which in Italy is a so-called destination category), we can capture the differences in pricing and price promotion strategies across retailers and geographic areas.

Therefore, this chapter responds to the following research questions:

1. What strategies are employed for pricing and price promotion in the Italian pasta retail market?
2. How are the strategies for pricing and price promotion distributed across regions, retailers and brands?

Pasta is an ideal sector for analysis to arrive at answers to those questions, which are relevant for marketing practitioners in CPG manufacturing and retail. Indeed, Italy is the world's leading pasta producer and the largest consumer of pasta (International Pasta Organisation, 2014).

Therefore, brand managers need to review the overall positioning of their products to consumers, spotting potential inconsistencies that may create confusion or strategies that are not consistent with their overall plan (Bolton, Shankar & Montoya, 2010). Retailers need to control and evaluate their pricing and promotional strategies vis-à-vis those of their competitors to ensure that they transmit the right message to consumers about which store to visit when they are shopping for this product.

The geographic aspect is particularly relevant, because the local competitive environment is considered a key determinant of the results of retailers' strategy, and some evidence indicates that retailer strategies tend to be homogeneous in a given area (Ellickson & Misra, 2008).

In this chapter, we employ a unique dataset of prices and temporary price reductions[3] for retailers across Italy and consider the type-brand-retailer-region combination as a statistical observation. Our empirical analysis is based on 738 items of weekly average price data from January 2011 to June 2015 segmented across 16 retailers, 18 brands and five regions.

In order to explore the various pricing and price promotional strategies used for pasta, we apply a fuzzy-set theory approach (Zadeh, 1965, 1968, 1977;

Dubois & Prade, 1980; Zimmermann, 2001), as properly designed membership functions (MF) enable us to achieve a better classification of the data, smoothing distortions caused by outliers while still including them in the analysis. Another advantage of the fuzzy-set theory approach is that it overcomes the limits from discrete classifications of data, preserving a higher degree of information for analysis.

We propose the use of multi-dimensional clustering that takes into account regular prices and temporary price reductions to derive the strategies implemented by retailers for different brands and classify them according to the characteristics revealed.

The remainder of this chapter is structured as follows. First, we review studies related to price promotion to determine the relevant dimensions to consider in our analysis. Then, we present the research methodology and describe the data used. Results are presented in the next section. Finally, we offer the managerial implications, limitations, suggestions for future research and conclusions.

Conceptual Framework

Price promotion is seen as the only tool that can drive an increase in sales in the short term, unlike advertising spending, which has long-term returns.[4] It is also perceived as less risky for small brands because the return on promotional spending is more certain in terms of demand generation (Anderson & Fox, 2019; Bogomolova, Szabo & Kennedy, 2017). Price promotions are another tool for manufacturers to use in maintaining brand awareness, as they nearly always accompany communication efforts by retailers (Anderson & Fox, 2019; Brito & Hammond, 2007; Blattberg & Briesch, 2012). Manufacturers of private label products for retailers also devote funding for promotional activities to support their sales, perhaps because product volume declines dramatically when products are not promoted (Anderson & Fox, 2019).

As mentioned earlier, the effects on retailer revenue are generally positive, especially retailers in CPG, as a majority of them historically rely heavily on price promotion as a competitive weapon, i.e. using a strategy known as 'HiLo' ('high price, low price') by retailers who offer periodic, temporary price discounts (low prices) in contrast to the regular prices (high prices). Other retailers, including Walmart, effectively built their success on an EveryDay-Low-Price (EDLP) strategy, used by retailers that maintain a low constant price without any discounts.

Some evidence shows that HiLo strategies lead to a higher profit margin, and moving from a HiLo to EDLP strategy entails high switching costs (Ellickson, Misra & Nair, 2012). Retailers' economic results are also highly influenced by the local context, as competitive activity and socio-economic background may effectively alter the payoff from a HiLo or EDLP strategy. Stores in the same chain in different locations might implement different strategies to better compete in the local market (Ellickson & Misra, 2008).

Moreover, promotions may be strongly habit-forming for consumers. For instance, when JC Penney tried to switch from a 'coupon sales' pricing strategy to an EDLP strategy, it experienced a dramatic decline in store visits and sales (Mourdoukoutas, 2017), and eventually it was forced to return to a HiLo strategy. When even prominent manufacturers such as Procter & Gamble (P&G) reduced spending on price promotions to move to an EDLP strategy, it faced severe backlash, as consumers perceived that P&G brands suddenly became more expensive (Slater, 2001). The EDLP strategy carried out in the 1990s cost P&G a sizeable share of the market as well, because competing brands maintained a HiLo strategy, effectively eroding P&G's position in several categories. Eventually, P&G returned to a HiLo strategy, even though some studies show that the EDLP strategy improved its profits as a percentage of sales. It seems likely that the drop in sales volume was of greater concern and had to be addressed (Ailawadi, Lehmann & Neslin, 2001).

The attractiveness of a price promotion is generally related to the magnitude of the discount versus the regular price. However, a particularly deep discount is a concern for brand managers. A retailer might offer an extremely low price to increase store traffic, but this move could also '*disrupt the marketplace, anger competing retailers, and damage brand equity*' (Anderson & Fox, 2019), with a detrimental long-term effect on overall brand performance (DelVecchio, Henard & Freling, 2006). According to Nielsen (2015b), price promotion is a driver that 45% of consumers report as important in store switching. It is widely documented that shoppers generally buy a basket of goods that includes both items on sale and those at the regular price (Anderson & Fox, 2019). Therefore, to maximise shopper traffic to a store, the retailer can use price promotion as a magnet to increase overall sales. The frequency of price promotion, i.e. the average number of times a specific brand is promoted over a specific period, is another key decision for brand managers and retailers (Allender & Richards, 2012).

In the retail context, a 'product category' is defined as '*a distinct manageable group of products that consumers perceive to be related and/or substitutable in meeting a consumer need*' (Blattberg & Fox, 1995). Specific product categories that are particularly well-suited for attracting consumers to a store are called 'destination categories'. Within those categories, the items that are most important for attracting shoppers are called 'key value items' (Briesch, Dillon & Fox, 2013). The considerations by retail managers in pricing and promoting those categories and items go beyond simple margin targets, as the main goal is to leverage those categories for attracting shoppers in the store and generate beneficial spillovers in other categories (the basket building effect) (Chevalier, Kashyap & Rossi, 2003).

Therefore, pricing and price promotion strategies are key elements in an overall sale strategy for CPG manufacturers and retailers. The research on this subject is vast and consolidated, as ascertained in several literature reviews over time (Kuntner & Teichert, 2016; Blattberg & Neslin, 1989; Blattberg, Briesch & Fox, 1995; Neslin, 2002; Ailawadi, Beauchamp, Donthu, Gauri & Shankar, 2009; Grewal et al., 2010; Fassnacht & El Husseini, 2013).

Bolton and Shankar (2003) derived an empirical taxonomy of pricing and price promotion strategies for grocery retailers in the US across several product categories using a multi-dimensional approach. Their study is a departure from the traditional classification of strategies (Zwanka, 2017) focused on HiLo and EDLP, either as a binary classification (Johnson, 2003; Bailey, 2008; Lal & Rao, 1997) or as a continuum with several intermediate strategies between those two extremes (Hoch, Drèze & Purk, 1994; Gauri, Trivedi & Grewal, 2008; Ellickson & Misra, 2008).

By referring to the Previous literature on price promotions (Bolton & Shankar, 2003; Hoch, Drèze & Purk, 1994; Blattberg & Briesch, 2012) we identify the following strategic dimensions to be considered for analysing retailers' price strategies for pasta in Italy: regular price level, regular price variability, price promotion level, price promotion variability and price promotion frequency. In the next section, the metrics used to capture these dimensions are reported.

Data and Methods

The dataset we used in this study has been obtained from ISMEA data, after having carried out analyses to delete inconsistencies and impute missing data.[5] The dataset includes 738 observations on regular prices (RP) and temporary price reductions (TPR), divided into two different tables, for pasta stock keeping units (SKUs) at different retail chains divided into NUTS1 regions in Italy. In this case, the 738 observations combine the type, brand, retailer and region.[6] Data are reported for 234 weeks, starting in January 2011, and provide information on RP and TPR for 18 pasta brands across 16 retailers in 5 NUTS1 regions. The data points total 153.182 in the RP table and 16.910 in the TPR table. RPs and TPRs are list prices for the retailers' chain in each region where they have stores.

The dataset is particularly valuable, as it enables us to follow the brand positioning across multiple retailers and regions. The addition of the pasta format to define the observations increases the granularity of our analysis and enables us to provide more insights for brands with more SKUs on retail shelves. Pasta, as a destination category with a large number of manufacturers of very different sizes, provides an ideal landscape for exploring different commercial strategies.

We propose multi-dimensional clustering that takes into account regular prices and temporary price reductions to derive the strategies implemented by retailers on the different brands and classify them according to the characteristics revealed. We used the partitioning around medoids (PAM) clustering algorithm, as it provides a higher level of robustness for noise and outliers than other methods, such as k-means. Furthermore, as the medoids identified in the PAM procedure are in our dataset, we can also use them as reference points for our MF.

As a first step in our procedure for analysing the dataset and searching for answers to our research questions, we calculate the following set of synthetic metrics (Table 20.1) to capture the dimensions identified above:

1. Average RP, calculated as the arithmetic mean of RP time series;
2. RP variability, calculated as the relative standard deviation (RSD) of RP time series;
3. TPR percentage, calculated as the difference between RP and TPR values divided by RP, and multiplied by 100;
4. TPR variability, calculated as the RSD of the TPR percentage time series;
5. TPR frequency, calculated as the number of TPR data points over the number of RP data points.

A graphical analysis of the five metrics shows the presence of outliers and skewed distributions that could potentially affect the analysis of the data, as shown in Figure 20.1 for RP variability and TPR frequency.

We use the PAM algorithm to cluster the observations into two sets, representing high and low clusters, based on each metric listed above. This operation divides the dataset into clusters characterised by the low (or high) value of the metric being evaluated, as a basis for the following empirical definition of pricing and price promotion strategies. For instance, we identify the observations characterised by a high RP, compared to the rest of our sample. This transformation, which classifies every observation as high or low, effectively removes potential bias caused by outliers in the distribution of each metric.

To overcome the limitations in the binary classification performed in the previous step, we use the fuzzy-set theory approach to smooth the transition from low to high classification for each metric, defining an MF that will associate each observation with a degree of belonging to the low classification m_L and consequently a degree of belonging to the high classification $1 - m_L$.

Several types of MF for fuzzification of a dataset have been introduced in the literature. Many of the simplest forms – for instance, triangular,

Table 20.1 Pricing and price promotion metrics

Dimension	*Metric*	*Min.*	*Median*	*Max.*	*RSD*
Regular price level	Average RP	0.460	1.780	3.392	28.04%
Regular price variability	RP variability	0.000	3.460	18.074	71.87%
Price promotion level	Average TPR%	0.000	18.489	55.556	80.53%
Price promotion variability	TPR% variability	0.000	0.197	1.124	100.25%
Price promotion frequency	TPR frequency	0.000	5.556	98.291	120.21%

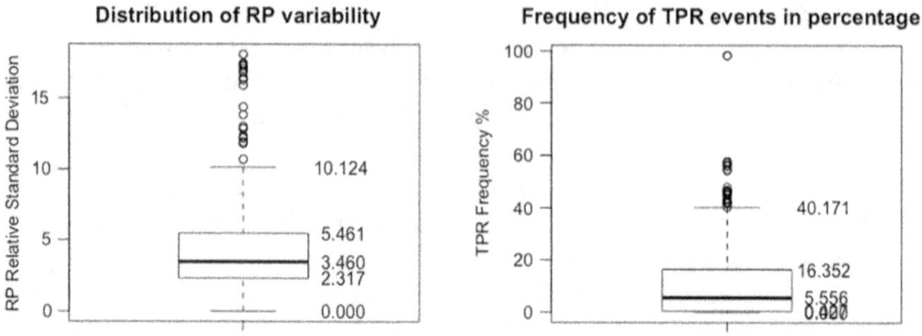

Figure 20.1 Dispersion of pricing and price promotion metrics.

trapezoidal or Gaussian – rely on arbitrary values for definition of the MF, which makes them prone to subjective evaluations. Other more sophisticated forms – for example, those based on a Lorentz distribution and its derivatives – offer a more objective approach to fuzzification.

In this case, we need the MF to do the following:

- avoid excessive change in membership levels at the edges of the distribution, as some metrics have outliers and hard limits at zero;[7]
- avoid reliance on any external parameters for their definition.

Keeping those points in mind, we define the MF in a series of stages based only on information derived from the dataset. The medoids found in the previous PAM procedure are used as partitioning points in the fuzzification. For each metric, data points below the low medoid have full membership in the low cluster ($m_L = 1$) and those above the high medoid have full membership in the high cluster ($m_L = 0$). For data points between them, we define the degree of membership in the low cluster for the data point i as the proportion of data points between the two medoids with a value higher than i.

$$m_{Li} = \begin{cases} if\ y_i < y_{Lmed} & \rightarrow & 1 \\ if\ y_{Lmed} < y_i < y_{Hmed} & \rightarrow & \dfrac{\sum_{k=i+1}^{n} y_k > y_i}{\sum_{k=2}^{n} y_k > y_1} \\ if\ y_i > y_{Hmed} & \rightarrow & 0 \end{cases}$$

The MF results are the basis for our PAM clustering aimed at discovering the different commercial strategies in the market. We select the optimal number of clusters for this operation based on average silhouette width.

For control purposes, we also perform the same clustering on the value of the original metrics, selecting the optimal number of clusters according to average silhouette width and forcing the same number of clusters that we found optimal for clustering on membership values.

We then characterise each strategy individuated in our procedure according to dimensions, region, retailers and brands.

Results

Table 20.2 lists the results from the initial clustering of values in high and low classifications according to each dimension. We show that some dimensions have a fairly skewed distribution of values.

Our MF attenuates this skewness to a certain extent, resulting in a relative majority of observations classified with a membership value blending high and low classifications, as shown in Table 20.3 and Figures 20.2–20.6.

Moving on to the results of our study, in a comparison of the different clustering procedures aimed at identifying pricing and price promotion strategies, two results are clear:

- clustering on membership values captures a deeper level of variability across the dataset, identifying nine clusters as optimal divisions, rather than the four clusters that were supposed to be optimal in clustering on the original metrics;
- clusters calculated on membership values are more consistent with the business logic behind pricing and price promotion strategies.

Table 20.2 Clustering results on each dimension

Metric	*Low Medoid*	*Low N*	*High Medoid*	*High N*	*Silhouette*
Average RP	1.515	393	2.385	345	0.709
RP Variability	2.875	527	6.982	211	0.607
Average TPR%	0.000	337	28.495	401	0.708
TPR% Variability	0.000	361	0.387	377	0.588
TPR Frequency	1.282	460	21.264	278	0.667

Note: The silhouette index is related to PAM clustering with two clusters for each metric. This is not necessarily the maximum silhouette index achievable for each metric, as a different number of clusters might have better performance. However, for the purpose of classifying pricing and price promotion strategies, this binary clustering enables us to link our analysis with business practices.

Table 20.3 Membership function results on each dimension

Metric	$M_L = 1$	M_L]0:1[	$M_L = 0$
Average RP	197	368	173
RP variability	264	368	106
Average TPR%	178	360	200
TPR% variability	248	302	188
TPR frequency	228	368	142

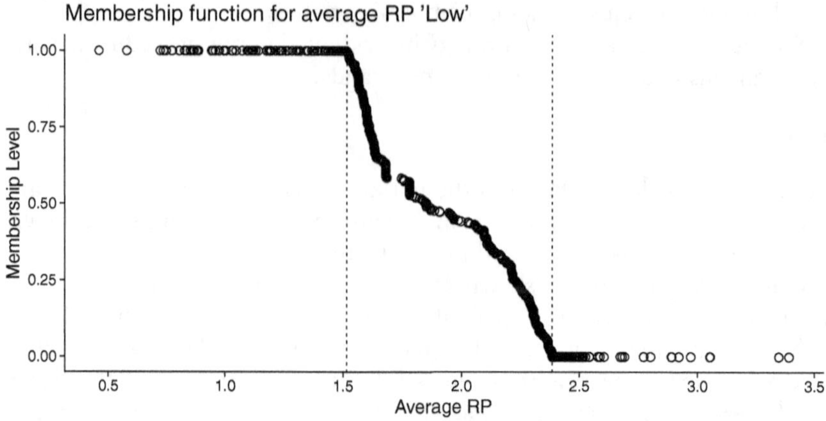

Figure 20.2 Membership function for average RP low.

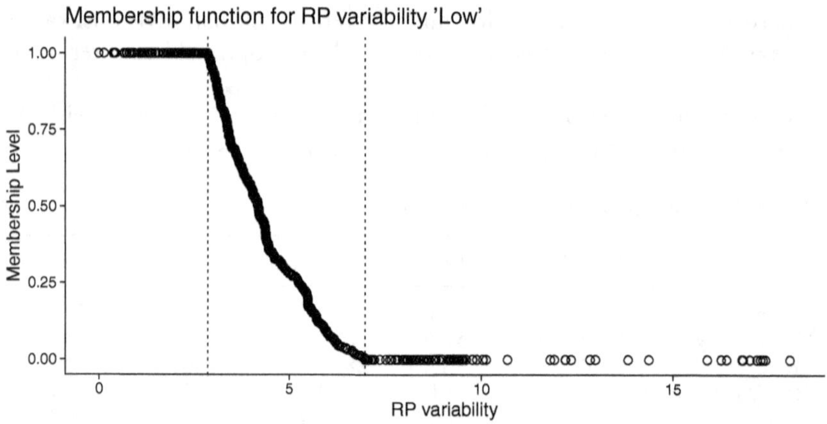

Figure 20.3 Membership function for RP variability low.

For example, to support this second point, we report the mapping of the different clusters against the average RP. The clustering derived on the membership values (Figure 20.7) is much more consistent with business logic than the one calculated with the original metrics. In contrast, the 'traditional' approach does not show a clear pattern consistent with the business logic when the optimal number of clusters is applied based on the original metric values (Figure 20.8) as well as when using the same number of clusters found to be optimal by clustering the fuzzy membership values (Figure 20.9).

Table 20.4 lists the results from cluster analysis based on fuzzy membership values measured with our observations, reporting mean scores of each original metric.

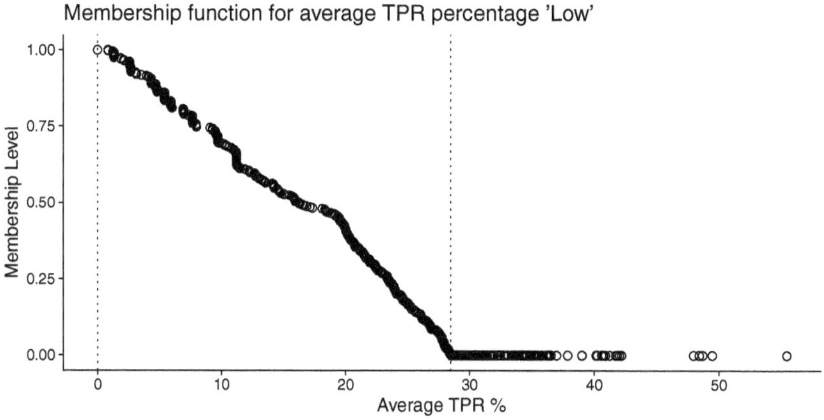

Figure 20.4 Membership function for TPR percentage low.

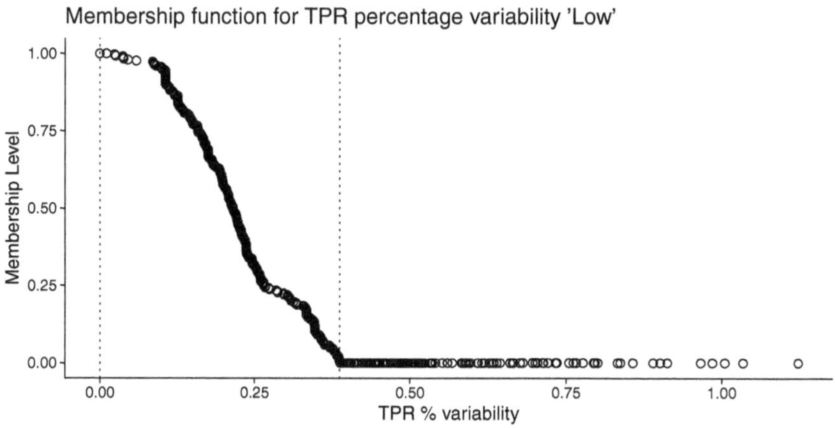

Figure 20.5 Membership function for TPR percentage variability low.

Using fuzzy clustering, we can derive our empirical taxonomy of the different pricing and price promotion strategies based on the peculiarities of each cluster. We label them: everyday new low price (EDNLP), everyday low price (EDLP), surprise promo (SP), stable premium promo (SPP), luxury (L), high variability luxury (HVL), stable value promo (SVP), high variability value promo (HVVP) and high variability premium promo (HVPP).

Table 20.5 shows the combinations of pricing dimensions for each pricing strategy, listing the characteristics of those clusters based on the business domain and the size of each cluster.

This clustering leads to a fairly balanced panel, with a wide variety of strategies. This finding is consistent with the overall business scenario for

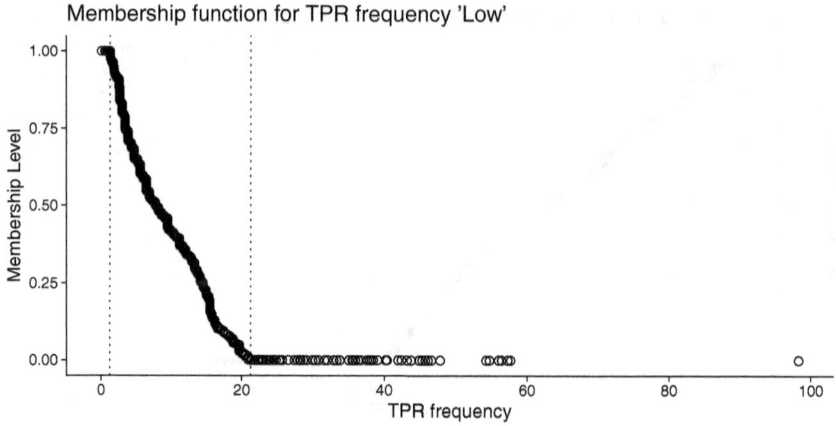

Figure 20.6 Membership function for TPR frequency low.

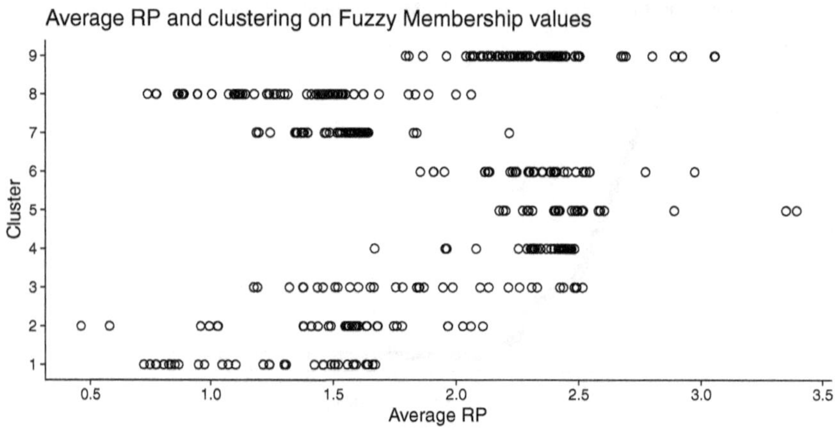

Figure 20.7 Average RP and clustering on fuzzy membership values.

pasta market in Italy, characterised by fierce competition and a large number of competitors,. The amount of high TPR frequency and TPR% value items in the value (clusters 7 and 8) and premium segments (clusters 4 and 9) are roughly equivalent, and they are probably frequently and deeply promoted to attract shoppers (Bolton & Shankar, 2003). In contrast, the number of prices that change infrequently – with both low RP and low TPR frequency – is remarkably higher in the value segments (cluster 2) than in the premium segments (cluster 5). A large share of observations has extremely high variability, probably a replacement for TPR events, in both the value (cluster 1) and premium segments (cluster 6). Finally, a large cluster shows a

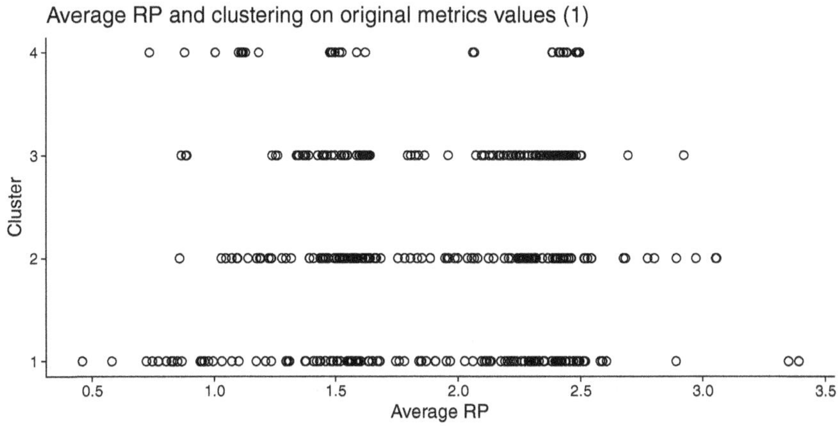

Figure 20.8 Average RP and clustering on original metrics.

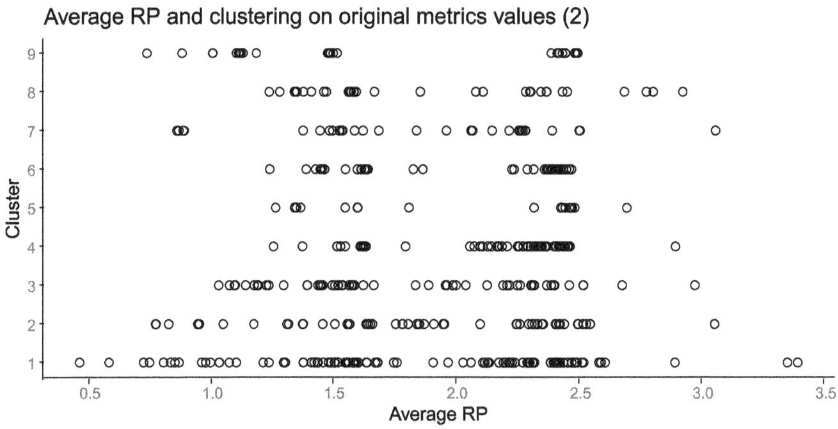

Figure 20.9 Average RP and clustering on original metrics values, forcing the same number of clusters identified with the clustering on fuzzy membership values.

characteristic of the category, with average pricing, relatively infrequent TPR events and extremely high TPR% variability (cluster 3). This might mean that some TPR events will be much more attractive to customers than others, but the latter will be much less appealing in term of monetary savings.

Some underlying macro groups emerge from this clustering, with some strategies that rely heavily on TPR (clusters 4, 7, 8 and 9) and others that instead decline to pull this promotional lever (clusters 1, 2, 3, 5 and 6). Another characteristic, this time based on RP positioning, shows that some

Table 20.4 Mean scores on the dimensions for each cluster

	N	*Average RP*	*RP Variability*	*Average TPR%*	*TPR% Variability*	*TPR frequency*
Min.	738	0.460	0.000	0.000	0.000	0.000
Median	738	1.780	3.460	18.489	0.197	5.556
Max.	738	3.392	18.074	55.556	1.124	98.291
Cluster						
1	52	1.225	6.502	5.661	0.013	0.509
2	104	1.569	1.437	3.507	0.010	0.793
3	81	1.874	2.803	6.702	0.520	6.691
4	73	2.378	3.119	32.353	0.147	13.229
5	51	2.540	2.123	2.048	0.001	0.107
6	59	2.325	6.374	5.214	0.027	0.636
7	102	1.530	2.349	29.979	0.222	17.647
8	98	1.316	5.474	22.283	0.405	18.675
9	118	2.330	7.311	26.780	0.435	20.815

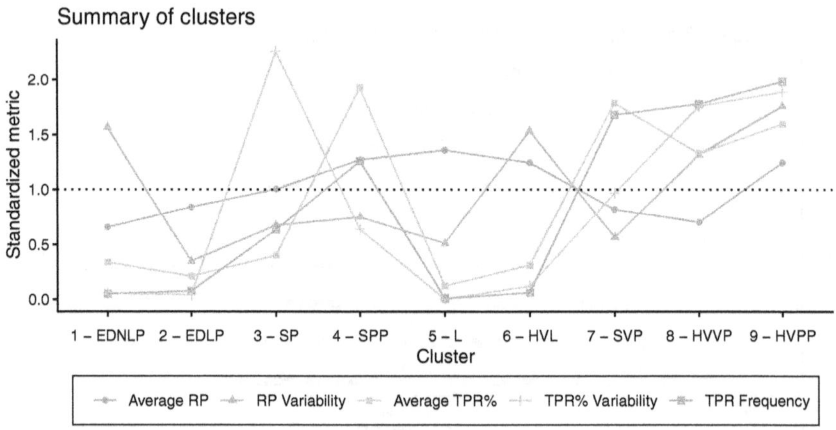

Figure 20.10 Summary of pricing and price promotion strategies. *Note*: Everyday new low price = EDNLP, everyday low price = EDLP, surprise promo = SP, stable premium promo = SPP, luxury = L, high variability luxury = HVL, stable value promo = SVP, high variability value promo = HVP and high variability premium promo = HVPP.

clusters use premium price positioning (clusters 4, 5, 6 and 9), while others use value positioning (clusters 1, 2, 7 and 8), and the remaining group positions itself around an average market price (cluster 3).

Having classified all observations based on our empirically derived taxonomy, we analyse how those classifications are distributed across regions, retailers and brands. We first examine group characteristics in the NUTS 1 regions, standardising each metric over the metric's overall average for easier comparison (Table 20.6).

Table 20.5 Characterisation of pricing and price promotion strategies

Cluster	*N*	*Label*	*Description*	*TPR reliance*	*RP positioning*
1	52	Every day new low price	Low RP, extremely high RP variability, extremely low TPR%, frequency and variability	Low	Value
2	104	Every day low price	Low RP and RP variability, extremely low TPR%, TPR frequency and TPR variability	Low	Value
3	81	Surprise promo	Average RP, extremely high TPR variability, relatively low RP Variability, TPR% and TPR frequency	Low	Average
4	73	Stable premium promo	Extremely high TPR%, high TPR frequency, low TPR and RP variability, high RP	High	Premium
5	51	Luxury	High RP, Low RP variability, extremely low TPR%, frequency and variability	Low	Premium
6	59	High variability luxury	High RP and RP variability, extremely low TPR%, frequency and variability	Low	Premium
7	102	Stable value promo	Extremely High TPR% and frequency, low TPR variability and RP, medium RP variability	High	Value
8	98	High variability value promo	High TPR%, frequency and variability, High RP variability, low RP	High	Value
9	118	High variability premium promo	High TPR%, frequency and variability, high RP and RP variability	High	Premium

Average regular prices are quite similar across regions. More evident differences appear in comparing TPR frequencies, with extremely high use of this promotional tool in Southern Italy and much less so by all the other regions. The Islands, in particular, stand out as having much lower TPR frequency and TPR percentage than other regions.

To compare the composition of strategies across regions, we plotted the percentage of observations in each region classified according to our taxonomy (Figure 20.11).

Table 20.6 Summary metrics by region

Region	*Average RP*	*RP Variability*	*Average TPR%*	*TPR% Variability*	*TPR Frequency*	*N*
Centre	1.024	0.662	0.992	0.730	0.826	226
Islands	0.980	1.032	0.569	1.334	0.417	64
North-east	1.032	1.194	1.066	0.738	0.760	180
North-west	1.022	1.175	1.063	1.094	0.898	113
South	0.921	1.127	1.066	1.491	1.848	155

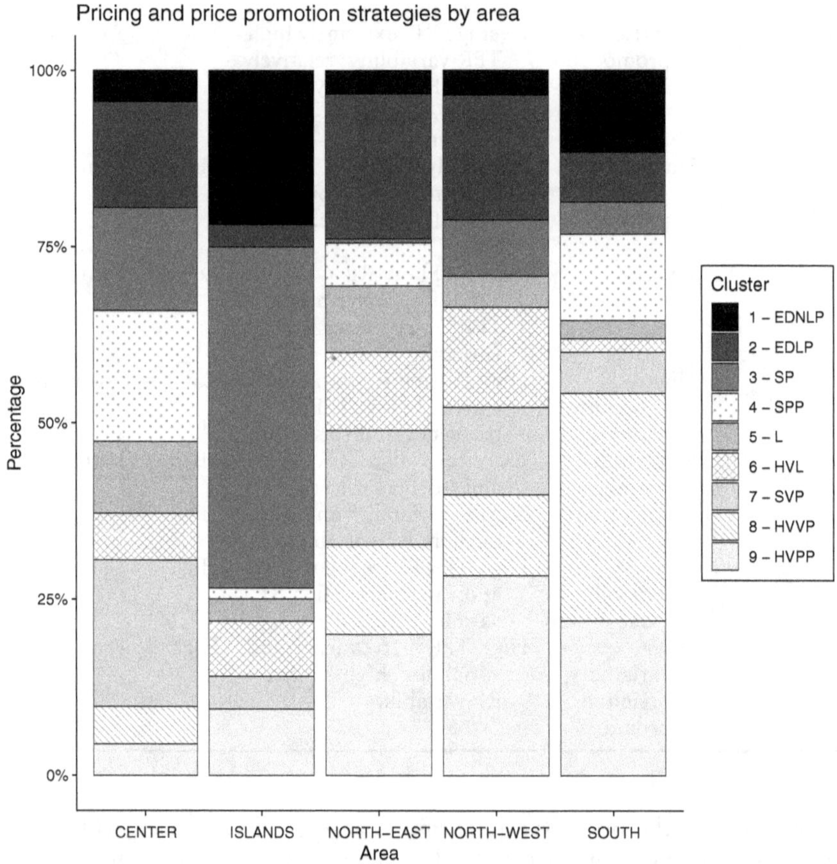

Figure 20.11 Pricing and price promotion strategies by region.

Southern Italy has a prevalence of strategies that rely heavily on TPR, but they are nearly absent in the Islands. Another notable characteristic is that the Islands present much less strategies that rely on value or premium pricing and much more strategies that position the RP near the market average.

Table 20.7 Summary metrics by retailer

Retailer	*N*	*Average RP*	*RP Variability*	*Average TPR%*	*TPR% Variability*	*TPR Frequency*
Auchan	86	0.927	1.269	1.302	1.105	0.782
AZ	11	0.687	1.075	1.160	1.034	2.160
SISA	79	0.974	0.816	1.650	0.844	0.789
Codè CRAI Ovest	8	1.091	0.623	0.067	0.000	0.030
Conad–Iper	178	1.047	1.251	1.588	1.540	2.150
Conad del Tirreno	89	0.986	0.680	0.335	1.743	0.460
Coop Centrale Adriatica	46	0.835	1.092	0.039	0.110	0.010
Etruria–SMA	7	1.065	1.104	1.558	0.678	1.175
Gabrielli	22	0.934	1.065	1.271	1.196	1.761
Il Gigante	12	0.892	1.174	1.415	1.795	1.221
Megamark	8	0.780	0.936	0.644	0.476	1.025
Multicedi	14	0.875	1.126	1.162	1.840	2.582
Nealco	86	1.153	0.417	0.125	0.000	0.047
SMA	55	1.083	1.279	0.423	0.237	0.088
Unicomm	15	1.031	1.285	1.451	1.023	1.369
Unicoop Tirreno	22	0.967	0.918	1.592	0.910	1.127

We then analyse our results by retailer chain, with the standardised metrics listed in Table 20.7. Note that the distribution of stores by retailer chain is not regionally uniform.[8]

Figure 20.12 shows the proportion of strategies employed by each retailer. The retailer profiles vary widely, from those that take a more balanced approach, such as Auchan, to those that clearly chose sides in terms of price positioning and the use of TPR, such as Il Gigante and Multicedi.

Finally, we analyse the strategies by brand, with the standardised metrics listed in Table 20.8.

We see large differences in size for each group. Those that are smaller might be private labels, which are distributed by only a single retailer, or a local brand with limited distribution, often in a single region. Pricing strategies are strongly heterogeneous among brands.

Figure 20.13, which illustrates the proportion of pricing and promotional price strategies by brand, shows many interesting facts about individual brand positioning. Some brands take a clear EDLP approach (i.e. Bianconi, Ceccato, Coop and Valdigrano), positioning themselves with value pricing and refraining from TPR. But other brands rely heavily on TPR for their commercial strategy, positioning their pricing as value (Il Gigante, Sisa) or using a mixed strategy (Multicedi). However, the brands mentioned so far all have smaller representation in our analysis. It is reasonable to expect that brands with a larger distribution adopt a wider variety of strategies. The remaining brands have different levels of reliance on TPR, and the brands

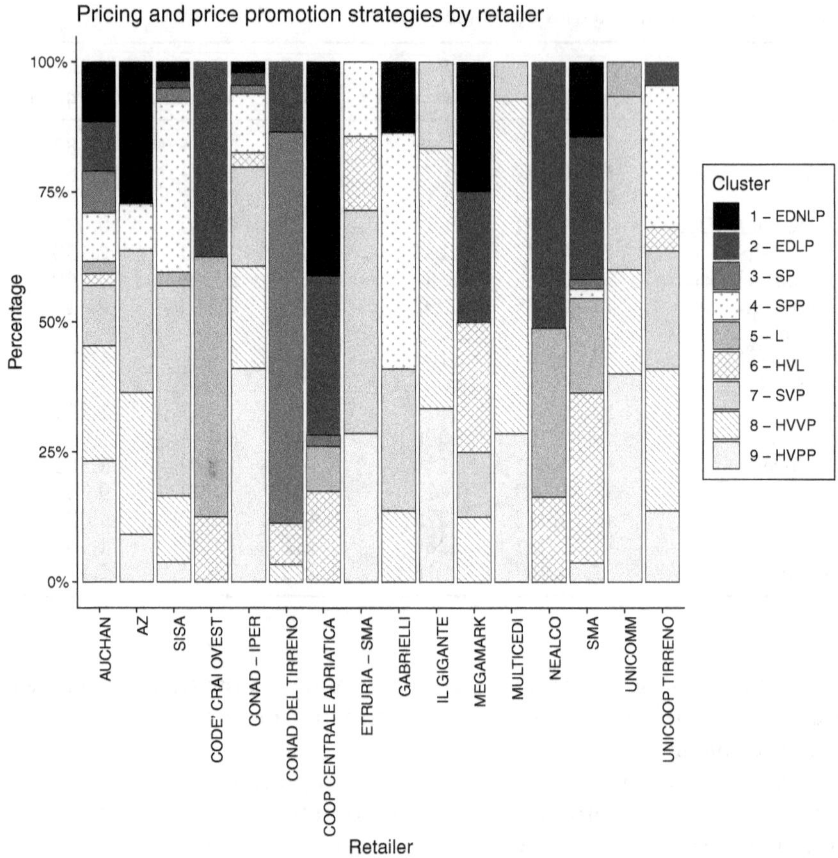

Figure 20.12 Pricing and price promotion strategies by retailer.

more represented in our dataset (Barilla, De Cecco, Divella and Voiello) show a slight prevalence in the use of TPR in marketing strategies.

Regarding the pricing level, most brands are fairly consistent, pursuing strategies with common characteristics. However, a few brands employ strategies with contradictory characteristics. This can affect the clarity of the brand image among consumers, if the same brand is positioned very differently across regions or retailers in the same region.

Conclusions

In this chapter, we empirically identify nine different pricing and price promotion strategies for pasta brands in Italy, characterised by different levels and mixtures of RP and TPR positioning: everyday new low price, everyday low price, surprise promo, stable premium promo, luxury, high variability

Table 20.8 Summary metrics by brand

Brand	*N*	*Average RP*	*RP Variability*	*Average TPR%*	*TPR% Variability*	*TPR Frequency*
Agnesi	11	0.987	0.523	0.693	0.647	0.502
Amato	10	0.801	0.709	0.494	0.608	0.214
Barilla	206	0.863	0.778	0.905	1.039	1.062
Bianconi	1	0.386	1.064	0.000	0.000	0.000
Ceccato	5	0.438	1.992	0.000	0.000	0.000
Colavita	4	0.412	1.887	0.438	1.047	0.122
Coop	20	0.625	0.717	0.018	0.000	0.004
De Cecco	218	1.290	1.066	1.189	1.048	1.263
Divella	82	0.699	0.932	1.414	1.136	1.442
G/Passione	3	1.748	0.688	0.254	1.241	0.434
Garofalo	27	1.297	0.787	1.375	0.780	1.244
Il Gigante	4	0.586	1.138	1.300	1.804	0.377
Jolly	26	0.929	0.288	1.014	0.180	0.199
Multicedi	2	1.164	1.791	1.132	2.369	0.835
Pallante Reggia	17	0.468	1.556	0.750	1.058	1.111
Sisa	9	0.653	0.808	1.349	1.394	0.334
Valdigrano	5	0.316	0.044	0.000	0.000	0.000
Voiello	88	1.155	1.709	0.738	1.285	0.593

luxury, stable value promo, high variability value promo and high variability premium promo.

We also show that fuzzification of the metrics that underlie the clustering enable us to identify clusters that are more consistent with the business logic in the pricing and price promotions strategies.

We developed a novel MF approach, based on preliminary clustering of the individual metrics and leveraging their medoids to derive membership values that: (1) are not influenced by arbitrary or exogenous values, (2) minimise the effect of outliers and (3) preserve the maximum information from the original metrics.

We use a dataset with weekly reported prices which has been filtered to remove inconsistencies and impute missing data. However, one limitation of our research is that our dataset does not contain information about display and features, two aspects that previous literature considers important in augmenting TPR results. In addition, the data refer to large regions, which might be characterised by a high level of heterogeneity in pricing strategies across sub-regions.

Further research using scanner data might be able to provide additional insights into retailers' and brands' pricing and price promotion strategies. Moreover, our clustering approach treats all variables as equally relevant for classifying the strategies. Clustering on weighted variables, giving certain dimensions of the marketing mix more relevance, might offer further insights and different perspectives on pricing and price promotion strategies.

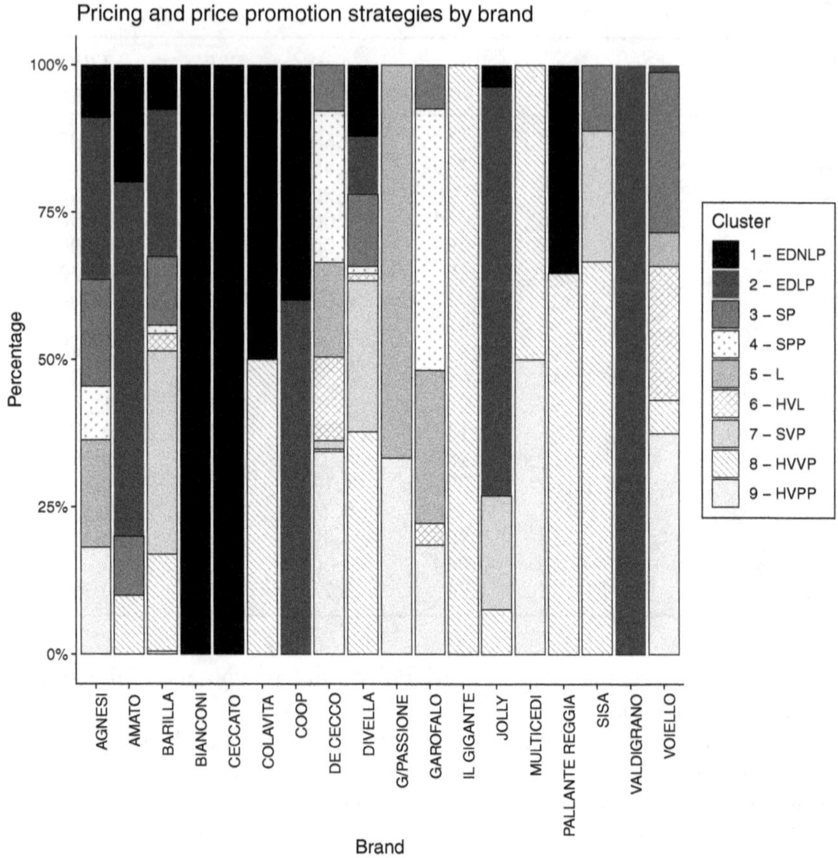

Figure 20.13 Pricing and price promotion strategies by brand.

Notes

1 Retail price promotions are generally backed by trade price promotions offered by CPG manufacturers to retailers. The degree of price reduction passed from retailers to consumers may vary widely across brands, categories (Besanko, Dubé & Gupta, 2005) and time (Meza & Sudhir, 2006).

2 Different sources use slightly different definitions in calculating these values.

3 TPR is only one of the possible promotional strategies in CPG. However, several studies show how TPR is used more widely than other promotional options (multi-buy, extra products free, etc.) (Gedenk, Neslin & Ailawadi, 2010; Bogomolova (unify the citations in a single parentheses), Dunn, Trinh, Taylor & Volpe, 2015). Therefore, our research concentrates on TPRs.

4 This bias towards short-term returns is deeply criticised by academics and practitioners who advocate the superiority of advertising in building customers loyalty, as stated by Ken Roman of Ogilvy & Mather: '*Promotions rent customers, advertising owns them*' (Pettie & Pettie, 2003). Recent studies, however, show

that brand loyalty is at an all-time low, despite increases in advertising spending (Jedidi, Mela & Gupta, 1999; Nielsen, 2019).

5 We thank ISMEA, in particular, Maria Nucera for giving us the dataset. We performed several elaborations to correct reporting inconsistencies in the dataset, such as: removing data on price promotions that are inconsistent with regular prices; reclassifying regular price points which follow a price promotion pattern; removing anomalous regular price points; and imputing missing regular price points.

In our elaboration, we identified as TPRs – in addition to those self-reported by retailers – a price reduction of at least 10% (Nielsen, 2020) over the regular price that lasts for less than five weeks and is followed by an increase in the shelf price. In a series of studies on the German food retail market, a TPR is defined as a reduction of at least 5% over the regular price that lasts for a maximum of four weeks and is followed by an increase in the shelf price. The regular price is observed in the four weeks preceding a sales promotion (Empen, Loy & Weiss, 2015; Herrmann, Moeser & Weber, 2005). Combining this information with the reference from Nielsen (2020) on the Italian market and the metrics derived from our data, we feel confident about the consistency of our TPR definition metrics.

6 The SKU is defined by a combination of format and brand.

7 We assume that variability at the edges of the distribution has less impact on differentiating two strategies than variability in the middle of the distribution.

8 As a result, in some cases a higher number of observations may be attributed to retailers by reporting the RP and TPR of more brands and SKUs and/or across multiple regions. Some retail chains in the analysis are in only a single region, resulting in smaller representation.

References

Ailawadi, K.L., Beauchamp, J., Donthu, N., Gauri, D.K., & Shankar, V. (2009). Communication and Promotion Decisions in Retailing: A Review and Directions for Future Research. *Journal of Retailing*, 85(1), 42–55.

Ailawadi, K.L., Lehmann, D.R., & Neslin, S.A. (2001). Market Response to a Major Policy Change in the Marketing Mix: Learning from Procter & Gamble's Value Pricing Strategy. *Journal of Marketing*, 65(1), 44–61.

Allender, W.J., & Richards, T. (2012). Brand Loyalty and Price Promotion Strategies: an Empirical Analysis. *Journal of Retailing*, 88(3), 323–342.

Anderson, E.T., & Fox, E.J. (2019). How Price Promotions Work: A Review of Practice. In J.-P. Dubé, & P.E. Rossi, *Handbook of the Economics of Marketing* (1st ed., Vol. 1, pp. 497–552). Amsterdam: North-Holland.

Bailey, A.A. (2008). Evaluating Consumer Response to EDLPs. *Journal of Retailing and Consumer Services*, 15(3), 211–223.

Besanko, D., Dubé, J.-P., & Gupta, S. (2005). Own-Brand and Cross-Brand Retail Pass-Through. *Marketing Science*, 24(1), 110–122.

Blattberg, R.C., & Briesch, R.A. (2012). Sales Promotions. In O. Özer, & R. Phillips, *The Oxford Handbook of Pricing Management* (pp. 585–619). Oxford: Oxford University Press.

Blattberg, R.C., Briesch, R., & Fox, E.J. (1995). How Promotions Work. *Marketing Science*, 14(3), G1–G236.

Blattberg, R.C., & Fox, E.J. (1995). *Category Management: A Series of Implementation Guides (Vols. I–V)*. Washington DC: Food Management Institute.

Blattberg, R.C., & Neslin, S.A. (1989). Sales Promotion: The Long and the Short of it. *Marketing Letters*, 1, 81–97.

Bogomolova, S., Dunn, S., Trinh, G., Taylor, J., & Volpe, R.J. (2015). Price Promotion Landscape in the US and UK: Depicting Retail Practice to Inform Future Research Agenda. *Journal of Retailing and Consumer Services*, 25, 1–11.

Bogomolova, S., Szabo, M., & Kennedy, R. (2017). Retailers' and Manufacturers' Price-Promotion Decisions: Intuitive or Evidence-Based? *Journal of Business Research*, 17, 189–200.

Bolton, R.N., & Shankar, V. (2003). An Empirically Derived Taxonomy of Retailer Pricing and Promotion Strategies. *Journal of Retailing*, 79(4), 213–224.

Bolton, R.N., Shankar, V., & Montoya, D.Y. (2010). Recent Trends and Emerging Practices in Retailer Pricing. In M. Krafft, & M.K. Mantrala, *Retailing in the 21st Century* (pp. 301–318). Berlin: Springer.

Boston Consulting Group (2012). *Consumer Products Trade Spend Benchmark*. Boston, MA: The Boston Consulting Group, Inc (BCG).

Briesch, R.A., Dillon, W.R., & Fox, E.J. (2013). Category Positioning and Store Choice: The Role of Destination Categories. *Marketing Science*, 32(3), 488–509.

Brito, P.Q., & Hammond, K. (2007). Strategic Versus Tactical Nature of Sales Promotions. *Journal of Marketing Communications*, 13(2), 131–148.

Buil, I., de Chernatony, L., & Martínez, E. (2012). Examining the Role of Advertising and Sales Promotions in Brand Equity Creation. *Journal of Business Research*, 66(1), 115–122.

Cacchiarelli, L., & Sorrentino, A. (2019). Pricing Strategies in the Italian Retail Sector: The Case of Pasta. *Social Sciences*, 8(4), 113.

Chevalier, J.A., Kashyap, A.K., & Rossi, P.E. (2003). Why Don't Prices Rise During Periods of Peak Demand? Evidence from Scanner Data. *The American Economic Review*, 93(1), 15–37.

DelVecchio, D., Henard, D.H., & Freling, T.H. (2006). The Effect of Sales Promotion on Post-Promotion Brand Preference: A Meta-Analysis. *Journal of Retailing*, 82(3), 203–213.

Drèze, X., & Bell, D.R. (2003). Creating Win-Win Trade Promotions: Theory and Empirical Analysis of Scan-Back Trade Deals. *Marketing Science*, 22(1), 16–39.

Dubois, D., & Prade, H. (1980). Systems of Linear Fuzzy Constraints. *Fuzzy Sets and Systems*, 3(1), 37–48.

Ellickson, P.B., & Misra, S. (2008). Supermarket Pricing Strategies. *Marketing Science*, 27(5), 811–828.

Ellickson, P.B., Misra, S., & Nair, H.S. (2012). Repositioning Dynamics and Pricing Strategy. *Journal of Marketing Research*, 49(6), 750–772.

Empen, J., Loy, J.-P., & Weiss, C. (2015). Price Promotions and Brand Loyalty: Empirical Evidence for the German Ready-to-Eat Cereal Market. *European Journal of Marketing*, 49(5/6), 736–759.

Fassnacht, M., & El Husseini, S. (2013). EDLP Versus Hi–Lo Pricing Strategies in Retailing – A State of the Art Article. *Journal of Business Economics*, 83, 259–289.

Gartner. (2015). *Market Guide for Trade Promotion Management and Optimization*. Stamford, CT: Gartner, Inc.

Gauri, D.K., Trivedi, M., & Grewal, D. (2008). Understanding the Determinants of Retail Strategy: An Empirical Analysis. *Journal of Retailing*, 84(3), 256–267.

Gedenk, K., & Neslin, S.A. (1999). The Role of Retail Promotion in Determining Future Brand Loyalty: Its Effect on Purchase Event Feedback. *Journal of Retailing*, 75(4), 433–459.

Gedenk, K., Neslin, S.A., & Ailawadi, K.L. (2010). Sales Promotion. In M. Krafft, & M.K. Mantrala, *Retailing in the 21st Century* (2nd ed., pp. 393–408). Berlin: Springer.

Gómez, M.J., Rao, V.R., & McLaughlin, E.W. (2007, August). Empirical Analysis of Budget and Allocation of Trade Promotions in the U.S. Supermarket Industry. *Journal of Marketing Research*, 44(3), 410–424.

Grewal, D., Janakiraman, R., Kalyanam, K., Kannan, P., Ratchford, B., Song, R., & Tolerico, S. (2010). Strategic Online and Offline Retail Pricing: A Review and Research Agenda. *Journal of Interactive Marketing*, 24(2), 138–154.

Herrmann, R., Moeser, A., & Weber, S.A. (2005). Price Rigidity in the German Grocery-Retailing Sector: Scanner-Data Evidence on Magnitude and Causes. *Journal of Agricultural & Food Industrial Organization*, 3(1), 1–35.

Hoch, S.J., Drèze, X., & Purk, M.E. (1994). EDLP, Hi-Lo, and Margin Arithmetic. *Journal of Marketing*, 58(4), 16–27.

International Pasta Organisation. (2014). *The World Pasta Industry Status Report 2013*. Roma, Italy: International Pasta Organization (IPO).

IRI. (2016, 11). *Price and Promotion in Western Economies*. Retrieved 02.23. 2020, from Iriworldwide.com: https://www.iriworldwide.com/IRI/media/IRI-Clients/International/Price-Promotion-in-Western-Economies-a-Pause-in-Promotion-Escalation.pdf

Jedidi, K., Mela, C.F., & Gupta, S. (1999). Managing Advertising and Promotion for Long-Run Profitability. *Marketing Science*, 18(1), 1–22.

Johnson, L.K. (2003). Dueling Pricing Strategies. *MIT Sloan Management Review*, 44(3), 10–11.

Kuntner, T., & Teichert, T. (2016). The Scope of Price Promotion Research: An Informetric Study. *Journal of Business Research*, 69(8), 2687–2696.

Lal, R., & Rao, R. (1997). Supermarket Competition: The Case of Every Day Low Pricing. *Marketing Science*, 16(1), 60–80.

McShane, B.B., Chen, C., Anderson, E.T., & Simester, D.I. (2016). Decision Stages and Asymmetries in Regular Retail Price Pass-Through. *Marketing Science*, 35(4), 619–639.

Mela, C.F., Gupta, S., & Lehmann, D.R. (1997). The Long-Term Impact of Promotion and Advertising on Consumer Brand Choice. *Journal of Marketing Research*, 34(2), 248–261.

Meza, S., & Sudhir, K. (2006). Pass-Through Timing. *Quantitative Marketing and Economics*, 4(4), 351–382.

Mourdoukoutas, P. (2017, 2 24). *A Strategic Mistake That Still Haunts JC Penney*. Retrieved January 11, 2020, from *Forbes*: https://www.forbes.com/sites/panosmourdoukoutas/2017/02/24/a-strategic-mistake-that-still-haunts-jc-penney/#4968b5041bcf

Neslin, S.A. (2002). Sales Promotions. In B.A. Weitz, & R. Wensley, *Handbook of Marketing* (pp. 310–338). London: SAGE Publications Ltd.

Nielsen. (2009a, 06 17). *Promotions Spur Growth In UK Grocery Sales*. Retrieved 02 23, 2020, from Nielsen.com: https://www.nielsen.com/us/en/insights/article/2009/promotions-spur-growth-in-uk-grocery-sales/

Nielsen. (2009b, 10 05). *Almost Half of U.S. Supermarket Purchases are Sold on Promotion*. Retrieved 02 23, 2020, from Nielsen.com: https://www.nielsen.com/us/en/insights/article/2009/almost-half-of-u-s-supermarket-purchases-are-sold-on-promotion/

Nielsen. (2015a, 02). *The Path to Efficient Trade Promotions*. Retrieved 02 23, 2020, from Nielsen.com: https://www.nielsen.com/wp-content/uploads/sites/3/2019/04/the-path-to-efficient-trade-promotions-feb-2015.pdf

Nielsen. (2015b, 06 25). *Consumer Loyalty Is Not Much Deeper Than Our Pockets*. Retrieved 03 05, 2020, from Nielsen.com: https://www.nielsen.com/us/en/insights/article/2015/consumer-loyalty-is-not-much-deeper-than-our-pockets/

Nielsen. (2018a, 08 03). *Are We Really Getting Value From Our Promotions?* Retrieved 02 23, 2020, from Nielsen.com: https://www.nielsen.com/au/en/insights/article/2018/are-we-really-getting-value-from-our-promotions/

Nielsen. (2018b, 05 15). *The $470M Opportunity: Changing The Game With Price and Promotions*. Retrieved 02 23, 2020, from Nielsen.com: https://www.nielsen.com/nz/en/insights/article/2018/the-470m-opportunity-changing-the-game-with-price-and-promotions/

Nielsen. (2019, 08 07). *Global Ad Spending Is Up, But You Can't Buy Loyalty in CPG*. Retrieved 03 05, 2020, from Nielsen.com: https://www.nielsen.com/us/en/insights/article/2019/global-ad-spending-is-up-but-you-cant-buy-loyalty-in-cpg/

Nielsen. (2020). *The Ultimate Guide to Nielsen Retail Measurement Services*. Retrieved 03 05, 2020, from Nielsen.com: https://www.nielsen.com/us/en/client-learning/retail-measurement-services/analyzing-promotion/

Pettie, S., & Pettie, K. (2003). Sales Promotion. In M.J. Baker, *The Marketing Book* (5th ed., pp. 458–484). Oxford: Butterworth Heinemann.

Slater, J. (2001). Is Couponing an Effective Promotional Strategy? An Examination of the Procter & Gamble Zero-Coupon Test. *Journal of Marketing Communications*, 7(1), 3–9.

Srinivasan, S., Pauwels, K., Hanssens, D., & Dikempe, M. (2004). Do Promotions Benefit, Manufacturers, Retailers, or Both? *Management Science*, 50(5), 617–629.

Zadeh, L.A. (1965). Fuzzy Sets. *Information and Control*, 8(3), 338–353.

Zadeh, L.A. (1968). Probability Measures of Fuzzy Events. *Journal of Mathematical Analysis and Applications*, 23, 421–427.

Zadeh, L.A. (1977). Fuzzy Sets and Their Application to Pattern Classification and Clustering Analysis. Classification and Clustering. *Proceedings of an Advanced Seminar Conducted by the Mathematics Research Center, the University of Wisconsin–Madison, May 3–5, 1976* (pp. 251–299). New York: Academic Press.

Zimmermann, H.-J. (2001). *Fuzzy Set Theory - and Its Applications* (4th ed.). New York: Springer Sience+Business Media.

Zoellner, F., & Schaefers, T. (2015). Do Price Promotions Help or Hurt Premium-product Brands? The Impact of Different Price-promotion Types on Sales and Brand Perception. *Journal of Advertising Research*, 55(3), 270–283.

Zwanka, R.J. (2017). Everyday Low Pricing: A Private Brand Growth Strategy in Traditional Food Retailers. *Journal of Food Products Marketing*, 24(4), 373–391.

Index

Page numbers in italic indicate a figure and page numbers in "bold" indicate a table.

www.ingramcontent.com/pod-product-compliance
Lightning Source LLC
LaVergne TN
LVHW021117300926
849160LV00010B/763
9780367514075